AF478044

Experiential Constructions in Yucatec Maya

Studies in Language Companion Series (SLCS)

This series has been established as a companion series to the periodical
Studies in Language.

Volume 87

Experiential Constructions in Yucatec Maya. A typologically based analysis of a
functional domain in a Mayan language
Elisabeth Verhoeven

Experiential Constructions
in Yucatec Maya

A typologically based analysis
of a functional domain in a Mayan language

Elisabeth Verhoeven
University of Bremen

John Benjamins Publishing Company
Amsterdam / Philadelphia

 The paper used in this publication meets the minimum requirements of American National Standard for Information Sciences – Permanence of Paper for Printed Library Materials, ANSI Z39.48-1984.

Library of Congress Cataloging-in-Publication Data

Verhoeven, Elisabeth.
Experiential constructions in Yucatec Maya : a typologically based analysis of a
      functional domain in a Mayan language / Elisabeth Verhoeven.
    p. cm. -- (Studies in language companion series ; ISSN 0165-7763 ; v. 87)
Includes bibliographical references and index.
1. Maya language--Grammar. I. Title.
PM3969.V47   2007
497'.41525--dc22   2007004707
ISBN 978-90-272-3097-3 (hb : alk. paper)

John Benjamins Publishing Co. · P.O. Box 36224 · 1020 ME Amsterdam · The Netherlands
John Benjamins North America · P.O. Box 27519 · Philadelphia PA 19118-0519 · USA

In Dankbarkeit, meinem Vater Heinrich Verhoeven

Contents

Figures and tables

List of constructions

List of figures

List of tables

Preface

This is the revised version of my doctoral dissertation. Several people deserve my special gratitude and thanks for helping and advising me during the writing of this dissertation and preparing it for publication.

I am most indebted to my first supervisor Christian Lehmann for many discussions concerning all aspects of this work and for his diligent comments and valuable advice. I am also grateful to my second supervisor Balthasar Bickel for numerous inspiring and helpful discussions and his comments on an earlier draft. This work has also benefited from fruitful discussions I had with numerous colleagues: Amani Bohoussou, Jürgen Bohnemeyer, Dagmar Haumann, Johannes Helmbrecht, Gerd Jendraschek, Yoko Nishina, Su-Rin Ryu, Eva Schultze-Berndt, my 'favorite' colleague Yong-Min Shin, and specially Stavros Skopeteas.

I thank Werner Abraham, who, as the series editor, gave me very helpful comments to improve the manuscript. Kees Vaes and Patricia Leplae provided me with all the necessary help during the production process.

Beginning in 1996, I undertook several stages of fieldwork in the Mexican states of Quintana Roo and Yucatán. Special thanks are due to Jürgen Bohnemeyer for introducing me into the village of Yaxley, which became my main field site, and for facilitating work and contact to the people when I was getting started. Barbara Pfeiler and Neifi Vermont Vermont facilitated a research stay in 1998 in Valladolid and the villages of St. Andrés and Yalcoba.

I am especially grateful to the people of Yaxley, especially Ramon May Cupul, Ernesto May Balam, Norma May Pool, Fuljencio Ek Ek and Sebastian Baas May for having been my language teachers and consultants during my fieldwork periods in 1996, 1998, 2000, 2002, 2002/2003, and 2004. Vicente Ek Catzin and Fuljencio Ek Ek and their families receive special thanks for providing accommodation and food during these trips.

Furthermore, special thanks go to Amedee Colli Colli and her family for their friendship and hospitality during my stays in Felipe Carrillo Puerto in 2002/2003 and 2004. Amedee was always ready to answer all my questions concerning Yucatec Maya during her visit to Erfurt in November 2002 as well as during my stays at Carrillo Puerto and afterward.

I thank Kirsten Brock, Elizabeth Medvedovsky and especially Rachel Montague for proofreading the manuscript.

I gratefully acknowledge the financial support I received from several institutions for my dissertation project including my fieldwork in Mexico. The state Thüringen supported my dissertation project in 2002/2003 with a grant (Graduiertenförderstipendium). My fieldwork from 1996 until 2002 was made possible by the DFG (Deutsche Forschungsgemeinschaft). The University of Erfurt financially supported my fieldwork in winter 2002/2003 and in 2004.

Finally, I want to thank my parents Heinrich and Sophia Verhoeven as well as Leonidas Skopeteas, Maria Sepsa, Leonidas Heinrich Skopeteas and especially Stavros Skopeteas for their indispensable support while I was working on my dissertation and preparing the manuscript for publication.

Berlin, January 2007
Elisabeth Verhoeven

Abbreviations

Glosses and categories

Ø	meaningless element		DEF	definite
1	first person		DEM	demonstrative
2	second person		DET	determiner
3	third person		DETF	determiner final
A	actor		DISTR	distributive
ABS	absolutive		DU	dual
ABSTR	abstract marker		DUR	durative
ABSOL	absoluble		DUB	dubitative
ACC	accusative		EF	extrafocal
ADJR	adjectivalizer		EMPH	emphasizer
ADV	adverb		ERG	ergative
ADVR	adverbializer		EXIST	exist(ential)
AN	animate		F	feminine
AOR	aorist		FACT	factitive
ART	article		FOC	focus
AUX	auxiliary		FUT	future
CAUS	causative		GEN	genitive
CL	noun class		GER	gerund
CMPL	completive		GERV	gerundive
CNJ	conjunction		HAB	habitual
CNTR	continuator		HUM	human
COLL	collective		IMP	imperative
CONTR	contrastive		IMPF	imperfective
CONV	converb		INAN	inanimate
COP	copular		INCMPL	incompletive
D1	1st person deictic		INF	infinitive marker
D2	2nd person deictic		INT	interrogative
D3	3rd person deictic		INTRV	introversive
DAT	dative		INV	inverse
DEAG	deagentive		IRR	irrealis
DEB	debitive		LD	locative-directional
DECL	declarative		LOC	locative

LOCF	locative final	PROG	progressive
M	masculine	PROSP	prospective
N	neuter	PRS	present
NEG	negative	PRSV	presentative
NEGF	negative final	PST	past
NEUT	neutral aspect	PUNCT	punctual
NOM	nominative	QUOT	quotative
NPST	non-past	RED	reduplicative
NR	nominalizer	REL	relationalizer
NSG	non-singular	REPORT	report marker
OBJ	object	RFL	reflexive
OBL	oblique	RSLTV	resultative
ORIG	origin	SBJ	subject
PART	participle marker	SBSTR	substantivizer
PASS	passive	SG	singular
PAT	patient	SPEC	specific
PE	plural exclusive	SPONT	spontaneous
PF	perfect	SR	subordinator
PFV	perfective	SS	same subject
PL	plural	SUBJ	subjunctive
PERS	personal	T/A(/M)	tense/aspect(/mood)
POSS	possessive	TEL	telic
POESS	postessive	TERM	terminative
PRDV	predictive	TOP	topic
PRED	predicative	TRR	transitivizer
PREP	preposition	USAT	usative
PROC	inchoative	VR	verbalizer

Grammatical categories

Adj	adjective		complex
Adv	adverb	IntrVStem	intransitive verb
CtNom	count nominal		stem
Det	determiner	ITR	independent time ref.
DRef	different reference	Mod	modal
DTR	dependent time ref.	N	noun
EPNom	extended possessed	NCl	nominal clause
	nominal	Nom	nominal
IntrVCo	intransitive verbal	NP	noun phrase
	core	NumCom	numeral complex
IntrVCom	intransitive verbal	PossNP	possessor NP

PP	prepositional phrase	TrVCo	transitive verbal core
Ptcl	particle	TrVCom	transitive verbal complex
S	clause		
SAdv	simple adverb	TrVStem	transitive verb stem
SFVCo	semi-finite verbal core	Trvd	transitive verboid
		V	verb
SPNom	simple possessed nominal	VCl	verbal clause
		VCo	verbal core
SRef	same reference	VP	verb phrase

Sources: Texts and persons

AAK	Romero Castillo, Moisés 1964, "Tres cuentos mayas." *Anales del INAH*, Tomo XVII, 64:307-309.
ACC	Amedée Colli Colli, Felipe Carrillo Puerto, Quintana Roo
AEF	Amalia Ek Falcon, Yaxley, Quintana Roo
AME	Antonio May Ek, Felipe Carrillo Puerto, Quintana Roo
BVS	Blair, Robert W. and Vermont-Salas, Refugio 1965/1967, *Spoken (Yucatec) Maya, 2 vols*. Chicago: University of Chicago, Dept. of Anthropology. Reprint: Columbia, Miss.: Lucas Brothers, 1979.
CHAAK	Tun, Bernardino 1931, *The Ch'á'cháak Ceremony* [transcribed by Manuel J. Andrade]. Chicago: University of Chicago Library (Microfilm Collections of Manuscripts on Cultural Anthropology, No. 262, Series XLIX, Text No. 35, pp. 211–215).
CHAN	Cemé, Eustaqueo 1931/1933, *Historia de Chan Kom* [recorded by Manuel J. Andrade; transcribed and translated by Refugio Vermont-Salas]. Chicago: University of Chicago Library (Microfilm Collections of Manuscripts on Cultural Anthropology, No.108, Series XIX, text No. 15).
CPP	Catalino Poot Pena, Yaxley, Quintana Roo
EMB	Ernesto May Balam, Yaxley, Quintana Roo
FCP	Vivas Cámara, Gregorio 1989, *U tsikbalil u kuxtal Don Felipe Carrillo Puerto* [recorded by Christian Lehmann in Yaxley].
FEE	Fulgencio Ek Ek, Yaxley, Quintana Roo
FKB	François Kipré Blé (University of Abidjan)
FOTOH	Justina Pat May 1996, [recorded by Elisabeth Verhoeven in Yaxley].

HALA'CH	Andrade and Máas Collí (eds.) 1991, "Huntuul hala'ach wiinik yeetel ooxtuul ma'ako'l winiko'b." In: *Cuentos mayas yucatecos; tomo II*. Mérida: Universidad Autónoma de Yucatán; 303-319.
HA'N	Andrade and Máas Collí (eds.) 1991, "Huntuul ha'n hach h tuus." In: *Cuentos mayas yucatecos; tomo II*. Mérida: Universidad Autónoma de Yucatán; 322-361.
HAPAIKAN	Dzul Poot, Domingo 1985, "Hapai kan". In: *Cuentos mayas; edición bilingüe: español – maya*. Mérida. Yucatán: Maldonado; INAH, SEP; 55-58.
HIJO	Vivas Cámara, Gregorio 1988, *El hijo pródigo* [recorded by Christian Lehmann in Yaxley].
HK'AN	Dzul Poot, Domingo 1986, "J-k'an yajaw". In: *Cuentos mayas; tomo II; edición bilingüe: español – maya*. Mérida, Yucatán: Maldonado; INAH, SEP; 89-114.
HLU'M_KÀAB	Tun, Bernadino 1930, "Hlu'm kàab". Andrade, Manuel J. and Máas Collí, Hilaria (eds.) 1990, *Cuentos mayas yucatecos; tomo I*, Mérida: Universidad Autónoma de Yucatán; 27-58.
HNAZ	Bolio, Antonio 1930, "H Nazario". Andrade, Manuel J. and Máas Collí, Hilaria (eds.) 1991, *Cuentos mayas yucatecos; tomo II*, Mérida: Universidad Autónoma de Yucatán; 64-127.
HOSEH	Andrade and Máas Collí 1991, *Cuentos Mayas Yucatecos, tomo II*, Mérida: Universidad Autónoma de Yucatán; 292-301.
HTS'ON	Romero Castillo, Moisés 1964, "Tres cuentos mayas." *Anales del INAH*, Tomo XVII, 64:309-311.
ICM	Ignacio Canul Mazun, Yalcobá, Yucatán
K'AXBIL	May Ek, José 1991, *How a traditional house is built* [recorded by Christian Lehmann in Yaxley].
MCK	Myung-Chul Koo (University of Seoul).
MPK	María Arimatea Puk Ciau, Yaxley, Quintana Roo
MUUCH	Pool Kaaw, Estéban 1989, *Xunáan mùuch* [recorded by Christian Lehmann in Yaxley].
NAH	Pool Kaaw, Estéban 1989, *How a traditional house is built* [recorded by Christian Lehmann in Yaxley].
NMP	Norma May Pool, Felipe Carrillo Puerto, Quintana Roo
NVV	Neifi Vermont Vermont, Valladolid, Yucatán
PEEK'	Dzul Poot, Domingo 1985, *Cuentos Mayas. Edición bilingüe: Español – Maya*. Mérida, Yuc.: Maldonado & INAH-SEP, 93–102.
PLC	Petronila Loria Cupul, St. Andres-XBac, Yucatán
RMC	Ramón May Cupul, Yaxley, Quintana Roo

SANTO	Camal Mas, Maria 1967, *The holy rain ceremony* [recorded by Ramón Arzápalo Marín in Chemax].
SBM	Sebastián Baas May, Yaxley, Quintana Roo
SME	Saturnino May Ek, Yaxley, Quintana Roo
T'UUP	May Pool, Norma 1996, *T'ùup* [recorded by Elisabeth Verhoeven in Yaxley].
UTSTS'	Tun, Bernadino 1930, "U Tsikbàal Ts'ono'b". Andrade, Manuel J. and Máas Collí, Hilaria (eds.) 1990, *Cuentos mayas yucatecos, tomo I*, Mérida: Universidad Autónoma de Yucatán; 59-64.
UUCHUL	May Pool, Norma 1996 [recorded by Elisabeth Verhoeven in Yaxley].
VEC	Vicente Ek Catzin, Yaxley, Quintana Roo
XTUUCHAH	Tun, Bernadino 1930, "Xtùuchah". Andrade, Manuel J. and Máas Collí, Hilaria (eds.) 1990, *Cuentos mayas yucatecos, tomo I*, Mérida: Universidad Autónoma de Yucatán; 519-529.
XWAAY	Romero Castillo, Moisés 1964, "Tres cuentos mayas." *Anales del INAH*, Tomo XVII, 64:305-306.
YMS	Yong-Min Shin (University of Jinju)

Chapter 1

Introduction

1.1 *Subject of investigation*

The present work is a study of the functional domain of experience in Yucatec Maya (henceforth YM), the Mayan language of the Yucatán Peninsula and parts of Guatemala and Belize. Experience is a basic phenomenon in human life. It constitutes a fundamental concept that must be rendered in every language in some way or another. The domain of experience, as understood here, covers more specific types of experiences that are ultimately related to the processing of inner and outer stimuli by the human (and animal) nervous system and other related systems. More specifically, this concerns (the faculty of) sensual perception, bodily sensations and feelings, cognitive processes, as well as emotional reactions.

There are a number of languages that code experiential situations in a special grammaticalized way. These include Caucasian languages that have a special case, sometimes called affective, otherwise dative, to code an experiencer of several types of experiences (Comrie 2001, Comrie and van den Berg 2003). The examples in (1) are from Lezgian (North Caucasian, Haspelmath 1993). Lezgian puts the experiencer of perceptual (1a), sensory (1b), volitional (1c), emotional (1d) and cognitive situations (1e) in the dative case.

(1)   a. *Zamira.di-z   Diana   aku-na.*
          Zamita-DAT   Diana   see-AOR
          'Zamira saw Diana.' (Haspelmath 1993:270)

        b. *Za-z   gisin-da.*
          1.SG-DAT   hungry-PRED
          'I am hungry.' (ibid:116)

        c. *Ča-z   kwe-q^h galaz k'wal-er degišar-iz k'an-zawa.*
          we-DAT [you.all-POESS with   house-PL change-INF] want-IMPF
          'We want to exchange apartments with you all.' (ibid:225)

        d. *Za-z   wun   k'an-zawa.*
          1.SG-DAT ABS.2.SG love-IMPF
          'I love you.' (ibid:137)

e. *Za-z   či-zwa.*
1.SG-DAT   know-IMPF
'I know.' (ibid:139)

English, in contrast, codes the experiencer shown in the translations of (1a-e) in all cases as the subject of experiential adjectives or verbs. Such a unified treatment by a language is judged as a clue that languages may conceptualize experiences in a unified way, and this is taken as the point of departure for the functional analysis of experience in language in the present work.

Furthermore, the verb type hierarchy presented in Tsunoda (1981), which is supposed to underlie an implicational hierarchy of transitive vs. non-transitive verb marking in a language, features experiencer verbs in three of six positions. This can be seen as an indication that experiencer verbs are semantically conspicuous in constituting a probable transition group with respect to transitivity, i.e., that they vary as to transitivity and grammatical coding in general. These are just a few examples from a growing body of literature on experiencer coding which clearly show that experiential predicates are likely to constitute a particular predicate class associated with a possibly distinctive argument structure in a language.

Further data, which comes predominantly from Asian and African languages, but also from native languages of the Americas, shows the predominant use of so-called psycho-collocations,[1] frequently body or person part constructions, which are a very characteristic means in these languages of rendering experiential situations. Compare the examples from Belhare (Sino-Tibetan, Eastern Kiranti; (2a)), Ewe (Niger-Congo, Kwa; (2b)) and Jacaltec (Mayan; (2c)) for illustration.[2]

(2)   a. *U-niũa   hab-yu.*
           POSS.3.SG-mind   cry-NPST
           'He is desperate.' (Bickel 1997[P]:145)

        b. *é-kpe   ŋu ná-m.*
           3.SG-weigh skin to-1.SG
           'I am ashamed of it.' (Ameka 1990:167)

        c. *ç-Ø-tz'a   hin   c'ul   s-to   naj.*
           NEUT-SET.B.3-burn SET.A.1.SG   stomach SET.A.3-go CLF/3.SG.M
           'I am sad that he is going.'   (Craig 1977:252)

---

[1] This term has been introduced in Matisoff (1986).

[2] Other languages which frequently use body or person part constructions to render experience include Tzotzil (Mayan, Haviland 1988), Dholuo (Western Nilotic, Reh 1998[L]), Mangap-Mbula (Austronesian/Western-Oceanic, Bugenhagen 1990, 2001), Wardaman (non-Pama Nyungan, Merlan 1994), and Sino-Tibetan languages (Matisoff 1986), to name just a few.

YM also uses the strategy of body or person part constructions in the expression of experiential situations (cf., e.g., Hanks 1990:87, Stolz and Stolz 1993 for a number of examples). In this respect, the language contrasts with Standard Average European (SAE) languages – following Benjamin L. Whorf's term – that exhibit such a phenomenon only marginally, being found only in fixed expressions (idioms). The 'seat' of bodily and emotional feelings in YM is *óol* 'mind, heart' and a number of internal experiences are ascribed to this entity instead of to the person as a whole. Compare (3a) for a plain body part construction and (3b) for a local body part construction.

(3)   a. *Míin   ma'   tòoh   in   w-óol-i'.*
         perhaps NEG   straight POSS.1.SG Ø-mind-NEGF
         'I think I am not well. (lit.: my mind is not straight)' (Blair and Vermont Salas 1965/1967:745)

      b. *In   w-uk'ul   hach   ki',*
         POSS.1.SG Ø-drink   really delicious
         ba'le'   a   hàanal mas ki'   t-in   chi'.
         however POSS.2 food   more delicious LOC-POSS.1.SG mouth
         'My drink is really sweet, but I like your food even more. (lit.: but your food is more delicious to my mouth)' (López Otero 1914:25)

The present work will present a comprehensive semanto-syntactic study of experiential expressions in YM. These will be described and evaluated with respect to a typologically relevant frame that will be established in ch. 3 based on typological and language-specific studies of the expression of experiential situations.

A function-oriented investigation of experience may be viewed as including descriptive as well as expressive words and expressions (cf., e.g., Kövecses 2000 with respect to the study of emotions). The former primarily embody the epistemic function of language,[3] i.e., the function that is concerned with 'talking about entities and states of affairs'. The latter type of expression embodies the social function of language; more specifically it is related to the speaker himself and the immediate reflection of his inner situation.[4] Against this background, the present work will deal with the study of descriptive means (i.e., lexemes, constructional patterns, grammatical regularities in the language about emotions and internal experiential states, processes and events), while

---

[3] This corresponds to the "Darstellungsfunktion" in Bühler (1934) and to the "referential function" in Jakobson (1960).

[4] This refers to the "Ausdrucksfunktion" in Bühler's terms, while Jakobson calls this function "emotive".

the immediate reflection of a speaker's emotions, e.g., by interjections, etc. will be excluded.[5]

1.2 *Theoretical approach*

The theoretical approach followed in the present work is a functional-typological one. In this, however, it does not rely on a single framework, but draws on various approaches.

From the UNITYP framework as developed in the research on language universals and typology in Seiler (1988), Seiler and Premper (eds., 1991), and Seiler (2000), this investigation has borrowed the conceptualization of functional domains as identifying the universally relevant communicative and cognitive functions that language is assumed to ultimately serve. A functional domain can be characterized by those techniques that are used in the languages of the world to fulfill these functions. Thus, the functional domain of participation is characterized by the techniques 'verb classes', 'valency', 'case marking', 'argument structure', etc. (Seiler 1988:100). The concepts identifying a given functional domain are partly linguistic, and partly extralinguistic in nature; in any case, they are independent of the structure of any particular language. For instance, the concept of the experiencer is a functional category that is different from its specific coding in a given language, e.g., as a dative marked noun phrase.

The universality of the functional domain of experience is based on the anthropological prerequisites that are common to and characteristic of every human being, independent of the cultural imprinting that he undergoes during life. These are the common anatomical and physiological attributes that human beings share. One of their most basic manifestations is human sentience, i.e., the faculty of sensual perception and bodily sensation as well as the faculty of cognitive processing and emotional reaction to external stimuli. From these basic biological facts, common to all human beings (and some of them to higher animals as well), the subdomains of the functional domain of experience can be deduced: bodily sensation, emotion, cognition, volition, and perception. These subdomains will be characterized in sect. 3.2.

The description of a linguistic phenomenon may proceed either from a form-based perspective or from a function-based perspective (cf. Seiler 1988, Lehmann 1989, 1998). The form-based approach is also called 'semasiological'. It begins with linguistic structures and then identifies their function. The function-based approach is also called 'onomasiological'. It operates the opposite way, presupposing cognitive and communicative functions and identifying

---

[5] A study devoted to the expression of emotions within linguistic structure is, for instance, Hübler 1998.

those linguistic structures that fulfill them. In the present investigation both views are used in different parts of the analysis.

The functional domain of experience as roughly outlined above deliminates the kinds of grammatical constructions of investigation. These, however, will constitute the perspective of the main description of experiential constructions in YM in ch. 5. A form-based outline has been chosen here since the domain of experience is predominantly lexically structured. The constructional outline starts with predicate types and their specific constructional patterns that are relevant to rendering experiential situations in YM. Which constructions pertain to which experiential subdomains will be analyzed from this perspective. The investigation of experiential predicates as propositional predicates in ch. 7, in contrast, takes a functional vantage point. A functionally oriented analysis is suitable for experiential matrix constructions since subordination patterns depend to a large degree on the semantics of the respective predicates (cf. Noonan 1985).

The analysis of experiential constructions in ch. 5 follows a constructional approach in the spirit of construction grammar as initiated by works such as Fillmore (1988), Kay and Fillmore (1999), Goldberg (1995) and others, which will be explained in sect. 2.3. Further theoretical assumptions taken as a basis for the empirical analysis will be referred to in ch. 2.

1.3   *The language under investigation: Yucatec Maya*
1.3.1 *Some general information*
YM belongs to the Yucatecan branch of the Mayan languages and is spoken on the Yucatán peninsula in southeastern Mexico and in the neighboring areas of Belize and Guatemala. The Mexican part of the language area includes the states of Yucatán, Quintana Roo and Campeche. Spoken by about 800,000 people it is the largest indigenous language of Mexico. The language is generally used for oral communication and only rarely for written communication. It is influenced more and more by its Spanish superstratum. The autodenomination of the language is *Maya t'àan* 'Maya speech', or simply *Maya*.

The whole language area is generally considered rather homogeneous regarding dialectal diversification. According to Pfeiler (1995), one can, however, distinguish between a western and an eastern variety based on some regular lexical and morphological differences. The western variety is spoken in the northwest of the peninsula, including the urban areas around Mérida and the city of Campeche, whereas the eastern variety covers the rest of the language area, especially Valladolid and the rural areas to the east and south of Valladolid.

YM is usually learnt as a first language. Bilingualism with Spanish is generally common in urban areas (such as Mérida, Valladolid, Chetumal, and Felipe Carrillo Puerto) and in villages near the main highways, while in more remote rural areas, monolingualism, though certainly in the process of vanishing, still exists.

The ancestor of the Modern variety of YM is called Classical or, more often, Colonial YM. It is dated between the middle of the 15th century and the middle of the 17th century, thus, including the time of colonial submission. During this period, a writing system based on the Spanish orthography was developed by missionaries. The transition to Modern YM is characterized by considerable changes in the areas of the lexicon, morphology and syntax (Lehmann 1990[L]:31f.). Colonial YM will not be a focus of the present study, but will occasionally be treated in comparison to Modern YM data.

1.3.2 *Previous research on Yucatec Maya*

In the following section, the current research status of YM will be briefly depicted. General results of research related to experiential constructions will be addressed in sect. 3.1.

To carry out the present investigation, I was able to rely on a considerable body of previous work on YM. An investigator of YM has at his disposal a number of historical and contemporary dictionaries. The *Diccionario Maya Cordemex* (Barrera Vásquez et al. eds. 1980) provides a compilation of a larger number of older dictionaries starting with the *Diccionario de Motul* (1573–1617). Also included are unpublished modern sources. Thus, this dictionary covers a time period from Colonial YM to the Modern variety spoken today. Comprehensive dictionaries of contemporary YM are Bricker et al. (1998) and the recent *Diccionario Maya Popular. Maya–Español, Español–Maya* of the Academia de la lengua maya de Yucatán. Essential work on Colonial YM includes McQuown (1967) and Smailus (1989).

Important works on YM from a structuralist tradition are Blair (1964) on the morphosyntax of nouns and verbs, and the grammar of Andrade, which, regrettably, could only be published posthumously in 1955 on microfilm as a kind of edited field notes (see Andrade 1955). Andrade's work is based on a huge corpus of spontaneous discourse and recorded texts, and the available grammar contains a great number of notated examples from these sources. Andrade's corpus is published on microfilm in Andrade and Vermont-Salas (1971), and part of it has been revised and printed in Andrade and Máas Collí (eds., 1991). Some of these texts have been included in my database and are the source of some examples in the present study. Texts from a language course by Blair and Vermont-Salas (1965/1967) are a further source of my data collection (which will be commented on in more detail in the following chapter).

Following the works of Blair and Andrade, a number of studies have appeared related to diverse aspects of the grammar of YM most of which are related to morpho-syntactic questions. One of these, Owen (1968), gives a thorough account of the verbal morphosyntax. Durbin and Ojeda (1978) discusses constituent order patterns of clauses and sentences. Bricker (1979) is an essential source for cleft constructions, which will enter the discussion of YM grammatical relations in sect. 4.3. Bricker (1981[I]) provides a grammatical introduction to verbal inflectional paradigms, and Bricker (1981[S]) analyzes the YM ergative split from a diachronic angle. Lehmann (1991) gives a general characterization of the language, providing basic information on the phonology, morphology, and syntax of the language. Lucy (1992) includes a study on number marking in YM and Lucy (1994) analyzes formal verb classes and the semantic motivation of the derivational relations between them.

Of immediate relevance to the present study are several works by Lehmann, Lehmann et al., and Bohnemeyer which have appeared in recent years. Lehmann (1993[P]) classifies a substantial set of predicates from all classes according to a number of semantic tests. Lehmann (1993[G]) discusses the syntax of aspect and mood auxiliaries. Lehmann (1998) is a comprehensive study of the functional and formal aspects of possession in YM, an area that is especially well developed in the language. Against this background, Lehmann et al. (2000[D]) and (2000[P]) analyze the preponderance of YM possessive constructions and their interaction with participant relations from a typological perspective. The results of these studies build one starting point in the typological analysis of YM experiencer constructions in the present work (cf. sect. 2.2.3).

A text which is very important for the present investigation is Bohnemeyer's (1998[T]) dissertation on the expression of time relations in YM. Bohnemeyer provides a thorough analysis of the aspect-mood system of the language, showing that the category tense is not semantically coded in YM, but instead transmitted by pragmatic inferences. Those parts relevant for the grammar of YM are published in Bohnemeyer (2002). Results of Bohnemeyer (1998[S]) which deal with the topicalization of clauses are referred to in sect. 4.2 of the present work dealing with complex constructions in YM. Finally, Bohnemeyer (2001) and (2004) on argument structure and linking in YM will be considered in the discussion of grammatical relations in sect. 4.3.

1.3.3 *Orthographical conventions*

In the present work the orthographic standards developed in the Yucatec Maya Research Project at the Universities of Bielefeld and Erfurt (Lehmann 1996[O]) are followed. It is largely compatible with the orthographic standard used in Mexico (cf. Academia de la lengua maya de Yucatán s.d.), but differs from the Mexican standard on three points. While lexical high tone is indicated in both orthographic standards by an acute accent, lexical low tone is indicated differently. The lexical low tone is not indicated at all in the Mexican standard. This is due to the fact that it only appears with long vowels, so that indication of long vowels, which is done by doubling the letter, is considered sufficient in the Mexican standard. In the Bielefeld/Erfurt orthography, however, the low tone is indicated by a grave accent. Furthermore, vowels followed by a glottal stop are shortly reverberated if they occur within a syllable, which is not orthographically represented in the Bielefeld/Erfurt orthography, therefore, e.g., <u'> represents [u'u] in the mentioned context. Finally, the voiceless glottal fricative /h/ is spelled <h> in the Bielefeld/Erfurt standard, while it is spelled <j> in the Mexican orthography, based on Spanish spelling.

1.4 *Methodological approach and data collection*

The descriptive and analytical parts of this work (ch. 5–8) are to a large extent based on fieldwork that was carried out in 5 stages between 1996 and 2003 in various places on the Yucatán Peninsula of Mexico. The main field site was the village of Yaxley, located in the state of Quintana Roo. Further work on the language was carried out in Felipe Carrillo Puerto (Quintana Roo) and Valladolid and in the surrounding villages of St. Andres-XBac and Yalcobá (Yucatán). Both areas of investigation belong to the eastern variety of YM as depicted in sect. 1.3.1. Furthermore, I worked with one of my main consultants, Amedee Colli Colli, for two weeks at the University of Erfurt in November 2002, and I had the opportunity to consult her during the writing up of this work via e-mail for the final checking of several points. Most of my consultants are bilingual to some degree, having acquired Spanish primarily in school. Those consultants who contributed to the present work are indicated in the list of text sources (sect. Abbreviations).

The methods of data collection used in the field can be assigned to either of the two approaches to language outlined in sect. 1.2, i.e., the onomasiological and the semasiological approach. Both approaches were used alternately. The onomasiological perspective was taken in the form of guided elicitation, which I used to collect native utterances containing experiential lexemes and constructions. I designed a questionnaire of experiential stimulus situations (similar to those used in the questionnaire of Dahl 1985), which the consultants were asked to translate into YM. Each situation contained a stimulus utterance for which the YM equivalent of a Spanish experiential term was sought. Furthermore, the consultants were asked to continue talking about the situation in YM. In addition, I asked directly for translations of Spanish experiential, and especially emotional terms. However, this lead to the discovery of hitherto unknown YM experiential lexemes in only a few cases.

Besides these types of direct elicitation, I tried to indirectly induce discourse on experience. I asked the consultants to talk about emotive situations, and to describe (sequences of) pictures of emotive scenes.

The semasiological vantage point could be taken once a considerable number of relevant experiential items was collected. In direct elicitation, semantics and structural behavior of the items were tested. This included acceptability tests, which, however, were mostly based on available discourse or isolated examples given by some consultant, possibly on other occasions. The semantics of YM emotion terms was systematically tested following a catalogue of parameters that have been identified as crucial in scenarios of emotions (cf. Wierzbicka 1999). Furthermore, tests concerning situation properties of predicates and particular constructions were conducted. These tests and the motivation of their use in this study are dealt with in sect. 5.1.2.

In addition to the data collected in this way and the data from published sources that were mentioned in sect. 1.3.2, I had the opportunity to use transcribed material from the abovementioned Yucatec Maya Project at the Universities of Bielefeld and Erfurt. The text database developed in this project consists of roughly 12,000 entries. It includes texts from different sources (see section "text sources"), such as several stories from Andrade and Vermont-Salas (1971), Dzul Poot (1985), and Andrade and Máas Collí (1991), and part of the dialogues provided in Blair and Vermont-Salas (1965/1967). Furthermore, a considerable number of texts have been recorded by different members of the abovementioned project, generally in the village of Yaxley.

Finally, it has to be mentioned that I occasionally collected material on experiential constructions in Bété (Niger-Kongo, Bendi) with François Kipré Blé (University of Abidjan) and in Korean with Yong-Min Shin (University of Jinju) and Myung-Chul Koo (University of Seoul). This has been included in the typological chapter 3, especially sect. 3.4. To identify the examples provided by these persons, I give their initials following the translation.

1.5 *General objectives and outline of the present work*

The aims of the present study are threefold. Firstly, it is intended to present a structurally as well as functionally comprehensive description of the domain of experience in YM. This is understood to be a contribution to the description of a language that can only be maintained with the support of linguists.

Besides this descriptive work, typological comparison with other languages is undertaken. A typological perspective can sharpen the analysis of a particular phenomenon in a language, and at the same time, language-specific results contribute to the typological knowledge about that phenomenon.

Finally, a study of the experiential constructions of YM should not only contribute to the theory of the linguistic coding of experience, but also to its cognitive foundations which are relevant for linguistic theory. For this purpose, the functional domain of experience and the experiential situation and its components are outlined. This outline has the status of a *tertium comparationis*, and should thus be applicable to any other language as well.

Following these objectives, the study will proceed as follows. Chapter 2 introduces the main theoretical assumptions underlying the investigation. These include a typology of situations and the participants relevant to them, questions of the interrelation of syntax and semantics, and an outline of the construction-based approach used for the description of the empirical facts in chapters 5–6.

In chapter 3, functional and formal prerequisites of experience and its linguistic manifestation are discussed. First the functional domain of experience is depicted (sect. 3.2), followed by a general outline of the experiential situation and its components in sect. 3.3. These parts present the functional apparatus for the analysis of experiential constructions in YM. Sect. 3.4 treats the grammatical coding of experience and thus identifies the structural background of the analysis of the YM experiential constructions. Finally, the role of figurative language in the investigation of experiential constructions is discussed in sect. 3.5.

With chapter 4, the language-specific part of the study begins. This chapter provides a description of the basic grammatical features of YM that are necessary to understand the analysis of the experiential constructions in the remaining chapters.

Chapter 5 constitutes the core of the empirical analysis of experiential constructions in YM. The presentation starts from a structural perspective and construction types are grouped by the word class of the predicative element, be it experiential in meaning, based on metaphor, or a kind of abstract predicator. It is shown that there is a rather straightforward correlation between the experiential subdomains and formal predicate types. Person part constructions containing the person part noun *óol* 'mind' are argued to constitute genuine experiential constructions, with *óol* functioning as a kind of desemanticized experiential marker.

The remaining chapters, 6–8, discuss more specific issues related to YM experiential constructions. Chapter 6 examines grammatical properties of experiencers against a typological background. It is shown that, due to a well-developed derivational system between stative and verbal classes, experiencers may occur in any syntactic function and generally behave canonically in these functions. Rather exceptional cross-linguistically however, is the grammatical behavior of indirect object experiencers in certain matrix and possessive constructions. In chapter 7, experiential predicates are investigated in their function as complement taking predicates. Here, it is shown that the semantic membership in a given experiential class determines the subordination patterns of a matrix predicate. Furthermore, YM experiential complementation patterns are roughly in accordance with the *binding* and *desententialization/deranking* hierarchies that have been claimed for subordination in typological literature. Chapter 8 proposes a semantic analysis of body and person part terms occurring in experiential collocations.

Finally, chapter 9 provides a summary of the empirical part of the investigation and examines the results from a cross-linguistic perspective. It is shown that the grammatical structure of the domain of experience in YM is largely influenced by its typological profile. Experiential constructions draw largely on more general construction types such as person part constructions, the existential construction, the transitive construction, etc. and most of their properties are inherited from these.

CHAPTER 2

Theoretical preliminaries

The present section introduces the main theoretical assumptions upon which the investigation of experiential constructions in YM in this work is based. This includes a typology of situations and their linguistic expression (sect. 2.1), general assumptions about the interrelation between semantics and syntax (sect. 2.2), and a description of the model used for the analysis of the data, i.e., the constructional approach (sect. 2.3).

2.1 *Conceptualization of a situation*

The following outline draws on various mainly function-based theoretical approaches in linguistic theory. The main points have been outlined in Lehmann et al. (2000[D]), (2000[U]), (2000[Z]), following Fillmore (1977), Comrie (1981), Dik (1978, 1997), Foley and Van Valin (1984), Givón (1984), Langacker (1987), Lehmann (1991[P]), (1993[P]), Croft (1991), and Van Valin and LaPolla (1997). A comparable approach to a functional typology of situations can be found in Halliday (1985).

2.1.1 *General*

A situation is defined as a cognitive representation. It is comprised of entities that are called participants. A participant can be related to one or more other participants in stative or dynamic relations. These relations may be thought of as criss-crossing through an immaterial center, which is called the situation core.[1] The situation core can thus be regarded as the reification of the relation(s) among the participants. On the linguistic level, it can have different degrees of complexity according to the specificity of the relation. More abstract relations such as, e.g., identification (cf. (4a) from Russian), class inclusion (cf. (4b) from YM), or possession may not be rendered linguistically by their own sign but may be inferred from context.

(4)   a. *Sadovnik – ubijca.*
            'The gardener is the murderer.' (Lehmann et al. 2000[D]:5)

---

[1] This corresponds to the *participatum* in Seiler (1984) and subsequent work.

> b. *hun-túul   x-wàay   le   ko'lel-o'*
>   one-CL.AN   F-sorcerer   DEF   lady-D2
>   'that lady is a witch' (Lehmann 1998)

With increasing specificity, however, an explicit linguistic expression becomes necessary. The common linguistic representation of the situation core is therefore the predicate, which is generally formed by a verb or by other predicating elements. These lexicalize different types of situation cores. In doing so, they may focus on only some of the numerous relations that exist among participants on a cognitive level. At the same time languages generally focus on certain aspects of the situation (core) including dynamicity, telicity, manner (of performance), number and kind of participants, etc., in their lexicalizations of situations, i.e., in their verbal lexicon. In a comparison between the linguistic encoding of the situation: breaking a window by means of throwing a stone at it, Van Valin and LaPolla (1997:87ff.) identifies several differences between English and Lakhota. Lakhota obligatorily codes properties of the affected object (flat, brittle vs. long, thin) and the manner of action (striking vs. action from distance) in the verb, while English leaves both types of information implicit if they are not relevant for discourse targets. Furthermore, the two languages differ as to which participants need to be expressed and in what way they may be expressed. While in English it is possible to code the instrument as the subject of the verbs *break* or *shatter*, this is not possible for the Lakhota equivalent *bléčha* 'break'.

Participants are commonly encoded as noun phrases. This is an iconic reflection of their status as entities. By virtue of assuming that there is a situation core, relations between the participants and the situation core can be identified. These characterize the role of a given participant in a situation, i.e., its participant role. On the linguistic level, participant relations are mirrored by the relations between the predicate and its arguments. These latter relations differ from participant relations by being linguistic in nature. They will be called semantic roles in this work (s. sect. 2.1.4). Furthermore, a participant bears properties that are independent of its relation to the situation core or other participants. These are called participant features[2] and include the participant's position on the empathy or animacy hierarchy (s. sect. 2.1.3).

Given the nature of situations as outlined above, the situation core and the participants are interdependent (correlative) notions (Lehmann 1991, ch. 2.2), i.e., neither the situation core nor the participants have priority. Rather, the

---

[2] Concerning the necessity of distinguishing between participant roles and participant features, cf. Comrie (1981, ch. 3.1), Lehmann (1991[P]), etc.

situation core is constituted by the relations between the participants.[3] In the following, aspects of the situation itself (sect. 2.1.2) and aspects of the participants, namely, participant features (sect. 2.1.3) and participant roles (sect. 2.1.4) will be discussed.[4]

2.1.2 *Situation types and their features*

The term situation is meant here as a generic term comprised of different more specific situation types (see Comrie 1976, Lyons 1977 and Lehmann 1991, 1993[P]). It largely corresponds to the notions "state of affairs" in Dik (1978, 1997) or Van Valin and LaPolla (1997), "process" in Halliday (1985), or "event" in Bohnemeyer (1998[T], 2002) and Schultze-Berndt (2000).[5]

Situation types vary according to different types of parameters.[6] Most important are those related to their internal temporal structure, i.e., their time stability.[7] Most theories dealing with the internal temporal structure of situations or their respective predicates are based on three parameters, namely, dynamicity (stative vs. dynamic), telicity (telic vs. atelic) and durativity (durative vs. punctual).[8] Dynamicity refers to the question of whether or not there is a change inside the situation or at its margins. Telicity refers to whether or not a situation has intrinsic or natural boundaries (either at its left or right margin or both) or if it is naturally unbounded. Durativity concerns the temporal extension of a situation, which contrasts with its being momentary. Numerous examples from different languages can be found in the literature to show the linguistic relevance of these parameters. These include derivational processes

---

[3] This seems to be the reason for why theories vary in assigning certain parameters either to the situation or to the participants, such as, e.g., the parameter of control to be discussed below. Van Valin and LaPolla (1997), in contrast, argues for the priority of the predicate and the complete dependency of the argument roles on the predicate.

[4] Cf. a similar approach in Van Valin and Wilkins (1996), which distinguishes between entity-related characteristics and event- or state-related characteristics.

[5] Terminological variation is due to the fact that there is no generic term in standard English (and supposedly in other languages) that covers all types of 'situations'.

[6] Furthermore, it may be assumed that the kind or domain of situation the participants are involved in, e.g., motion, position, action, experience, communication, possession, transfer, etc., constitutes a situation type parameter. This information, however, is to a large degree defined by participant features and role features.

[7] This term is introduced in Givón (1979, ch. 8) and used in Lehmann (1993[P]) to cover different parameters concerning the internal temporal structure of the situations to be introduced below.

[8] Cf. Bohnemeyer (1998[T], 2002) for a detailed description of concepts of time semantics and Sasse (2002) for a detailed overview of aspect theories.

such as processive, inchoative, resultative, semelfactive, and iterative derivations between verb classes.[9]

The parameters of dynamicity, durativity and telicity can be projected on a
one-dimensional scale where more specific situation types can be located.[10]
These show a specific combination of values of the abovementioned parameters (cf. Lehmann 1991, 1993[P]). Such a scale is schematized in Figure 1,
which has been adapted from Lehmann (1991[P]:203, 1994:3298).

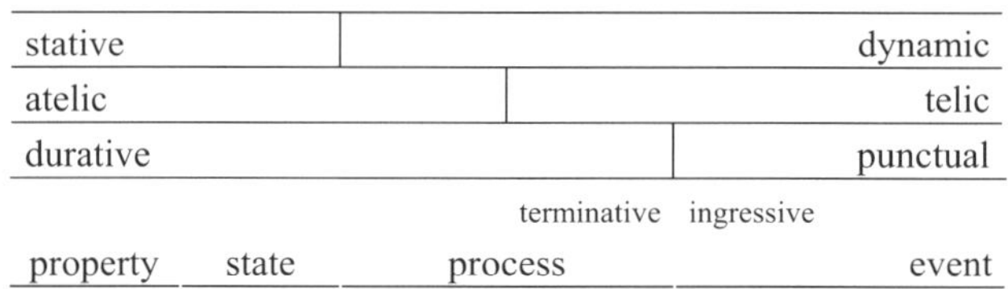

Figure 1. Scale of time stability

Figure 1 reflects the implicational relations among the parameters given (cf.
Bohnemeyer 2002:34). Thus, stative situations are necessarily atelic, and atelic
situations are necessarily durative. Punctual situations are always telic, and
telic situations are by necessity dynamic. Thus, the combination of the parameters resulting in more specific situation types is limited due to the exclusion of
certain combinations.[11]

Below, some characteristics of the more specific situation types, which are
located in the lower part of Figure 1, will be outlined. Properties, in contrast to
more dynamic situation types, do not have potential boundaries and cannot be

---

[9] Some of these derivational processes have traditionally been referred to as *Aktionsarten*. Me-
anwhile, the term *Aktionsart* is also used to refer to the internal temporal structure of verbs independent of overt marking (cf. Van Valin and LaPolla 1997, Bickel 1997[A]/2000). Other
terms used in this sense are *aspectual type, aspectual character, verbal character, lexical a-
spect*, etc. (cf. Lyons 1977, Lehmann 1994, Bohnemeyer 2002, Sasse 2002). In this work the
term *aspectual character* is used when referring to the internal temporal structure of a lexical
predicate.

[10] The idea of projecting a combination of binary oppositions on a one-dimensional scale is also common in phonology; cf. Blevins (1995:211) with respect to sonority.

[11] Several scholars (e.g., Mourelatos 1981, Smith [2]1997, Bertinetto 1997, Van Valin and La-
Polla 1997) have reconstructed the Vendlerian (1967) *Aktionsart* types state, activity, achievement, and accomplishment in a typology of verb/predicate classes, each type being characterized by a set of specific values of the parameters of dynamicity, telicity and durativity. These
can be allocated in Figure 1 in the following way: activities are dynamic, atelic and durative,
accomplishments are dynamic, telic and durative, and achievements are dynamic, telic and
punctual. These concepts will be used only sporadically, generally when referring to research
done within this framework. Activities partly correspond to processes as used above, but they
involve a controlling main participant. Accomplishments correspond to terminative processes,
and achievements to ingressive and punctual events.

located in time. Property concepts are generally lexicalized as adjectives if a language possesses a genuine class of adjectives. In those languages that possess a closed class of adjectives, these exclusively represent property concepts (cf. Givón 1979). Properties can be characterized as absolute states and they can in this way be distinguished from contingent states (cf. Comrie 1976, ch. 5.2.1.2, Lyons 1977:717, Lehmann 1991:197). The latter do not have intrinsic boundaries, but they can be located in time and allow for durational specification. A prototypical state, as opposed to a process, is described as involving no energy to go on or be kept going. Processes, as opposed to states, involve a change in time (cf., e.g., Comrie 1976, Lehmann 1991, Van Valin and LaPolla 1997). As concerns lexicalization, states often pertain to different parts of speech, i.e., nouns, adjectives and verbs. While languages such as Korean, which has a small closed class of adjectives which only denote property concepts, lexicalize stative concepts as (stative) verbs, languages such as English, which possesses a large and productive class of adjectives, code many stative concepts as adjectives.

Dynamic situations are either processes, i.e., if they involve duration, or events, i.e., if they are punctual. More specific subtypes arise from the parameter of telicity. Those processes that are bounded at the end or right margin are called terminative, while situations that are bounded at the start or left margin are called ingressive. Finally, punctual situations are bounded at both margins without involving a temporal extension inbetween them. Dynamic situations are generally lexicalized as verbs.

Processes and events, as characterized in Figure 1, may involve changes of state in the sense of Dowty (1979), Jackendoff (1990) and others who undertake a decompositional analysis in the representation of situations. A change of state focuses on the transition between states. Changes of state may be either gradual or absolute. Absolute changes are naturally telic (e.g., Engl. *die, burst*). Gradual (or incremental) changes (e.g., Engl. *grow, melt, vaporize, cross, etc.*) may either involve a discrete end state or not. In the former case the predicate or construction is telic (e.g., *This flower grew five inches in six months*), in the latter case it is atelic (e.g., *This flower grew for years*). Typical activity verbs such as Engl. *dance, walk,* etc. are atelic in bare use but telic when a goal is specified (e.g., *walk to the sea*). These examples show that two levels of application of the parameters of time stability must be distinguished, i.e., a lexeme-semantic level and a construction-semantic level.[12]

---

[12] Cf., e.g., Fabricius-Hansen (1991), Lehmann (1994), Bickel (1997[A]), Bohnemeyer (2001, 2002), Primus (1999:41), and Sasse (2002) for further examples concerning differences in telicity and durativity based on the type or role of the participant involved (e.g., its referential specificity, its quantification, its total vs. partial affectedness, etc.) and/or the larger construction in general.

Semantic tests that operationalize the abovementioned parameters are a crucial means of identifying a given situation type or semantic predicate class. Thus, in a given language, a property may be distinguished from a state by the impossibility of combining it with time adverbials such as 'yesterday', 'last month', etc. In languages like English or German, telicity can be satisfactorily tested by inserting a given predicate into a frame which indicates duration of the situation (*X for an hour*) vs. a frame which indicates its limits (*X in an hour*). Since these tests are semantic in nature, they are largely language specific. Those tests used in the present study for the analysis of YM will be introduced in sect. 5.1.2.

Other parameters, such as control and causation, have occasionally been ascribed to the situation core (e.g., Dik 1978, 1997[13]) or used in the decomposition of predicates (cf., e.g., Dowty 1979, Croft 1993, Van Valin and LaPolla 1997). These will be thought of here as participant relations,[14] which will be discussed below in sect. 2.1.4.[15]

2.1.3 *Participant properties*

A participant bears certain properties independently of its relational properties in a situation. These are features such as [animate], [human], [speech act participant], [abstract], [individuated], etc. The properties of a participant can be viewed as its position on the so-called animacy hierarchy (cf. Comrie 1981, ch. 9) or empathy hierarchy (cf. Kuno and Kaburaki 1977, Kuno 1987 and Langacker 1991, ch. 7.3.1.1) which is represented in Figure 2 (based on Lehmann et al. 2000[P]). Distinctions in such hierarchies have been identified as relevant to many grammatical features, among them split ergativity (Silverstein 1976), pronominal systems, inverse systems (e.g., Palmer 1994, ch. 8.2.2.), the assignment of grammatical relations (e.g., Lehmann et al. 2000[P]), etc.

With respect to predicates it is relevant whether or not the participant is able to become involved in a given situation as determined by features such as [animate], [volitional], [sentient], [motive], etc. These features have different

---

[13] For example, Dik (1997, ch. 5.2.) views the parameter [+/- control] as part of the state of affairs based on the view that there is a mutual dependency between state of affairs and semantic functions of the first argument.

[14] Cf. also Primus (1999:39) on the issue of the interrelation between internal aspectual (i.e., *Aktionsart*) properties of the verb and thematic properties of the arguments (corresponding to our semantic roles), especially with respect to the notions active and activity.

[15] Notice that in this respect Bohnemeyer (2001, 2002:30) argues, with reference to a YM verb classification, that role parameters such as agentivity/control and situation parameters such as state change and telicity must be kept apart since there is no universal entailment or matching between the two. On a language-specific level, predicate classes cluster with respect to certain participant properties and relations along with specific situation types.

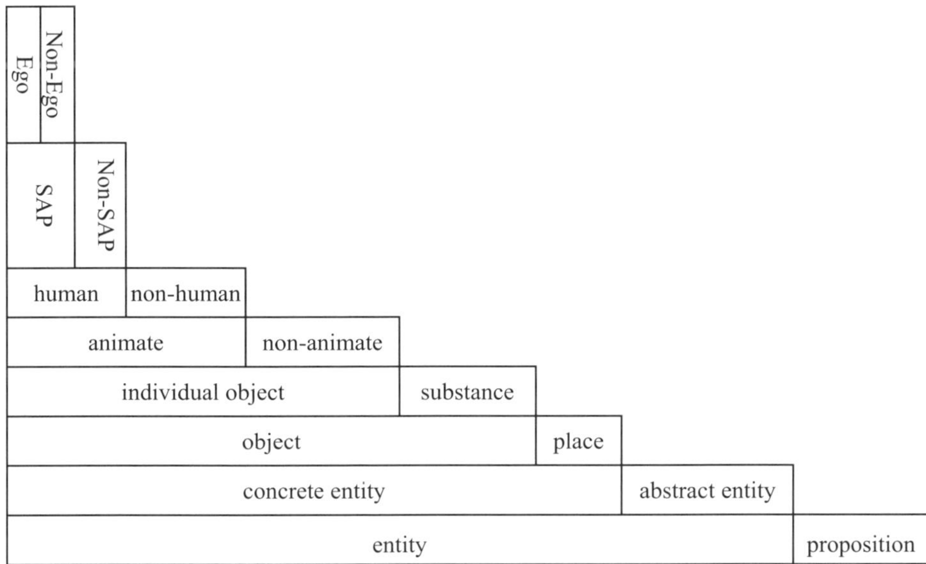

Figure 2. Participant properties

relations to the categories mentioned in Figure 2, e.g., entailment (cf. Van Valin and Wilkins 1996:313ff.). For instance, the feature [human] entails features such as [rational], [intentional], [volitional] and [animate]. In certain cultures young children or infants may be judged as lacking the features [intentional] and/or [rational], so that if they are combined as actors with verbs like *break*, it may result in an interpretation of accidental action. The feature [animate] entails the features [living], [motive] and [sentient]. Languages differ as to whether they allow only animates to combine as actors with certain verbs of action, or if they also allow natural forces or (dependently motive) objects in this function (cf. the different behavior of Lakhota vs. English with respect to the possibility of coding an instrument as the subject of verbs meaning 'break' or 'shatter', as described in sect. 2.1.1).

The participant feature [place] allows for any participant that can function as a place, and the feature [object] allows for anything that can be treated as a thing, including animate beings. Figure 2 further distinguishes between abstract entities and propositions due to their linguistic instantiations as nouns vs. as (possibly reduced) clauses. While some *verba dicendi* (e.g., *say*) exclusively take propositional participants, *verba sentiendi* often allow abstract entities as well as propositions as stimuli participants.

2.1.4 *Participant roles and semantic roles*
The relation of a participant to the situation core constitutes its participant role. Participant roles are thus derived from conceptual relations at a non-linguistic

level. Relations between a predicate and its arguments at the linguistic level correspond to these conceptual relations.[16] In the present work these are called semantic roles.[17] In accordance with general conventions the same role labels will be used on both levels, distinguishing them in the following way: the participant role will be given in normal typeface (e.g., agent), and the semantic role in small capitals (e.g., AGENT).

A number of parameters will be used to define or describe semantic roles. Most important are the notions of control and affectedness, which are part of most characterizations of semantic roles. These are particularly related to the agent–patient pair, or the macrorole pair ACTOR–UNDERGOER (cf. Foley and Van Valin 1984, Van Valin 1993, Van Valin and LaPolla 1997). Control and affectedness are gradient parameters which are opposed to each other, but at the same time, mutually dependent (cf. Givón 1975, Comrie 1981:53ff., Bugenhagen 1990, Lehmann 1991). A controlling participant can be viewed as responsible for the initiation, realization and the end of the situation. It is involved in the situation at least to some degree, although mediated control is possible. Affectedness refers to a participant that is disposed or even acted upon in the situation, generally undergoing some change (of state). Lehmann (1991[P] and subsequent work) has tried to describe the whole range of roles by these parameters, arguing, however, that the less involved a role becomes with respect to the situation at hand, the less it is determined by these two parameters. Thus, roles such as experiencer, beneficiary, emitter, recipient and local roles are less determined by the features control and affectedness.

Involvement is a further parameter along which semantic roles vary. The notion of involvement is based on the relationality of the situation core, which is linguistically reflected in the valency of verbs. Central participants are inherent in the situation and the respective roles can be characterized as inherent

---

[16] A similar distinction of the roles at different levels can be found in typological (e.g Van Valin and LaPolla 1997) as well as in psycholinguistic studies (e.g., Härtl 2001). Note that Van Valin and LaPolla (1997) uses the term 'participant role' similarly, i.e., with respect to the role of the participant in a state of affairs, this being roughly identical to what is here called situation. The labels have been changed with respect to earlier work (Lehmann et al. 2000[D]) for the sake of consistency, accounting for the fact that the term participant is clearly located at the non-linguistic level in the present work. In Lehmann et al. (2000[D]), the label 'cognitive role' is used for what is here called 'participant role' and 'participant role' for what is here referred to as 'semantic role' here.

[17] There is a rather large terminological variety in this area with respect to different theoretical frameworks and conceptions. Earlier expressions include case roles (Fillmore 1968), semantic roles (e.g., Comrie 1981), semantic functions (Dik 1997), participant functions (Halliday 1985), thematic relations (e.g., Jackendoff 1987, Foley and Van Valin 1984, Van Valin 1993, Van Valin and LaPolla 1997), thematic roles (e.g., Givón 1984, Jackendoff 1990, Dowty 1991, Croft 1983, 1991, 1993, 1998), or theta-/θ-roles (e.g., Chomsky 1981, Grimshaw 1990, Chomsky 1995, Pesetzky 1995).

in the lexical semantics of the predicate. This is true for the agent and the patient of a dynamic transitive verb, the recipient of a verb of change of possession or the experiencer in an experiential situation. Peripheral participants, in contrast, are not constitutive in a given situation; their relation to the situation core has to be established. Peripheral roles generally presuppose the existence of other participants. For example, a beneficiary is generally added to situations displaying a beneficient and a benefactum.[18] An instrument and comitative prototypically accompany the agent in dynamic situations and local roles can be added to a large number of situation cores. Thus, the degree of involvement of a participant also depends on the (degree of) involvement of other participants in the same situation.[19] Specific participant roles are only shaped in the periphery of a situation. In the situation core, the identity of the participants becomes indistinct and the participants are merely classified as controlling or affected, i.e., as ACTORS or UNDERGOERS. If peripheral participants are centralized by diverse morphological and syntactic processes, their roles are neutralized in the macroroles ACTOR and UNDERGOER.

The concept of semantic macroroles developed in Role and Reference Grammar and its advancements (Foley and Van Valin 1984, Van Valin 1993, Van Valin and Wilkins 1996, Van Valin and LaPolla 1997) is used in the present work. Semantic macroroles are abstractions over the more specific semantic (micro)roles and have immediate relevance for the syntactic coding of arguments. They are used to link semantics and syntax, i.e., they map semantic roles onto grammatical relations (cf. sect. 2.2.2 for further discussion). Role and Reference Grammar assumes the two macroroles ACTOR and UNDERGOER which are linked to subject and object of a transitive verb in accusative languages. In Lehmann et al. (2000[D]), a third macrorole INDIRECTUS, which links the indirect object, is proposed. This macrorole roughly corresponds to what others have called dative[20] (e.g., Givón 1984), beneficiary (a grammatical role in Palmer 1994), goal (e.g., Croft 1991), or proto-recipient (Primus 1999 following the proto-role approach of Dowty 1991).

On the syntactic level, the difference between central and peripheral roles corresponds to that between complement and adjunct. Complements and adjuncts differ prototypically by the degree of grammaticalization of their relator: while complements are generally marked by more grammaticalized signs such as case, fixed word order, etc., adjuncts are semantically more specific and thus their relation to the situation core is frequently coded by adpositions.

---

[18] For the terminology used, cf. Lehmann et al. (2000[P]).

[19] This point is acknowledged in Croft (1983:87) by his claim that semantic roles must not only be defined paradigmatically but also syntagmatically.

[20] This term seems to be quite unfortunate since it traditionally designates a case. Givón (1984: 107f.) subsumes at least the experiencer and the addressee under the role dative.

Semantic roles, as they have been used in many theoretical approaches, are hybrid notions that combine relational functions (in terms of the parameters involvement, affectedness, controlledness) and absolute properties of participants, namely, their position on the animacy hierarchy and related features of these positions such as, e.g., volitionality, sentience, motiveness, etc. A number of roles are distinguished by the empathy of the respective participant rather than by its relational function (e.g., recipient vs. goal, comitative vs. instrument). A combination of role features and absolute participant features is, however, not sufficient to identify the commonly used roles or to distinguish them from each other. A number of roles, e.g., recipient, experiencer, emitter, etc. are clearly bound to a specific situation type. This implies the necessity of defining participant roles with respect to the situation type they prototypically occur in as a central or peripheral participant.[21] Here the dynamicity of the situation plays a role. Certain roles prototypically occur in dynamic situations (e.g., agent, force, instrument, comitative, patient, recipient, emitter, beneficiary, goal, source), while others are prototypically bound to stative situations (e.g., theme, locus). The more dynamic a situation is, the more participant roles it may potentially include. Peripheral roles such as beneficiary, instrument, comitative, source and goal typically occur in dynamic situations. The parameters of control and affectedness are bound to dynamic situations. In prototypically stative situations (e.g., those referring to properties or states), there is generally only one elementary relation, which is not necessarily related to the predicate by the parameters control and affectedness. concept

At a low level of abstraction, a given verb may be thought of as bearing its specific semantic roles.[22] In this sense, a perception verb bears the specific semantic roles of perceiver and perceived, a cognition verb takes the roles cognizer and cognized. At a higher level of abstraction, perceiver and cognizer may be combined into an experiencer role, the perceived and the cognized into a stimulus role. At an interlingual level as well as at a language-specific level, participant roles may be combined differently to yield more abstract semantic roles. Croft (1991:157) identifies for Mokilese a semantic (macro)role GOAL comprising the recipient, the beneficiary and the allative, while English groups the recipient and the goal against the beneficiary and Russian the recipient and the beneficiary against the allative through formal marking. This example attests to the fact that language typology needs semantic roles at different levels of abstraction.

---

[21] This concept can be found in Dik (1978), Jackendoff (1987), Van Valin (1993), Van Valin and LaPolla (1997), etc. The last two works consider semantic roles (their 'thematic relations') exclusively in terms of argument positions in the 'decomposed' semantic structure of verbs. Participant roles and semantic roles do not have an independent status of their own but are completely derived from the situation core or verb, respectively.

[22] This view is advocated, e.g., in Givón (1984), Croft (1991), Van Valin and Wilkins (1996).

Following from the general characterization of an experiential situation in sect. 1.1, an initial provisional definition can be given for the central semantic roles in an experiential situation, namely, the experiencer and the stimulus. The experiencer is a sentient being that experiences an internal bodily or mental state, process or event. More specifically, the experiencer may be a senser, emotor, cognizer, wanter, or perceiver. The stimulus is an entity or proposition that triggers the experience or to which the experience is directed. More specifically, the stimulus may be the emoted, the cognized, the wanted, or the perceived entity or proposition. In situations of bodily sensation, the stimulus is not a central role. These definitions will be specified and justified with respect to the abovementioned parameters in sect. 3.3.2.

Languages use grammatical coding strategies to render participant relations linguistically. These coding strategies mirror certain possible perspectives of conceptualization of a situation. For example, coding strategies may reflect a causative scheme, an instrumental scheme, etc. Certain participants may be conceptualized as generalized actors or undergoers according to common properties. Against this background, languages tend to extend a preferred coding perspective onto other conceptually homogeneous situations. This is conceived as the basis for argument structure constructions and is used as one means of analyzing the YM data in ch. 5. The integration of the construction approach in the present work will be discussed in sect. 2.3.

Semantic roles are language-specific and at the same time cross-linguistic notions. They are located on the semantic side of a language-specific expression, and gain cross-linguistic relevance in so far as several languages use comparable means or coding strategies for the expression of the same participant role. Thus, semantic roles are not necessarily universal concepts. Peripheral participant roles especially vary considerably in their interlingual coding, both with respect to expression vs. non-expression as well as to the kind of coding a language chooses. The same holds true for those participants that are bound to specific situation types such as experiencer or addressee. Languages differ as to whether they have developed a specific grammatical coding for a given semantic role (e.g., a case for the experiencer in Caucasian languages) or if they map a role onto one or more existing construction types, e.g., coding an experiencer as an ACTOR or an UNDERGOER. In contrast, macroroles such as ACTOR and UNDERGOER as well as specific roles such as AGENT (instigator, initiator) and PATIENT may well be considered as (near-)universal, in so far as most languages displays specific means of coding agent and patient/actor and undergoer in their verbal alignment.

2.2   *On the interrelation of syntax and semantics*
2.2.1 *A hierarchy of grammatical relations*
The syntactic prominence of a participant can be evaluated with respect to a hierarchy of grammatical relations (or syntactic functions), as is shown in Figure 3. Such a hierarchy can be established on the basis of criteria such as the accessibility of the nucleus of a relative clause to a given relation (cf., e.g., Keenan and Comrie 1977, Lehmann 1984, ch. IV.3.1.1), its structural markedness concerning case marking and verb agreement (cf., e.g., Lehmann 1983, sect. 4, Croft 1990, ch. 5.3.2), or its dependency on the valency of verbs.

subject   <   object   <   indirect   <   adjunct   <   adnominal   <   gram. relation in
                              object   relation   subord. clause

Figure 3. Hierarchy of grammatical relations[23]

Figure 3 has to be read as an implicational hierarchy that works from left to right, i.e., if one of the aforementioned criteria is true for a given relation in Figure 3 it will be true for all other relations located to its left. Thus, if a given language allows adjuncts to function as the head of a relative clause, then it will also allow relativization for complements, i.e., subjects, objects and indirect objects. Figure 3 is assumed to apply in a given language and is at the same time true cross-linguistically.

Concerning the structural markedness of grammatical relations, generally those relations located further to the left in Figure 3 are morphologically less marked than those located to the right. The morphological marking of a participant correlates in an inverse way with its potential to trigger verb agreement. Thus, participants on the left side of Figure 3 are more prone to triggering verb agreement than the participants on the right.

The adverbial functions in Figure 3 can also be ranked with respect to their dependency on the valency of verbs. Thus, the single argument of a monovalent verb generally receives subject function. Bivalent verbs are either transitive, taking a subject and a direct object, or they are intransitive, taking a subject and a prepositional object. The ranking of the second (non-subject) argument with bivalent verbs may be deduced from the argument structure of transitive verbs that code prepositional objects as adjuncts outside their valency frame. Finally, a trivalent verb generally takes its third argument as an indirect (or secondary) object.

---

[23] Figure 3 is a simplified version of the hierarchy of syntactic functions given in Lehmann et al. (2000[P]:10).

2.2.2 *Linking between semantic roles and grammatical relations*

Hierarchies of semantic roles have been proposed as linking mechanisms to grammatical relations from the very beginning (cf. Fillmore 1968, Dik 1978, 1997, Foley and Van Valin 1984, Dixon 1989, Grimshaw 1990, Van Valin and LaPolla 1997, etc.).[24] More specifically, in the macrorole approach of Role and Reference Grammar (Foley and van Valin 1984, Van Valin 1993, Van Valin and LaPolla 1997) semantic roles are located on an actor–undergoer hierarchy which indicates their probability of being marked as an actor or undergoer in a language.

In general, rules of the following kind hold true: A single participant in an intransitive situation is always linked to the subject function, irrespective of its participant role, which is determined by the semantic type of the situation core. In a transitive situation, two participants have to be mapped onto subject and object function. In a typical accusative language the highest-ranking macrorole, i.e., the actor, is linked to the syntactic subject, while in a syntactically ergative language the lowest-ranking macrorole, i.e., the undergoer, is linked to the syntactic subject. In a prototypical three participant situation, the participants will be linked to subject, direct object and indirect object functions. Optional participants generally receive oblique syntactic functions, e.g., the instrument, local roles, etc.

However, these are general correlations that work for prototypical cases. Other factors that interfere with a straightforward mapping of semantic roles onto grammatical relations are participant features such as animacy and general force-dynamic relationships[25] among participants. Approaches such as Van Valin and LaPolla (1997) have implicitly incorporated such situation structural properties by identifying thematic roles as argument positions in the logical structure (event structure) of verbs/predicates. In the present work, linking between semantic roles and grammatical relations is generally seen as an interaction of different factors which have been introduced as situation type features and participant properties and roles.

2.2.3 *A typology of person vs. relation prominence*

The influence of a participant's animacy on the assignment of grammatical relations is the focus of a typology of person prominence vs. relation prominence, developed in Lehmann et al. (2000[P]). This typology shows that a language may consistently position animate participants high on Figure 3, irre-

---

[24] The proto-role approach (Dowty 1991, Primus 1999) is similar in ascribing (prototypical) agent (e.g., control, sentience, cause etc.) and patient properties (e.g., affectedness, change of state, etc.) to other roles and claiming these properties as a semantic correlative for linking to subject/A or object/P of a transitive verb.

[25] This refers to the position of participants in the causal chain of an event in terms of transmission of force (cf. Croft 1998:23).

spective of their role in a situation. Many SAE languages follow such a principle and consistently foreground animates in syntactic structure. For example, in German, affected possessors must be coded as dative adjuncts, as in (5). Furthermore, semantically impersonal modal verbs such as the modal of necessity/obligation are construed with a personal subject, as in (12).

(5)   *Du tratst mir auf den Fuß.*
        'You stepped on my foot.'

(6)   *Ich muß gehen.*
        'I have to go.'

If a language does not foreground persons in syntactic coding, but consistently codes them corresponding to their semantic function or relationality, one may speak of relation prominence as a typological trait of the language. In this sense, a typical trait of relation prominence consists of the precedence of inherent relations over established relations in linguistic coding. This means that, e.g., inherent possessive relations are always syntactically coded, even at the expense of simultaneously existing established participant relations. Thus, external possessors are excluded in relation-prominent languages. In YM, the inherent relation between *òok* 'foot' and its first person possessor in (7) is necessarily coded, while, in contrast, there is no possibility of coding the indirect affectedness of the possessor, as in (5). This can be referred to as a strategy of person backgrounding.

(7)   *T-a   ya'-chek'-t-ah   in   w-òok.*
        PFV-SBJ.2 step-foot-TRR-CMPL   [POSS.1.SG Ø-foot]
        'You stepped on my foot.' (EMB 047)

Furthermore, semantically impersonal modal verbs such as the modals of necessity/obligation are construed in an impersonal construction in YM (8a). This strategy is even extended to semantically personal modal verbs such as *tàak* 'anxious, want' (8b).

(8)   a. *K'abéet   in   bin.*
           necessary [SBJ.1.SG   go]
           'I have to go.' (BVS_07.01.24)
        b. *Tàak   in   bin.*
           anxious [SBJ.1.SG   go]
           'I want to go.'

Person foregrounding vs. person backgrounding strategies of participant coding will be discussed against a typological background with respect to experiencer coding in sect. 3.4.4.

2.3 *A construction-based approach*

The notion of construction as a meaningful entity in linguistic analysis is used in many diverse approaches to grammar, including cognitive grammar (e.g., Langacker 1987, Lakoff 1987), construction grammar (e.g., Fillmore 1988, Goldberg 1995, Michaelis and Lambrecht 1996, Kay and Fillmore 1999), radical construction grammar (Croft 2001), and other typologically oriented, generally function-based approaches to language (e.g., Wierzbicka 1988, 2001, Van Valin and LaPolla 1997, etc.). It can be traced back to the work of structuralists such as Bloomfield (1970 [1933]), Hockett (1958), and Frei (1962).[26]

Constructions are viewed here as complex, non-compositional[27] patterns which are linguistic signs in their own right, consisting of a formal and a semantic/functional layer (cf. Zwicky 1987, 1994, Fillmore 1988, Goldberg 1995, Kay and Fillmore 1999, Schultze-Berndt 2002, etc.). They are symbolic units that are (at least partly) schematic (i.e., uninstantiated) and may be partly filled with lexical or grammatical items (cf. the English 'X *let alone* Y' construction discussed in Fillmore et al. 1988, the '*What's* X *doing* Y?' construction discussed in Kay and Fillmore 1999 or the Jaminjung (Australian, Djamindjungan) 'NP-*gu* V' construction treated in Schultze-Berndt 2000). Thus, constructions can be described by means of indicating (classes of) lexical fillers or by indicating other constructions they consist of. Constructions are patterns or templates (cf. Langacker 1990, Van Valin and LaPolla 1997) that have to be distinguished from actually occurring linguistic expressions. Linguistic expressions are rather viewed as instantiating constructions.

At the heart of the present study are argument structure constructions (Goldberg 1992, 1995, 1999), otherwise called linking constructions (cf. Michaelis and Lambrecht 1996, Kay and Fillmore 1999).[28] Goldberg (1995:59) has proposed "a constructional approach to argument structure in which the semantics of the verb classes and the semantics of the constructions are integrated to yield the semantics of particular expressions." In such a conception

---

[26] Cf. Schultze-Berndt (2002, sect. 1.1) for an overview of construction-based models of grammar.

[27] This does not mean that a construction is completely arbitrary, but that there is a unique patterning of form/function which is not predictable from the semantics of its parts. The psycholinguistic 'reality' of such a view can be deduced from the fact that constructions are learned as a unit, similar to lexical items (cf., e.g., Tomasello 2000).

[28] These contrast with other construction types such as sentence type constructions, constituency constructions (e.g., the verb phrase), information structure constructions, etc. (cf., e.g., Lambrecht 1994, Michaelis and Lambrecht 1996).

arguments are not viewed as being (exclusively) licensed by the inherent grammatical relationality/valency of a lexical item but rather as parts of argument structure constructions which are assumed to exist independently of lexical items.[29] Following such an approach, a distinction has to be made between constructional arguments, i.e., those arguments that refer to a constructional argument slot, and semantic arguments, which are licensed by the semantic relationality of a predicate.

Using a construction approach to argument structure the concept of semantic role as introduced in sect. 2.1.4 has to be further specified. Semantic roles are motivated by the lexical semantics of a relational predicative lexeme (e.g., a verb, a relational adjective or a relational noun). Argument structure constructions possess specific argument roles, i.e., roles that are associated with the arguments of an argument structure construction. These are naturally more general roles which occur in cognitively relevant schemata such as the macroroles actor, undergoer and indirectus (cf. Foley and Van Valin 1984, Lehmann et al. 2000[D]), theme and location in a local construction, the instrument or comitative in a concomitant construction, etc. Semantic roles and argument roles are 'fused' when a verb integrates with a construction according to general unification rules[30] (cf. Goldberg 1995, ch. 2.4). In the same way as semantic roles, argument roles are language specific as well as interlingual notions. Their relation to a construction as a language-specific sign is parallel to that of a semantic role to a lexical predicate. Following a convention established in Schultze-Berndt (2000), argument roles will be indicated by a capital initial letter.

Arguments of a construction may correspond to complements or adjuncts of a verb. This can be shown with respect to the analysis of the examples in (9) from Goldberg (1995:9).

> (9)　　a. *He sneezed the napkin off the table.*
> 　　　　b. *She baked him a cake.*

Regarding lexical valency, *sneeze* is an intransitive verb and *bake* is a transitive verb. In a constructional approach, *sneeze* can be analyzed as integrating with the caused-motion construction 'X causes Y to move Z', and *bake* can be analyzed as integrating with the ditransitive construction. These constructions account for the arguments that do not make up part of a verbs' valency, i.e., the

---

[29] Note that this view differs from the approach in Kay and Fillmore (1999:11), which claims that arguments are licensed exclusively by a verb's valency.

[30] For further details, cf. Goldberg (1995:50) on the "Semantic Coherence Principle" and the "Correspondence Principle".

direct object and the source NP in (9a) and the NP in beneficiary function in (9b).

In the constructional account, there are central (or 'profiled'[31]) arguments as well as peripheral arguments both on the lexical level and the constructional level. These correspond to central and peripheral participants based on their involvement in the situation (cf. sect. 2.1.4). The above analysis of (9) has shown that there may be mismatches concerning the argument status of a given participant in a construction vs. in the lexical valency frame. Central arguments of a lexical predicate are those that remain stable across all constructions in which it occurs. This generally corresponds to what has been called the 'syntactic valency' of a lexical item. Against this background, Goldberg (1995:45ff.) identifies the difference in argument structure between Engl. *rob* (e.g., *he robbed the rich (of all their money)*) and *steal* (e.g., *he stole money (from the rich)*) as follows. The 'target' *the rich* is a central argument of *rob* but peripheral for *steal*, while the 'goods' *money* is a central argument of *steal*, but peripheral for *rob*.

Constructions will be represented as indicated in Construction 1.[32] Construction 1 is an abstract representation of an argument structure construction with one argument. The syntactic layer of a construction is indicated in a constituent structure representation with category labels. It is linked with the semantic layer of the construction via lines which are given for corresponding elements. The semantic layer indicates construction specific argument roles. Argument roles are understood to be unified with lexically determined semantic roles for which the lexemes that integrate with the construction are subcategorized (cf. Goldberg 1995, ch. 2.4). These are optionally indicated in a line between the semantic and the syntactic layer of the construction, identified in Construction 1 as instantiation. The layers semantics and instantiation contain several variables (e.g., PRED, SEMANTIC CLASS, Arg. role), which are further specified (if necessary) by means of constraints at the bottom of the construction. These constraints may restrict the application of the variables to a specific semantic class or to particular lexemes. Furthermore, square brackets are used in the constituent structure representation, pointed brackets are used for the set of arguments in the semantic representation.

(10) gives examples from German that may be integrated into a construction equivalent to Construction 1, as is shown in Construction 2. For the sake of illustration it may be assumed that German verbs like *schwitzen* 'sweat', *grübeln* 'brood', etc. instantiate a more abstract argument structure construction, consisting of a dynamic predicate indicating a process and one argument that may

---

[31] Cf. Goldberg (1995) based on Langacker (1987).

[32] Similar linking schemes are also used outside construction grammar to analyze argument structure as e.g. in RRG (cf. Van Valin and LaPolla 1997) and LFG (cf. Bresnan 2001).

semantics:	SEMANTIC CLASS	<Arg. role>
instantiation:	PRED	<SEM. ROLE>
syntax:	[V	NP]ₛ
constraints:	PRED/SEMANTIC CLASS ∈ {item1, ..., itemN}/ {sem.class}; SEM.ROLE/Arg.role ∈ {participant properties}	

Construction 1. Argument structure C.

be called a Theme. The verbs *schwitzen* 'sweat' and *grübeln* 'brood' are sub-categorized for the specific semantic roles 'sweater' and 'brooder', which can be identified as the semantic role THEME, and which are mapped onto the constructional argument role Theme. For the verbs *schwitzen* and *grübeln* the THEMES are animate and human, respectively. The argument structure construction these verbs instantiate is, however, not restricted to these features, given that intransitive process verbs may take arguments at other positions in Figure 2 as well.

(10)   *Peter schwitzt/grübelt* etc.
          'Peter is sweating/brooding.'

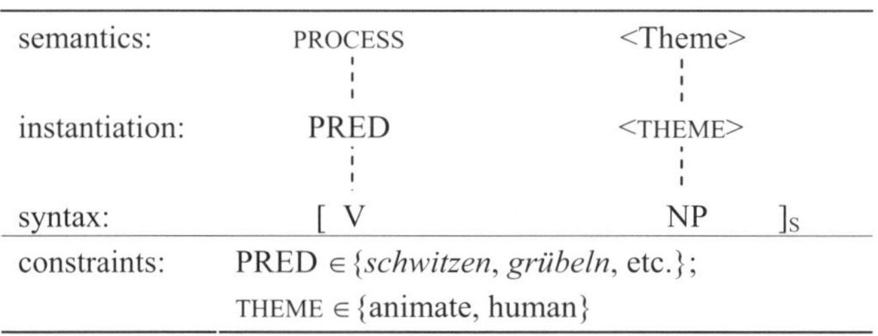

semantics:	PROCESS	<Theme>
instantiation:	PRED	<THEME>
syntax:	[V	NP]ₛ
constraints:	PRED ∈ {*schwitzen, grübeln*, etc.}; THEME ∈ {animate, human}	

Construction 2. Instantiated process C. with Theme argument

Now compare the semantically similar examples from German and English in (11).

(11)   *Peter kommt ins Schwitzen/ins Grübeln* etc.
          'Peter begins to sweat/to brood etc.'

In these examples the main verb *kommen* 'come' does not identify the situation core on its own. It is identified by the whole predicate, i.e., the verb including the prepositional complement. Such a structure is semantically more complex and involves two steps from the structural representation to the semantic representation of the whole construction. Thus, a constructional representation of

(11), which is carried out in Construction 3, needs an additional semantic level in comparison to (10). In Construction 3 the first semantic line, i.e., the one closer to the syntax line, indicates an immediate or literal representation of the syntactic part of the construction. A second derived semantic level is added on top of the immediate representation, giving the 'proper' or idiomatic meaning of the construction. This second semantic level may be derived from the first by different types of semantic processes such as metaphor or metonymy. The specific semantic relation will be indicated at the right side of the figure, between the two 'semantic' lines. Semantic representations in both lines use the same terms. They do not constitute hierarchically different levels.

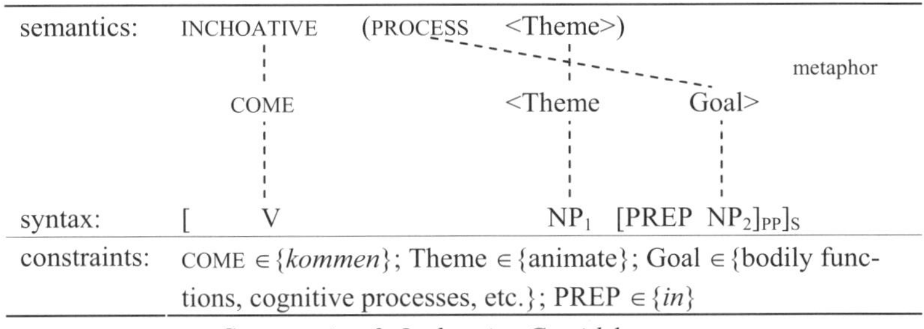

Construction 3. Inchoative C. with kommen

The verb *kommen* in examples like (11) is called a *Funktionsverb* (lit. 'function verb') in German linguistics. It adds an inchoative meaning to the basic situation as expressed in (10). Structurally, *kommen* is the main verb displaying an argument structure as indicated in the immediate semantic representation, i.e., taking the argument roles Theme and Goal.[33,34] On the derived semantic level, representing the semantics of the whole construction, the grammatical semantics of the *Funktionsverb* and the lexical semantics of the nominalized part of the predicate (i.e., *Schwitzen, Grübeln*, etc.) together constitute a complex predicate corresponding to the situation core.

Construction 3 is represented as an independent construction. Note however, that in addition to *kommen*, there are other *Funktionsverben*, like *gelangen* and *geraten*, which also impose an inchoative reading on the situation, but which collocate with other (kinds of) nouns as heads of the prepositional phrase (e.g., *in Verwirrung/Wut etc. geraten* 'begin to be confused/furious etc., *in Vergessenheit/Abhängigkeit etc. geraten* 'become forgotten/dependent etc.',

---

[33] The argument role Goal is understood to have an abstract reading as opposed to the semantic role of a motion verb GOAL.

[34] The 'literal' semantic representation can be taken as the basis for event structure metaphors as introduced in Lakoff (1993). It is at the same time the basis of the grammaticalization of *kommen* into a *Funktionsverb*.

zur Erkenntnis gelangen 'realize', *zur Aufführung gelangen* 'be performed', etc.). These collocations vary as to preposition selection, namely, *in* 'in' with *geraten* and *zu* 'to' with *gelangen*. Furthermore, the nominal part of the predicates represent different situation types, namely, states, processes or events. These may constitute a more general construction which determines part of the structure of Construction 3. It may be represented as shown in Construction 4.

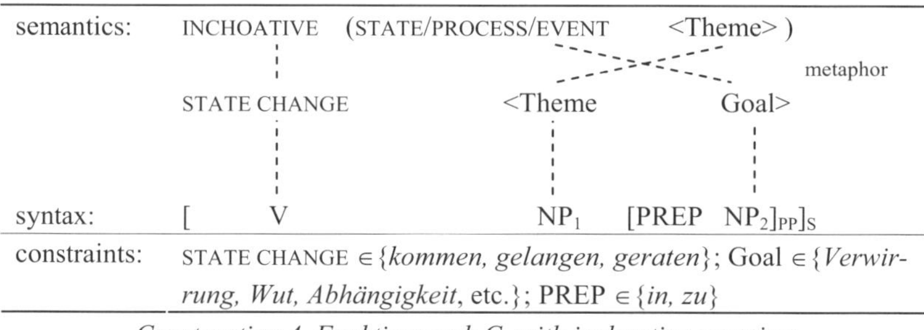

Construction 4. Funktionsverb C. with inchoative meaning

Thus constructions exist in relation to other constructions. There are several kinds of inter-constructional relations. Constructions have paradigmatic relations to other constructions by virtue of taking the same fillers (e.g., in voice alternations, sentence types; cf. Schultze-Berndt 2000:26). They may be in meronomic, i.e., 'part–whole' relations in cases of complex constructions, e.g., NP is part of the Jaminjung 'NP-*gu* V' construction mentioned above.[35] The example given above is a case of a taxonomic relation, i.e., a given construction may be a special instance of a more general construction, if it is more fully specified. Furthermore, a given construction may be a metaphorical extension of another construction (cf. Goldberg 1995:81ff.). In these cases, the more general constructions are said to motivate the more specific constructions (cf., e.g., Goldberg 1995, ch. 3, Michaelis and Lambrecht 1996:242, Bickel 2004, sect. 6). This motivation is reflected in those elements that the more specific or more complex construction inherits from the more basic construction. Thus, inheritance relations (or 'links', as these relations are commonly called by construction grammarians) are a way to describe and represent structural and functional correspondences among constructions and to make language-internal generalizations. In this sense, Construction 4 can be regarded as being a superordinate construction of Construction 3. Similarly, the representation at the intermediate semantic level of both constructions can be said to reflect the semantic part of a superordinate construction motivating the overall semantics of the respective constructions.

---

[35] This relation is called 'subsumption link' in Michaelis and Lambrecht (1996), 'subpart link' in Goldberg (1995:78), 'meronomic relation' in Croft (2001:21), and Schultze-Berndt (2002:271) speaks of 'subconstructions'.

The constructional approach is well suited for the description of collocations as well as idiomatic phrases, which frequently occur in the experiential domain. Construction grammar had its origin in the need to capture relatively idiomatic constructions that could not easily be accounted for by simply referring to the general grammatical rules of a language. At the same time, by invoking (partial) inheritance from more abstract constructions for specific and idiomatic constructions, possible generalizations are not overlooked. Thus, most general and productive as well as highly specific and idiomatic phenomena can be treated in a construction-based approach.

Finally, construction grammar assumes the existence of very general and abstract constructions such as, e.g., the 'headed phrase construction' identified in Kay (2002), the transitive (verb) construction, the possessed nominal construction, etc. which are assumed to be shared cross-linguistically. Those constructions that represent general cognitively based schemes are presumed to be shared by many languages. Thus, a constructional approach is also well suited for the typological comparison of languages (cf. especially Croft 2001).

CHAPTER 3

Universals and typology of experiential constructions

This chapter discusses the theoretical and empirical foundations of experiential constructions from a cross-linguistic point of view. Sect. 3.1 reviews the state of the art concerning the investigation of experiential constructions. Sect. 3.2 outlines the structure of the functional domain of experience. Those concepts prototypically belonging to the five subdomains of experience, namely, bodily sensation, emotion, volition, cognition and perception, are identified and these domains will be distinguished from neighboring but different domains. Following this in sect. 3.3, the experiential situation as a conceptual unity underlying experiential coding in language will be characterized, identifying and outlining those components that are considered to be constitutive. In particular, role properties of the crucial participants, experiencer and stimulus, will be discussed in some detail. Sect. 3.4 presents an overview of important cross-linguistic features of the grammatical coding of experience. It determines the analytical parameters for the investigation of YM experiential constructions in ch. 5, 6, and 7. Sect. 3.5 defines the necessary concepts concerning the analysis of figurative language, focusing especially on collocational structures in the language of experience. Finally, sect. 3.6 discusses the issue of the diachronic development of experiential verbs and constructions.

3.1 *Earlier approaches to experiential constructions*

In recent years the linguistic expression of experiential situations has attracted more and more attention in linguistic research, but work has been mostly confined to language-specific studies (cf. Ameka 1990, Bugenhagen 1990, Clark 1996, Jaisser 1990, Bickel 1997[P], Klein and Kutscher 2002, Becher 2003, etc.). Areal as well as typologically oriented studies are still rare but nevertheless do exist. Here, the following should be mentioned: Verma and Mohanan (eds., 1990) discusses experiencer subjects as defining India and South Asia as a linguistic area. Bickel (2004) examines experiential constructions in the Himalayas. Reh (ed., 1998) summarizes preliminary results from a typological research project on experiencer constructions in African languages. This study develops a framework for the analysis of experiencer constructions, defining an experiential situation and its components and identifying typologically relevant coding strategies. The domain of experience is subdivided into six subdomains, namely, emotion, cognition, conception, volition, perception and physical sensation. Each domain is represented by a number of concepts varying in number from two (for perception) to ten (for emotion). Bossong (1998) investigates experiencer coding in 40 European languages from different families, based on ten experiential concepts.

Important works focusing mainly the semantics of emotions are Wierzbicka (1999) and the collection of papers in Harkins and Wierzbicka (eds., 2001). Wierzbicka (1999) also considers typological and comparative questions. She identifies parameters that are proposed as having universal or near-universal status in the definition of emotions and their linguistic coding. First of all, it is assumed that all languages possess terms for emotions. Some of these emotions can be described as good and some as bad (while others may be neutral in such an evaluation).[i] Furthermore, it is presumed that in all languages emotions can be described via external bodily symptoms (e.g., blush, get pale, etc.) and that all languages do this to a certain degree. Moreover, Wierzbicka claims that all languages can describe emotions via internal bodily images and that most languages provide means for describing emotions via sensations (e.g., feeling hot etc. as a reaction to an emotional situation). With regard to specific emotions, Wierzbicka supposes that most languages lexicalize concepts equivalent to 'afraid', 'angry' and 'ashamed'. She presumes furthermore that all languages provide for alternatives in their grammatical construction of emotions which are related to parameters such as control, voluntariness, etc.

The papers in Harkins and Wierzbicka (eds., 2001) are mainly language-specific studies on emotion concepts or words. The latter is also true for a number of articles in a volume of the *Australian Journal of Linguistics* dedicated to the language of emotions (see for instance, Dineen 1990). These articles use the Natural Semantic Metalanguage developed by Wierzbicka and her research group to define emotion concepts. Similar in spirit, but more confined to the grammatical structure of experiential constructions, are approaches that highlight the functional motivation of, or correlation with, specific kinds of experiential constructions, e.g., Ameka (1990), Bugenhagen (1990), Chun and Zubin (1990), Mohanan and Mohanan (1990), Croft (1993), Van Valin and Wilkins (1993), Dabrowska (1994).

The conceptualization and linguistic coding of emotions are at the focus of many papers from the collections in Niemeier and Dirven (eds., 1997) and Athanasiadou and Tabakowska (eds., 1998). Both volumes follow a mainly cognitive approach to the language of emotions. A number of the papers make up part of a large body on emotion research in cognitive linguistics, initiated by Lakoff and Johnson (1980), Johnson (1987), Lakoff (1987). A great deal of further work exists in this area including Kövecses (1986, 2000), Lakoff and Kövecses (1987), Manney (1990), Belz (1992), Fesmire (1994), McVeight

---

[i] Feelings often described as 'neutral' are, e.g., surprise and interest (cf. Goddard, 2001:177).

(1996) and many others. Many of these studies operate with the concepts of metaphor, metonymy, and synecdoche to "explain" experiential and especially emotional language and its respective constructions (cf. Lakoff and Johnson 1980, Matisoff 1986, Goossens 1989, Jaisser 1990, Reh 1998[M], Kövecses 2000, Niemeier 2000, Haspelmath 2001 and especially Klein and Kutscher 2002).

Since the late 80s, experiencer verbs have been discussed as a test case for argument linking. Universal (or language-specific) argument linking rules have been proposed for the so-called psychological predicates or psych-verbs from a syntactic (e.g., Postal 1971, Belletti and Rizzi 1988) as well as from a semantic point of view (e.g., Tenny 1987, Grimshaw 1990, Croft 1993, Pesetzsky 1987, 1995, Filip 1996, Van Valin and LaPolla 1997, Anagnostopoulou 1999, Härtl 2001, Klein and Kutscher 2002, etc.). Some of them relate the linking mechanisms (exclusively or partly) to the internal temporal structure of the predicate/verb (e.g., Tenny 1987, Grimshaw 1990) and/or to its causal structure (Dowty 1991, Croft 1993, 1998, Van Valin and LaPolla 1997, Härtl 2001). It is assumed that there are two to three basic types of experiencer verbs or constructions, i.e., the *fear/temere* type (taking the experiencer in subject function), the *frighten/preoccupare* type (taking the experiencer in direct object function), and finally the *appeal/piacere* type (taking the experiencer in oblique object function). The latter type is not discussed in many of the above works (but cf. Belletti and Rizzi 1988, Croft 1993, Anagnostopoulou 1999, Klein and Kutscher 2002). Croft (1993) notes further groups such as inchoative and activity mental verbs, which he claims universally display experiencer-subjects. Among the works mentioned, Croft (1993) is the only one to recognize that typological variation is expected in subject assignment with experiential verbs designating a state due to their indecisive or two-way causal structure, i.e., the experiencer directs its attention to the stimulus and the stimulus is (at the same time) the cause of the experiencer's mental state. As most of these approaches almost exclusively discuss data from a few European languages (mainly English, Italian, Greek, German) they fall short of recognizing and discussing other experiential construction types, e.g., possessor-experiencers.

Some more recent work has focused on experiencer coding from the perspective of a mismatch between morphological marking and syntactic properties. Bickel (2004) calls this morphological downgrading of experiencers, and investigates experiencer coding in the Himalayas from this perspective. Aikhenvald et al. (eds., 2001) use the term non-canonical marking of subjects and objects in a similar context. Papers in this volume which apply it to experiencers are most notably Haspelmath (2001) and Shibatani (2001). Both approaches highlight the observation that experiencers may be coded in morphologically 'lower' cases but nevertheless display some or most subject properties. In light of this observation, Croft (2001:158f.) writes that in Georgian the experiencer is coded as dative, but verb agreement may be triggered if the experiencer is higher in animacy and definiteness than the stimulus. Morphologically downgraded experiencers are also discussed in the collection of papers on experiencer subjects in Verma and Mohanan (eds., 1990) and a number of further papers, among them Gupta and Tuladhar (1979).

The semantic role of the experiencer has been addressed in different role theories (e.g., Dowty 1991, Filip 1996, Van Valin and LaPolla 1997, Jackendoff 1987, 1990). Most theories identify semantic roles as arguments in the semantic decompositional structure of a relational lexeme. The semantic role of the experiencer and the relevant literature will be addressed in detail in sect. 3.3.2.

Diachronical aspects of experiencer coding are investigated in Croft (2001), Haspelmath (2001) and Klein and Kutscher (2002). The main hypotheses concerning evolution and change of experiencer constructions will be addressed in some detail in sect. 3.6 below.

There are a number of language-specific studies investigating experiential, especially emotional constructions, involving (body-)part expressions or idioms (e.g., McElhanon 1975, 1977, 1978, Matisoff 1986, Jaisser 1990, etc.). Such complex experiential constructions have been studied under the terms of 'body image idiom' (McElhanon 1975, 1977, 1978) or 'psycho-collocation' (Matisoff 1986). These often use a body or person part term combined with a predicative expression to yield an experiential expression. Such expressions seem to be especially widespread in Africa and in Asia. Many languages display one or more special (often immaterial/formal) body parts as the seat of emotional and/or cognitive experiences. These body parts are used in experiential expressions and in this way the latter designate feelings and emotions.

Some special aspects of experiential verbs have been studied with regard to several grammatical domains. For instance, Horie (1985) studies experiential predicates as matrix predicates, Dik and Hengeveld (1991) analyzes perception verb complements. Others (e.g., Givón 1980, Bolinger 1984, Noonan 1985, Wierzbicka 1988) discuss experiential predicates as part of more general accounts of complementation.

Finally, as has already been remarked on in the introduction, experiential verbs have always played a prominent role in research on transitivity (cf. Hopper and Thompson 1980, Tsunoda 1981, 1985, Rice 1987). They are generally associated with parameter values of reduced transitivity.

3.2   *The functional domain of experience*

The functional domain of experience can be identified by concepts that are contained in lexemes as well as in constructions of a given language or language type. Apart from lexeme-specific semantics or semantic networks, languages may possess specific experiential constructions such as the 'possessive of experience' construction in Belhare (Bickel 1997[P]), the dative/affective case in Caucasian languages (cf. sect. 1.1), the dative subject constructions in many South Asian languages (cf. Verma and Mohanan 1990) or the double nominative constructions in Korean and Japanese (Shibatani 2001). The latter constructions generally include most or all types of experiencers, but are not necessarily confined to them. Such construction types may identify a given semantic domain relevant to a language, which may reflect language-specific categorization. Interlingual relevance of a functional category can be shown to the extent that languages show similar constructions or construction types, i.e., combining a given structure with given semantics (cf. Comrie 1981, Dik 1978, 1997, Lehmann 1991, Croft 1991, 2001).

The following outline of the functional domain of experience draws on typological as well as language-specific studies. It is assumed to present a functional grid for the comparative analysis of experience in a language. However, before addressing the structure of the functional domain of experience in sect. 3.2.2, the question of universality vs. culture-specificity of the concepts in the domain will be tackled in sect. 3.2.1. This question has been discussed with great controversy, especially with respect to emotional concepts.

3.2.1 *Universality vs. culture-specificity*

As was introduced in sect. 1.2, the domain of experience contains those concepts that are related to the consciousness of human beings and higher animals. More specifically, bodily feelings and sensations, feelings of emotions, concepts related to cognition, volition, and perception are included.

With respect to the categorization of emotions, semantic universals have been proposed in various contexts. In ethno-psychological and ethno-biological literature (cf., e.g., Johnson-Laird and Oatley 1989, 1992, Russell 1991, 1995, Ekman 1992, Ekman and Davidson eds. 1994) it is claimed that there are a number of basic culturally independent emotions that are characteristic of every human being and can be found in every culture, and must therefore be reflected in each language in some way. In contrast to this is the claim that emotions are (to a large extent) culture-specific and formed by social and cultural processes (cf. Lutz 1988, Wierzbicka 1999). In the latter view, which is present in anthropological (e.g., Lutz 1982, 1987, Leavitt 1996), (ethno-)psychological (e.g., Doi 1981, Russell et al. eds. 1995) as well as linguistic research (cf. Bugenhagen 1990, 2001, Wierzbicka 1990, 1992, 1995, 1999), emotions are viewed as "cultural artifacts of the mind" (cf. Geertz 1973:81).[2]

---

[2] Enfield (2001:164) even observes that to some degree situations that provoke a given bodily reaction, such as, for instance, situations provoking 'disgust' may vary considerably across cultures.

Wierzbicka (1996, 1999) tries to reconcile these opposing assumptions by claiming a number of very basic semantic universals in the domain including emotion, cognition, and volition, which are presumed to be present in all languages: THINK, KNOW, WANT, FEEL. Many works done in the spirit of Wierzbicka try to show that similar emotional concepts may differ in specific aspects from language to language but can be decomposed using the same semantic universals.[3]

The question of universality vs. culture-specificity of concepts in the domain of experiences has been thoroughly discussed, especially with respect to emotions, as is shown by the above references. For the subdomain of perception as well, there has been discussion as to how far the 'western-based/biased' perceptual modes are universally recognized. The classification of five senses can be traced back to Aristotle and may be judged as a Eurocentric cultural conceptualization. From a scientific point of view it is by far insufficient to describe all sensual perceptions (cf., e.g., Stadler et al. 1975:79). Comparative work on the history and culture of perception has shown that "some cultures recognize more senses, and other cultures fewer" (Classen 1993:2). Language-specific and typological work on perception verbs has also shown that the categorization of perceptions is clearly not identical in all languages. On the other hand, the study of Viberg (1984) suggests that an implicational hierarchy exists concerning the expression vs. lexical fusion between some perceptual modes (cf. further sect. 3.2.2.6). Evans and Wilkins (1998) supports the implicational order of 'sight < hearing' made in Viberg (1984) for Australian languages. This is in accordance with Wierzbicka (1996, ch. 2.17) who proposes SEE and HEAR as semantic primitives in the subdomain of perception.[4]

Setting aside the debate on universality, it will be assumed that universal and culture-specific properties correspond to different levels of analysis. The same concept of cross-linguistic comparison based on Lehmann et al. (2000[D]) that has been outlined with respect to semantic roles will be followed here. It is assumed that the analytical problems concerning semantic roles work in the same way for the classification of more specific semantic domains such as experience and emotion. First, it has to be acknowledged that on a language-external level of 'reality' all human beings share the same bio-

---

[3] Cf. for instance Bugenhagen (1990:208) on the concept of *fear* and its variants in Mangap-Mbula, Harkins (2001) on concepts of anger in Arrernte and neighboring languages, Kornacki (2001) on concepts of anger in Chinese and articles from Harkins and Wierzbicka (eds., 2001) among others.

[4] Note however, that in Wierzbicka (1999) a case from Tariana (Arawak, Brazil; Aikhenvald) is reported in which the same verb is used for SEE and HEAR, the latter being distinguished from the former by adding an 'auditory' object such as ('words', 'sounds', 'language' etc.). Wierzbicka analyzes this case as polysemy in the same way as cases where one word means, e.g., 'see' and 'know'.

logical, i.e., anatomical, neurological, physiological, etc. prerequisites that are the basis for experiences such as perception, sensation, emotion, volition, and cognition. In addition to these universals, a language-independent cognitive level, where universal concepts are located may be conceived of. These naturally include concepts related to emotion, cognition, volition, perception, and bodily sensation. Lexical items in natural languages encode representations at the cognitive level in their specific structure.

On a cross-linguistic level, semantic generalizations such as, for instance, LOVE and HATE are possible. At this level of analysis, cross-linguistic generalizations can be made, which does not, however, imply that concepts at this level are necessarily identical in all the languages of the world.[5] At the same time, languages provide for special implementations of these concepts, i.e., a concept LOVE1 in German (as expressed through *Liebe*) and a concept LOVE2 in YM (as expressed through *yàabilah*) are not necessarily identical, but they display a significant overlap of meaning which enables us to recognize them as translation equivalents.[6] For the core elements of the domain the view will be adopted that they may constitute universal concepts which are expected to be found across cultures.

3.2.2 *The structure of the subdomains of experience*
3.2.2.1 *Introduction*

The functional domain of experience is part of the more comprehensive domain of participation (cf. Seiler 1988). Grammaticalization or grammatical means of expression in the domain of experience reside mainly in a special coding of argument structure, e.g., the experiencer may receive a special case (as has been shown for Lezgian in (1), cf. furthermore Comrie and van den Berg 2003); an experiential construction may be identified by a special alignment configuration,[7] e.g., experiencer-subject/stimulus-object (*fear*-type) or stimulus-subject/ experiencer-object (*frighten*-type). Apart from this, the domain of experience can be characterized by its lexical and specific predicate structure[8] and therefore differs from other more 'grammaticalized' or gram-

---

[5] It is my understanding this view does not contradict the existence of basic 'emotions' as innate human internal reactions to certain stimuli, as, e.g., a baby's feeling of contentment or discontent, feelings of anger or happiness. However these feelings are understood as socially and culturally shaped and reflected in lexical concepts that are much more complex than these so-called basic emotions.

[6] Thus, translations given for the YM emotional terms (and presumably others as well) must be taken with this proviso.

[7] The alignment configuration of a construction is the constructionist counterpart of the valency frame in a dependency grammar view.

[8] This includes the techniques 'verb classes' and 'valency' as identified in Seiler (1988:100) as so-called indicative techniques in the universal dimension of participation as opposed to predi-

matically relevant domains (as are outlined in Seiler 1988), e.g., the domain of possession (e.g., Lehmann 1998, Shin 2004) or the domain of localization (cf. Skopeteas 2002). Note, for example, that the domain of possession is characterized in many languages by a grammatical verb expressing an ascription of possession to the possessor (cf. Engl. *have*, Germ. *haben*) or the existential verb (YM *yàan*). This may correspond to the existence of a generalized verb of experience in the experiential domain, e.g., Germ. *fühlen*, YM *u'y*. Such verbs however, are not generally grammaticalized in the languages of the world.[9]

The following outline of the experiential domain gives a definition of each subdomain and a characterization of the prototypical concepts within it. This includes their characterization concerning features of situation type (cf. sect. 2.1.2). It delimits each subdomain against neighboring subdomains. Those parameters concerning the participant roles and features of experiencer and stimulus are dealt with in sect. 3.3.2.

The experiential subdomains to be outlined below show certain overlaps. For instance, there are a number of concepts known from SAE languages that cannot be clearly assigned to a single subdomain. This is especially true for rather complex and culture-specific notions as, e.g., 'surprise', 'jealousy', 'envy', etc. The concept of 'surprise' involves cognition and emotion, the concepts 'jealousy' and 'envy' involve emotion and volition, the concept of Germ. *es verlangt jdn. nach jdm./etw.* 'sb. longs/ yearns for sb./sth.' involves volition and bodily sensation, etc. For this reason, the subdomains are viewed as having fuzzy boundaries, and thus a given item may belong to more than one subdomain.[10]

The notion of evaluation is metonymically linked to most of the experiential subdomains. Evaluation of an entity or a proposition can be based on sensation, emotion, cognition, or perception. This is the reason why, for instance, perception verbs shift to evaluation verbs in many languages.

3.2.2.2 *Bodily sensation*

The functional subdomain of bodily sensation is concerned with feelings related to the experiencer's body. Concepts belonging to the subdomain of bodily

---

cative techniques. The above mentioned techniques of argument structure and case marking belong to the latter.

[9] Note however that such verbs may be slightly more grammatical than prototypical lexical verbs in that they occur as main predicates in combination with more specific experience coding nouns (cf. Construction 31) or in evaluative constructions with a secondary predicate (cf. Construction 34 in sect. 5.3.2.1.4).

[10] This is in accordance with Wierzbicka's view, which, e.g., considers the semantic primitive WANT as crucial part of many emotion concepts (cf., e.g., Wierzbicka 1994, 1999). At the same time she argues that emotions are cognitively based feelings, i.e., English emotion terms always involve the semantic primitive THINK.

sensation are: feelings concerning a state of saturation, e.g., 'hungry', 'thirsty'; feelings of temperature, e.g., 'feel hot'/cold', feelings of 'aching', 'itching', 'tiredness', and feelings related to general bodily or health condition such as 'feel good/bad', 'recover', etc. A bodily sensation is prototypically not related to a source or a goal but conceived of as self-motivated and occurring by itself.

Concepts of bodily sensation are prototypically states, but more dynamic situations are also included such as changes of state or processes. Furthermore, the causation of bodily sensation makes up part of the subdomain under consideration.[11] The prototypicality of states for the subdomain of bodily sensation may be deduced from the observation that states of bodily sensation are primary lexicalizations in many languages, while more dynamic concepts and the causative lexemes are often systematically derived.

A bodily sensation is related to a bodily or physical state, change of state or process, but it cannot be equated with these. This is important to note, since languages like English (and possibly many others) do not necessarily distinguish explicitly between the former and the latter. Thus, the expression *Peter is cold* can refer to Peter's bodily state or to his feeling of being cold.[12] It is also possible to explicitly refer to the feeling of being cold by combining the general sensation verb *feel* with a bodily state adjective as in *Peter is feeling cold*. The necessity of distinguishing between a bodily sensation and a bodily state, change of state or process, becomes obvious given that there may exist a certain sensation without the underlying state being true, and vice versa. Thus, it is possible *to feel sick* without *being sick*, and *to be sick* without *feeling sick*. Given this distinction, the terms corresponding to Engl. *ill, pregnant, drunk,* etc. are not considered bodily sensations but bodily states. Only bodily sensations but not bodily states or respective changes of state or processes are considered to be part of the domain of experience.[13]

According to Van Valin and LaPolla (1997:103), Bonggi (Malaysia, Western Austronesian) distinguishes between bodily states and bodily sensations by a different affixation on stative stems expressing 'be.cold' etc. German, like English, provides the option of using a number of lexemes denoting bodily or physical states with the general sensation verb *fühlen* 'feel'. To explicitly convey bodily sensation, the reflexive form *sich fühlen* is used with respect to

---

[11] Cf. Van Valin and LaPolla (1997, sect. 3.2.1) for the systematic relationship between basic situation types and their causation.

[12] provided that Peter communicated this feeling to the speaker, so that the latter is able to know of his feeling

[13] Furthermore, a physical state may not be that of the experiencer itself but of another entity. Also in this case, expressions like *it is cold* referring to weather condition or *the water is cold* referring to a physical state of the water may be used. However these convey an evaluation based on the perception of touch, and as such, they will be treated as being part of the experiential subdomain of perception (cf. sect. 3.2.2.6).

one's own body, e.g., *ich fühle mich krank* 'I am feeling ill', while the deagentive form *sich anfühlen* can be used to explicitly convey the sensation of a physical state of another entity, as, e.g., in *X fühlt sich kalt an* 'X is/feels cold'.

Furthermore, bodily sensations are distinguished from bodily functions such as those conveyed by Engl. *sweat, bleed,* etc. Bodily functions as well as bodily states can be considered neighboring domains with respect to the subdomain of bodily sensation. As a result of metonymy, notions of these neighboring domains may enter the subdomain of bodily sensation. This seems to have happened with the YM equivalent of Engl. *pregnant* and *give birth (to a baby).* The collocations *ma' tòoh* POSS[14] *óol (ti' chàampal)-i'* (NEG straight POSS mind (LOC baby)-NEGF) 'pregnant' and *tòohtal* POSS *óol ti' chàampal* (straight-PROC POSS mind LOC baby) 'give birth (to a baby)' are related to the collocation *tòoh* POSS *óol* (straight POSS mind) 'be fine, well, healthy' (cf. sect. 5.2.1.3 and sect. 5.3.1.2).

3.2.2.3 *Emotion*

The subdomain of emotion is clearly the most varied among the experiential subdomains from a semantic as well as grammatical point of view and has therefore been the motivation of most studies. Following Wierzbicka (1999), emotions can be defined as cognitively based feelings. Emotions are thought-related as opposed to bodily sensations or feelings. They are biologically founded, interpersonal and have a social basis. Scientific as well as folk-theories of emotion generally consider them as involving a causal chain. More specifically, three events have to be distinguished: an emotion-arousing or triggering, generally external event; an emotional state; and a physiological re-action and/or other behavioral responses (Radden 1998:273).[15] Linguistically, all three points are mirrored in semantic and structural aspects of experiential constructions. The causing event corresponds linguistically to the stimulus (cf. sect. 3.3.2). Many emotion terms are semantically stative and thus correspond to their ontology. Physiological and biochemical reactions (e.g., blush, get pale, increase of heart rate, etc.) or behavioral reactions (e.g., spitting, frowning, etc.) to emotions often constitute metonymically based expressions of a given emotion in language (cf. Wierzbicka 1999, Lakoff 1987, Kövecses 2000).

In the majority of languages, the emotions which have the highest probability of being linguistically coded are those that have been identified in eth-

---

[14] In the citation form of YM collocations, possessor and subject clitics are indicated by their respective abbreviations. For the grammar of these clitics cf. sect. 4.1.2.

[15] The Wierzbicka school accommodates this internal structure of emotions in prototypical scenarios of emotion terms (compare the numerous 'definitions' of emotion terms in form of prototypical scenarios in various languages in Wierzbicka 1992, 1999, 2001, Ameka 1990, Bugenhagen 1990 etc.).

nopsychology as basic (or even innate). However lists of proposed basic emotions differ from author to author in number and content. Frequently included are 'happiness', 'sadness', 'fear', 'anger', 'disgust', 'shame', and 'surprise' (cf., e.g., Izard 1977, Johnson-Laird and Oatley 1989, 1992, Ekman 1992, Ekman and Davidson eds. 1994, Wierzbicka 1999). Acknowledging the bias mentioned in sect. 3.2.1, these concepts can thus be supposed to possess near equivalents in many languages. Concepts expressing positive and negative feelings towards other human beings such as 'love', 'like', 'sympathy', 'hate', 'dislike', etc. may be added to these basic items. More complex, socially determined emotions include 'worry', 'disappointment', 'pity', 'jealousy', 'envy', 'pride', etc. These are based on the more basic emotions, e.g., 'worry' includes 'fear', 'disappointment' and 'pity' include 'sadness', 'pride' includes 'happiness', etc.

Emotion concepts vary in their internal temporal structure. This corresponds to the distinction between emotion vs. mood vs. temperament (affective style), which is frequently made in the psychological literature (e.g., Ekman and Davidson eds. 1994). Emotions are defined in psychology as passing short term reactional systems which are triggered by certain events. Moods have a larger temporal extention and may last hours or days. They are perceived as a kind of permanent, diffuse shading of subjective experience. Contrary to emotions, moods are not directed to persons, objects or events. Temperament or affective style may be described as an emotional disposition to manifest a certain emotional reaction or a mood and may be so thought of as a character trait of a person.

Such a distinction may possibly find expression in the linguistic structure of a language (if conceptualized in this way), possibly in the structure of predicate classes. For example, a word class (part of speech) distinction may be used to reflect the difference in time stability and relationality described above. So it seems more probable that a language would choose adjectives to render temperament and verbs to render emotions. The intrinsic relationality of emotions may be expressed by bivalent verbs while mood and temperament are prone to occur in monovalent structures (i.e., adjectives and possibly intransitive verbs).

In some areas of emotional type there are systematic correspondences between (some of) the mentioned dynamicity types. For instance, German contrasts the emotion term *(sich) erschrecken* 'be/get shocked' with the temperament/disposition term *schreckhaft sein* 'be jumpy, easily startled'. Further pairs are *Angst haben/bekommen* 'be/become afraid' vs. *ängstlich sein* 'be frightened', *sich aufregen* 'get worked up/excited' vs. *(leicht) erregbar sein* 'be easily annoyed'. However there are clearly limits to such regular lexical relations (cf., e.g., *traurig sein/ trauern* 'be sad'/ 'mourn' vs. *depressiv/ melancholisch sein* 'be depressive' etc.).

Some "emotions" as, e.g., Germ. *Neugier* 'curiosity' may be linguistically conceived as dispositions or character traits while others are thought of as clearly limited to stative situations (e.g., Germ. *Trauer* 'sadness', *Freude* 'joy', etc.). Furthermore it may be assumed that a number of emotion terms in a language are open to interpretation as to their time stability (i.e., as to their interpretation as either emotion or mood or temperament) and that a given meaning results from the context (cf. discussion with respect to YM in sect. 5.2.1.1). Ameka (1990:159f.) shows that for Ewe, a given emotional expression may refer either to an emotional disposition or to an emotional reaction, chosing either the habitual or the present progressive, as follows.

(12)   a. *ɖevi má   kpe-a   ɲu.*
            child DEM weigh-HAB side
            'That child is shy.'

        b. *ɖevi má   le   ɲu   kpe-ḿ.*
            child DEM be:PRS side   weigh-PROG
            'That child is feeling shy/is embarrassed.' (Ameka 1990:150f.)[16]

By virtue of being properties, temperament expressions are not prototypical representatives of the subdomain of emotion, but are rather at its fringes. It is assumed that the experiencer of a temperament expression is prone to be linguistically coded as a holder of a property.

Besides emotional properties and states, there are also more dynamic emotion concepts such as, e.g., Germ. *(sich) erschrecken* 'be/get shocked', *sich aufregen* 'get worked up, to get excited', etc. constituting changes of state. Examples of emotional activities seem to be rarer, but Germ. *wüten* 'rage, riot' and *schmollen* 'sulk' may be included. These latter concepts designate actions based on a certain emotion, and again are not prototypical representatives of the subdomain of emotion.

Concepts of the expression of emotion such as 'laugh', 'cry', etc. or verbs denoting the communication of an emotion, e.g., Engl. *scold*, Germ. *schimpfen, sich beschweren* should be excluded from the subdomain of emotion. These are thought of as representing action or communication concepts. Other lexemes may have an emotional as well as an expressional reading at the same time, depending on the context, as will be shown for YM in ch. 5.

---

[16] To understand the Ewe example some further clarification seems to be in order: *kpe ɲu* 'be ashamed, shame' is a phrasal predicate consisting of the verb root *kpe* and the nominal complement *ɲu*. The nominal behaves syntactically independently, i.e., it is not incorporated. This is visible in (12a) vs. (12b). In (12a), *ɲu* follows the verb, while in (12b), it precedes the verb. The verbal complex in the progressive form differs from that in the habitual form in that it has an analytical structure: a tense marking element precedes the (first) object in transitive constructions (*ɲu* in (12b)). The latter is followed by the verb, which is itself marked for aspect.

As has been stated above with respect to bodily sensation, not only those lexemes and constructions denoting emotion have to be included in the domain but also lexemes and constructions denoting the causation of emotion such as German *ärgern* 'annoy', *langweilen* 'bore', etc.

3.2.2.4 *Cognition*

The subdomain of cognition subsumes internal experiences based on mental functions. It includes situations that involve the presence or absence of information, i.e., concepts similar to 'know', 'understand', 'learn', 'remember', 'forget', situations of conceptual activity, i.e., concepts similar to 'suppose', 'consider', 'imagine', and attitudes towards (the truth of) propositions, i.e., concepts similar to 'think', 'believe'. Causative members of the subdomain include concepts like 'show', 'teach', 'remind'. Cognitive concepts are prototypically related to a content.

Reh (1998[M]:27) divides the abovementioned concepts into two separate subdomains, i.e., cognition and conception, following Horie (1985), who himself bases his classification on the behavior of the respective verbs with respect to complementation.[17] In this view, cognition is the more stative part of the subdomain "which relates to the presence or absence of information in the mind" (Horie 1985:39) while conception is the more active part; including imagination and attitudes (in terms of Horie 1985:40 "conceptual activities from imagination to belief"). Since the parameters of dynamicity and control are crucial in other domains as well, they are not reflected by creating a separate subdomain, but stative and dynamic as well as active and inactive concepts are part of the subdomain of cognition.

Like the aforementioned subdomains of bodily sensation and emotion, the subdomain of cognition contains stative (e.g., 'know') as well as dynamic concepts (e.g., 'think', 'remember'). More than these subdomains, it is also characterized by activity concepts (e.g., 'suppose', 'consider', etc.). Cognitive property concepts such as 'be intelligent', 'think/know a lot', 'be wise', etc. are considered marginal for the same reasons as emotional dispositions are considered marginal to the subdomain of emotion (cf. sect. 3.2.2.3).

3.2.2.5 *Volition*

The functional subdomain of volition is semantically narrower than the other experiential subdomains. It is understood here as being comprised of two main areas of meaning, i.e., psycho-physical meanings which are expressed by con-

---

[17] There is a distinction between Horie's conception and cognition verbs in the truth status of the complement clause which is adopted in the investigation of YM complementation with cognition verbs in terms of knowledge predicates and predicates of propositional attitude (cf. sect. 7.3). In the current study, the distinction between Horie's cognition and conception verbs is treated as a more specific one within the subdomain of cognition.

cepts such as 'like', 'wish', 'desire', etc., and meanings connected to intention as implied in concepts such as 'intend', 'plan', etc. It is thus made up of conscious as well as unconscious forms of will (cf. Van Valin and Wilkins 1996: 313). Cross-linguistically, it can be noted that both meaning components are often encoded in one lexical item, as, e.g., in the German modal verbs *wollen* and *mögen*, Span. *querer*, Modern Greek *θélo*, YM *k'áat*, etc. (cf. Harkins 1995, Diewald 1999, sect. 4.3.2). Like cognition concepts, volition concepts are related to a content.

Given this description, the subdomain of volition seems to have an affinity to the experiential subdomains of emotion and cognition. Like most cognition predicates, volition predicates prototypically combine with propositions in stimulus function. As complement taking predicates, volition predicates often show a special grammatical behavior regarding types of complements. In light of this observation, Noonan (1985) makes a distinction between 'hope' vs. 'wish' vs. 'want' type predicates based on their relation to reality (possibility of realization) and their temporal structure (cf. ch. 7 for an analysis of complement types with experiential predicates in YM). A number of emotion concepts are closely related to volition, i.e., 'long', 'miss', 'jealous', 'envious' (cf., e.g., Wierzbicka 1999 etc.).

Furthermore, it seems to be reasonable to include the (bodily) needs of a person in the subdomain of volition, as Reh and Simon (1998:42) does. A bodily need can be understood as a will (concerning the realization of a situation) based on person-immanent physical necessities. Engl. *need* or Germ. *brauchen*, *bedürfen* convey related meanings. Terms conveying need(s) are occasionally used in contexts of emotional dependence in interpersonal relationships as well.

As becomes obvious from the preceding characterization of the subdomain of volition, there is an overlap with the domain of modality concerning the concepts 'want', 'need', 'like', etc., which in many languages are grammaticalized verbs or modals. Such verbs are often polyfunctional, displaying full verb use as well as a participant-oriented modality use or a deictic (e.g., epistemic) use related to the factitivity of a proposition. This can be exemplified with German modal verbs. Some modals such as Germ. *wollen* 'want' and *mögen* 'like' can be argued to be experiential in meaning in their full verb use (13a), as well as in their use of expressing a participant-oriented modality (13b/c). They impose restrictions on subject selection, generally occurring with sentient participants.

> (13)   a. *Der Junge will/möchte/mag Eis.*
>   'The boy wants/likes ice-cream.'
>
>   b. *Er will nun täglich schwimmen gehen.*
>   'He now wants/intends to go swimming daily.'

    c. *Er möchte in diesem Jahr gerne nach Spanien fahren.*
       'He would like to go to Spain this year.'

Other (more rare) uses[18] of these verbs are more strongly grammaticalized and no longer convey an experiential reading. This is true for the quotative reading in (14a) and the non-experiential reading in (14b).

(14)   a. *Er will nichts davon gewußt haben.*
       'He claims not to have known anything about it'
    b. *Diese Flasche will nicht aufgehen.*
       'This bottle does not open.'

In (14b) it is presumed that the subject of *will* 'want' has an internal disposition which prevents it from opening. In these situations *wollen* can be combined with non-sentient participants as subject.

3.2.2.6 *Perception*

The functional subdomain of perception includes those concepts that refer to the intake of information through the senses. Perceptual senses allow animate entities to access the surrounding world and to gain knowledge about it. As has been said above, 'western' cultural conceptualizations recognize five sensual modes: sight, hearing, touch, taste, and smell. From a biological-scientific point of view however, these are not sufficient to describe all sensual modes of perceptions. Thus, it has to be acknowledged that some languages may lexicalize more and/or different senses. For those languages which code (some of) the mentioned modes, the following implicational hierarchy seems to be at work: sight < hearing < touch < smell/taste (Viberg 1984).[19] A lexical item at a given point in this hierarchy may encompass those concepts to the right of it in the hierarchy. For instance, within this hierarchy, YM distinguishes between sight and the rest, i.e., the language covers hearing, touch, smell and taste by a single lexeme *u'y* (cf. sect. 5.3.2).

Perception is a relation between a perceiving entity, i.e., the experiencer and a perceived entity or situation, i.e., the stimulus. The internal temporal structure of perception concepts varies from stative to dynamic. Basic perception verbs corresponding to 'see', 'hear', etc. are often stative, while verbs of controlled perception such as Engl. *watch, stare*, etc. are durative processes, and verbs of unintentional perception such as Germ. *erblicken* 'catch sight of' are

---

[18] Cf. Diewald (1999:283) for remarks on the meaning and the frequency of the non-experiential use of *wollen.*

[19] This hierarchy, especially with respect to the 'vision first' claim, is supported by the findings of Evans and Wilkins (1998) for Australian languages.

punctual events. Stative perception is prototypical for the experiential subdomain of perception since such situations are linguistically prone to having a special experiential coding, as will be shown below.

Perception may be active (implying attentive, directed, voluntary and intentional) or inactive (implying unattentive, undirected, involuntary, and unintentional).[20] The distinction between active and inactive perception is expressed lexically and/or grammatically in many languages. Inactive perception is often coded as reduced transitivity. The inactive see-er/perceiver may be a morphologically downgraded subject, e.g., a dative subject as in Lak, Lezgian, Hunzib and other Daghestanian languages. These languages code the active perceiver as an ergative or absolutive subject, depending on the larger construction (cf. Comrie 1981:55, Haspelmath 1993, van den Berg 1995, Comrie and van den Berg 2003), or the stimulus may not occur as a direct object with inactive perception verbs. For instance, Samoan (Austronesian, Nuclear Polynesian) codes inactive perception in an intransitive frame, coding the perceiver in the absolutive and the stimulus in a directional phrase while active perception shows a regular transitive frame with an ergative perceiver and an absolutive theme (Mosel and Hovdhaugen 1992:733).[21]

In some languages inactive perception is rendered by a stimulus-oriented construction, i.e., a construction with a stimulus subject. Such constructions are often related to active perception by voice (e.g., in Korean) or inverse operations, as, e.g., shown for Ewe in (15). The inverse construction in (15b) is chosen if the perception happens involuntarily.

(15) a. *Kofí   kpɔ́   ama   le   mɔ́-á   dzí.*
         Kofi   see   Ama   at   way-DEF   top
         'Kofi saw Ama on the way.' (Ameka 1990:153)

      b. *Ama   nyá   kpɔ́-ná   (ná-m).*
         Ama   INV   see-HAB   to-1.SG
         'Ama looks well (to me).' (Ameka 1990:175)

Stimulus-oriented verbs of perception are often intransitive (e.g., *seem*, *look*, *sound*, etc.), but in addition to these, there are also transitive verbs such as *dazzle* etc..

The subdomain of perception shows a closer connection to two of the other subdomains, namely, cognition and bodily sensation. Perception is related to

---

[20] This may correspond to the distinction between state and activity perception verbs discussed in Van Valin and Wilkins (1996:310) which is captured by the addition of a *do'* component (taking an effector as first argument with the activity verb).

[21] Further examples include Finnish which shows reduced transitivity with perception verbs coding the stimulus in the partitive (Hopper and Thompson 1980:265).

cognition through its primary aim, namely, gaining knowledge about the world. The metonymic shift from 'seeing' to 'knowing' is documented in many languages with diverse cultural backgrounds (cf. Sweetser 1990). In Australian languages, a shift from hearing to knowing is common (cf. Evans and Wilkins 1998). A connection between perception and bodily sensation is given through the sense of touch. This is found in many languages (including German and YM) in which a polysemous lexeme 'feel' covers both subdomains.

3.3   *The experiential situation*

The nature of the subtypes of experiential situations has been discussed in some detail in the preceding sections. The current chapter characterizes the experiential situation by identifying its components and their prototypical linguistic expression (sect. 3.3.1). The participant roles of experiencer and stimulus are discussed in sect. 3.3.2 before experiential situation types are addressed with respect to their internal temporal structure in sect. 3.3.3.

3.3.1 *Components of an experiential situation*

On a conceptual level, several components of an experiential situation, as exemplified in (16) from Wolof (Niger-Congo, Atlantic) have to be distinguished, namely, an experiencer, its person part, the expertum, and the stimulus.[22]

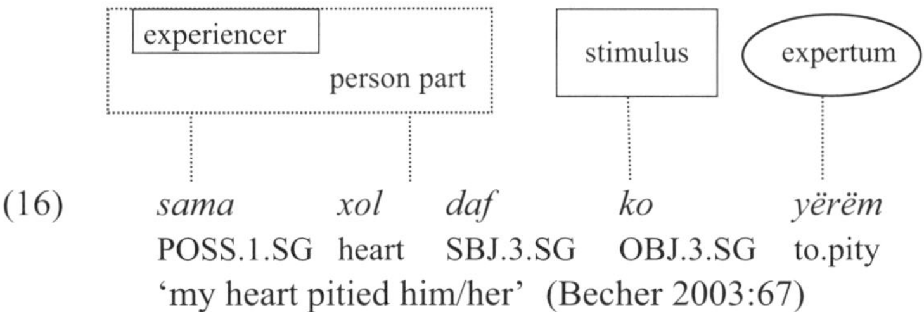

(16)   *sama   xol   daf   ko   yërëm*
       POSS.1.SG   heart   SBJ.3.SG   OBJ.3.SG   to.pity
       'my heart pitied him/her'   (Becher 2003:67)

Figure 4 arranges the components graphically and represents a conceptualization of the relations between them. There are several options for rendering a basic experiential situation linguistically. Both the experiencer and the stimulus may be initial or causal in the situation (cf. Croft 1993). In addition there are more conceptualizations which vary according to the situation type and the number and presence of participants in the specific experiential situation. Coding strategies which are identifiable cross-linguistically will be addressed in sect. 3.4.

---

[22] Compare, e.g., Reh and Frühwald (1996), Reh (1998[E]) which recognize three cognitive units, i.e., experiencer, experitum and phenomenon.

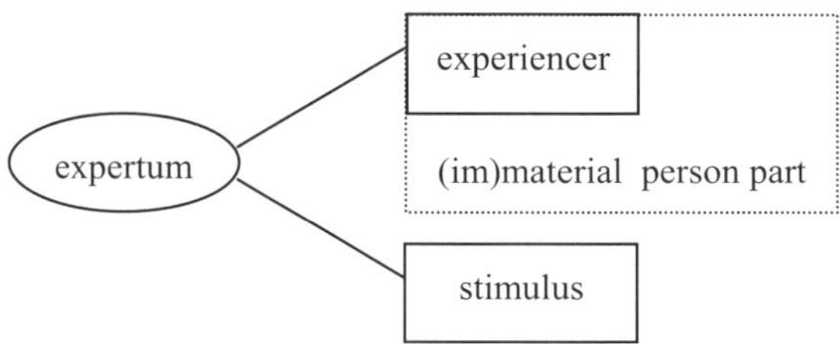

Figure 4. Components of a basic experiential situation

The experiencer is a sentient, usually human participant, that is in, undergoes or is affected by an internal state, process or event; prototypically a feeling, or a mental or perceptual situation. The experiencer participates through
its physicalness and intellectuality in the situation which may be linguistically
rendered by the use of material or immaterial body or person part nouns.[23]
(Im)material person parts are involved in the situation as parts of the experiencer. They are thus thought of as being on a secondary level; their participation being given by the experiencer. This is shown in Figure 4 by broken lines.
The experiencer is sympathetically[24] affected when its parts are affected. The
expertum refers to the situation core of an experiential situation and is generally expressed by the predicate. The expertum constitutes the experience, i.e.,
the sensation, feeling, cognition, or perception. The stimulus is used here as a
cover term for the participant that triggers, causes, initiates the experience, or
that which the experience is directed to.

The notion of experience is an essential component of experiential situations. Therefore, they have to be separated from situations that may imply an
experience, for example, situations of physical or bodily affectedness of an
animate undergoer, e.g., conveyed by verbs like *hit, wound, injure*, etc. These
may implicate the experiential affectedness/bodily sensation of the undergoer
but do not profile it. At a conceptual level the participant in question may be a
patient and an experiencer at the same time, whereas at the linguistic level the
undergoer of verbs like *hit, wound, injure*, etc. is always a PATIENT. Further
cases of delimitation from neighboring domains have been addressed in sect.
3.2.2, for instance, the distinction between bodily states and bodily sensations
in sect. 3.2.2.2.

However a variant of an experiential situation is a situation which includes
(in addition to those participants found in Figure 4) a causing participant that is
generally an agent, i.e., an animate sentient participant that brings about the

---

[23] In this work the term 'person part' is used to include material and immaterial body parts as
well as reified products of the human mind, e.g., thought, speech etc.

[24] This term 'sympathetic' is derived from the 'dativus sympatheticus' introduced in Havers
(1911); for the concept see Lehmann et al. (2000[D]).

experiential situation of its own volition. Such situations are rendered by verbs such as *remind, show, teach,* etc. which require – apart from a causer – a sentient/rational affected participant. It could also be argued that the latter is an experiencer. In this situation type, the agent has a causal relation to the experiential situation. Such a derived experiential situation is shown in Figure 5.

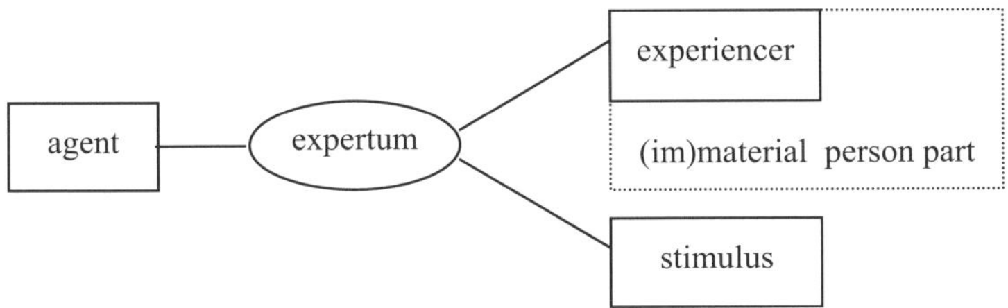

Figure 5. Components of a derived experiential situation containing an agent

Other experiential verbs such as Germ. *stören* 'disturb', *nerven* 'get on s.o.'s nerves', *ärgern* 'annoy', etc. may also take an agent in their valency, as illustrated in (17a). These also match Figure 5. The stimulus may be optionally coded in instrument function with this type of agentive causative experiential verb (cf. Croft 1991, 1993, Klein and Kutscher 2002).

(17)   a. *Maria störte/nervte Peter* (*absichtlich*) (*mit ihrer Fragerei/durch ihre Fragerei*).
'Maria disturbed/annoyed Peter (intentionally) (with her questions/ by her questions).'
b. *Marias Fragerei störte/nervte Peter* (**absichtlich*).
'Maria's questions disturbed/annoyed Peter (*intentionally).'

Verbs, like those shown in (17), belong to a systematically ambiguous pattern of causative experiential verbs that take either an agent (one potential reading in (17a), or a stimulus (alternative reading of (17a), (17b)) in subject function (cf., e.g., Grimshaw 1990:28ff., Jackendoff 1990:140f., van Voorst 1992 for discussion of respective verbs in English). The stimulus reading yields a stative interpretation of the situation, while the agent reading requires that the verb is understood as an action/activity. Only in the latter reading can a processive passive be formed, while the stative reading only allows the so-called adjectival or stative passive.

On a conceptual level, the components mentioned in Figure 4 are all constitutive of an experiential situation. They differ however, in their involvement in the experiential situation according to the more specific types of experience.

As will be seen in sect. 3.3.2.2.3, the involvement of the experiential participants can contribute to the definition of the experiential subtypes.

Linguistically, a large number of different construction types encoding experiential situations are found. Not all of the components of an experiential situation must be linguistically realized in a given construction. A cross-linguistic survey of experiential construction types will be given in sect. 3.4.3.

3.3.2 *Participant roles in an experiential situation*

There are two members constituting participant roles among the components of a prototypical experiential situation as represented in Figure 4, namely, the experiencer and the stimulus. Figure 4 shows further components that are not role terms, i.e., person part and expertum. These receive their semantic and argument roles with respect to a given verb and the construction (type) with which they integrate. For instance, a person part noun often takes the role of Theme, Patient or Locus in experiential constructions. For example, in (3a) from YM the body part noun is a Theme with respect to a qualifying adjective. In (3b) the person part noun takes the argument function of a Locus. The expertum noun may be integrated into constructions in which it takes Agent function, as, e.g., in (69) from Wolof. In (62), it displays Theme/Possessum function in a construction with a possessive verb. A discussion of such construction types will take place later in sect. 3.4.3.

Many works discussing the functional basis of experiential constructions underline theirs deviations and differences with respect to agent-patient relations (e.g., Rice 1987, Croft 2001:89). The alleged counterparts in an experiential situation, experiencer and stimulus, are not as opposed as, e.g., agent and patient are; and this kind of partial opposition results in a large variety of coding strategies. The stimulus triggers the experience, but the experiencer may be said to initiate the experience in that it is its origin. Furthermore the experiencer undergoes the experience and can control it only to a certain degree, varying from case to case.[25] It is the experiencer that is undergoing a (conceptual) change, not the stimulus, which distinguishes it from an agent and makes it more like a patient. The following subsections will examine the roles of the experiencer (sect. 3.3.2.1) and of the stimulus (sect. 3.3.2.2) in some detail.

3.3.2.1 *Experiencer*

Many definitions of the experiencer role focus on just a few aspects of experiential situations as outlined in sect. 3.2.2. Often the semantic role of experiencer is related to the situation type state and the experiencer is described as

---

[25] In a Proto-role approach in the sense of Dowty (1991), this is captured by the theory that "experiencer-stimulus verbs select fewer Proto-role properties for their arguments and are accordingly less stable with respect to their argument pattern across languages and very often also within one language" (Primus 1999:44f.).

undergoing the experiential situation.[26] From a conceptual point of view however, a multi-faceted participant role experiencer which covers the diverse subtypes of experiences has to be provided for (cf., e.g., Dik 1997). On the language-specific level, languages differ as to whether they choose to code the participant role experiencer as a unified semantic role EXPERIENCER, such as many Caucasian languages seem to do (cf. sect. 1.1),[27] or whether they map them onto several other schemes. A given language may also choose to combine only part of more specific experiencers to code them in a semantic role EXPERIENCER, e.g., experiencers of bodily sensation and emotion, or experiencers of states (but not of more dynamic situation types), etc.

In the following sections, the experiencer role will be reviewed with regard to its participant properties and the role properties control and affectedness.

3.3.2.1.1 *Participant properties*

In terms of participant properties (cf. Figure 2) the experiencer is prototypically animate, or even human. As was explained in sect. 2.1.3, the feature [animate] entails, in addition to other features, the feature [sentient]. In a given situation, the feature [human] may entail, among others, features such as [rational], [intentional], [volitional]. The subtypes of experience require a refinement of their definitions with regard to participant properties. The capacity of sentience, which is essential for experience, is ascribed to human beings in general and sometimes to higher animals such as dogs (this may vary culturally[28]). The experiencer in all subdomains of experience necessarily has the feature [sentience]. For the experiencer of bodily sensation and perception as well as of some basic emotions (e.g., happiness, sadness, and fear) the feature [sentience] is a sufficient condition. These subdomains are accessible to animates in general.

The feature [volitional] is essential to the subdomain of volition and to some (more complex and/or socially defined) emotions (e.g., jealousy, envy, etc.) and it may be ascribed to human beings and to higher animals. More complex

---

[26] These include definitions of the experiencer as "an argument of an as yet unexplored State-Function having to do with mental states" (Jackendoff 1987:387, 1990:47), "sentient beings that experience internal states, such as perceivers, cognizers and emoters" (Van Valin and La-Polla 1997:85), "the person whose mental state is being described" (Croft 2001:155f.), "the locus of an internal event" (VanValin 1993:42).

[27] Following Comrie (1981:53) a given semantic role is justified as a cross-linguistic or language-specific category if there is a (reasonable number of) language(s) which provide(s) a special grammatical coding for it. Regarding the experiencer, this may be true either with respect to the whole range of subtypes of experiencers, (e.g., in Caucasian languages) but with respect to deviant subtypes as well, i.e., if, e.g., affected experiencers are marked by a specific kind of coding (cf. Dik 1997).

[28] Note that the ascription of participant properties may in general vary culture-specifically (cf. Van Valin and Wilkins 1996:314).

emotion terms as well as the subdomain of cognition furthermore presuppose the feature [rational]. While higher animals may be thought of as having access to basic cognitive states such as 'know', they may not be understood as, e.g., 'thinking' or 'reasoning'.[29] Thus, the whole range of experiences seems to be accessible only to human beings, while more basic concepts of certain subdomains may select features further down in Figure 2.

Various studies on experiencer coding (Gerdts and Youn 1988, Chun and Zubin 1990, Reh 1998[L]) suggest that the Ego or first person has a privileged role as experiencer. Experiential constructions sometimes display differences in interaction with evidentiality or mediativity[30] systems, in accordance with person marking. For instance, in Korean (as in Japanese), unmarked emotion expressions only occur in the first person (and in the second person in questions) (18a). In order to reference the emotions of a third person either a dynamic verb form[31] is used, pointing to the visible effects of the emotion, as in (18b), or the verb is marked evidentially, e.g., by the hearsay suffix (18c).[32]

    (18)   a. *Na-nɯn   kae-ka   musɵp-ta.*
             1.SG-TOP   dog-NOM be.afraid-DECL
             'I am afraid of/dislike/like dogs.'

          b. *Uli   ai-nɯn   kae-lɯl   musɵ-wɵ-ha-n-ta.*
             1.PL   child-TOP   dog-ACC be.afraid-GER-do-PRS-DECL
             'Our child is afraid of/fears dogs.'

---

[29] It goes without saying that cases of anthropomorphization are excluded in this evaluation.

[30] There has been some debate concerning terminology in the domain of evidentiality/mirativity/mediativity in recent years (cf. DeLancey 1997, Lazard 1999). Lazard (1999) points to the necessity of distinguishing two subcategories of a more general category that may be called evidentiality (in a larger sense) or in French terminology *médiatif*. The relevant subcategories are 'mediative proper' for marking an utterance as 'unassimilated knowledge' for the speaker and 'evidentials proper' for marking the source of evidence for an utterance. The first category is grammaticalized, for example, in Balkan languages, Tibeto-Burman languages, etc. The second category is grammaticalized in a number of Amerindian languages such as Tuyuca (Tucanoan), Wintu (Penutian), etc. Since there may be languages in which both values co-occur these categories have to be set apart (possible cases discussed in Lazard (1999, sect. 3.5) include Korean and Caxinaua (Pano)).

[31] The dynamic form on the contrary is unusual with a first person declarative construction with experiential verbs, cf. Chun and Zubin (1990) for a detailed analysis of the Korean experiential vs. agentive (i.e., dynamic) construction of experiential verbs and their interaction with person marking.

[32] In narrative discourse where the deictic center is moved to a third person, he or she can be conceived of as having direct evidence so that an experiential construction can be used with respect to that person (cf. Chun and Zubin 1990).

    c. *Uli   ai-nɨn   kae-ka   musɘp-tae.*
    1.Pl   child-TOP   dog-NOM   be.afraid-DECL:HS
    'Our child is afraid of dogs (they say).' (MCK)

The functional basis of this intimate relation is the fact that inner states and feelings are most accessible to the experiencer itself.

3.3.2.1.2 *Role properties*

In sect. 2.1.4, the parameters control and affectedness and involvement of a given participant in a situation were introduced as role properties. These parameters will now be discussed as they relate to the experiencer.

The experiencer's characterization in terms of control and affectedness is under debate and needs to be refined. These parameters need to be objectivized and operationalized by suitable tests. There are a number of well known semantic tests that indicate the control or affectedness of an argument. One of the most used and discussed control tests is the imperative test.[33] As a test for control however, it can not simply be used to check the grammaticality of a given imperative form; the semantic implications have to be considered as well. Thus, only with control verbs is an imperative assumed to be a true command (Lehmann 1993[P]:207). Utterances such as *be happy!* or *dream nicely!* merely represent wishes of the speaker. Conversely, the grammatical impossibility of forming an imperative (i.e., the non-existence of an imperative form for a given verb or class of verbs) can be judged as indicating a lack of control.

A further control test that is judged to be more reliable than the imperative test is to subordinate the argument to be tested under a control verb such as *hesitate, try, intend,* or *dare.* Only control verbs should make sense in such a frame. The specific verb has to be chosen according to semantic compatibility with the items to be tested. Other control tests include modification with adverbials like *deliberately, voluntarily,* or the insertion of the item to be tested in a purposive construction (*do X in order to Y*). Compare the application of some of these test frames for German *anekeln* 'disgust' in (19) from Klein and Kutscher (2002, sect. 3.2). The acceptability judgments come from a larger group of native speakers.

    (19)   a.**Ekle deine Großmutter nicht an.*
           'Don't disgust your grandmother!'
        b.[??]*Er versuchte, ihn anzuekeln.*
           'He tried to disgust him.'

---

[33] For comments on this test and some of the following cf. Dik (1978), Lehmann (1991[P], 1993[P]).

c.?*Er benahm sich wirklich widerlich, um seinen Nachbarn anzu-
ekeln.*
'He really behaved awfully in order to gross his neighbor out.'

The fact that a given item shows differences in acceptability in different
control frames may be judged as indicating that there are different degrees of
control. This fits with the theory that control can be seen as a continuum (cf.
sect. 2.1.4). Examples such as (19) make clear that in cases of unclear acceptability, the semantic and pragmatic conditions for a given judgment have to be
taken into account. Suitable semantic tests are to a certain degree language-
specific and need to consider the language-specific semantics of the construction or the lexical items used as indicators. For YM, combinability with impersonal vs. personal phase verbs has turned out to be a good control test. It is
explained and illustrated in sect. 5.1.2.

Control and affectedness of the experiencer vary according to the subtypes
of experience outlined in sect. 3.2, but also within the subdomains, sometimes
in correlation with the internal temporal structure of the situation. In order to
make this more clear more specific role terms for the experiencer of the subdomains outlined in sect. 3.2.2. are adopted from Van Valin and LaPolla
(1997): the experiencer of a perception will be called a perceiver, the experiencer of a cognitive situation a cognizer, the experiencer of an emotion an
emoter, the experiencer of a volitive situation a wanter, and the experiencer of
a bodily sensation a senser.[34] These are understood here as more specific participant roles, which may or may not be part of a more general semantic role
EXPERIENCER in a given language.

In the approach followed here, i.e., which assumes a strong relationship between syntactic structure and semantic content, grammatical coding strategies
are seen as reflecting semantic and conceptual content. A given structure however can not be judged *a priori* as indicating control or affectedness since such
an approach would be circular. If, on the basis of an independent justification
(such as the mentioned tests), a strong correlation between syntactic transitivity
and semantic control/affectedness can be established (e.g., in terms of Hopper
and Thompon 1980), one can draw an inverse conclusion and associate high
control with a given role if respective verbs are generally transitive.[35] On this

---

[34] Terminology and conceptualization of these role terms are (slightly) different in Van Valin
and LaPolla (1997). The term 'experiencer' is (at least in the argument role reading, see
pp.115, 125) used for what is called 'senser' in this work, i.e., the experiencer of a bodily sensation. Otherwise, these authors also use 'experiencer' as a participant role comprising more
specific roles in terms of perception, cognition and emotion (cf. p.85).

[35] Cf. however the study of Maratsos et al. (2000), which calls into question the immediate
connection between grammatically high and grammatically low/oblique coding and (perceived) control. Croft (1993:61) argues in favor of an association of control and coding in subject

basis perceivers and cognizers may be judged as having the most control among the experiencers since they occur most often as subjects or as A of transitive verbs cross-linguistically. Bossong (1998) and Haspelmath (2001) confirm this with reference to a larger number of genetically and areally diverse European languages.[36] Blake (1994:57) notes that perceivers are more likely to be coded in the same way as the agent of a transitive verb than as the experiencers of emotion; Primus (1999:70) confirms this as a weak preference for German.

Cognizers include those experiencers that are selected by mental activity verbs such as *think (about), wonder (about), consider*, etc. in languages like English and German. Following the analysis in Croft (1993:62), these take a volitional and controlling experiencer being the initiator in the situation (cf. also Van Valin and LaPolla 1997:126). This raises the question as to whether there are corresponding activity verbs in the other experiential subdomains. For perceivers, this question has already been positively answered in sect. 3.2.2.6: perceivers are 'traditionally' subdivided into active and inactive groups, the former pertaining to the activity of perception, the latter to the experience of perception. Many languages reflect this distinction in control structurally, e.g., by case marking, transitivity of the verb, etc. Concerning the subdomain of emotion, it was shown in sect. 3.2.2.3, that there are activity verbs involving an emotion or a feeling as, e.g., Engl. *scold, quarrel* or Germ. *schimpfen, sich beschweren*, etc. *Flehen* 'beg with insistence and submission' is similarly related to the subdomain of volition. These verbs however are primarily communication verbs. Nevertheless, the existence of emotional activity verbs which take a possibly controlling experiencer cannot be excluded. Examples may be Germ. *wüten* 'rage, riot' and *schmollen* 'sulk' which both seem to involve an action or activity based on emotion. Korean displays a systematic distinction between stative and dynamic experiential verbs (e.g., *tulyəp-ta* revere-DECL 'be reverent in front of s.b.' vs. *tulyə-wə-ha-ta* revere-GER-do-DECL 'revere s.b.'; cf. also (18.a/b) above). This distinction is associated not only with a difference in dynamicity but also with a difference in control. Thus, only the dynamic verb may form an imperative while the stative can not (20).

(20)   *Hanɨnim-ɨl   tulyə-wə-ha-la*!
        god-ACC   revere-GER-do-IMP
        'Revere God!' (MCK)

---

function. For instance, the subject of symmetric predicates is interpreted as having more control than the partner (e.g., with *fight* etc.).

[36] Cf. as well the more detailed study in Klein and Kutscher (2002) on German.

Finally, the subdomain of bodily sensation does not seem to have activity verbs implying control.

In comparison with cognitive concepts, emotional concepts seem more often to imply a lack of control of the experiencer; i.e., there are generally more emotional concepts implying a lack of control of the emoter than there are cognitive concepts.[37] Emoters seem to vary to a higher degree in terms of control properties, in that they depend on more specific emotion lexemes (cf. Kemmer 1993, sect. 4.2, Filip 1996). The experiencer of a bodily sensation also seems to have low control or no control. If the typological study in Bossong (1998) on experiencer coding is taken as an index (taking into account subject/nominative vs. object/dative/accusative/oblique coding together with morphological marking of the verb (as, e.g., reflexivity)), then control (and conversely affectedness) of the experiencer increases in the following order: bodily sensation/emotion < cognition < perception.[38] Note however, that the data pool is rather small: Bossong tested 10 items per language and the items are not equally distributed in number over the subdomains. Thus, this study can only be seen as a hint of the given order, notwithstanding the above mentioned inverse conclusion which was drawn from structure to control semantics.

---

[37] This statement may be biased with respect to a Western conceptualization of the domain. Talmy (1985, sect. 1.9.2) finds a significantly higher number of stimulus-subject verbs than emoter-subject verbs for English emotion verbs while for 'cognitive' verbs this is reverse. Similarly, Klein and Kutscher (2002) note for German that cognition verbs are mostly experiencer-subject (one exception being *dünken* 'sth. seems to sb.') while verbs of sensation and emotion vary in subject assignment. However non-European data seems to point to the same conceptualization with respect to control. Croft (1993:69f) states for Acehnese that most intransitive emotion verbs show either undergoer cross-reference marking or belong to a variable class which may take their experiencer either as agent or as undergoer (only a few take an agent-experiencer). With intransitive cognition verbs, most items take agent-experiencers and some variable experiencers while there seem to be no intransitive cognitive verbs with an undergoer-experiencer. Reh (ed., 1998) reports with repect to a number of African languages (e.g., Mande and Chadic languages) that subject experiencers are predominant with perception, cognition and volition while non-experiencer subjects are found with emotion and bodily sensation expressions. In Wolof emotion and bodily sensation are predominantly expressed by expertum oriented constructions "which depict the experiencer-participant as a victim of the emotion or the physical condition respectively" (Becher 2003:56). This construction type does not appear within the subdomain of cognition.

[38] Bossong (1998:261) gives a characterization of the increasing activity and control in this order, including bodily sensation and emotion. His data however is not clear in this point. There are some languages (e.g., Latvian, Russian, Finnish, Mari, Udmurt, Georgian) that are consistent in coding the senser 'more obliquely' than the emoter. With most other languages there is either no (significant) morpho-syntactic difference between senser and emoter, or the emoter is coded 'more oblique' (e.g., in Welsh, Breton, Italian, Dutch, Classical Greek). Rather, most (but not all) languages show a rather clear difference in the coding of bodily sensation and emotion on the one hand and cognition and perception on the other hand.

Affectedness appears to be more difficult to test. A criterion that can be used to judge the affectedness of a given subtype of experiencer is the probability of its showing middle constructions. Kemmer (1993:130) explains: "As we have seen in connection with other middle domains, one of the main functions of a middle marker is to code the affectedness of an initiating entity. Therefore, we might hypothesize that increased affectedness of an Initiator would result in increased likelihood for a situation type to be subsumed under middle marking." According to Kemmer's investigation of cross-linguistic data concerning middle constructions in the experiential subdomains of emotion, cognition and perception, the subdomain of emotion is most likely to show middle constructions (cf., e.g., Germ. *sich fürchten*[39] 'be/become frightened' etc., Hungarian *dühös-köd* 'be furious', *gyülölköd* 'bear malice, bear a grudge', etc. Twi *onū nehō* 'he repents' etc. and many examples from other languages) followed by that of cognition (cf., e.g., Latin *meditor* 'ponder, meditate', *interpretor* 'interpret', etc., Fula *miilo* 'ponder', *hiiso* 'calculate', etc.). Perception verbs do occur as middle verbs but much less frequently. If perception verbs show middle marking, then they generally belong to the stimulus-oriented type (cf. sect. 3.2.2.6, e.g., *sich gut anhören* 'sound good' etc.). This type of middle construction however is functionally akin to a passive construction in that it deemphasizes the agent.[40] Evidence from middle constructions therefore points to a decreasing affectedness in the following way: emotion > cognition > perception. This conforms to the above mentioned results from Bossong (1998).

Finally, a few words need to be said about the involvement of the experiencer in an experiential situation. The experiencer is a central participant in all types of experiential situations. This is reflected linguistically by the fact that it is coded as a complement to experiential predicates. However, with one type of predicate, i.e., with a subgroup of stimulus-oriented predicates, the experiencer is less central (e.g., *be visible/be known to sb.*, etc.). The experiencer is demoted to an adjunct with such predicates (which correspond to stative passives). In contrast, evaluative predicates (like *tasty, nice, dangerous*, etc.) generally do not adjoin an oblique experiencer. These correspond to deagentive forms of active verbs that cut off the experiencer completely. It can be argued that they are not primarily experiential but denote properties of their subject which may be optionally related to an evaluating participant.

---

[39] The middle marker is underlined in these examples.

[40] Furthermore, note that in German there are reflexive constructions with *ansehen* 'watch' and *anhören* 'listen to' as in *Ich sehe mir einen Film an.* 'I am watching a film (to my benefit)'. A similar construction is possible with *wünschen* 'wish' (e.g., *Ich wünsche mir ein Auto.* 'I would like to have a car (for my own)'. In these cases, the reflexive construction identifies the experiencer as an auto-beneficiary. It may point to simultaneous control and affectedness of the latter.

3.3.2.2 *Stimulus*
3.3.2.2.1 *The nature of the stimulus*

The stimulus is a very heterogeneous participant role. It is comprised of cause and goal of an experiential situation, authority of a social feeling such as 'shame' or 'pride', or simply the object or target of an affect or a perception. Terminology varies according to theoretical frames as well as with respect to the experiential subtypes at the focus of a given analysis. Frequently the term 'theme' is chosen instead (e.g., Grimshaw 1990, Van Valin 1993, Pesetzsky 1995). Halliday (1985) and Reh (ed., 1998) use the term 'phenomenon'. In this work the term 'stimulus' is preferred (following Blansitt 1978, Croft 1993 and many others) to indicate the specificity of this role in experiential situations as opposed to 'theme', which is used with other definitions as well, e.g., as non-mechanically/non-physically affected undergoer or as localized or moving participant in situations of motion (e.g., Van Valin and LaPolla 1997:85). The stimulus role may be specified as corresponding to the subtypes of the experiencer role, resulting in subtypes such as perceived, cognized, wanted, emoted.[41]

With respect to the conceptualization of a causal structure of a situation based on force-dynamic relations among participants (cf. Croft 1993, 1998), it seems that the various more specific stimulus subroles can be captured by two more general variants, namely, those stimuli that are more cause- or source-like (i.e., that precede or trigger the experiential situation) and those stimuli that are more goal-like (i.e., that follow the experiential situation), e.g., in the sense that the experience is directed towards them.[42] These two subroles, namely source-stimulus and goal-stimulus, can encompass the various shadings of the stimulus role. Source or goal conceptualizations may be, e.g., expressed by the use of specific prepositions or cases in the coding of stimuli arguments (cf. (21a) vs. (21b) from English and (22) from Dutch).[43]

---

[41] Van Valin and LaPolla (1997) chooses the following more specific terms: stimulus (with perception), content or judgment (with cognition), desire (with volition), target (with (relational) emotion), sensation (with bodily sensation). These are all (such as the subtypes of the experiencer) in a paradigmatic relationship with respect to linking, i.e., subtypes of a role never occur syntagmatically. They are thus, together with other more specific roles, thought of as being part of a more basic thematic relation which for the experiencer-subroles is the first argument x of a stative predicate pred'(x,y) and for the stimulus subroles the second argument y of a stative predicate pred'(x,y).

[42] Cf. Blansitt (1978) for an overview of the treatment of the stimulus in early semantic role studies. Approaches to the stimulus often vary in subsuming it either under cause (e.g., Fillmore 1971) or goal (e.g., Longacre 1976). Cf. as well Van Valin and LaPolla (1997) who call the stimulus of the emotion word *love* a 'target'. This view of the stimulus role is also articulated in Bolinger (1977, 1984) with respect to English emotions terms.

[43] For an analysis of English prepositions in emotional constructions cf. Osmond (1997). Her detailed analysis shows that source- and goal-semantics are certainly not the only semantic content of the stimulus joining prepositions.

(21)   a. *I was annoyed by the barking of the dogs.* (source)
        b. *The old dog is devoted to you.* (goal)

(22)   *De leraar houdt van deze bloemen.* (source)
        'The teacher likes these flowers.' (Blansitt 1978:323)

Along with coding a stimulus as a source or as a goal, a construction may also be neutral to a source or a goal conceptualization, which is typically true of experiential states that do not involve a force-dynamic distinction between experiencer and stimulus (cf. Croft 1993:62). Consider (23) in this respect. The example comes from Japanese and displays a double nominative construction.

(23)   *Ai ga   Ken ga   suki da.*
        Ai NOM   Ken NOM   like   COP
        'Ai likes Ken.' (Shibatani 2001:311)

Source- or goal-stimuli do not seem to be especially subdomain-specific, with the possible exception of the subdomain of volition, which seems to be inherently goal-oriented. Specific lexemes are often subcategorized for either a source- or a goal-stimulus. This becomes obvious in preposition selection. The combination of more specific stimulus subtypes is possible, as, e.g., a source-like and goal-like stimulus with verbs like 'ashamed', which may include the reason for shame and the authority with respect to which shame is felt. Compare (24) from German.

(24)   *Ich schäme mich vor dir für mein grobes Verhalten.*
        'I am ashamed of my bad behavior in front of you.'

However, a given experiential expression most often adds only one type of stimulus, a reason why the role of stimulus is generally not further subdivided in works in the domain. Furthermore, as Van Valin and LaPolla (1997) notes, the domain-specific stimulus types, e.g., perceived, wanted, emoted, etc. do not co-occur syntagmatically.

Klein and Kutscher (2002, sect. 1) has introduced the notion of a 'split stimulus' with respect to verbs such as Germ. *jdm. etw. gönnen* 'not to begrudge sth. to so.', *jdm. etw. neiden* 'envy sb. [for] sth.', *jmd. etw. wünschen* 'wish so. sth.' (25). These are obviously three-place/ditransitive verbs based on a transfer or beneficiary/maleficiary situation. The stimulus refers to a complex situation containing an animate participant bene-/malefiting from the mental state/activity expressed by the verbs *gönnen, neiden* and *wünschen*. The latter is coded as a RECIPIENT/BENEFICIARY/MALEFICIARY in the dative, while the entity or proposition wished/not begrudged is coded as an UNDERGOER.

(25) a. *Ich gönne dir den Sieg/dass du siegst.*
          'I don't begrudge you the victory/that you win.'
      b. *Ich wünsche Peter den Sieg/dass er siegt.*
          'I wish Peter the victory/that he wins.'

Another case of split stimulus is presented in (26).

(26) a. *Die Arbeit beeindruckt vor allem durch ihren Umfang/ aufrund/*
          wegen ihres Umfangs.
          'The work impresses above all by its size/ because of its size.'
      a'.*Der Umfang der Arbeit beindruckt vor allem.*
          'The size of the work is above all impressing.'
      b. *The article angered Bill by its content.* (Grimshaw 1990:23)
      b'.*The article's content angered Bill.*

The examples in (26) display a metonymic relationship between the stimulus
argument in subject function (*die Arbeit* in (26a), *the article* in (26b) and the
'second' stimulus or cause which appears in adjunct function in both examples
(cf. Grimshaw 1990:23). This can be shown by the paraphrases in (26a'/b')
where the respective participants appear in a possessive NP. Adjuncts, which
are characterized by not being governed by the verb, can be added freely and
their semantic role is thus not given/licenced by the verb, but rather, e.g., by a
governing adposition. Such cases, thus, do not affect the claim that each semantic role can only occur once in a clause. It is generally true that a stimulus-
like causal participant in adjunct function can be added to experiential situations if semantically appropriate. Such cases will not be discussed in the current work since they follow general rules of adverbial or adjunct marking.
    Furthermore, as has been said in sect. 3.3.1, a stimulus may co-occur with
an agent in a derived experiential situation, i.e., it may occur in a syntagmatic
relation to an agent. The stimulus as a participant role is in paradigmatic relation to other participant roles. Both the stimulus and the agent are potentially
triggering or causal in a situation. In sect. 3.3.1, it has been said that with
causative experiential verbs such as *frighten, bother*, etc. the actor argument
may be interpreted as either a stimulus or an agent. If the stimulus is animate it
provides the potential for agentivity and may be integrated into agentive constructions, e.g., a construction with an instrument phrase. Such a participant is
an agent as well as a stimulus on the conceptual level, and, theoretically, very
often if not always an AGENT and ACTOR at the linguistic level.

3.3.2.2.2 *Participant properties*

Besides the theme, the stimulus is the only role which is open to the whole range of participant properties (cf. Lehmann et al. 2000[D]). Like the theme, it may involve propositional or abstract participants. This holds true in particular for members of the subdomains of perception, emotion, volition and cognition. Cognition verbs such as *think, suppose*, etc. exclusively select propositional stimuli. Perception verbs are in principle open to the whole range of participant properties given in Figure 2. However, members of the subdomain of bodily sensation are an exception since they prototypically are not subcategorized for a stimulus participant. In general, it may be concluded that the stimulus (similar to the theme and the patient) is unmarked for a specific position in the animacy hierarchy (cf. Figure 2).[44]

Following what has been said above, propositional stimuli are only considered in this work to the extent that they constitute obligatory participants of a given experiential situation. This is due to the fact that a modifying adverbial sentence can be added to all experiential sentences as (27) shows.

(27)   *I am hungry because I didn't eat the whole day.*

3.3.2.2.3 *Role properties*

As regards the role properties of the stimulus, it is generally not at all, or only weakly affected in all subtypes where it occurs. Linguistically, this is reflected by the fact that the stimulus is often coded by oblique or prepositional arguments (e.g., with experiential activity verbs such as *think (about), worry (about)*, etc., cf. Croft 1993:62). Differences may exist according to participant properties of the stimulus. Thus, an inanimate participant is certainly not affected by feelings as love, scorn or disgust. An animate participant however, may be affected by such feelings (if he is aware of them). Among the perception verbs, the active verbs (e.g., *gaze (at)* etc.) can be argued as having a possibly affected stimulus-undergoer which may be more similar to a patient.[45] Active perception verbs are generally transitive verbs which can be then distinguished from inactive ones in taking an AGENT and a PATIENT as semantic roles (cf. discussion of languages that regularly distinguish between inactive and active perception in their constructions in sect. 3.2.2.6).

If the stimulus is at the same time an agent, as in (17a), it exerts a rather high degree of control in the situation. This is shown in (17a) by the option of

---

[44] This does not however mean that specific lexemes in the domain do not display more specific selectional restrictions as to their stimulus argument. Rather, the domain contains groups or types of verbs/predicates on different positions in Figure 2.

[45] With verbs like *anstarren* 'stare at', the perceived entity may well be affected if it is sentient itself and perceives the situation.

adding an adverb that indicates volition or by the option of adding an instrumental phrase. Inanimate stimuli such as those in (26), correspond to agent-stimuli in their causal function. They do not, however, exert control in the situation, given the definition of control as being exerted by an entity that is responsible for the initiation, realization and the end of a situation. Inanimate stimuli may be judged as being initiative due to their causal effect. They do not however have any effect on the development of a situation.[46]

The abovementioned subtypes of experience differ as to whether a stimulus participant is obligatory or not, which is reflected in its involvement in the situation. While predicates of bodily sensation are often not subcategorized for a stimulus, predicates of the other subtypes generally do take a stimulus argument. The subdomains may be ordered according to how obligatory the stimulus is in the following way: bodily sensation > emotion > cognition/volition/perception. The subdomain of bodily sensation most often contains members of a stative class as basic items (mostly adjectives, stative verbs or abstract nouns occurring in light verb constructions, e.g., Germ. *ich habe Hunger/Durst* 'I am hungry/thirsty'). These are conceptualized mostly as autonomously existing, i.e., they are not conceived of as directed towards a stimulus participant or triggered by one. Only seldomly are they subcategorized for a stimulus (e.g., *hungry for*). On the other hand, many emotion terms may optionally take a stimulus argument. In German or English, emotion adjectives like *sich freuen (über)* 'be glad about', *Angst haben (vor)* 'be afraid of' select a specific preposition if they take a stimulus argument. The subdomains of cognition, volition and perception are characterized by transitive (or at least bivalent) verbs, a fact that points to an obligatory stimulus (in addition to the experiencer).

3.3.3 *Experiential situation types*

As has been outlined in sect. 3.2.2 for the specific experiential domains, experiential situations may pertain to any of the basic situation types introduced in sect. 2.1.2. There, prototypical situation types were identified for the more specific experiential subdomains. Experiential properties such as, e.g., emotional dispositions or character traits of temperament (cf. 3.2.2.3) were, however, identified as non-prototypical members of the domain of experience since they are prone to be linguistically coded like other properties, i.e., the experiencer will be conceptualized as a holder of a property in most languages. Correspondingly, experiential activities are more likely to be coded like other activities, i.e., conceptualizing the experiencer as an actor.

---

[46] Causing stimuli are similar to those roles that Van Valin and Wilkins (1996) subsumes under the effector role, namely, agent, force, and instrument. One crucial criterion of effectors however is not fulfilled by the causing stimulus, namely, it does not have any potential for dynamicity.

Analyses of the 'basic' aspectual character of experiential lexemes vary extremely. Given the fact that the aspectual character must first be analyzed with respect to a specific language and secondly with respect to a given construction in which a lexeme occurs, the issue of aspectual character types of experiential predicates can be discussed only quite generally, i.e., pursuing the question of which aspectual characters generally occur with certain types of experiential lexemes. Given the controversial discussion of the aspectual character of more specific types of experiential predicates (cf., e.g., Blansitt 1978, Grimshaw 1990, van Voorst 1992, Croft 1993, Van Valin and LaPolla 1997, etc.) two issues need to be commented on: the distinction between experiential states and more dynamic experiential situations, and the aspectual character of causative experiential predicates.

Emotion lexemes such as 'love', 'fear', 'admire', bodily sensation terms such as 'be sick', 'feel hot', etc., cognition lexemes such as 'know', 'believe' and perception verbs such as 'see', 'hear' are generally categorized as stative in the literature (cf., e.g., Grimshaw 1990, Croft 1993, Van Valin and LaPolla 1997, etc.). However, it is unclear if such concepts may rather (or alternatively) designate a durative process, especially for those concepts expressed as verbs in a language. A prototypical state (as opposed to a process or other more dynamic situation types) is often described as involving no energy to go on or to sustain it (cf. Comrie 1976, Lehmann 1991). Thus, a test frame with adverbs indicating the input of energy like *vigorously* (or Germ. *mit aller Kraft* 'with all one's strength') may help distinguish experiential states from more dynamic situation types. In this respect, German emotion verbs like *lieben* 'love' and *hassen* 'hate' may combine with the adverbial *mit aller Kraft*. The German equivalents of the other mentioned concepts, however, are negative in this frame. For German *lieben* 'love' and *hassen* 'hate' two different readings, a stative and a durative reading, are assumed. The stativity of the mentioned English experiential verbs and adjectives is usually shown by the failure of combination with the progessive.

Furthermore, it has been mentioned in sect. 3.2.2 that the subdomains of cognition, perception, and emotion, may involve rather systematic correspondences between state and activity conceptualizations (e.g., perception: *see* vs. *watch*, cognition: *know* vs. *think*, emotion: Germ. *wütend* 'furious, enraged' vs. *wüten* 'rage, riot'). The latter represent atelic durative processes according to Figure 1. This regular distinction with respect to dynamicity is implemented in diverse languages at different levels of the grammar of experience. With respect to (18), it can be seen that dynamicity is at the base of the Korean grammatical distinction between the stative (i.e., experiential) and the dynamic (i.e., agentive) construction of emotion verbs (cf. Chun and Zubin 1990).[47] Similarly, in Jaminjung some coverbs of bodily and emotional condition combine with the generic verb *-yu(nggu)* 'SAY/DO' to render an internal condition observable from outside, e.g., by a certain behavior (Schultze-Berndt 2000, sect. 6.4.3). Observe (28) which refers to the lively and happy bouncing of a child.

(28)   *Nganthan-nyunga   jalug   gan-unggu-m*
         what-ORIG   lively   3.SG:3.SG-say/do-PRS
         yirra=mulu   thanthu   jalig?
         1.PL.EXCL.OBL=COLL   DEM   child
         'Why is he being lively "at us all"', that child?' (Schultze-Berndt 2000:462)

The concepts discussed above are basically atelic, but there are also telic concepts in the domain of experience. Dynamic ingressive and punctual event denoting verbs, e.g., Germ. *sich erschrecken, sich erinnern, vergessen,* etc. belong to these. Moreover, languages often seem to provide for inchoative or ingressive correspondences to stative experiential lexemes of the type 'get sick/cold/hungry', 'get mad/bored/angry', cf. also Germ. *wissen ~ erfahren* '(get to) know', etc.

In sect. 3.3.1, the class of causative experiential verbs taking either an agent or a stimulus in subject function (i.e., the *frighten*-type) was introduced. Several approaches (that are generally concerned with English causative experiential verbs) argue for a uniform behavior of the members of this class with respect to situation structure, either analyzing them as accomplishments (i.e., terminative processes according to Figure 1, e.g., Grimshaw 1990) or as achievements (i.e., ingressive or punctual events according to Figure 1, e.g., Van Voorst 1992, Croft 1993). Considering data from German, causative experiential verbs belong to different situation types (cf. Klein and Kutscher 2002). Verbs like *jmd. erschrecken* 'give sb. a fright', *jmd. überraschen* 'surprise sb.', combine with neither adverbials of duration nor with adverbials indicating a time limit. The first test indicates that they are not durative (atelic). The second test indicates that they are not terminative or ingressive. Rather, they seem to have a punctual reading. Other causative experiential verbs, for instance *jmd. amüsieren* 'amuse sb.', *jmd. ärgern* 'annoy sb.', *jmd. nerven* 'get on sb.'s nerves' combine with adverbials of duration. They are, therefore, durative. Combination with an agentive stimulus seems to favor an activity reading while in combination with an inactive stimulus the verbs may have a state reading. This latter analysis is in accordance with Van Valin and LaPolla (1997:100f.) who

---

[47] Similarly, Drossard (1991, ch. 3) reports that Abkhaz possesses a stative and a dynamic class of experiential verbs.

classify verbs such as *frighten, upset, nauseate, amuse* as causative states, and remark that the more active and dynamic the causing state is, the better it combines with a progressive.

3.4 *Grammatical coding of experience*

3.4.1 *Introduction*

It has been widely recognized, explained functionally (cf. sect. 3.3) and exemplified with numerous languages that experiential constructions differ from prototypical transitive constructions in various ways (e.g., Rice 1987, Bickel 1997[P], 2004, Haspelmath 2001, and many others). As has been discussed above, experiential predicates differ from other non-experiential predicates and also class-internally according to a number of parameters. These parameters are the functional basis for the crystallization of more specific grammatically coded predicate classes. In this respect, it has been shown that participant-related factors such as properties, role and number of participants, and participatum-related factors such as (semantic) valency and transitivity of the predicate, its orientation and aspectual character, and the function of evidentiality/ mediativity play a role in shaping predicate classes which may correlate with subtypes of experience.

The mentioned parameters manifest themselves either on the predicate or the arguments, or sometimes on both at the same time, since predicate and argument coding are strongly interrelated. In the following, grammatical coding of experience will be discussed from a cross-linguistic perspective. Sect. 3.4.2 will focus on experience-typical marking of predicates, while sect. 3.4.3 will investigate argument coding in experiential constructions from a constructional point of view. Finally, sect. 3.4.4 discusses some prominence effects in the syntactic coding of the experiencer.

3.4.2 *Types of predicates*

In this section, predicate- or participatum-related phemomena that occur with experiential verbs in the languages of the world will be discussed. These include word classes and their semantic implications relevant to the expression of experience in sect. 3.4.2.1, the orientation of the predicate towards one of the components of the experiential situation in sect. 3.4.2.2, and, finally, transitivity-related phenomena relevant to experience in sect. 3.4.2.3.

3.4.2.1 *Parts of speech and predicate classes in experience*

Many languages code a basic part of their experiential lexemes as adjectives. This correlates with the stativity of many experiential situations (cf. sect. 3.3.3). Those languages that only possess a small class of adjectives may code stative experiences as stative verbs, as shown for Korean in (29) (for Korean cf. Chun and Zubin 1990, for Abkhaz cf. Drossard 1991).

(29)   *Na-nɯn   ne-ka   coh-ta.*
        1.SG-TOP   2.SG-NOM   good-DECL
        'I like you/think a great deal of you.' (YMS)

Furthemore, experiential situations are frequently coded as verbs and these often render stative as well as dynamic experiences. Thus, equivalents of basic emotion terms such as 'love', 'hate', etc., and of basic cognitive and volitive situations corresponding to 'know', 'want', etc. are coded as transitive (or intransitive) verbs, not only in SAE languages, but also in many other languages. Compare for 'love' (1d) from Lezgian, (30) from Amharic (Afro-asiatic, Ethiosemitic, Amberber 2001) and (57) from Bété, for 'know' (1e) from Lezgian, (31a) from Samoan and (36) from Tamil (Dravidian), and for 'want' (1c) from Lezgian, (31b) from Samoan and (32) from Maori (Austronesian, Eastern Polynesian). In Amharic, emotions are all expressed by verbs.

(30)   *Aster   ləmma-n   wəddədə-čči-w.*
        Aster   Lemma-ACC   love.PF-3.F.SBJ-3.M.OBJ
        'Aster loves Lemma.' (Amberber 2001:61)

(31) a. *E   iloa   uma   lava   pese   e   Seu.*
        T/A/M know   all   EMPH   song(SPEC.PL) ERG Seu
        'Seu knows all songs.' (Mosel and Hovdhaugen 1992:712)

     b. *'Ua   manaʻo   le   ulugāliʻi   ʻi   le   mea   ʻai.*
        PF   want   ART   couple   LD   ART   thing   eat
        'The couple wanted something to eat.'   (Mosel and Hovdhaugen 1992:432)

Many African languages code experiences as substantives using an auxiliary or a 'metaphorical' verb as predicator. The latter may be one-place (e.g., an existence predicate) or two-place (e.g., *have, put.on, take, see, hit,* etc., i.e., Experiencer *sees* Expertum vs. Expertum *beats* Experiencer, cf. also Germ. *ich habe Hunger*). These strategies will be referred to in more detail below.

More specific predicate classes can be identified with respect to the specific experiential domains. Perception verbs are generally subdivided into three typologically relevant types which have already been discussed indirectly in sect. 3.2.2.6: active perception verbs (e.g., *look at, listen to*, etc.), inactive perception verbs (e.g., *see, hear, feel*, etc.), and stimulus-oriented perception verbs (e.g., *look, sound*, etc.).[48] Experiential predicates differ as to whether they can function as matrix predicates. Perception predicates, cognition and volition

---

[48] Viberg (1984) calls them activity verbs, experience verbs, and copulative verbs, respectively.

predicates, and some of the emotion predicates usually take complement clauses, while predicates of bodily sensation do not.

3.4.2.2 *Orientation of predicates*

The orientation of the (experiential) predicate towards one of the components of the experiential situation (cf. sect. 3.3.1) will be used as a principle for structuring the discussion of YM experiential constructions in ch. 5. The goal of orientiation is defined as the grammatical subject (generally the S or A argument) of the construction. Thus, the following orientations can be identified: experiencer-oriented as in (32) from Maori, stimulus-oriented as in (33) from Tamil, expertum-oriented as in (34) from Mangap-Mbula (Austronesian, Western-Oceanic), and body part-oriented as in (35) from Lezgian.

(32)   *I   piirangi a   Hata ki   te   whare.*
        PST   want   PERS Hata to   the   house
        'Hata wanted the house.' (Bauer 1983:11)

(33)   *Plai-kaḷ eŋkaḷ-ai   santosa-paṭuti-n-arkaḷ.*
        child-PL   1.PL-ACC   glad-do-PST-3.HUM.PL
        'The children amused us.' (Lehmann et al. 2000[P]:80)

(34)   *Mete   i-kam   yo.*
        disease 3.SG-get 1.SG.ACC
        'I am sick.' (Bugenhagen 2001:73)

(35)   *Zi   q'il   t'a-zwa.*
        1.SG.GEN   head   hurt-IMPF
        'My head is aching.' (Lehmann et al. 2000[P]:74)

Non-oriented constructions including impersonal subjectless constructions (36), (37a) and those with an expletive subject (37b) have to be added in order to gain a cross-linguistic view.[49]

(36)   *Avar-e   en-akku   teri-yaatu.*
        3.SG.M-ACC   1.SG-DAT   know-FUT:NEG
        'I do not know him.' (Asher 1982:105)

---

[49] Here the Korean/Japanese double nominative constructions mentioned in sect. 3.4.3.5 may be added. If one adopts the analysis that both nominatives have equal syntactic status, then these constructions are non-oriented.

(37)   a. *Mir ist kalt/übel/angst und bange.*
         'I feel cold/sick/scared.'

       b. *Es fröstelt mich.*
          'I shiver.'

The orientations shown are sufficient for a description of YM experiential constructions, since the language does not display non-oriented constructions of the mentioned type.

3.4.2.3 *Valency and transitivity of experiential verbs*

Experiential verbs may be intransitive, transitive, or ditransitive. However, ditransitive verbs seem to be a marginal class, containing causative, mostly cognitive, verbs as, e.g., *show, explain, remember.* Others are non-causative and belong to the subdomain of emotion, e.g., Germ. *gönnen* 'not to begrudge', *neiden* 'envy', or volition, e.g., Germ. *jmd. etw. wünschen* 'wish so. sth.'.

Cross-linguistically, experiential verbs are especially characteristic of and frequent among those intransitive verbs that add an oblique complement. This verb type is called extended intransitive verb type in Dixon and Aikhenvald (2000:3). Languages such as Tibetan (Sino-Tibetan), Motuna (Papuan, Bougainville), Newari (Sino-Tibetan), etc. are reported as using this verb type for concepts such as 'see', 'like', 'want', etc. Indonesian also codes concepts of emotion and cognition that are expressed as transitive verbs in many other languages, e.g., 'love' etc. as extended intransitives (cf. Sneddon 1996:88, 245).

If a language has a class of medial or reflexive verbs, this class is very likely to host experiential verbs (cf., e.g., Drossard 1991, Kemmer 1993, etc.). Medial and reflexive verbs, the latter as *reflexiva tantum*, are used especially frequently in conveying experiential meaning, and, more specifically, emotional meaning in many languages of different affiliations. Drossard (1991, sect. 3.4.2) lists a number of languages, among them the well known cases in Indo-European (e.g., Ancient Greek, Slavic languages, Roman languages, Germanic languages) as well as Turkish, Quechua, and Mojave which display a great many experiential verbs with reflexive morphology.[50]

In sect. 3.2, it was shown that the domain of experience includes plain as well as causative experiential notions. Languages differ as to whether they have implemented the plain or causative notions as basic lexemes. Lexemes of the other orientation are generally derived from the basic item, either by causativization or by decausativization. Thus, German has a large number of derivational pairs of the causative – decausative type as, e.g., *jmd. erschrecken ~ sich erschrecken* 'frighten sb. ~ to be frightened', *jmd. langweilen ~ sich langweilen* 'bore sb. ~ to be bored' (cf. Kemmer 1993:132 for further languages).

---

[50] Cf. furthermore Manney (1990) on Modern Greek and Haspelmath (2001) for SAE.

Korean (38) and Tamil (39) are examples of the converse type. Basic emotional lexemes are frequently adjectives or intransitive verbs that may be causativized. In (38) and (39), both languages use a form meaning 'do' to that end.

(38)   *Suni-ka   na-lɯl   hwana-ke   haess-ta.*
        Suni-NOM   1.SG-ACC   angry-ADVR   do:CMPL-DECL
        'Suni annoyed me.' (Lehmann et al. 2000[P]:80)

(39)   *Plai-kaɭ eŋkaɭ-ai   santosa-paɖuti-n-arkaɭ.*
        child-PL   1.PL-ACC   glad-do-PST-3.HUM.PL
        'The children amused us.' (loc. cit.)

Finally, it has to be mentioned that in many languages transitive experiential verbs are restricted in their passive formation, i.e., they do not form a regular passive. This holds especially true for the stimulus-oriented type. For instance, stimulus-oriented transitive verbs may only form a so-called adjectival or stative passive (cf. (40c) for German), and can not form a processive passive (cf. (40b), furthermore sect. 3.3.1).

(40)   a. *Dieses Kind beeindruckt mich immer wieder.*
           'This child impresses me again and again.'

        b. **Ich werde immer wieder von diesem Kind beeindruckt.*
           intended: 'I am impressed by this child again and again.'

        c. *Ich bin immer wieder von diesem Kind beindruckt.*
           'I am impressed by this child again and again.'

Experiencer-oriented transitive verbs are less or not at all restricted in their passive formation, at least in German and English. In German, both a processive (41a) and a stative or adjectival passive (41b) are possible. As the examples show, the stative or adjectival passive is less regular and in some cases involves a full adjectival form.

(41)   a. *Unser Chef wird von vielen gefürchtet/ geachtet/ bewundert/ gemocht/ gehaßt/ geliebt.*
           'Our boss is feared/respected/admired/loved/hated/loved by many people.'

        b. *Unser Chef ist bei vielen gefürchtet/ geachtet/ verhaßt/ beliebt.*
           'ditto'

In contrast, experiencer-oriented verbs with dative-subjects do not form regular passives, as is reported for Icelandic (cf. Grimshaw 1990:118).

3.4.3 *Experiential construction types*

The present section shall give an overview of typical experiential construction types found cross-linguistically. The discussion will focus on their argument structure. Sections 3.4.3.1 - 3.4.3.4 discuss experiential constructions according to the valency of predicate. Sect. 3.4.3.5 deals with topic constructions and sect. 3.4.3.6 with possessive constructions.

3.4.3.1 *Simple adjectival and intransitive constructions*

Under this heading, those experiential constructions that take monovalent verbs or adjectives as their predicate will be discussed. These may be either experiencer-oriented or body part-oriented.

It is very common in the languages of the world to find experiential adjectives and intransitive verbs which take the experiencer in subject function, coding it as a nominative or absolutive argument. Compare (42) from Samoan, showing the experiencer in absolutive function with respect to a non-ergative verb, and (43) from Korean showing a nominative-marked experiencer as subject of a stative verb of bodily sensation.

(42)   *'Ua   'ou   ma'alili.*
        PF   1.SG   cold
        'I am cold.' (Lehmann et al. 2000[P]:72)

(43)   *Nae-ka   chup-ta.*
        1.SG-NOM   cold-DECL
        'I am cold.' (ibid:72)

Correspondingly, many languages also show possessed body part nominals combined with monovalent experiential adjectives or verbs in subject function, such as Samoan in (44a/b) and Korean in (45a/b). (44c) and (45c) show parallel constructions with possessed expertum nominals in subject function.

(44)   a. *Ua   ma'alili o='u   lima.*
          PF   cold   POSS=1.SG   hand
          'My hands are cold.'

       b. *Ua   tīgā   l=o'=u   ulu.*
          PF   hurt   ART=POSS=1.SG   head
          'I have a headache.' (Lehmann et al. 2000[P]:73)

       c. *Ua   faanoanoa o='u   lagona.*
          PF   sad   POSS=1.SG   feeling
          'I am sad.' lit.: 'My feelings are sad.' (Mosel and Hovdhaugen 992:771)

(45)   a. *Nae   mom-i   an-coh-ta.*
      1.SG body-NOM NEG-good-DECL
      'I am not well.'

     b. *Nae   pae-ka   aphɨ-ta.*
      1.SG   belly-NOM   ill-DECL
      'My belly hurts.' (Lehmann et al. 2000[P]:74)

     c. *Nae   kipun-i   coh-ta.*
      1.SG   mood-NOM   good-DECL
      'I am glad.' (ibid:81)

Some languages may foreground an experiencer which is at the same time the possessor of a body part noun, and code it as the subject of the experiential verb. For instance, in Jaminjung such an experiencer is coded as an absolutive subject (being cross-referenced on the verbs, cf. (46)), while the body part noun occurs at the same time as an absolutive-marked noun phrase. Such constructions have been discussed under the heading of external possessor constructions in the extant literature (cf., e.g., Chappell and McGregor eds. 1996, König and Haspelmath 1998, Payne and Barshi eds. 1999).

(46)   *Warlad   nga-yu   durlu.*
      sore   1.SG-be.PRS   heart
      'I have a sick heart' (Schultze-Berndt 2000:463)

Furthermore, the experiencer is often coded in a non-subject case with monovalent experiential predicates. This may result in either an impersonal construction (cf. von Seefranz-Montag 1983:71f.) or a non-canonical case of subject marking (cf. Aikhenvald et al. eds. 2001, Bhaskararao and Subbarao eds. 2004).[51] A number of languages choose the indirect object case, the dative, while others choose the 'primary' or direct object case for the experiencer. In Chickasaw (Muskogean, Payne 1982:356ff. apud Drossard 1991:168, (47)) the experiencer is coded in the same way as the recipient in the dative (differing from agent and patient).

(47)   a. *Am-aalhi.*
      DAT.1.SG-tired
      'I'm tired/worn out.'

---

[51] Cf. sect. 3.1 for the term 'non-canonical marking' and sect. 3.6 for the role of this marking type in diachrony.

  b. *An-chokma.*
   DAT.1.SG-good
   'I feel good.'

In (48) German can be seen as an example of a language with both dative and accusative marking of the experiencer with monovalent predicates. The latter marking however is nowadays largely obsolete.

(48) a. *Mir ist schlecht.*
   'I feel sick.'
  b. *Mich hungert.*
   'I am hungry.'

Also with some monovalent verbs of emotion and bodily sensation, Amharic (49) may optionally code the experiencer in the accusative.

(49) a. *aster(-in)* *čənnək'-at*
   Aster(-ACC) worry.PF.3.M.SBJ-3.F.OBJ
   'Aster is worried' (Amberber 2001:62)
  b. *aster(-in)* *rabb-at*
   Aster(-ACC) be.hungry.PF.3.M-3.F.OBJ
   'Aster is hungry' (ibid:41)

For languages such as Icelandic, (e.g., Barðdal 2002, (50)) or Lezgian (Haspelmath 1993, cf. (1)), it has been argued that the dative-marked experiencers behave (more or less) like regular subjects in the these languages.

(50) *Mér* *er* *kalt.*
   me:DAT is cold
   'I am cold' (Barðdal 2002)

3.4.3.2 *Extended adjectival and intransitive constructions*

As introduced in sect. 3.4.2.3, those adjectival and intransitive predicates and their respective constructions that take an oblique complement are called 'extended'. The oblique complement can be added, for instance, through dative-marking or by a specific adposition. As concerns respective experiential constructions, either the stimulus (sect. 3.4.3.2.1) or the experiencer (sect. 3.4.3.2.2) may occur as the oblique complement, the other participant occurring in subject function. A third possibility provided for in a number of languages, is that both experiencer and stimulus are coded in an oblique way (sect. 3.4.3.2.3).

3.4.3.2.1 *With oblique stimulus*

This construction type is represented, for example, in some Austronesian languages as in Samoan and Tongan. The experiencer is coded in the absolutive and the stimulus occurs in the dative, locative, or in a directional case (cf. Tsunoda 1981 and (51) from Samoan for illustration).

(51) a. *Sā̄   'ou   ita   'i   l=o='u   uso.*
            PST   1.SG   angry   LD   ART=POSS=1.SG   brother
            'I was angry with my brother.' (Mosel and Hovdhaugen 1992:106)

      b. *Na   va'ai   le   fafine   i   le   tama.*
            PST   see   ART   woman   LD   ART   boy
            'The woman saw the boy.' (ibid:416)

German and English both display a large number of emotional adjectives and intransitive verbs that add the stimulus argument with a specific preposition while the experiencer takes subject function, e.g., *sich fürchten vor* 'be afraid of, to fear', *sich schämen vor* 'be ashamed of', *sich freuen über* 'be glad about', *sich aufregen über* 'get excited about', *sich amüsieren über* 'be amused about', *wütend sein über* 'be furious about', *glücklich sein über* 'be happy about', etc. Furthermore, active perception verbs such as, e.g., *schauen auf* 'look at', *horchen auf* 'listen to', *riechen an* 'smell sth., have a sniff of', etc. belong to this valency type.

3.4.3.2.2 *With oblique experiencer*

Oblique experiencers in extended intransitive constructions are well established in the languages of the world. For instance, the ancestors of today's Indo-European languages display oblique experiencers. Ancient Greek shows diverse case marking with experiencers, e.g., genitive and dative (52). The stimulus is in the nominative.

(52) a. *moi   enok^hleîs*
           1.SG:DAT   bother:2.SG
           'you bother me' (Heliodorus, *Aethiopica* 10.9.5, 3AD)

      b. *sképsai   eàn   tóde   soi   mâllon*
           think:AOR:INF   if   that:NOM.SG.N   2.SG:DAT   rather
           aréskēi
           please:SUBJ:3.SG
           'think if rather that pleases you' (Xenophon, *Mem.* 4.4.12, 4BC)

Furthermore, the experiencer may occur in local or directional cases as well as ith adpositional marking, as in (53) from Ewe.

(53)   *Ama nyá kpɔ́-ná ná-m.*
        Ama INV   see-HAB to-1.SG
        'Ama looks well to me.' (Ameka 1990:175)

In the above examples, the stimulus argument occupies subject function. A further construction type takes a body part noun in subject function and takes the experiencer, which is at the same time the possessor of the body part, as an oblique object. This is the case in (54) from German. This construction type is again an example of an external possessor construction (cf. (46) above for another kind of external possessor construction).

(54)   *Der Bauch tut mir weh.*
        'My belly hurts.'

In a further construction scheme, an expertum noun may take subject function with respect to a more abstract predicate, e.g., a copula or an existential predicate. The experiencer generally occurs as an oblique object, as in (55) from Ewe.

(55)   *é-nyé   núxaxa   ná   m.*
        3.SG-be   worry   to   1.SG
        'It is a worry to me.' (Ameka 1990:151).

3.4.3.2.3 *With oblique experiencer and oblique stimulus*
In Ancient Greek, a dative experiencer may also combine with a genitive stimulus (56). A similar pattern occurred in Old English (cf. Allen 1995, Harris and Campbell 1995).

(56)   *mélei   moi   toútōn   hôn   erōtâis*
        care:3.SG 1.SG.DAT that:GEN.PL.N that:GEN.PL.N ask:SUBJ:2.SG
        'I care about what you ask' (Xenophon, *Oeconomicus* 11.9.4, 4.BC)

As has been mentioned above, languages differ as to whether non-canonically marked or morphologically downgraded experiencers display 'subject' properties (e.g., in some Caucasian languages, Icelandic, etc.), or not (e.g., German, Russian).[52]

---

[52] For a detailed analysis of subject properties of SAE oblique experiencers cf. Haspelmath (2001).

3.4.3.3 *Transitive constructions*

Many languages follow an actor – undergoer coding scheme with some of their experiential verbs. One participant of the experiential situation is then mapped onto the actor/subject function and another participant onto the undergoer/direct object function of a transitive verb. This is usually the canonical transitive scheme which is otherwise used for action verbs, effect verbs and the like. There are a number of different constellations of experiential participants taking the actor and the undergoer function. These will be discussed in the following sections.

3.4.3.3.1 *Experiencer as Actor*

In one construction scheme, the experiencer is coded as an Actor/subject and the stimulus as an Undergoer/direct object (cf. the *fear*-type in Belletti and Rizzi 1988). Compare the examples from Bété (Niger-Congo, Bendi, (57)), Mangarayi (Australian, Gunwingguan, (58)), and Korean (59). Further examples are, among others, (13a), (15a), (30), and (31a).

(57)　　*ń　ʄíɓǎ ná　　gú.*
　　　　 1.SG　love　POSS.1.SG　child
　　　　 'I love my child.' (FKB)

(58)　　*Jaḷug　wuran-ya-j.*
　　　　 forget　3.SG/3.DU-AUX-PST.PUNCT
　　　　 'He forgot them (DU).' (Merlan 1982:61)

(59)　　*Suni-ka　ne-lɨl　　musɘwɘha-n-ta.*
　　　　 Suni-NOM　2.SG-ACC　fear-PRS-DECL
　　　　 'Suni is afraid of you.' (MCK)

Languages differ as to whether they use this scheme for all or most of their two-place experiential verbs or only for some of them. Among the experiential subclasses, perception verbs are cross-linguistically the most likely to appear in an Actor – Undergoer scheme, which is in accordance with the alignment type nominative – accusative or ergative – absolutive. In the Australian languages Djaru, Warrungu and Guugu (cf. Tsunoda 1981, 1985), perception verbs appear in the ergative – absolutive scheme. Indoeuropean languages generally show nominative – accusative marking with perception verbs.

In another construction scheme, an expertum noun may take the undergoer/direct object function. This is the case if a generalized experiential verb is the predicate, e.g., verbs meaning 'feel', 'suffer', etc. Compare (60) from Modern Greek.

(60)   *O*   *jánis es θánete me γálo   póno.*
          DEF:NOM.SG.M Janis feel:3.SG   great:ACC.SG.M   pain:ACC.SG.M
          'Janis feels great pain.'

Other languages may use certain verbs in a metaphorical or semantically bleached way in order to add an expertum noun in direct object function (e.g., Ewe uses the perception verb *kpɔ́* 'see' in (61)).

(61)   *Me   kpɔ́   dzidzɔ.*
          1.SG   see   happiness
          'I was happy.' (Ameka 1990:140)

A more grammaticalized example of this construction type exists if a possessive verb meaning 'have' is used as the predicate, as, e.g., in Germ. *ich habe Hunger/Angst/Lust* etc. 'I am hungry, afraid, I feel like, etc.', in (62) from French or in (63) from Wolof .

(62)   *J'ai faim/soif/froid.*
          'I am hungry/thirsty/cold.'

(63)   *am   naa   naqar*
          have SBJ.1.SG   bitterness
          'I have bitterness' (Becher 2003:36)

3.4.3.3.2 *Stimulus as Actor*

A 'reverse' Actor – Undergoer scheme is used for stimulus-oriented transitive experiential verbs (i.e., the *frighten*-type in Belletti and Rizzi 1988). With this verb-type, the stimulus takes Actor/subject function and the experiencer takes Undergoer/direct object function as in (64) from German and in (65) from Ewe.

(64)   *Die Geschichte hat mich gelangweilt/geärgert.*
          'The story bored/annoyed me.'

(65)   *Agbeli   tsri   ama.*
          cassava hate   Ama
          'Ama is allergic to cassava.' (Ameka 1990:154)

In many languages, experiencer object verbs are causative verbs, derived overtly from basic experiencer-oriented adjectives or verbs, as in Tamil or Korean (cf. Lehmann et al. 2000[D]:80 and sect. 3.4.2.3, (38) and (39)).

3.4.3.3.3 *Expertum or person part noun as Actor*

Similar to this strategy is a strategy where an expertum or a person part noun is in Actor/subject function and the experiencer in Undergoer/direct object function. Here again, metaphorical or semantically bleached verbs may be used as predicates. This construction type seems to be especially widespread in African languages, cf. (66) from Bété, (67) from Ewe, (68) from Dholuo (Nilo-Saharan, Western Nilotic), and (69) from Wolof (furthermore Reh ed. 1998).[53] It is also attested in Asian languages (Bickel 1997[P], 2001), as well as in Papuan and Austronesian languages (McElhanon 1977, Bugenhagen 1990, 2001, cf. (70)).

(66)   *wōtròkō/ ɟɔ́lú̀/   zú́/   ŋān ɔ̄/ ŋwãní   wù̀-ʊ̃́   líɓǎ-lḛ̃́*
      coldness/ boredom/ shame/ fear/ happyness PROG-1.SG hit-PART
      'I am cold/bored/ashamed/afraid/happy' (FKB)

(67)   *dɔ   wu-m*
      stomach   kill-1.SG
      'I was hungry' (Ameka 1990:164)

(68)   *Koro   kibaji   nene   omako   Owiny ...*
      now   nervousness PST   3.SG:PFV:seize Owiny
      'Owiny became nervous (...)' (Reh 1998[L]:395)

(69)   *tiit-aange   moo   ko   jàpp*
      fear-NR   SBJ.3.SG OBJ.3.SG   catch
      'fear seized him' (Becher 2003:34)

(70)   *Mete   i-kam   yo.*
      disease 3.SG-get ACC.1.SG
      'I am sick.' (Bugenhagen 2001:73)

Note that in German and English this construction type is only represented by a few collocations such as *die Wut packte ihn* lit.: 'anger seized him' or *Furcht ergriff/überkam ihn* 'fear seized him', etc.

Lele (Niger-Congo), in contrast, has to a large extent generalized this strategy in the subdomains of bodily sensation and emotion, using a more abstract predicate, namely, the verb *nè* 'make'. Internal states of bodily sensation and emotion are expressed in a construction taking either a body part noun (71a) or an expertum noun (71b) in subject function while the experiencer takes direct object function.

---

[53] This is referred to as 'anthropomorphism strategy' in Reh and Frühwald (1996), Reh (1998[E]).

(71)   a. *kus-iy   ne-y*
         body-3.M   make-3.M
         'he is sick', lit. 'his body makes him' (Frajzyngier 2001:116)
       b. *kàsìyà   nè   tamá-ŋ   néy*
         shame   make   woman-DEF very.much
         'the woman was very ashamed' (loc.cit)

3.4.3.4   *Ditransitive constructions*

As has been discussed in sect. 3.4.2.3, ditransitive verbs are not frequent among the experiential verbs. Those mentioned, e.g., *show, explain, remember,* etc. generally take the experiencer in indirect object function while agent and stimulus are mapped onto the Actor/subject and Undergoer/direct object functions, respectively.

Some languages may possess explicitly causative constructions, using a causative verb such as, for instance, *dó* 'put on' in Ewe (72) or *machen* 'do' in German. Such verbs take an expertum noun in direct or primary object function adding the experiencer in indirect or secondary object function (cf., e.g., Germ. *er macht mir Freude/Angst/Sorgen* etc. 'he causes joy/fear/worries to me'). In Ewe, the experiencer may be coded either as a secondary object (72a) or as a prepositional object of a dative preposition (72b).

(72)   a. *Kofi   dó   vɔvɔ̃-m.*
         Kofi   put.on fear-1.SG
         'Kofi frightened me.' (Ameka 1990:169)
       b. *Kofi   dó   dzikú   ná   ama.*
         Kofi   put.on anger   to   Ama
         'Kofi made Ama angry.' (ibid:170)

Finally, some languages have non-causative ditransitive experiential verbs. Examples from German have been examined in (25). These represent extensions of the experiencer-actor/stimulus-undergoer scheme. In sect. 3.3.2.2.1, they were analyzed as taking a split stimulus, consisting of an animate participant and an abstract or propositional participant. The animate stimulus is coded as an indirect object while the propositional stimulus takes direct object function.

3.4.3.5   *Topic constructions*

Korean (73) and Japanese (74) are well-known for their double nominative constructions which are also pertinent to the domain of experience (cf., e.g., Inoue 1974, Jo 1988, Chun and Zubin 1990, Palmer 1994:49, Shibatani 2001). In both languages the experiencer may be coded in the nominative or as the topic with stative verbs in bivalent constructions. The stimulus invariably appears in the nominative (cf. also Chun and Zubin 1990).

(73) a. *Nae-ka paem-i   musɐp/silh/coh-ta.*
         I-NOM snake-NOM afraid.of/dislike/like-DECL

      b. *Na-nɯn paem-i   musɐp/silh/coh-ta.*
         I-TOP   snake-NOM afraid.of/dislike/like-DECL
         'I am afraid of/dislike/like snakes.' (Jo 1988:13)

(74) *Ai ga/wa   Ken ga   suki da.*
       Ai NOM/TOP Ken NOM like COP
       'Ai likes Ken.' (Shibatani 2001:309)

The double nominative and the topic-nominative constructions also appear with body part expressions, e.g., in bodily sensation, where the body part is invariably in the nominative and the possessor-experiencer is either marked as topic or as nominative. Compare (75) from Korean and (76) from Japanese.

(75) a. *Na-nɯn/nae-ka   mom-i   an   coh-ta.*
         1.SG-TOP/1.SG-NOM body-NOM NEG good-DECL
         'I am not well.'

      b. *Na-nɯn/nae-ka   pae-ka   kophɯ-ta.*
         1.SG-TOP/1.SG-NOM belly-NOM hungry-DECL
         'I am hungry.' (Lehmann et al. 2000[P]:75)

(76) *Taroo ga/wa   atama ga   itai.*
       Taroo NOM/TOP head   NOM hurting
       'Taro has a headache.' (ibid:313)

3.4.3.6 *Possessive constructions*

This section focuses on the expression of a possessive relation between certain participants of an experiential situation. More specifically, possessive constructions involving the experiencer and its body part, the experiencer and an expertum noun, the experiencer and the stimulus, and the stimulus and an expertum noun will be examined. Examples of some of these possessive constructions have already been given in the above discussion. There however, the focus was on the relations between the predicate and those participants of an experiential situation which are coded as its dependants. In the current chapter, possessive relations within the NP will be focussed on. External possessor constructions have also been discussed above, since within these constructions the possessor-experiencer is coded as a verb dependant.

3.4.3.6.1 *Experiencer-as-possessor constructions*
Constructions featuring the experiencer as possessor are recurrent in the languages of the world. The experiencer can occur as the possessor of a person part noun, as the possessor of an expertum noun, or as the possessor of the stimulus.

Person part constructions coding the experiencer as a possessive attribute of a person part noun are frequent in the expression of experience. For instance, in Bété, bodily sensation is often expressed by body part expressions. Depending on the type of verb and construction, the experiencer may be either the possessor of the subject (77a) or the possessor of the object (77b). Both construction types seem to be well established and recurrent in Bété and many other African languages (cf. Ameka 1990, Reh ed. 1998, Becher 2003).

(77)   a. *Ná   wǔlǘ   wǔ   pa-lě.*
          POSS.1.SG head   PROG hit-PART
          'I have a headache.' (FKB)

       b. *Wōtròkō   wǔ   ná   kɔ̀tì   lḭ̂bá̰-lě.*
          cold   PROG   POSS.1.SG hand   hit-PART
          'My hands are cold.' (FKB)

Wolof (78) in addition to the types shown above, displays experiential person part constructions with the experiencer as a possessor within a local prepositional phrase.

(78)   *Nen a   nekk   ci   sama   xel.*
        egg   FOC be.located LOC POSS.1.SG   mind
        'I think of eggs.' (Becher 2003:48)

In addition to body part nouns, expertum nouns also occur as possessed nominals, taking the experiencer in possessor function. Since the expertum itself is represented as a noun, either a general experiential verb, e.g., (79) from Belhare or a semantically more abstract verb will take the predicate function, e.g., a copula, an existential predicate, or an auxiliary as in (80) from Camling (Sino-Tibetan, Eastern Kiranti) and (81) from Bangla (Indo-European, Eastern Indo-Aryan)).

(79)   *ŋ-waepma   lus-e   i?*
        POSS.2.SG-thirst.NOM (3.SG)perceptible-PST   INT
        'Are you thirsty?' (Bickel 1997[P])

(80)   *A-bulma*   *la-e.*
         POSS.1.SG-anger.NOM   (3.SG)AUX-PST
         'I am angry.' (Ebert 1997:38 apud Bickel 2004, sect. 3)

(81)   *Tomār   Bāṅlā   sun-e*
         GEN.2.SG   Bangla.NOM   hear-CONV
         āmār   āscorjo   ho-lo.
         GEN.2.SG   surprise.NOM   become-PST.3
         'I was surprised when I heard your Bangla.' (Klaiman 1989 apud
         Bickel 2004, sect. 3)

It has been mentioned previously that oblique experiencers show subject
properties in some languages. Similarly, possessor-experiencers may display
subject properties, e.g., in Belhare (Bickel 1997[P], 2004). In certain experiential constructions, namely, in those that possess a transitivized verb and contain
a stimulus with a specific reference, the possessor-experiencer triggers agreement on the verb, i.e., with the actor suffix (82b). Note that in the intransitive
base construction in (82a), the verb agrees with the possessed body part noun
phrase (which is zero for third person singular).

(82)   a. *Cia   a-niũa   ti-yu.*
          tea   POSS.1.SG-mind   pleased-NPST
          'I like tea.'
       b. *Cia   a-niũa   tiu-t-u-ŋ.*
          tea   POSS.1.SG-mind   pleased-NPST-3.U-1.SG.A
          'I like that tea.' (Bickel 1997[P]:148)

Furthermore there are behavioral properties (e.g., in same subject constructions, reciprocal formation and nominalization) that identify the possessor-
experiencer as a subject in Belhare (Bickel 1997[P], sect. 4).[54]
Finally, person part constructions coding the experiencer as a possessive attribute of the stimulus noun seem to be very rare, but Samoan provides some
examples of this case as shown in (83). Such a construction can be used if there
is a possessive relation between the experiencer and the stimulus.

---

[54] Further examples of the development of possessor-experiencers to independent clausal arguments are discussed in Bickel (2004, sect. 3) with respect to the Indo-Aryan languages Bangla
and Assamese.

(83)   *'Ua galo se'evae   o   Miliama.*
         PF   forget shoe(SPEC.PL) POSS Miliama
         'Miliama has forgotten her shoes.'
         (Mosel and Hovdhaugen 1992:423)

3.4.3.6.2 *Stimulus-as-possessor constructions*

Cases in which the stimulus is coded as a possessor of an expertum noun seem
to be recurrent in some African languages. For instance, the Bété construction
represented in (66) may be expanded by adding the stimulus as a possessive attribute of the expertum noun in subject function (84). A further example is
(87b) from Bambara (Niger-Congo, Mande).

(84)   *Nà   tő   wừ-ő   lí6á-lẽ.*
         POSS.2.SG longing PROG-1.SG hit-PART
         'I long for you.' (FKB)

3.4.4 *Experiencer coding and syntactic prominence*

The preceding overview of cross-linguistically occurring experiential constructions shows that the experiencer can take a great variety of syntactic positions
in the hierarchy of grammatical relations given in Figure 3. As an animate being the experiencer is topical. A syntactically prominent coding, e.g., as the
subject, reflects the natural topicality of the experiencer. Examples of subject
experiencers have been given in sect. 3.4.3.1, sect. 3.4.3.2.1, and sect.
3.4.3.3.1. Role properties such as low control or lack of control and the affectedness of the experiencer are, on the other hand, reflected by a syntactically
lower prominence according to Figure 3. Examples of oblique experiencer coding have been mentioned in sect. 3.4.3.1, sect. 3.4.3.2.2, sect. 3.4.3.2.3, and
sect. 3.4.3.4. In the examples examined in sect. 3.4.3.3.2 and sect. 3.4.3.3.3, the
experiencer is coded as direct object. As a possessive attribute (cf. sect.
3.4.3.6), the experiencer is in an adnominal relation to a verbal dependant, and
is thus, in a rather low position on Figure 3.

Furthermore, the contradicting properties of natural topicality on the one
hand, and low control and high affectedness on the other, manifest themselves
in cases of mismatches between morphological coding and syntactic behavior
as has, for instance, been addressed with respect to dative experiencer subjects,
(cf., e.g., sect. 3.4.3.1) or with respect to subject properties of possessor-
experiencers in Belhare (cf. sect. 3.4.3.6.1).

On the basis of the principles of person foregrounding vs. person backgrounding (cf. sect. 2.2.3), experiencer subjects represent syntactic person
foregrounding while oblique and possessor-experiencers represent syntactic
person backgrounding. The mentioned mismatches can be viewed as person
foregrounding strategies, since morphologically lower marked elements dis-

play a syntactic behavior that is otherwise common for elements positioned higher on Figure 3. Furthermore, a diachronic picture concerning experiencer coding argues for the constant development from syntactically backgrounded experiencers such as oblique and possessor-experiencers to syntactically fore-grounded experiencers in subject function. This development is discussed in more detail in sect. 3.6.

The strategies of person foregrounding and person backgrounding can be thought of in two ways. The relative position of a given animate participant with respect to another less animate participant in Figure 3 can be the basis of judgment. In this respect, an object experiencer is syntactically backgrounded compared to a subject stimulus (cf., e.g., (52), (64)). The syntactic prominence of a given animate participant can also be evaluated with respect to its syntactic coding in another functionally equivalent construction. The latter is the basis if external possessor constructions are compared to 'internal' possessor constructions. For instance, in person part constructions designating the affect-edness of the part, the possessor is sympathetically affected (cf., e.g., Lehmann et al. 2000[P], sect. 5.3.5). A number of languages represent this kind of affect-edness by coding the experiencer as an immediate argument of the verb. Com-pared to the alternative coding of the experiencer as possessive attribute to the body part noun, such a coding is a case of syntactic person foregrounding and may appear as a trait of person prominent languages (cf. sect. 2.2.3).

3.5 *Figurative language and types of collocations*

The domain of experience has traditionally been analyzed using metaphorical and other transfer operations relating a concrete ('material') state of affairs to the abstract and immaterial domain of experiential states of affairs (cf. Lakoff and Johnson 1980, Matisoff 1986, Goossens 1989, Jaisser 1990, Reh 1998[M], Kövecses 2000, Niemeier 2000, etc.). The bulk of the mentioned work in the domain of experience is based on the theory of cognitive linguistics (Lakoff and Johnson 1980 and subsequent work). This approach recognizes metaphor as being crucial in determining language in its structure. In the analysis of YM experiential constructions (sect. 5) however, I will refrain from intensively re-ferring to metaphorical processes and the like since it seems to be difficult to prove that a given lexeme is understood as metaphorical with respect to a more basic, concrete sense.[55] Instead, I will confine myself to noting certain semantic domains with which experiential collocations operate. This chapter is organ-ized as follows: In sect. 3.5.1, some general issues concerning the identifica-tion of figurative language will be briefly discussed. Sect. 3.5.2 will introduce the main figures in the language of experience, namely, metaphor, metonymy,

---

[55] Compare, e.g., the view advanced in Levinson (1994) with respect to the semantics of body part terminology in Tzeltal (Mayan).

and synecdoche. Sect. 3.5.3 will address the issue of how to apply the notion of the semantic roles to figurative language, and, finally, sect. 3.5.4 will discuss types of collocations occurring in the domain of experience.

3.5.1 *Distinguishing between figurative and literal language*

At the foundation of a metaphorical/figurative approach to language (meaning) is a polysemous conception of the meaning of a lexical item. Thus a lexical item may possibly have a basic sense (default, least restricted) and an extended sense/extended senses which can be distinguished by a number of criteria (cf. Schultze-Berndt 2000:33 with respect to Cruse 1986:72 and Taylor 1989:116). A figurative sense of a lexical item is present if it is used in another semantic domain or applied to an item from a domain other than is its literal sense.

We may recognize different steps in the evolution of figurative language (such as metaphor and metonymy), varying (possibly forming a continuum and undergoing a development) from ad hoc formation to being fully established in the language (and possibly having replaced the former 'concrete' meaning). This is accompanied by parameters such as frequency of use, co-existence with a 'basic' sense, etc. If the extended metaphorical meaning has fully replaced the former basic meaning, it is no longer metaphorical or metonymical.

As regards terminology, a proposal in Reh (1998[E]:11) based on Halliday (1985) will be adopted in order to distinguish between congruent (i.e., literal) expressions and metaphorical expressions in the domain of experience. The latter will be called non-congruent expressions here. Congruent expressions are expressions in which the (verbal) predicate alone carries the experiential meaning, as is the case with semantically experiential verbs. (85a) is an example from Mangap-Mbula, (85b) is from Wolof.

> (85) a. *Ni   petel=i.*[56]
>   NOM.3.SG   be.hungry=ACC.3.SG
>   'He is hungry.' (Bugenhagen 2001:71)
>
>   b. *danga   foog   ne   dama   caaxaan*
>   SBJ.2.SG   to.assume that SBJ.1.SG   to.joke
>   'you thought/assumed that I was joking' (Becher 2003:77)

With non-congruent expressions, the (verbal) predicate alone refers to a different semantic domain than the whole expression does. It is important to note that it is not the whole predicate – including a possible complement – that is meant here, but rather the verbal predicate in its function as the predicator of the construction. Only the combination of the verbal predicate with a further

---

[56] Mangap Mbula has group of experiential verbs which code the experiencer in the nominative and the accusative, at the same time.

linguistic entity renders the experiential meaning of the whole expression. This is true in cases like those shown in (86), where a possessive verb (as in (86a) from German) or a locative verb (as in the Wolof example (86b) repeated here for convenience from (78)) constitute the predicator of the construction. The fact that the whole expressions refer to the semantic domain of experience is coded by (the combination with) other elements, i.e., the expertum noun *Hunger* 'hunger' in (86a), and the person part noun *xel* 'mind' in (86b).

(86)   a. *Ich habe Hunger.*
         'I am hungry'

       b. *Nen   a   nekk   ci   sama   xel.*
          egg   FOC   be.located   LOC   POSS.1.SG   mind
          'I think of eggs.' (Becher 2003:48)

Non-congruent expressions are morphologically more complex than congruent expressions since only the combination of the non-congruent predicator with a further linguistic entity results in the experiential meaning of the whole expression.

3.5.2 *Figures in the target domain*
3.5.2.1 *Metaphor*

A metaphor is based on the similarity between two domains, the donor or source domain and the target domain. Matisoff (1986, sect. VI) comes to the conclusion with respect to the expression of emotion, cognition, and qualities of character that a large number of metaphors are based on universal patterns.[57] He notes, e.g., that the following languages express the notion of 'decide' using the concept/word for 'cut, sever': Lahu, Jingpho, Burmese, Thai, Hmong, Chinese, Japanese, Russian, Latin, English (and German and YM can be safely added to these). This will not be taken as a proof of a putative universality of this metaphor (since there may well be other ways in which it may have been spread from language to language). The analysis of YM will be confined to recognizing similarities or differences in metaphorical strategies in other languages in the domain of investigation.

Frequent metaphors in the domain of experience include: mental processes are associated with motion or action; character and personal traits are often associated with physical quality such as color/clarity, temperature, seize, shape, height, weight, moral value, etc., which are often antonymically organized (cf., e.g., Matisoff 1986, Jaisser 1990 for White Hmong); certain types of emotion

---

[57] His observations however are based mainly on Southeast Asian languages and English. In addition Matisoff (1986) acknowledges the existence of culture-specific as well as areal metaphors.

(e.g., anger) are frequently associated with physical agitation (cf. Jaisser 1990: 169); a positive emotional relation with closeness and position; and intensity of emotion is often associated with fire.[58]

Apart from lexical semantics, constructional semantics in the domain investigated shows some widespread construction schemes that can be seen as based on event structure metaphors as, e.g., STATES ARE LOCATIONS, CHANGES ARE MOVEMENTS, etc. (Lakoff 1993). In Bambara (Mande, Niger-Kongo), a situation related to thinking can be expressed in several ways, among them an existence/location construction (containing the existential/locative copula *bɛ* as indicated in (87a)), or a (loco)motion construction (87b) (Reh 1998[M]:29).

> (87) a. *n' a miiri bɛ saraka la*
> and 3.SG thought be sacrifice LOC
> 'and she thought of the sacrifice', lit. 'and his/her thinking/thought was at the sacrifice'
>
> b. *ni saraka miiri nan' a la.*
> and sacrifice thought come:PST 3.SG LOC
> 'and she thought of the sacrifice', lit. 'and the thinking/thought of the sacrifice came to him/her' (Reh 1998[M]:29)

It has been proposed that event structure metaphors underlie such constructions (cf. Kövecses 2000, ch. 4). In the domain of experience (but surely not only there) several other schemes play a role. The use of a grammaticalized verb of possession is common in many languages as in Germ. *ich habe Hunger/Durst/Angst*, Fr. *j'ai faim/soif/froid*, Wolof (cf. (63)), etc. Belhare and other Kiranti languages have a possessive of experience construction (Bickel 1997[P], 2004). Many African languages employ an action scheme to render notions of bodily sensation and emotion, often using a specialized verb of physical affect which is combined with an expertum noun in subject function (cf. (77b), (84) from Bété). Constructional metaphors and metonymies are said to be used especially frequently for coding experience in Papuan and Austronesian languages (cf. Bickel 1997[P] with reference to McElhanon 1975, 1977).

3.5.2.2 *Metonymy*
While metaphor is based on the similarity of two domains, metonymy is based on their contiguity (e.g., Ullmann 1962:212 apud Goossens 1989, Heine et al.

---

[58] Cf. the following metaphors related to specific emotions ANGER IS A HOT FLUID, LOVE IS FIRE, HAPPINESS IS UP indicating the intensity aspect of the emotions concerned (Lakoff and Kövecses 1987, Lakoff 1987, Kövecses 1986).

1991).[59] In this sense, Goossens (1989:7) states that the occurrence of body parts as donor domains in experiential expressions is often metonymic, only seldomly metaphorical. Thus, reference to physiological or bodily processes or actions accompanying or expressing certain emotions used for reference to the emotion itself is a kind of metonymy. These include external behavioral reactions (as shown in (88) from Belhare) and bodily symptoms such as facial expression as well as internal physiological reactions.

(88)   *U-chiat*   *kolo*   *hoĩ-yu.*
       POSS.3.SG-spit   CONTR   appear-NPST
       'But he despises it.' (Bickel 1997[P]:145)

Metonymies are based on the folk understanding and conceptualization of the connection between emotional and cognitive states and processes and the accompanying physiological reactions, such as increase in heart rate or body temperature (cf. Lakoff 1987:38f.). Compare the examples from English in (89), which are analyzed as being related to the English emotion *anger* by metonymy, invoking the physiological reaction of an increasing body temperature. (90a) is a parallel example from Amharic, (91) codes a related sense in Wolof. (89), (90a), and (91) are internal "bodily images" in the sense of Wierzbicka (1999) which are based on metonymy, while (90b) from Amharic, equally based on metonymy, refers to an external bodily symptom.

(89)   a. *He lost his cool.*

       b. *You make my blood boil.* (Lakoff 1987:380f.)

(90)   a. *dəm-u*   *fəlla*
          blood-POSS.1   boil.PF.3.M
          'he is incensed' (Amberber 2001:60)

       b. *fit-u*   *aməd*   *məssələ*
          face-POSS.3.M   ash   be.alike.PF.3.M
          'his face became ashen (with fright)' (Amberber 2001:57)

---

[59] Note the difference to the Lakoff school in the following citation from Kövecses (2000:5): "Conceptual metonymies (…) involve a single domain, or concept. The purpose of metonymy is to provide mental access to a domain through another part in the same domain.(…) Thus linguistic examples for these two emotion concepts include *to be upset* for anger and *to have cold feet* for fear. The first is an instance of the conceptual metonymy PHYSICAL AGITATION STAND FOR ANGER, while the second is an example of the conceptual metonymy DROP IN BODY TEMPERATURE STANDS FOR FEAR". These two approaches differ in the definition of what is a domain in the theory of metonymy. Since this theoretical question is of no further relevance for the present work, this point is not further deepened here.

(91)   *sama   xol   dafa   tàng*
        POSS.1.SG   heart   SBJ.3.SG   be.hot
        'I am angry', lit.: 'my heart is hot' (Becher 2003:57)

Recall in this respect the universality claims made in Wierzbicka (1999) that
every language can describe emotions through their bodily effects or symptoms
as well as through bodily images (cf. sect. 3.1).

3.5.2.3 *Synecdoche*

Halliday (1985:319f.) defines synecdoche as follows: "A word is used for
some larger whole of which that which it refers to is a part." Thus, synecdoche
can be viewed as being a special kind of metonymic relation because of the
contiguity relation between part and whole. (92) from Belhare may be an example of the case in question.

(92)   *A-mik   yus-e.*
        POSS.1.SG-eye   sleepy-PST
        'I am sleepy.' (Bickel 1997[P]:146)

Ascription of an experiential state, process or event to a person part noun is
a frequent structural means in many languages. Examples such as (93) from
Wolof illustrate this strategy for emotional and cognitive concepts. A number
of languages exclusively or predominantly use such a strategy to express experiential situations. In these languages, such a strategy however, may not represent a stylistic figure, but rather, the underlying construction may be judged as
more precise in ascribing the experience to an appropriate person part instead
of ascribing it to the person as a whole.

(93) a. *sama   xol   dafa   bék*
         POSS.1.SG   heart   SBJ.3.SG   be.happy
         'my heart is happy' (Becher 2003:60)

      b. *sama   xol   daf   ko   yërëm*
         POSS.1.SG   heart   SBJ.3.SG   OBJ.3.SG   to.pity
         'my heart pitied him/her' (Becher 2003:67)

      c. *xel-am   xal-aat-u   ko*
         mind-POSS.3.SG   mind-VR-NEG   OBJ.3.SG
         'her/his mind didn't think (of) it' (Becher 2003:76)

Thus, a distinction has to be made between those cases in which an experience is ascribed to a person part without being a synecdoche, and those cases
where it indeed represents a synecdoche as a stylistic means. In these latter

cases the possessor of the person part noun can be identified as the experiencer. In the former cases, there may be an inference that the possessor of the person part is an experiencer. Such an inference however does not need to be part of the semantics of these constructions.

3.5.3 *Semantic roles in the analysis of figurative language*

Two levels are needed in the analysis of metaphorical and metonymical expressions and constructions of the mentioned types.[60] This is indicated in the representation of respective constructions, as, e.g., in Construction 3. First a literal level has to be assumed which is necessary for the alignment of the participants. At this level, the participants receive their semantic role with respect to the literal meaning of the predicate. For instance, in an example such as (89a), the first argument of *lose* is the 'loser' which is mapped onto the constructional Actor role, given the fact that it is syntactically coded as a subject of a transitive verb. Regarding the semantics of the whole expression, the first argument of *lose* in (89a) corresponds to the participant role experiencer.

If a figurative experiential expression is an instantiation of an experiential construction, a constructional role Experiencer will be assigned at the secondary semantic level, representing the semantics of the whole construction (cf. Construction 3). In this sense, the possessor of a body part noun in an experiential body part construction, which may be analyzed for the Wolof examples in (93), is a Possessor at the literal semantic level, but an Experiencer at the derived semantic level.

3.5.4 *Types of experiential collocations*

A collocation is a conventionalized combination of words. Such a combination may be idiomaticized to different degrees, ranging from a simple preference to a strong idiomaticization. In the latter case, the whole expression bears a composite meaning that cannot be deduced solely by relying on the meaning of its parts. It is generally based on possibly culture-specific ways of interpreting such combinations, which may or may not be based on metaphor or metonymy. The term 'experiential collocation' is used here instead of 'psycho-collocation' (Matisoff 1986) with the intention of including the subdomain of bodily sensation in the investigation of collocations as well. Matisoff defines psycho-collocations as consisting of a psycho-noun and a psycho-mate, usually an (action) verb or an adjective, i.e., the predicate of the construction. The psycho-noun is assumed to have explicit psychological reference. It is generally either a person part associated with a given experience or a noun referring to the experience itself. The expression as a whole refers to a mental process, quality or

---

state (cf. Matisoff 1986:9). This terminology will now be used to analyze experiential collocations.

In analyzing the lexical-semantic structure of collocations, Bickel (1997[P]) will be used as a reference for distinguishing between compositional and non-compositional collocations. In non-compositional collocations an experiential verb/predicate is combined with only one noun,[61] which means that the latter does not add experiential information that is not expressed by the verb/predicate alone. It may however be related to a full-fledged lexical item.[62] This holds true for the Belhare examples in (94), where *munma* 'forget' and *yama* 'pity' only combine with *niũa* 'mind' and *mik* 'eye', respectively.

(94) a. *Na   u-niũa   muĩ-kha   ma ʔi.*
    DEM   POSS.3.SG-mind   forget-NPST.NR   person
    'He is a forgetful person.'

  b. *A-mik   ya-yu.*
    POSS.1.SG-eye   pity-PST
    'I feel pity (so I can't kill).' (Bickel 1997[P]:142)

In compositional collocations, there is no unique combination of noun and verb/predicate. Either the noun or the verb/predicate has a general meaning while the other item caries the specific experiential meaning. In the Belhare examples in (95), the nouns have a general meaning, while the verb is specifically experiential in meaning.

(95) a. *Unchi-sua-bu   tuk-khar-e.*
    POSS.3.NSG-muscles-REPORT   hurt-TEL-PST
    'They became tired (of walking).

  b. *A-phok   tug-he.*
    POSS.1.SG-belly hurt-PST
    'My stomach aches. (Bickel 1997[P]:142)

In the second case, the verb possesses a general meaning while the noun is explicitly experiential, as shown in (96).

(96)   *U-remsumik   hond-he.*
    POSS.3.SG-envy   appear-PST
    'He is jealous.' (Bickel 1997[P]:144)

---

[61] These are psycho-mate and psycho-noun in the Matisoff's (1986) terminology introduced above.

[62] Bickel (1997[P]) calls such semantically empty (but potentially related to full morphemes) signs 'eidemes'.

The first case of a compositional collocation is reported to be especially frequent in Southeast Asian languages (cf. Matisoff 1986, Bickel 1997[P]) while the second case is frequent in African languages (cf., e.g., (66), (68), (69)).

Experiential collocations may be figurative and built on metaphor or metonymy. An example of a metonymic collocation was given in (88); (89), (90a), and (91) involve both metaphor and metonymy. The experiential meaning generally results from culture-specific ways of combining and interpreting noun and verb/predicate. Some metaphors and metonymies may have cross-cultural or even universal status, as has already been discussed above. The present work however does not intend to prove this claim.

An experiential collocation may be either a unique literal or figurative combination of lexemes expressing experience at the lexical level, or it may be an instance of a construction type which itself conveys experiential meaning. The latter case is analyzed for the Belhare 'possessive of experience' construction in Bickel (1997[P]). The Belhare examples given above in (82), (92), (94), and (95) are all instances of this construction, which is shown to display a unique grammatical behavior in several points.[63]

3.6 *Diachronic development*

Finally, some words have to be said about the development of experiential lexemes and constructions. Two kinds of changes, one referring to the experiential lexemes and their meaning and one concerning the argument structure of experiential constructions, will be addressed.

It has been reported with respect to diverse languages that experiential lexemes and expressions develop from non-experiential ones, e.g., from expressions pertaining to the concrete material domains of action, physical affect, motion, etc. (cf. Halliday 1985:109, Haspelmath 2001, Klein and Kutscher 2002). Such a development can be shown for experiencer-oriented as well as stimulus-oriented verbs (Klein and Kutscher 2002, sect. 4.3). Experiencer-oriented verbs may develop from (non-experiential) agent-oriented verbs, e.g., NHG *sinnen über* 'brood/muse over sth., to ponder/reflect on sth.', *sinnen auf* 'devise/think of sth.' has developed from Germanic *sinþan 'go, make a journey'). Further examples include cognition verbs such as Germ. *erfassen, begreifen* 'understand, comprehend, grasp' which originate in agent-oriented transitive verbs. Furthermore, patient-oriented intransitive verbs designating a state change such as Germ. *durchdrehen* 'crack up', *ausrasten* 'freak out', etc. may also be the source of experiencer-oriented verbs. These verbs originally referred exclusively to the material domain and have nowadays acquired expe-

---

[63] E.g., the combination with the impersonal reference marker *-i* distinguishes the possessive of experience from ordinary possessive constructions (Bickel 1997[P], sect. 2). Further special behavior of this construction type has been described above with respect to (82).

riential meaning in the colloquial language. With these verbs, the experiencer matches with the original semantic patient in subject function. Besides the experiencer-oriented verbs, there are stimulus-oriented experiencer-object verbs that come from non-experiential (agentive or causative) verbs of motion or physical force transmission which take affected or controlled objects. In the metaphorical experiential reading the experiencer corresponds to the affected object (e.g., Germ. *packen* 'seize', *bewegen* 'move', *bedrücken* 'depress, trouble', etc., Engl. *worry* < 'strangle, seize by the throat', *preoccupy* < 'seize beforehand'; see Haspelmath 2001:79).

The second type of change deals with the argument structure of experiential constructions. There seems to be a cross-linguistically attestable development for experiencers coded at lower functions in Figure 3 to attain higher syntactic prominence. This holds true for oblique verb-dependent experiencers as well as for possessor-experiencers, which both tend to acquire higher syntactic functions in Figure 3 diachronically. This generally results in the ultimate change to subject function. The first development has been described for a number of SAE languages as well as for Georgian and Maltese[64] (cf., e.g., Lightfoot 1979, Cole et al. 1980, Seefranz-Montag 1983, Allen 1995, Harris and Campbell 1995, Croft 2001, sect. 4.3.3, Haspelmath 2001). It is supposed that originally oblique experiencers gradually acquire behavioral subject properties (e.g., ellipsis in coordinate constructions etc.) followed by coding properties such as case marking and agreement.[65] In this way, for example, Old English dative experiencers changed to subject experiencers in Modern English. Compare (97), cited from Haspelmath (2001:76).

(97) *Þam   wife   þa   word   wel   licodon.*
      the.DAT   woman.DAT those.NOM words.NOM well liked.3.PL
      'The woman liked those words well.' (Beowulf 639)

The development from oblique to subject experiencer coding is believed to be unidirectional (cf. Croft 2001, Haspelmath 2001). This is functionally motivated by the fact that the experiencer is a highly empathic and definite participant that has a tendency to occur as topic. Since most human topics are subjects, the acquisition of morphosyntactic subject properties is a logical consequence.

Possessor-experiencers may also acquire subject properties and/or may (finally) change to 'full' subjects. For instance, in Mangap-Mbula the body part

---

[64] Haspelmath (2001:77f) gives evidence that the mentioned change is ongoing in contemporary Maltese.

[65] A different explanation is favored, e.g., in Lightfoot (1979) and Harris and Campbell (1995) which suppose that the change happened as a reanalysis of grammatical roles due to reduced case patterns which created ambiguities in case assignment.

noun in experiential body part constructions forms part of a complex verb, while its possessor is reanalyzed as the subject of the whole construction according to Bugenhagen (1990, 1995). This analysis is based on a diverging adverb placement; adverbs which normally occur between the subject and the predicate cannot be placed between the body part noun and the verb, but rather occur between the possessor NP and the body part noun. See (98) for this analysis: in (98a) in a non-experiential part-whole construction the adverb *ko* 'uncertain' cannot be placed between the possessor *ruumu* 'house' and the possessum *uteene* 'its roof', but it can occur between the entire NP and the verb. In contrast, in the experiential body part construction in (98b) the adverb cannot be placed between the possessed body part noun *lele-n* 'their insides' and the verb, but rather it has to occur between the possessor NP *zin* 'they' and the body part noun.

(98)   a. *Ruumu   (*ko)   ute-ene*
          house   uncertain head-GEN.3.SG
          (ko)   i-saana.
          uncertain 3.SG-deteriorate
          'The roof of the house might/will be bad.'

       b. *Zin   (ko)   lele-n*
          NOM.3.PL   uncertain insides-GEN.3.PL
          *(*ko)   i-saana.*
          uncertain 3.SG-deteriorate
          'They might/will be upset.' (after Bugenhagen 1995:257)

Furthermore, the fact reported in sect. 3.4.3.6.1, namely, that certain possessor-experiencers in Belhare show subject properties such as verb agreement etc. can be seen with respect to foregrounding experiencers in syntax. Finally, Bangla is an example of a language showing diachronic syntactic foregrounding regarding the lower area of Figure 3, i.e., the genitive experiencer which originally represented the possessive attribute of a body part or expertum noun has been reanalyzed as a clausal argument of its own (cf. Bickel 2004 based on Klaiman 1980).

   While the change of oblique experiencers and possessor-experiencers to subject experiencers seems to be indeed unidirectional, this is not necessarily the case regarding the development of lexemes with a concrete meaning to lexemes with an abstract experiential meaning (but cf. Haspelmath 2001:79). Lexemes with an experiential meaning may change to or be in variation with lexemes with a more concrete actional meaning. For instance, the German verb *sich kümmern* 'look after, take care of' refers to an action but is derived from the experiential noun *Kummer* 'grief'. Verbs like *deplore* etc. develop their meaning and function as emotive speech activity verbs later than their experiential meaning (cf. Kemmer 1993). The issue of variation and change with respect to experiential meaning will be addressed with respect to YM in ch. 5. It will be argued there that concrete activity readings of experiential lexemes are derived from basic experiential meanings and are thus, secondary.

CHAPTER 4

Introduction to Yucatec Maya

This chapter is intended to present the basic structures of the language under investigation which will be crucial to the analysis of the experiential constructions in ch. 5-8. Sect. 4.1 is an introduction to the basic structures of YM, introducing clause structure, nominal and verbal categories, and the features of word classes which can function as predicates. Sect. 4.2 and 4.3 treat more specific issues, namely, subordinative structures and grammatical relations.

4.1 *Basic structures*

The current section gives an outline of the basic grammatical structures of YM. The main resources of this chapter are Lehmann (1991[Y], 1993[P], 1993[G], 1998) and Bohnemeyer (1998[T], 2002) which are based in turn on earlier work on the language such as Andrade (1955), Blair (1964), Blair and Vermont-Salas (1965/1967), Owen (1968), Bricker (1979), (1981[I]), Bricker et al. (1998). First some general typological information about YM will be given in sect. 4.1.1 before some basic aspects of YM grammar will be addressed, such as the basic clause structure in sect. 4.1.3, the system of dependent and independent pronouns in sect. 4.1.2 and deictic clitics in sect. 4.1.4. Further topics to be discussed include nominal morphology and the morpho-syntactic structure of nominal possessive constructions (sect. 4.1.5) and the internal structure of the verbal core and the verb and its categories (sect. 4.1.6). The aspectual system will be introduced in sect. 4.1.7 while sect. 4.1.8 will discuss the grammatical aspects of those word classes which can function as predicates in YM.

4.1.1 *Short typological characterization*

As a morphological type, YM can be characterized as mildly polysynthetic in that it shows incorporation of nouns and adverbs. A verb or a noun together with its cross-reference markers may exhaust a clause. The main morphological strategy is agglutination, with some traits of fusion in the verbal complex.

Nominal morphology is relatively simple. There is no case marking and number marking is optional. Nominal syntax, however, is quite complex. The language has numeral and possessive classifiers. The grammar of possession is well developed, showing morphological and syntactic distinctions between various classes of alienable and inalienable nouns. Verbal morphology displays a higher complexity than nominal morphology. Aspect/mood is obligatorily marked on the verb (dependent on a system of preverbal aspect/mood markers to be described in detail in sect. 4.1.6). There is rich verbal derivation to change valence and aspectual character and a regular passive operation.

From a syntactic point of view, YM is exclusively head-marking, i.e., the head – verb, stative predicate, possessed noun, or preposition – is marked for the dependant by cross-reference indices. The main constituent order in simple sentences is as follows: VUA(G) in transitive clauses, VS(G) in intransitive clauses.[1] Thus, the subject follows the predicate, and the nominal and adverbial dependants are placed after the verb. In addition, nominal, adpositional and interclausal syntax is generally right branching, that is, attributes generally follow the head noun (apart from simple attributive adjectives, occurring in prenominal position, cf. sect. 4.1.8), adpositions are followed by their complements, and dependent clauses are placed after their matrix clause.

The organization of grammatical relations in Yucatec Maya is still an unsettled question. With regard to coding properties, YM shows a split-intransitive system of argument marking which depends on overt aspect/mood marking on the verb. In the incompletive aspect, the sole actant of an intransitive verb is marked like the actor of a transitive verb, while in the completive and subjunctive, it is marked like the undergoer of a transitive verb. Behavioral properties however, seem to point to a weakly pronounced S=A subject. The issue of grammatical relations will be discussed in 4.3.

4.1.2 *Dependent and independent pronouns*

YM has two paradigms of dependent pronouns that function as cross-reference markers within verbal and nominal clauses. One paradigm consists of preverbal/prenominal clitics, usually referred to as 'set A marker' in Mayan structural linguistics. The other paradigm is suffixal and is called 'set B marker'. Set A clitics and set B suffixes will be called here subject/possessor clitics and absolutive suffixes respectively because of their agreement pattern. These are purely structural concepts which are not directly mappable onto grammatical relations, let alone semantic roles. The functions of the subject clitic include marking the actor of a transitive verb, the possessor, and the sole actant of intransitive verbal cores with incompletive status. The absolutive suffix includes the undergoer of a transitive verb, the sole actant in stative clauses and in intransitive verbal cores with completive or subjunctive status. Morphologically this is a split-intransitive system of argument marking. How this corresponds to

---

[1] S stands for the single argument of an intransitive verb, A und U stand for the actor and the undergoer of a transitive verb, respectively, and G stands for the 'goal' of an (in)transitive verb, i.e., corresponding to its oblique object.

possible grammatical relations and accusativity vs. ergativity traits in syntax will be discussed in some detail in ch. 4.3.

Subject clitics trigger a glide if they immediately precede a vowel-initial verb or noun.[2] The third person clitic *u* may be dropped in front of the glide *y*, which, in this case, attains the indexical function. Furthermore note that the plural paradigm of the subject clitic is discontinuous; the plurality marker suffixes to the verb or noun. This behavior with respect to the first person plural is optional and seems to be a recent analogical development. The absolutive markers are suffixed to nouns, adjectives and verb stems, following all other verbal categories (cf. Figure 6 in the following section). Third person suffix *-ih* only attaches to intransitive verbs in clause-final position. The complete list of cross-reference markers is given in Table 1 (cf. Lehmann 1998, sect. 2.3, Bohnemeyer 2004, sect. 3).

	subject/possessor clitics		absolutive suffixes	
	singular	plural	singular	plural
1 person	*in (w-)*V/N	*k* V/N*(-o'n)*	*-en*	*-o'n*
1 p. incl.	/	*k* V/N*-o'n-e'x*	/	*-o'n-e'x*
2 person	*a (w-)*V/N	*a (w-)*V/N*-e'x*	*-ech*	*-e'x*
3 person	*u (y-)*V/N	*u (y-)*V/N*-o'b*	*-Ø/-ih*	*-o'b*

Table 1. Pronominal cross-reference markers

Next to the dependent pronominal markers, YM has a set of free personal pronouns, which is illustrated in Table 2. Historically, this has developed from a contraction of the most grammatical preposition *ti'* 'LOC' and the absolutive markers. The independent pronouns may occur in emphatic contexts, namely, in topic or focus positions. There, they may be co-referent with a dependent cross-reference marker. Otherwise, they appear mainly in indirect object or oblique function, or as the complement of a preposition. Lehmann (1998:21) distinguishes between a strong and weak form of the paradigm, which is visible in the third person, the strong form displaying the element *le-*. While the strong forms occur in topic or focus position and after a preposition, the weak forms are oblique pronouns which generally follow the verb (for an exception cf. 4.3.4).

	singular	plural
1st person	*teen*	*to'n*
2nd person	*tèech*	*te'x*
3rd person	*(le-)ti'*	*(le-)ti'o'b*

Table 2. Independent personal pronouns

---

[2] For some minor exceptions cf. Lehmann (1998, ch. 3.2.1.1.1.4).

4.1.3 *Internal clause structure*

The current section introduces the structure of a basic verbal clause followed by that of a basic nominal clause. In the structural representation used here and in the following sections, in general the conventions established in Lehmann (1998) will be observed. Morphological as well as syntactic information will be given to a degree necessary to understand the analysis of the YM data in ch. 5 to 8. For illustration, a constituent structure representation with category labels is used. Each structure is rendered by means of a glossed example. A more abstract representation of the structures introduced here will be used in the notation of the structural layer of the constructions in ch. 5 ff.

The basic verbal clause is illustrated in Figure 6. It consists of a preverbal marker/auxiliary indicating aspect or mood categories and the verbal core[3] which itself is internally complex. The latter is composed of the preverbal subject clitic (cf. 4.1.2) and the verb. Furthermore, there is a slot inbetween the subject clitic and the verb, which can be optionally filled with a simple adverb (complex adverbials are clause-final). The verb hosts a number of suffix positions, which will be discussed in sect. 4.1.6, and it carries the absolutive suffix (cf. 4.1.2). The verbal core may optionally contain argument NPs and adjuncts, which follow the verb.

A/M marker/aux ≺	Verbal core				
	Sbj.clitic ≺	(SAdv) ≺	Root	Status	Abs.suffix
[ts'o'k	[in	chéen	hats'	-ik	-ech] VCo]VCl
TERM	SBJ.1.SG	just	beat	-INCMPL	-ABS.2.SG
'I have just beaten you'					

Figure 6. Structure of the independent verbal clause

The verb is obligatorily marked for a status category (termed after Kaufman 1990), which is chosen from one of the three aspect/mood categories incompletive, completive or subjunctive. These categories (cf. Table 3 for the complete paradigm) are triggered by the preverbal A/M markers/auxiliaries as indicated for the more frequent in A/M markers/auxiliaries in sect. 4.1.7, especially Table 8.

The AM markers/auxiliaries can be divided into morphologically bound and unbound groups, the former being prefixed to the subject clitic such as the perfective marker *t-* in (99a). Verbal clauses with bound and unbound preverbal markers/auxiliaries differ as to which constituent is the main predicate of the clause. The main predicate can be identified by its potential to attract the question focus marker *wáah* 'INT' in polar questions as is shown in Bohnemeyer

---

[3] The term 'verbal core' is recurrent in Mayan linguistics to name the unit identified in Figure 6 as such. It should not be confused with the term 'core' as established in Role and Reference grammar (cf. Van Valin and LaPolla 1997).

(1998[T]:182). In clauses with bound AM markers, the lexical verb plus the bound marker can be shown to constitute the predicate (99a), while in clauses with unbound AM auxiliaries the AM auxiliaries attract the question focus marker (99b). The answer repeats the main predicate, as is shown in the primed examples of (99) (cf. also Lehmann 1993[G]:314).

(99) a. *T-u   hats'-ah-ech   wáah?*
       PFV-SBJ.3 beat-CMPL-ABS.2.SG INT
       'Did he beat you?'

      a'.*T-u   hats'-ah-en.*
       PFV-SBJ.3 beat-CMPL-ABS.1.SG
       'He did.'

      b. *Táan   wáah   u   hats'-ik-ech?*
       PROG   INT   SBJ.3   beat-INCMPL-ABS.1.SG
       'Is he beating you?'

      b'.*Táan.*
       PROG
       'He is.'

In their construction and function, the AM markers/auxiliaries seem to resemble Indo-European auxiliaries in analytic verb constructions.[4] Bricker (1981[I]) and Lehmann (1993[G]) indeed classify (most of) them as impersonal auxiliaries which are grammaticalized from (impersonal) lexical matrix predicates with aspectual and modal functions that take the verbal core in absolutive function. In the course of their development, they lose their AM marking and their verbal inflection, resulting finally in aspectual and modal markers that do not carry a valency relation with respect to the core. The unbound markers will be referred to as aspect/mood (or A/M) auxiliaries and the bound ones simply as A/M markers. They will be discussed as a distributional class in sect. 4.1.8.

Nominal clauses can be clearly distinguished from verbal clauses in that they lack an AM marker or auxiliary. They cannot bear any aspectual or modal marking. The nominal constitutes the predicate. This may be a member of the class of stative predicates (cf. Table 13 below), either a noun as in Figure 7 and in (100b), an adjective (100a) or a verboid (e.g., a transitive verboid[5] as in (100c)). Nominal predicates take the same cross-reference markers as verbs do. Monovalent predicates (100a/b) only take the absolutive suffix, which repre-

---

[4] Both Lehmann (1993[G]) and Bohnemeyer (1998[T], 2001) discuss the apparent contradiction that, from a cross-linguistic perspective, an auxiliary should carry verbal inflectional categories while the YM aspect/mood auxiliary is exclusively impersonal.

[5] The class of transitive verboids will be referred to in detail in sect. 4.1.8 and sect. 5.2.2.2.1.

sents their sole actant, while bivalent predicates take the set A clitic in possessor function and the set B suffix in subject function. An independent nominal clause with a bivalent predicate is illustated in Figure 7.

Poss.clitic ≺	N	
	(Nominal) root	Abs.suffix
[in	tàatah	-ech]$_{NCI}$
POSS.1.SG	father	-ABS.2.SG
'you are my father'		

Figure 7. Structure of the independent nominal clause

(100) a. *k'oha'n-ech*
           ill-ABS.2.SG
           'you are ill'

       b. *pàal-ech*
           child-ABS.2.SG
           'you are a child'

       c. *in   k'ahóol-ech*
           SBJ.1.SG   acquaint-ABS.2.SG
           'I know you'

As can be deduced from the examples presented in the current chapter, pronominal cross-reference markers are able to fully establish reference on their own. The verbal as well as the nominal clause may, however, be optionally followed by coreferent full NPs in subject or object function.

(101) a. *t-u   hats'-ah-ech   le   máak-o'*
           PFV-SBJ.3   beat-CMPL-ABS.2.SG   DEF   person-D2
           'the man beat you'

       b. *in   k'ahóol   le   máak-o'*
           SBJ.1.SG   acquaint   DEF   person-D2
           'I know the man'

       c. *k'oha'n   le   máak-o'*
           ill   DEF   person-D2
           'the man is ill'

4.1.4 *Deictic clitics*

YM has a set of 4 deictic enclitics which follow an independent clause. These elements are in general either obligatorily or optionally triggered by a number of items which may occur in the clause. Thus, if a clause contains an NP that is marked by the determiner *le* 'DEF', it is followed either by the proximal marker

-a' D1 or by the distal marker *-o'* D2 (cf., e.g., (102c), (112b)). Other demonstrative or deictic elements such as *way* 'here', *te'l* 'there', *he'l* 'PRSV', *be'òorah* 'now', *bèey* 'thus', etc. also trigger one of these clitics or the 'textual' deixis enclitic *-e'* D3 (cf., e.g., (103a)). Possessive clitics may optionally trigger a proximal or distal deixis marker (cf. Lehmann 1998, sect. 3.2.4.2; for an example (111)). Without any triggering element, the enclitic *-e'* may also function as a topic marker (TOP) (102b) or a continuator (CNTR) (102a), the latter signaling that the thus marked clause is not the final clause in the sentence. Finally, the particle *-i'* NEGF/LOCF follows most clauses containing the negation marker *ma'* NEG[6] (102b) and occurs in locational focus constructions (102c).[7]

(102) a. *Huntéenaki' bin   káa h hóok' u   bin-bal-e'*
          once   QUOT CNJ PFV exit SBJ.3 go-INTRV-CNTR
          h   tu'b u   bis-ik   u   nu'kul …
          PFV   forget SBJ.3 carry-INCMPL POSS.3 instrument
          'Once when he left, he forgot to take the keys (…)' (HK'AN_045)

     b. *Ko'lel-o'b-e' ma' táan   u   bin-i'.*
          lady-PL-TOP   NEG PROG SBJ.3 go-NEGF
          'Women don't go there.' (SANTO_056)

     c. *te'l   túun ti' le   óox-p'éel   che'-a'*
          there then LOC DEF three-CL.INAN tree-D1
          ti' ken   a   chuy-i'   yéetel àak'.
          there SR.FUT SBJ.2 sew-LOCF with   liane
          'there at the three trees, there is it where you are going to sew them together with a liane' (NAH_089)

4.1.5 *Nominal categories*

In terms of inflectional morphology, NPs are marked for plurality by the suffix *-o'b*, which follows the noun stem. However, plurality marking is not obligatory but correlates with the empathy and specificity of the referent of the NP (cf. Lucy 1992, Lehmann 1998:19). The simplest structure in the nominal sphere is a nominal consisting of a head noun optionally preceded by a simple adjective attribute, as schematized in Figure 8.

---

[6] For exceptions cf. Bohnemeyer (1998[T], ch. 4.2.1.5.) and, e.g.,(107).

[7] Hanks (1990) is a comprehensive work on deixis in YM from an anthropological point of view.

<table>
<tr><td colspan="2">(Adj) ≺   N</td></tr>
<tr><td>[mehen</td><td>xibpal]_{Nom}</td></tr>
</table>

(Adj) ≺	N
[mehen	xibpal]_{Nom}
small	man:child
'small boy'	

Figure 8. Structure of the nominal

Adjectives can function as the head of a nominal without overt marking (103a). As head of a plural NP, however, they take the suffix *-tak* (103b/c).

(103) a. *Mùuk' che' yéetel mehen bèey-o' ...*
strength wood and   small   thus-D2
'A strong plank and a small one like that, (...)' (NAH_085)

b. *Le   u   chuk-a'n   mehen-tak*
DEF   POSS.3   suffice-RSLTV   small-SBSTR.PL
ken   u   bèet-bil-o' ...
SR.FUT   SBJ.3   do-GERV-D2
'Enough of the small ones have to be made, (...)' (CHAAK_026)

c. *Le   ch'uhuk-o'b k-u   ko'n-ol-o'b-o'   hach*
DEF sweets-PL   IMPF-SBJ.3   sell\PASS-INCMPL-3.PL-D2   really
mehen-tak-o'b.
small-SBSTR.PL-PL
'The sweets that are sold are really small ones.' (ACC_0260)

We now turn to the description of possessed nominals. Lehmann (1998) distinguishes between a 'simple possessed nominal' and an 'expanded possessed nominal', the latter differing from the former in that it displays a lexical noun or independent pronoun in possessor function. A simple possessed nominal (cf. Figure 9) consists of a nominal as represented in Figure 8 and a preposed possessor clitic which is governed by the head nominal. The possessor clitic has a discontinuous part, marking plurality, which follows the nominal (cf. sect. 4.1.2).

Poss.clitic ≺	Nom		
[u	[mehen	xibpal]_{Nom}	-o'b]_{SPNom}
POSS.3	small	man:child	-3.PL
'their small boy'			

Figure 9. Structure of the simple possessed nominal

An expanded possessed nominal (cf. Figure 10, example (104)) consists of a simple possessed nominal followed by a lexical noun or independent pronoun in possessor function which is the head of a possessor NP (cf. Figure 11 for the internal structure of the YM NP). Government of the possessor clitic by the head nominal extends to the possessor NP via coreference. Furthermore note that the possessor clitic agrees with the possessor NP in person and number.

SPNom				≺	PossNP
[[a	[mehen	xibpal]$_{Nom}$	-e'x]$_{SPNom}$		te'x]$_{EPNom}$
POSS.2	small	man:child	-2.PL		you.PL
'your (pl.) small boy'					

Figure 10. Structure of the expanded possessed nominal

(104)   *u*   *mehen xibpal(-o'b)*   *in*   *w-íits'in-o'b*
       POSS.3 small   man:child-3.PL   SBJ.1.SG 0-younger.sibling-PL
       'my younger brothers' small boy'

A possessed nominal may be the predicate of a clause as was described in sect. 4.1.3 and illustrated in Figure 7. Note here that the absolutive suffix indexing the subject of the clause is attached to the simple possessed nominal, and not to the expanded possessed nominal because it is a word-level suffix (105). It sequentializes with the discontinuous plural marker of the possessor clitic according to their positions in the animacy hierarchy (cf. sect. 2.1.3).

(105)   *u*   *pàal-e'x-o'b*   *h-k'áaxil-o'b*
       POSS.3 child-ABS.2.PL-3.PL   M-farmer-PL
       'you are the children of farmers' (Lehmann 1998:42)

A nominal (simple, simple possessed or expanded possessed) may combine with outer nominal specifiers such as, e.g., a numeral complex (consisting of a numeral plus a numeral classifier (106a), or a mensurative) and/or the determiner (106b) forming a (possessed) NP, as indicated in Figure 11 (cf. Lehmann 1998:92).

(106) a. *yàan*   *hun-p'éel*   *u*   *nah-il*
        EXIST   one-CL.INAN   POSS.3   house-REL
        'he had a house, (…)' (MUUCH_090)

       b. *le*   *in*   *w-íits'in-o'*
        DEF SBJ.1.SG 0-younger.sibling-D2
        'that younger brother of mine' (ACC_0279)

Det ≺	CtNom				≺	Ptcl
	Num.Complex ≺		EPNom			
[le	[[hun-	túul]$_{NumCom}$	[[u	k'éek'en]$_{SPNom}$	Pedro]$_{EPNom}$]$_{CtNom}$	-a']$_{NP}$
DEF	one-	CL.AN	POSS.3	pig	Pedro	D1
'this one pig of Pedro'						

Figure 11. Internal structure of the NP

4.1.6 *Verbal categories*

YM distinguishes between transitive (Figure 12) and intransitive verbs (Figure 13, Figure 14). Figure 12 and show that the subject clitic is discontinuous with the plural marker, i.e., the plural marker of the subject clitic is suffixed to the verb. Relative order with respect to the absolutive suffix depends on their positions in the animacy hierarchy.[8] In Figure 12 the discontinuous number suffix follows the absolutive suffix, but it would be the other way around if the undergoer were lower in animacy than the actor. Following the root, there are (at least) two optional derivational slots, which in Figure 12 are filled by the distributive marker *-la'n* and the transitivizer *-t*. *-la'n* seems to occur exclusively with *-t* and one could argue that these constitute one morpheme (parallel to the factitive marker *-kint/-kins*), but with incorporation, the incorporated noun intercedes between the two derivational suffixes, hence two positions are assumed. Note however, that the language seems to avoid multiple derivational suffixes. It either drops one (as, e.g., *-t* in front of *-bil, -a'n, -mah* etc.) or it tends to merge them (cf. Bohnemeyer 1998[T]:273, 225f.). Figure 12 does not represent a maximal morphological template of a transitive verb since composition and incorporation are not considered.

Sbj.clitic ≺	(SAdv) ≺	Stem	Status	Abs.suffix	(Num.suf._{Sbj})
[u	háan	[mach-la'n-t]_{TrVStem}	-ik	-e'x	-o'b]_{TrVCom}
SBJ.3	right.away	seize-DISTR-TRR	-INCMPL	-ABS.2.PL	-3.PL
'they seize all of you (Pl.) (one after another) right away'					

Figure 12. Structure of the transitive verbal complex

With intransitive verbs the occurrence of subject clitics vs. absolutive suffixes depends on the AM marking. Therefore two morphological templates are required for intransitive verbs, one for incompletive status as given in Figure 13 and one for the remaining status categories as shown in Figure 14.

The verb classes to be introduced in sect. 4.1.8 reflect their morphological differences in status inflection. Each class shows its own inflectional paradigm for the three status categories already introduced: incompletive, completive and subjunctive.

Sbj.clitic ≺	(SAdv) ≺	Stem	Status	(Num.suffix_{Sbj})
[u	háan	[chuk-pah]_{IntrVStem}	-al	-o'b]_{IntrVCom}
SBJ.3	right.away	suffice-SPONT	-INCMPL	-3.PL
'they get complete right away'				

Figure 13. Structure of the intransitive verbal complex for incompletive status

---

[8] Cf. Hanks (1990:162) and Lehmann (1998, sect. 3.2.1.1.1.2) for the complete paradigm of combinations of discontinuous subject and absolutive markers which may also occur on a possessed nominal.

(SAdv) ≺	Stem	Status	Abs.suffix
[chéen	[chil-lan-kil]$_{IntrVStem}$	-nah	-en]$_{IntrVCom}$
just	lie-DUR	-CMPL	-ABS.1.SG
'I just lay about'			

Figure 14. Structure of the intransitive verbal complex for other status categories

Furthermore, YM has a regular passive voice that applies to all transitive verbs. It is considered a syntactic process which demotes the A and allows for the U of a transitive verb to appear as the subject in the passive clause. The action denoted by the verb is understood to be caused by an agent, which is optionally added by means of the preposition *tumen* 'by, because of'. However like derivational processes passivization renders the verb intransitive. Cross-reference marking is identical to that of intransitive verbs. The paradigm of status inflection in Table 3 (cf. Bohnemeyer 1998[T]:221) shows that the passive verb inflects for all status categories, just as the other verb classes do. There are two ways to form the passive which are in complementary distribution. In (most) root transitive verbs, a glottal stop is inserted into the root and the status suffixes, identical to those of the intransitive inactives are added. This is indicated by the notation " '/…-suffix" in Table 3. With derived transitive verbs, the passive is formed by adding the suffixes indicated in the second line of the passive forms in Table 3. Note that in this case the glottal stop is inserted into the suffix while the verbal stem does not change.

	incompletive	completive	subjunctive
tr. active	*-ik*	*-ah*	*-Ø/-eh*
passive (intr.)	*\'/…-Vl*[9]	*\'/…-Ø*	*\'/…-Vk*
	l-a'l	*l-a'b*	*l-a'k*
intr. inactive	*-Vl*	*-Ø*	*-Vk*
intr. active	*-Ø*	*-nah*	*-nak*
intr. inchoative	*-tal*	*-chah*	*-chahak*
intr. positional	*-tal*	*-lah*	*-l(ah)ak*

Table 3. Status inflection according to verb classes

Additionally, there is a fourth inflectional category which is related to the completive. It is called extrafocal as it marks the out-of-focus predicate of some focus constructions. It might be a relic from a more complete system in Colonial YM which may have occurred with all three categories completive, incompletive and subjunctive in certain types of subordinated clauses/cores. Today it occurs only in the extrafocal part of a cleft construction within manner focus constructions (cf. sect. 5.3.2.1.4, (283), (284b)). With transitive verbs

---

[9] V is a vowel in harmony with the verbal root vowel.

the extrafocal suffix is *-il*, with intransitive verbs and the passive the suffix is *-ik*, as indicated in Table 4.

	extrafocal
tr. active	*-ah-il*
passive (intr.)	\ʼ/...*-Ø-ik*
	/-aʼb-ik
intr. active	*-nah-ik*
intr. inactive	*-Ø-ik*
intr. inchoative	*-chah-ik*
intr. positional	*-lah-ik*

Table 4. Extrafocal inflection

The members of all verb classes, apart from those of the intransitive class of inchoatives, form a morphological imperative, as listed in Table 5. For transitive verbs the morpheme is *-eh*, which is identical with the subjunctive marker (cf. Table 3). Just like the subjunctive form, it only surfaces in clause final position. Intransitives form their imperative with *-en* following the 'thematic' element *-n-* for active intransitives and *-l-* for positionals.[10] The imperative morpheme is in opposition with the status morphemes in Table 3. It is never accompanied by AM marking.

	imperative
tr. active	*-Ø/-eh*
intr. active	*-nen*
intr. inactive	*-en*
intr. inchoative	/
intr. positional	*-len*

Table 5. Imperative formation

Restrictions on imperative formation correlate with the degree of control on the part of the addressee (i.e., the main argument). This fact is grammatically implemented for inchoative verbs, whose main argument is a semantic patient/theme (cf. sect. 4.1.8). A further group of verbs, i.e., those that are formed with the spontaneous markers *-chah/-kʼah/-pah* (cf. Table 6), do not form a morphological imperative, although they do formally join the inactive class of intransitive verbs which has an imperative form. This behavior correlates with

---

[10] Blair and Vermont-Salas (1965/1967:758) analyzes the completive stem as the basis for imperative formation with the segment *ah* being syncopized, i.e *-l-* with positionals is from *h kulahen* 'PFV sit:CMPL-ABS.1.SG' => *kulen!*, *-n-* with actives: *h meyahnahen* => *meyahnen*, Ø with inactives *h òoken* => *òoken*.

the meaning of the derivation, which renders the action denoted by the base (verb) as occurring by itself, perhaps against a potential agent's will. Furthermore, it has to be noted that the imperative form does not occur in negative contexts. The form that is functionally equivalent to a negative imperative is constructed as in (107), i.e., the verb appears in its incompletive form and the cross-reference marking is that of the second person. Compare (107a) for an inactive intransitive verb, with (107b) for an active intransitive verb, and (107c) for a transitive verb.

(107) a. *Ma' a   he'l-el*!
         NEG SBJ.2 rest-INCMPL
         'Don't take a rest!'

      b. *Ma' a   w-áalkab-e'x!*
         NEG SBJ.2 0-run(INCMPL)-2.PL
         'Don't (Pl.) run!'

      c. *Ma' a   w-a'l-ik-e'x   mixba'l!*
         NEG SBJ.2 0-say-INCMPL-2.PL   nothing
         'Don't (Pl.) say anything!' (HK'AN_252)

YM demonstates a rich variety of options for changing the class of a predicate (see sect. 4.1.8 for details). Some of these operations are highly regular and applicable to most (if not all) members of the base class. This applies, for example, to the deadjectival derivation with the inchoative suffix *-tal* or with the factitive suffixes *-kint/s* or *-kunt/s*. In general, the derivations to at least a certain degree are base specific: Thus adjectives and sometimes nouns are changed to verbs by means of the suffix *-tal*. Causativization with *-s*, and, more seldomly, with *-bes*, applies to verbs of the inactive intransitive class. Factitivization (with *-kint/s/-kunt/s*[11]) applies to adjectives and positionals resulting in transitive verbs. Extraversive transitivization by means of the suffix *-t* applies to active intransitive verbs.[12] Like many other Mayan languages, YM displays an antipassive[13], demoting the U argument of the transitive base verb and an

---

[11] The variation in the vowel is due to disharmony with the vowel of the stem. The coda consonants *-s/-t* following *ki/un* seem to be in free variation (though consultants display preferences with most verbs).

[12] For some exceptions to the class-bound *-s/-t* derivations see Bohnemeyer (2004) which hypothesizes that *-s/-t* are merely allomorphs with a transitivizing function, the class of the base being decisive for either causative or applicative semantics. Cf. further Lehmann and Verhoeven (2006) on extraversive/applicative formation in YM.

[13] It is also called 'introversive' in Lehmann (1993[P]), 'deaffective' in Lucy (1994).

anticausative[14], demoting the A argument of the transitive base. In contrast to the passive operation introduced in the preceding chapter, the causing A argument is excluded and the action is rendered as self-occurring. While the passive is regularly applied to all transitive verbs and has therefore been classified as an inflectional category, anticausative (henceforth deagentive) and antipassive (henceforth introversive) are accessible only to limited groups of transitive verbs. The deagentive is reported as applying only to underived transitives, while the introversive is said to be formed from basic and causativized transitives (cf. Bohnemeyer 1998[T]:219). Sporadic tests among my consultants hint that the formation of the introversive is also semantically limited (108b). (108) exemplifies the possible voice alternations for the root-transitive verb *sat* 'lose' in imperfective aspect: (108a) is in the active voice, (108b) in the introversive, derived by low tone on the root vowel, (108c) displays passive voice and (108d) the deagentive formed by high tone on the root vowel.

(108) a. *tíin*   *sat-ik*   *hun-p'éel*   *pèeso*
         PROG:SBJ.1.SG lose-INCMPL one-CL.INAN   peso
         'I am losing a peso' (NMP)

      b. **tíin*   *sàat*
         PROG:SBJ.1.SG   lose\INTRV
         'I am losing' (NMP, ACC, RMC)

      c. *túun*   *sa't-al*   *hun-p'éel*   *pèeso*
         PROG:SBJ.3   lose\PASS-INCMPL   one-CL.INAN   peso
         'a peso is (being) lost (by someone)' (NMP)

      d. *túun*   *sáat-al*   *hun-p'éel*   *pèeso*
         PROG:SBJ.3 lose\DEAG-INCMPL   one-CL.INAN   peso
         'a peso gets lost' (NMP)

In Table 6 and Table 7 those derivational operations that are relevant for experiential expressions are summarized. Table 6 summarizes the valency changing operations and divides them into valency increasing and valency decreasing operations, which are mirror cases of valency change. In Table 6 corresponding arguments of the base and the goal construction are given in the same line so that respective changes in argument structure can be easily compared. The operations indicated by a/a' affect the U and those under b/b' and c/c' affect the A. Furthermore, b/b' concerns operations that remain inside the verbal predicate class while c/c' includes changes between the stative and the verbal class.

---

[14] It is also called 'deagentive' in Lehmann (1993[P]), 'decausative' in Lucy (1994), 'middle voice' among other Mayanists.

operation		base construction	goal construction	marker
valency increasing				
a	extraversion[15]	V(act.intr.)	V(tr.)	*-t*
		S	A	
		-	U	
b	causativization	V(inact.intr.)	V(tr.)	*-s, -bes*
		S	U	
		-	A	
c	factitivization	N/Adj/Positional	V(tr.)	*-kint/s/-kunt/s*
		S	U	
		-	A	
valency reducing				
a′	introversion	V(tr.)	V(act.intr.)	low tone[16]
		A	S	
		U	-	
b′	deagentivization	V(tr.)	V(inact.intr.)	high tone
		U	S	
		A	-	
b′	spontaneous formation[17]	V(tr.)	V(inact.intr.)	*-chah /*
		U	S	*-k'ah /*
		A	-	*-pah*
c′	resultative formation	V(tr.)	Adj(stat.)	*-a'n*
		U	S	
		A	-	
c′	gerundive formation	V(tr.)	Adj(stat.)	*-bil*
		U	S	
		A	-	

Table 6. Valency changing operations

Not all derivational changes are valency changing. Those not affecting argument structure but dynamicity, i.e., causing a change from the class of stative predicates to verbal predicates, are listed in Table 7. The split is made according to the increase or the reduction of dynamicity. The same letters in the leftmost column again indicate mirror cases of derivation. Thus, the operations under a/a' involve two arguments, A and U, while those under b involve only one argument, generally S. Those dynamicity changing operations which are also valency changing are only listed in Table 6, namely, resultative formation from transitive verbs and gerundive formation.

---

[15] This is simple undergoer-focused transitivization, an essentially lexical counterpart of applicative formation (cf. Lehmann and Verhoeven, 2006).

[16] Derived verb stems may form their introversive with *-ah*, e.g., *xóoyt* 'detour sth.' => *xóoyt-ah* 'detour-INTRV', *túucht* 'send sth.' => *túucht-ah* 'send-INTRV'.

[17] A further term is 'extended deagentivization' in Lehmann (1993[P]).

operation	base	target	marker
dynamicity increasing			
a verbalization	N(rel.)/Verboid(tr.)	V(tr.)	*-t*
b durative formation	Adj	V(act.intr.)	*-(lank)il*
b inchoative formation	N/Adj/Mod	V(inchoa.intr.)	*-tal*
b spontaneous formation	N/Adj	V(inact.intr.)	*-chah /-k'ah /-pah*
dynamicity reducing			
a' perfect formation	V(tr.)	Verboid(stat.)	*-mah*
b' resultative formation	V(intr.)	Adj(stat.)	*-a'n*

Table 7. Dynamicity changing operations

There are also category-preserving operations like the derivation of transitive verbs with the distributive marker *-la'n-t*. Furthermore, there are shifts inside/between the intransitive classes: the durative marker *-lan-kil* may be attached to positionals and inactive intransitives yielding active intransitive verbs. The spontaneous marker *-chah/-k'ah/-pah* seems to be largely unspecific as to the 'input class' of its base. In addition to the cases mentioned above, it can also combine with positionals and active and inactive intransitive verbs. In the latter case the operation is category-preserving as well.

There are limits to the combined application of different operations. It is generally possible to dynamize a stative predicate or increase its valency and subsequently re-stativize it. This can be seen in (109) where members of the stative class are first formed with the inchoative *-chah* in (109a) or factitive morphemes *-kint/-kuns* in (109b/c) and are then followed by the resultative *-a'n* in (109a/b) or by the gerundive *-bil* in (109c).

> (109) a. *k'àas-chah-a'n*
>   bad-PROC.CMPL-RSLTV
>   'gone bad/stale'
>   b. *ch'uy-kint-a'n*
>   hang-FACT-RSLTV
>   'hung up'
>   c. *kàah-kuns-bil*
>   village-FACT-GERV
>   'to be populated' (Bohnemeyer 1998[T]:225)

In contrast, if verbs have been stativized there is no possibility of re-dynamization. A succession of several transitivization and detransitivization operations is limited, but possible, i.e., introversion following causativization (cf. *lúub-s-ah* (fall-CAUS-INTRV) 'fell (unspecified objects)').

The rest of this section will be used to discuss those derivations resulting in stative predicates that frequently co-occur with experiential expressions, namely, the resultative formation in *-a'n* and the perfect formation in *-mah*. The resultative in *-a'n* is compatible with all transitive and intransitive verbs, but in natural discourse it occurs preferably with members of those intransitive classes that denote a change of state such as inactive intransitives, inchoatives and positionals.[18] Thus, resultative formation seems to presuppose an undergoer (of a state change). With intransitive verbs, *-a'n* follows the completive stem, which is unmarked with inactive intransitives but marked with all other groups (cf. Table 3; e.g., inactive: *lúub-a'n* 'fall-RSLTV', inchoative: *k'ùux-chah-a'n* 'angry-PROC.CMPL-RSLTV', active: *xíimbal-nah-a'n* 'stroll-CMPL-RSLTV'). The resultative generally occurs in postnominal position; its occurrence in prenominal position seems to be restricted to fixed expressions and lexicalized forms that are clearly part of the class of (attributive) adjectives (cf. *káala'n* 'drunk' in (110)).

(110)   *mèeki'n   u   tàal   le   káal-a'n   máak-o'*
         zigzag   SBJ.3.SG   come   DEF   drunk-RSLTV person-D2
         'in a zigzag way the drunk man is coming' (EMB_0116)

Resultative *-a'n* also combines with transitive verbs (111). Like the passive verb it can add an actor phrase by means of *tumen* 'by, because of'.

(111)   *le   in   w-íits'in-o',*
         DEF   POSS.1.SG   0-younger.sibling-D2
         t-u   síih-ah   le   much'pàax
         PFV-SBJ.3   give.as.present-CMPL   DEF   unite:musician
         póol-a'n   ti'   che'
         trim-RSLTV   LOC   tree
         síih-a'n   tèen   tumen   in   na'-o'
         give.as.present-RSLTV   me   by   POSS.1.PL   mother-D2
         'my brother gave away the group of musicians trimmed in wood, given to me as a present by my mother' (ACC_0439)

Perfects in *-mah* combine exclusively with transitive stems. The two-place structure is preserved after derivation. Similar to resultatives, perfects are generally excluded from occurring in prenominal position. The perfect form of the transitive verb resembles relational nouns in structure, as both occur with both a subject/possessor clitic and an absolutive suffix (zero for the third person

---

[18] Bohnemeyer (1998[T], 2002) only has evidence for resultative forms of active intransitives from elicitation.

singular in (112)) and both are incompatible with AM markers or auxiliaries
(cf. 4.1.8). The A argument may be understood to be the possessor of the U argument with respect to the situation designated by the base verb. In typical
translations given by consultants, this is rendered as 'un tercio de leña tiene
encargado' (112a) or 'tengo visto esa casa' (112b).

> (112) a. *le   máak-o',   hun kuch   si'*
>   DEF   person-D2 one   load   firewood
>   *u   k'óoch-mah   t-u   ho'l*
>   SBJ.3   carry.on.shoulder-PART.PF   LOC-POSS.3   head
>   'that person, one load of firewood he is carrying on his head'
>   (RMC_0748)
>
> b. *in   w-il-mah   le   nah k-a   w-a'l-ik-o'*
>   SBJ.1.SG 0-see-PART.PF DEF   house IMPF-SBJ.2 0-say-INCMPL-D2
>   'I have seen the house that you are talking about' (ACC_0454)

Perfects in *-mah* and resultatives in *-a'n* designate the post-state of the situation encoded by the verb stem (cf. Bohnemeyer 1998[T]:271). This implies that
the situation designated by the verb stem has taken place before the state sets
in. If the base verb belongs to one of the state change classes (cf. sect. 4.1.8.2),
the implication is that the participant in question has achieved the target state.
A nuance of this reading is the experiential post-state reading, which implies
that the main participant is in the state of having had the experience of the situation designated by the verb stem (112b).

4.1.7 *Aspectual and modal markers and auxiliaries*

Yucatec Maya has a set of aspectual and modal markers and auxiliaries which
precede the verbal core (cf. sect. 4.1.3). In principle, all of them may occur
with verbs of all predicate classes, i.e., transitive verbs and the four classes of
intransitive verbs, active, inactive, inchoative and positional. The aspect/mood
markers and auxiliaries trigger status inflection on the verb in the way given in
Table 8. AM markers and auxiliaries can be identified by a number of critera
including the following two: they do not inflect for status and they exclusively
combine with verbal cores as identified in Figure 6 (cf. Bohnemeyer 1998[T],
sect. 4.2.1.4). Aspectual and modal predicates can be distinguished according
to their meaning. These distinctions are largely inferrable from the labels given
in Table 8.

As already explained in sect. 4.1.3, the items in the list can be further distinguished by their morphological status of being bound vs. unbound. Some of
the frequent A/M auxiliaries do also have (more grammaticalized, cf. Lehmann
1993[G]) portmanteau forms 'incorporating' the subject clitic (*táan in* 'PROG
SBJ.1.SG' > *tíin* 'PROG:SBJ.1.SG', *táan u* 'PROG SBJ.3' > *túun* 'PROG:SBJ.3') or

amalgamating with it (*ts'o'k in* 'TERM SBJ.1.SG' > *ts'in* 'TERM:SBJ.1.SG', *ts'o'k u* 'TERM SBJ.3' > *ts'u* 'TERM:SBJ.3').

label	marker/auxiliary	status triggered
perfective	*t-/h-*[19]	completive
imperfective	*k-*	incompletive
progressive	*t(áan)*	
terminative	*ts'(o'k)*	
necessitive	*k'abéet*	
	k'a'náan	
desiderative	*tàak*	
predictive	*bíin*	subjunctive
prospective	*muka'h*[20]	tr.verb: subjunctive
		intr. verb: incompletive

Table 8. Status assignment

The aspectual and modal meanings rendered by the AM markers and auxiliaries will be introduced once they are needed in the discussion of the experiential predicates in chs 5 - 7. According to Bohnemeyer (1998[T], 2002), none of the AM markers convey temporal meanings of event order and location in time. Instead, these are inferred from aspectual and modal meanings by pragmatic implicatures with respect to context situations and world knowledge.

Regarding the aspectual interpretation of a clause in discourse, it is assumed that the aspectual character of YM verbs may be neutralized or overridden by status inflection and aspectual marking. This can be deduced from the observation that all verbs are largely compatible with all status and aspect markers and auxiliaries. This must be kept in mind for the analysis of experiential predicates which change from the stative to the verbal class (cf. sect. 5.3.2.1.1).

4.1.8 *Word classes in predicate function*
4.1.8.1 *The distinction between stative predicates and verbs*
Since the system of word classes that can appear in predicate function is crucial for the analysis of experiential constructions in YM, an overview of its organization will be presented and characteristics of each class will be discussed in opposition to other (sub)classes. The subdivision of predicate classes given in Table 9 will be taken as a starting point. It follows Bohnemeyer (1998[T], 2002), which is itself based on Lehmann (1993[P]) and Lucy (1994).

---

[19] The perfective allomorphs *t-/h-* occur depending on whether the combination is with a transitive or intransitive verb, respectively.

[20] Allomorphs are *mika'h* and *bika'h*.

stative predicates			verbs				
stative predi-cates proper	noun	adjective	intransitive				transitive
			active	inactive	inchoative	positional	

Table 9. Predicate classes (Bohnemeyer 1998[T]:231/2001:155)

As has already become apparent in the above treatment of verbal and nominal clauses and categories, YM distinguishes sharply between stative and verbal predicates not only by syntactic properties but also morphologically. Stative predicates are further subdivided into nouns, adjectives and stative predicates proper. Nouns function as heads of noun phrases without further ado, while adjectives can be used attributively as dependants of noun phrases without further marking of the NP head as would be necessary if a noun functions as modifier of another noun (cf. Bohnemeyer 2002, sect. 5.1.1, Lehmann 1998, sect. 2.2.2 and 3.2).

At the center of the following discussion are members of a class labled 'stative predicates proper' in Table 9. In contrast to nouns and adjectives, this group of items can neither be the head of noun phrases nor can its members be used as attributes within a noun phrase.[21] It is largely comprised of items functioning as propositional predicates (e.g., aspect/mood auxiliaries, other modals, evaluative adjectives), the transitive verboids and all derived statives (cf. sect. 4.1.6). The auxiliaries are further subdivided into aspectual and modal auxiliaries since the latter are of special interest due to their relation to the domain of experience (cf. sect. 5.2.2.1.1).[22]

In YM, adjectives modifying a noun may precede the noun or they may follow it.[23] There are (probably very few) adjectives that occur exclusively in prenominal position (e.g., *chàan* 'little'), and a number of adjectives that ex-

---

[21] This holds true with the exception of certain gerundive forms of *-bil*, since cooking terminology is full of gerundive forms modifying a noun as in *chakbil bu'l/he'/kàax* etc. (boil:GER bean/egg/chicken etc.) 'boiled beans/eggs/chicken etc.'. These may however be judged as cases of lexicalization similar to lexicalized resultatives (110). Lexicalized resultatives show the characteristic behavior of adjectives and the same derivational potential as adjectives. This point has to be investigated in more detail in the future.

[22] The bound aspect markers (*k-* 'IMPF', *t-/h-* 'PRF' , *ts'-* 'TERM') are left out of this discussion since they differ from the unbound aspect/mood auxiliaries in that they do not constitute the main predicate of the clause (cf. sect. 4.1.3).

[23] Bohnemeyer (1998[T]:232) identifies the prenominal occurrence of adjectives with attributive function and their postnominal occurrence with predicative function. In the latter case, the adjective is analyzed as representing a stative relative clause. Bohnemeyer further states that "actual attributive (non-predicative) use of adjectives is quite rare." I did not test this hypothesis systematically, but in sporadic tests many adjectives were possible in prenominal position. Cf. sect. 5.2.1.1 for a discussion of experiential adjectives.

clusively follows their head noun (e.g., *sùuk* 'tame', *àal* 'heavy', etc.),[24] but most adjectives can occur in prenominal or in postnominal position. Adjectives may also function as predicates, apart from those occurring only in prenominal position and having exclusively attributive function. It is in this predicative use that adjectives are discussed in the reminder of this section.

In the following, the distributional properties of the abovementioned stative predicates will be discussed with respect to other stative and verbal predicates. As the main aim of this section is to lay a foundation for the division and treatment of the experiential constructions in ch. 5, those items especially relevant to the domain of experience will be in focus, i.e., transitive verboids, stative derivations in *-a'n*, *-mah*, and modal auxiliaries. Further discussion of explicitly experiential classes follows in ch. 5 and ch. 6. Other word classes like numerals, interrogative pro-forms, etc., which may also function as stative predicates, will not be treated here since there is no special relation to the domain of experience.

As has already been said, the main categorical division of word classes in predicate function is between stative predicates and verbs. These are clearly distinguishable by two characteristics shown in the first column of Table 10 (representing morphological and morphosyntactic distribution) and in Table 11 (showing syntactic evidence for the subclassification of predicate types). The first column of Table 10 indicates that verbs, and never stative predicates, are obligatorily marked for status as given in Table 3.

	status marking	participant properties
aspect auxiliaries		impers./(pers.)
modal auxiliaries		impersonal
nouns	no	
adjectives		
gerundive (*-bil*)		
resultatives (*-a'n*)		all persons
tr. verboids		
perf. part. (*-mah*)		
yàan	*-il/-ik/-ak*	
tr. verbs	full status	
intr. verbs	paradigm	

Table 10. Morphosyntactic properties of stative predicates vs. verbs

Exclusively transitive and intransitive verbs are marked for the full range of status categories, while the members of the stative predicates do not generally

---

[24] In order to occur in prenominal position these adjectives have to be reduplicated, cf. sect. 5.2.1.1 for a similar behavior of experiential adjectives.

show status inflection. Only the existential predicate *yàan* (113) may be marked with the extrafocal suffix *-il/-ik* (cf. Table 4) in certain cleft construction, e.g., in manner focus constructions. Furthermore, *yàan* may take the subjunctive suffix *-ak* (200d).

(113)   *Bix   yàan-ik   a   tsikbenil?*
        how   EXIST-EF   POSS.2   honour:ADJR:ABSTR
        'How is your Honor?'

The extrafocal suffix cannot, however, be added to adjectives, transitive verboids (114) or to the other stative subclasses mentioned in Table 10. The grammatical behavior of the transitive verboids is discussed in detail with special reference to the syntactic status of experiencers in ch. 6.

(114)   *Wáah   bèey   u   k'áat   yùum   ahaw* ...
        if   thus   SBJ.3   wish   lord   chief
        'If it is the chief's will, (…)' (HK'AN_565.1)

Furthermore, Table 10 shows in its second column that the aspectual and modal auxiliaries differ from the rest of the predicates investigated by being construed impersonally (the only exception being the prospective auxiliary *muka'h* which takes an absolutive suffix for a personal main participant (357)). Participant association is not specifically indicated in Table 10. Among the stative predicates (as, naturally, among the class of verbs) there are monovalent as well as bivalent items. The bivalent stative predicates include: Items with a further oblique complement; the closed class of transitive verboids (e.g., *p'èek* 'hate', *ohel* 'know', etc.), which is discussed in detail in sect. 5.2.2.2.1; perfect participles (cf. sect. 4.1.6); and possessed nouns in predication. Perfect participles retain the relational structure of their base transitive verbs, which may be monotransitive or ditransitive. Just like adjectives, resultatives and gerundives, intransitive verbs are either monovalent or bivalent and take a further oblique complement. S is in general the only (main) argument of the gerundive. Gerundives and resultatives may, depending on the valency of the base verb, preserve an oblique argument (cf. Bohnemeyer 2002:210, E178 *bis-bil ti' a kumpàale* (go:CAUS-GERV LOC POSS.2 compadre) 'to be taken to your compadre' may be analyzed as a case in point). Concerning the parameters discussed, gerundives and resultatives do not differ from predicatively used adjectives.[25]

---

[25] Another common trait of resultatives and gerundives is that they may add the actor of a potential basic transitive verb in a prepositional phrase added by means of *tumen* 'by' (cf., e.g., (111) and (133e)).

As has already been mentioned above, verbs and not stative predicates can combine with the class of modal and aspectual markers and auxiliaries (cf. first column in Table 11). Since there are contexts such as, for example, a subordinative *káa*-clause (cf. sect. 4.2 on subordination), where verbs appear without being accompanied by one member of this class, but a verb never occurs without being marked for status, this criterion can be taken as the most important and definitive one for membership in the class of verbs.

A further criterion which matches nearly fully with that of the combinability with aspect/mood markers and auxiliaries is given in the second column in Table 11, namely, the ability to be the main predicate in an embedded complement clause, which is possible for verbs but impossible for all subtypes of stative predicates with the exception of the gerundive form (cf. (133.e)).[26] This is a peculiarity of gerunds which distinguishes them from all other stative predicates.

	combines with AM marker	main pred. in emb. compl. clause
aspect auxiliaries	no	no
modal auxiliaries		
nouns		
adjectives		
resultatives (*-a'n*)		
tr. verboids		
perf. part. (*-mah*)		
yàan		
gerundive (*-bil*)		yes
tr. verbs	yes	
intr. verbs		

Table 11. Syntactic properties of stative predicates vs. verbs

Finally, the derivational properties of some stative predicates will be looked at in order to obtain additional evidence for their subclassification (cf. Table 12). Inchoative derivation in *-tal* is accessible not only to adjectives, but also to most underived statives such as nouns, the existential predicate *yàan* and even to some aspectual and modal auxiliaries, namely, *k'abéet/k'a'náan* 'necessary' and *tàak* 'be anxious, want'. This latter characteristic is another point toward the morphosyntactic heterogeneity of the class called AM markers in Bohnemeyer (1998[T], 2002, cf. Table 8 in sect. 4.1.7), which only behaves uniformly from a syntactic point of view. Morphological (bound vs. unbound

---

[26] See sect. 4.2.1, especially (119) and (120) for the argumentation for why nominal predicates do not occur as embedded complement clauses.

status) and morphosyntactic heterogeneity (cf. Table 10, last column) is due to the fact that the items belonging to this grammatical class joined it at different stages in their history (cf. Lehmann 1993[G]).

<table>
<tr><td></td><td>-tal
'PROC'</td><td>-ki/unt/s
'FACT'</td><td>-t
'TRR'</td><td>-int
'USAT'</td></tr>
<tr><td>adjectives</td><td rowspan="5">yes</td><td rowspan="2">yes</td><td rowspan="9">no</td><td rowspan="2">no</td></tr>
<tr><td>modal auxiliaries</td></tr>
<tr><td>nouns[27]</td><td rowspan="9">no</td><td rowspan="3">yes</td></tr>
<tr><td>aspect auxiliaries[28]</td></tr>
<tr><td>yàan</td></tr>
<tr><td>resultatives (-a'n)</td><td rowspan="6">no</td><td rowspan="6">no</td></tr>
<tr><td>gerundive (-bil)</td></tr>
<tr><td>perf. part. (-mah)</td></tr>
<tr><td>tr. verbs</td></tr>
<tr><td>tr. verboids</td><td rowspan="2">yes</td></tr>
<tr><td>intr. verbs[29]</td></tr>
</table>

Table 12. Derivational potential of stative predicates and verbs

Derivation in *-ki/unt/s* 'FACT' groups together adjectives and the modal auxiliaries *k'abéet/k'a'náan* and *tàak*. While the derivational potential of *k'abéet/ k'a'náan* may also be due to their adjectival counterparts, *tàak* does not have such a counterpart, but combines nevertheless with both *-tal* and *-ku/int/s* in derivation. Furthermore, all members of the class of transitive verboids can be combined with *-t* 'TRR' to yield transitive verbs, a characteristic they share with intransitive verbs of the active class (cf. sect. 4.1.6). Combination with the usative marker *-int* is reserved for nouns ((115), cf. Lehmann 1998 for further details on this derivation).

(115)   *Ba'n   ken   a   k'áan-int-eh?*
         what   SR.FUT   SBJ.2   hammock-USAT-SUBJ
         'What are you going to use as a hammock (= where are you going to sleep)?' (RMC_2248)

---

[27] Nouns do not regularly combine with *-t*, but there are some exceptional cases, e.g., *k'áak'(t)* 'fire, (roast)', etc. In most other cases, putative nominal bases possess intransitive verbal equivalents of the active class which may be argued to be their bases.

[28] Only some of the unbound, less grammaticalized aspect auxiliaries, namely, *sáam* and *úuch*, may be bases of derivation by means of *-tal*.

[29] Positional roots like *chil* 'lie', *kul* 'sit' etc. never occur as free forms but only as intransitive verbs (taking the status suffixes as indicated in Table 3) or as transitive verbs with the affixes *ki/unt/s*.

Those stative predicates shown in Table 10 – Table 12, which occur neither as attributes nor as heads of noun phrases, may be termed verboids, taking into account their main function in predication. The class of verboids consists of three subclasses: the aspect and modal auxiliaries,[30] the transitive verboids, and the predicative adjectives (cf. Table 13, which is slightly revised with respect to Table 9). The existential predicate *yàan* has been shown to display verbal as well as stative traits. However, the stative traits seem to prevail as showing status inflection is the only verbal trait, and this is limited to a reduced set. Therefore *yàan* will be also classified here as a verboid. Furthermore, as has been addressed above, the gerundive in *-bil* and the resultative in *-a'n* belong to the class of predicative adjectives, while the perfect in *-mah* belongs to the class of transitive verboids.

nouns	adjectives	verboids		
		auxiliaries	pred. adjectives	trans. verboids

Table 13. Stative predicate classes in YM

4.1.8.2 *The verb classes*

Having investigated the issue of stative predicate classes, the discusssion will turn to the verbal classes given in Table 9. These are mirrored completely by the morphological classes given in Table 3, which are in turn motivated by argument and situation structure features (cf. Bohnemeyer 2001, Bohnemeyer 2002, ch. 5.1).

The active intransitive class is comprised of activities and processes, i.e. dynamic situations that involve internally-caused activities (e.g., *áalkab* 'run') as well as non-internally-caused processes (e.g., *balak'* 'roll').[31] These include active verb roots, introversives of transitive verbs (e.g., *k'àay* 'sing'), composed stems on the basis of noun incorporation (e.g., *ch'akche'* 'chop wood/trees'), and all intransitive roots borrowed from Spanish. The class of active intransitives hosts, among others, manner of motion verbs (e.g., *áalkab* 'run', *balak'* 'roll', *harax* 'slide') and emission verbs (*che'h* 'laugh', *he'síin* 'sneeze', *òok'ol* 'cry', etc.).

The inactive, inchoative, and positional intransitive subclasses are comprised of verbs that lexicalize different kinds of state changes. Members of the inchoative intransitive class as well as those of the inactive intransitive class lexicalize either 'gradual' state changes with no discrete end state (e.g., *ka'n* 'get tired', *káaltal* 'get intoxicated/drunk', *wi'htal* 'get hungry'), 'incremental'

---

[30] Recall that the bound aspect markers are strongly grammaticalized and, in contrast to the unbound auxiliaries, do not function as the main predicate of a clause (cf. sect. 4.1.3).

[31] The distinction between 'internally caused' vs. 'non-internally caused' activities is used in Bohnemeyer (2004) based on Levin and Rappaport-Hovav (1995).

state changes with a discrete end state (e.g., *báan* 'drizzle', *wéek* 'drip, spill') or 'absolute' state changes (e.g., *káah* 'begin', *kim* 'die'). Inactive verb roots as well as deagentive and spontaneous derivations of transitive verbs belong to the class of inactive intransitive verbs. Semantic groups such as verbs of creation and destruction (e.g., *kim* 'die', *síih* 'be born', *la'b* 'deteriorate', etc.), change of location (*em* 'descend', *hóok'* 'exit', *máan* 'pass', etc.), and phase verbs (*chúun, k'áah* both 'start\DEAG', *ch'éen, xúul* 'stop\DEAG', *ho'p'* 'begin', etc.) also belong here. Inchoative intransitives are exclusively derived from stative roots, which have been described before (e.g., *áak'abtal* 'night:PROC', *bòoxtal* 'black:PROC', etc.). Positional intransitives are all based on positional roots (e.g., *chil* 'lie', *kul* 'sit', etc.) which may be considered ambi-categorical since they regularly produce transitive (on *-kunt/s/-kint/s*) as well as intransitive verb stems.

The class of transitive verbs contains basic transitive stems, extraversives which are mainly derived from active intransitives, causatives derived from inactive intransitives, and transitive derivations from statives and positional roots. These include verbs representing the basic meaning of caused state change with respect to physical objects (e.g., *xot* 'cut', *kach* 'break', *kins* 'die: CAUS', etc.), caused motion (e.g., *bis* 'go:CAUS', *tàas* 'come:CAUS', *ts'a'* 'put', etc.), contact verbs (*yet'* 'massage' etc.), exchange of possession (*síih* 'give as a present', *òokolt* 'steal', etc.), and verbs of perception and cognition (*il* 'see', *na't* 'understand', *u'y* 'hear, feel, sense', etc.).

A distinction between transitive and intransitive verbs according to their derivational potential has already been shown in sect. 4.1.6: only transitive verbs can concatenate with *-bil* (gerundive) and *-mah* (perfect participle). The resultative in *-a'n* is most productively formed from the intransitve classes denoting state changes, i.e., inactives, inchoatives and positionals.[32] Transitive verbs also generate a resultative with *-a'n* (cf. Table 3) while intransitive verbs of the active class seem to be unnatural in the resultative form.

There seems to be a prototypical correlation that states are rendered by stative predicates and dynamic situations by verbs. This is in line with the fact that verbs co-occur with aspect/mood marking while stative predicates are excluded from being modified by such marking. Given, however, that there is a considerable derivational apparatus (cf. sect. 4.1.6) for turning stative predicates into verbs and vice versa, the question arises if and in how far aspectual character properties are changed by these operations. This issue is taken up again with respect to experiential lexemes in ch. 5.

---

[32] Positional stems stativize also in *-Vkbal*.

4.2 *Complex constructions*

Since many experiential predicates may take propositional stimuli that appear as subordinate cores or clauses, some basic structures of embedding and subordination under lexical predicates will be introduced here. This introduction is meant to sketch out the structural basics for understanding ch. 7, where experiential predicates are discussed in their complement taking function. The first subsection of the current chapter will introduce different types of subordination, namely, embedding of dependent verbal cores and subordination of verbal and nominal clauses (sect. 4.2.1). The subsequent section deals with predicate marking in these structures (sect. 4.2.2).

4.2.1 *Subordination and embedding*

First, syndetic and asyndetic subordination must be distinguished. In the three examples given in (116), the subordinate clause (indicated by square brackets in the morpheme glosses) functions as the direct object of the transitive verb *tuk(u)l* 'think' and the transitive verboid *k'áat* 'want, wish' despite of the structural differences. In (116a), the subordinate clause is introduced by the subordinative conjunction *káa*, while in (116b) and (116c) the juncture is asyndetic, i.e., without any segmental marker of subordination.

(116) a. *In   k'áat káa k'áax-ak   ha'.*
　　　　SBJ.1.SG wish [that rain-SUBJ   water]
　　　　'I wish that it rains.' (RMC)

　　　b. *Tiin   tukl-ik-e'   yan   u*
　　　　PROG:SBJ.1.SG think-INCMPL-CNTR [DEB   SBJ.3
　　　　k'áax-al   ha'.
　　　　rain-INCMPL   water]
　　　　'I am thinking that it will rain.' (ACC, NMP, EMB)

　　　c. *Tiin   tukl-ik   u   k'áax-al   ha'.*
　　　　PROG:SBJ.1.SG think-INCMPL [SBJ.3   rain-INCMPL water]
　　　　'I think/fear it is raining/going to rain.' (ACC, EMB)

(116b) and (116c) differ in the fact that the b-example displays subordination of an independent verbal clause, while the c-example exhibits subordination of a dependent verbal core. The difference is in the presence vs. absence of the AM marker. A verbal clause must have an AM marker while a verbal core is defined by not displaying an AM marker (cf. 4.1.3).[33] This distinction correlates on the syntactic level with the distinction of juxtaposition vs. embedding

---

[33] This is compared in Bohnemeyer (1998[T], ch. 4.2.1.1, 2000) with finite vs. non-finite clauses in Indo-European languages. The former convey independent time reference (116b) while the latter convey determined time reference (116c) in the sense of Noonan (1985).

the 'semantic complement clause'. In the first case, the complement clause is
not embedded in the matrix clause, a fact that can be inferred from the option
of inserting a clause-final particle (cf. sect. 4.1.4) at the end of the first clause.
The structure in (116b) is, thus, biclausal. The complement clause is analyzed
as being coreferential with the complement, in this case the direct object argument of the transitive verb in the 'matrix' clause.[34] In the second case, on the
contrary, insertion of a clause-final particle is ungrammatical (117). Here, the
dependent verbal core constitutes the direct object of the matrix clause (and is,
thus, cross-referenced with the absolutive marker, which however, is always
zero in those cases that apply here).[35]

(117)   *Tíin   tukl-ik-e'   u   k'áax-al   ha'.
        PROG:SBJ.1.SG think-INCMPL-CNTR [SBJ.3 rain-INCMPL water]
        intended: 'I think/fear it is raining/going to rain.'
        (ACC/NMP/EMB)

Following the criterion of the option of insertion of a clause-final deictic particle, subordinate clauses introduced by the subordinative conjunction *káa* are
not embedded in the matrix clause (cf. Bohnemeyer 1998[T]:171). The possibility of inserting such a particle in (116a) is illustrated in (118).

(118)   *In   k'áat -e'   káa k'áax-ak   ha'.*
        SBJ.1.SG wish-CNTR [that rain-SUBJ water]
        'I wish that it rains.'(RMC)

Note, however, that contrary to verbal clauses which depend on the matrix
predicate only semantically (cf. (116b)), *káa*-clauses depend syntactically on

---

[34] This corresponds to 'paratactic complements' in the sense of Noonan (1985, sect. 1.3.3.).
Thus, in this case, there is no syntactic subordination. This type of complement clause encom-
passes the typology of clause linking proposed in Dixon (1995) which distinguishes between
co-ordinate and non-embedded subordinate constructions on the one hand and complement
clauses on the other hand. In terms of Foley and Van Valin (1984) it may be cosubordination
(although dependence is only semantic in the above YM case, so that cosubordination may better fit with the *káa*-clause which is clearly syntactically dependent but not embedded). Cf. also
Van Valin and LaPolla (1997).

[35] In the case that the matrix predicate is a verb, e.g., with the modal verb *páahtal* 'be possible'
the complement clause in subject function gets cross-referenced by the subject clitic as in the
following example:

K-u páah-tal a k'uch-ul ich ka'-p'éel òorah xíimbal-il.

IMPF-SBJ.3 possible-PROC [SBJ.2 arrive-INCMPL in two-CL.INAN hour walk-ADVR]$_{VCo}$

'You can get there in two hours (by) walking.' (BVS_08.01.06)

the matrix clause. Table 14 summarizes the three types of subordination illustrated in (116) and their main characteristics.

Subordination of	Juncture	AM marker	Dependency status
independent verbal clause	asyndetic: juxtaposition	yes	syntactically independent
dependent verbal core	asyndetic: embedding	no	syntactically dependent
káa-clause	syndetic	no	syntactically dependent

Table 14. Types of subordination

The three types of subordination in Table 14 are independent of their grammatical function with respect to the matrix predicate. That means that all three kinds of clauses/cores may function as a complement of the matrix predicate. Furthermore, complement clauses invariably follow the matrix predicate (cf. Bohnemeyer 1998[S]:61). This is independent of the grammatical relation the complement clause has with respect to the superordinate clause.

A further fact important to the analysis of experiential predicates and constructions in ch. 5 is that only verbal cores can be embedded under higher order predicates, not nominal clauses, i.e., those clauses that have a stative predicate as their main predicate (cf. sect. 4.1.3 and Table 13). Thus, stative predicates need to be verbalized in order to be embedded in a matrix predication. In (119a) the transitive verboid *ohel* 'know' is transitivized (and thus verbalized) by means of the transitivizing suffix *-t* and in (119b) the adjective *uts* 'good' is verbalized through the inchoative suffix *-tal*.

(119) a. *He'bix señor Christian*
       like   mister Christian
       u   k'áat   u   y-ohel-t-eh ...
       SBJ.3 wish [SBJ.3 0-know-TRR-SUBJ]
       'Like Señor Christian wants to learn it, (…)' (FCP_397)
     b. *Kláaroh peroh wáah a   k'áat uts-tal-e' ...*
       true   but   if   SBJ.2 wish [good-PROC]-CNTR
       'True, but if you want to recover, (…)' (BVS_13.01.24)

Furthermore note that it is also impossible to have a nominal clause introduced by the subordinative conjunction *káa*. Nominal clauses can be subordinated either in an asyndetic way (120a) or by means of the subordinative conjunction *wáah* 'if, that' (120b). The first case is parallel to the 'semantic subordination' of full verbal clauses: the nominal clause is not embedded but juxtaposed to the matrix clause. Again this can be deduced from the fact that the clause-final particle *-e'* 'CNTR' can follow the matrix clause in (120a). The

nominal clause is analyzed as being coreferent to the U argument of the matrix
verb. After negated matrix predicates (as well as questioned and hortative matrix predicates) *wáah* may introduce the subordinated nominal clause. A clause
introduced by *wáah* is also syntactically juxtaposed to the matrix clause, as is
again visible by the presence of the clause-final particle *-e'* following the matrix clause.

>(120) a. *In   w-ohel(-e')   tèech u   tàatah-ech   Juan.*
>   SBJ.1.SG 0-know(-CNTR)   [you POSS.3 father-ABS.2.SG Juan]$_{NCl}$
>   'I know that you are Juan's father.' (ACC)
>
>   b. *Ma' u   y-ohel-e'   wáah h-p'óokinah   tsùuk.*
>   NEGSBJ.3   0-know-CNTR   [if   M-hat:USAT:NR   paunch]$_{NCl}$
>   'He did not know that it was Paunchhat.' (HK'AN_554)

4.2.2 *Predicate marking under subordination*

There are roughly three patterns of predicate marking in subordinated cores
which occur subordinated to experiential matrix predicates. These include two
types of embedded verbal cores[36] which follow the matrix clause asyndetically,
and a further type of verbal core following the subordinative conjunction *káa*.
The three construction types differ in their manner of marking the main argument of the subordinate verb as well as in their verbal status category. They are
summarized in Table 15 and will be explained in the following paragraphs.
Table 15 lists the categories according to which subordinate verbal cores vary
in its head line. These include the transitivity of the subordinate verb, the type
of verbal core, the status category marked on the verb, and different vs. same
reference of an argument in the matrix clause with the subject of the subordinate clause. The two values of this latter parameter will be referred to by DRef
(different reference) vs. SRef (same reference) henceforth. The type of verbal
core identifies the kinds of categories it is marked for. At this point a verbal
core as represented in Figure 6 must be distinguished from a semifinite verbal
core (SFVCore) which lacks person marking. Finally, the last column of Table
15 gives a summary of the main semantic features of the three construction
types.

---

[36] There are further patterns to be included in a complete list of embedded verbal cores as, e.g.,
the subjunctive core occurring independently of the verb's transitivity after some AM markers
(cf. Table 8), which has however little to do with experiential predicates. Embedded verbal cores occurring in cleft constructions will be referred to in the discussion of grammatical relations in sect. 4.3.

Construction type	Tr. of V	VCoType	Status Ct.	Reference	Semantics
incompletive-marked verbal core	tr./intr.	VCore	Incompl.	DRef, SRef	simultaneous; realis/factive/actual
'split'-marked verbal core[37]	intr.	SFVCore	Incompl.	SRef	purposive;
	tr.	VCore	Subj.		irrealis/non-factive/potential
káa-introduced verbal clause	tr./intr.	VCore	Subj.	DRef, SRef	irrealis (non-assertive)

Table 15. Some types of verbal cores under subordination

The incompletive-marked verbal core mentioned in the first line of Table 15 can be characterized by the fact that transitive and intransitive verbs are marked in the same way, i.e., both retain the subject clitic and are marked for incompletive status (recall the verbal core in Figure 6 for transitive verbs). A large number of experiential and non-experiential predicates take such an embedded verbal core as direct object or subject argument, among them perception verbs (e.g., *il* 'see' in (121a) and *u'y* 'hear' in (121b), phase verbs[38] (e.g., *káah* 'start\DEAG' in (122a) and *kah* 'start' in (122b) and evaluative predicates (e.g., *uts tin t'àan* 'I like', etc.). In (121) and (122) the subordinate core is included in square brackets in the glosses.

---

[37] There is a further 'similar' pattern which is characterized by not displaying the subject clitic with transitive as well as with intransitive verbs (i.e., displaying a semi-finite verbal core for transitives as well as intransitives). The verb is marked for incompletive status and transitive verbs retain the absolutive marker. This pattern optionally replaces the 'split' pattern in cases of object control of 'equi-deletion' in a verbal core in adjunct/adverbial function (cf. (134a/b)). Furthermore, it may occur after motion verbs (and object control verbs) in extrafocal clauses with prospective aspect/mood marking, as is noted in Bricker (1981[S]:98) and supported by some instances in my text base, e.g.,

teen kin   *bin*   *il-ik*

me   SR.IRR:SBJ.1.SG go   [see-INCMPL(ABS.3.SG)

u   *kim-s-a'l.*

[SBJ.3   die-CAUS-PASS.INCMPL]$_{Vco}$]$_{SFVCo}$

'(…) it is me who will go (and) see him being killed.' (FCP_237)

These cases are approved by my consultants, and replacement by the 'split' pattern of Table 15 is ungrammatical. Conversely, replacement of the 'split' pattern in (125b) by this pattern is judged ungrammatical as well. Thus, it is not just a variant of the 'split' pattern shown above. Since it does not seem to be notably related to experiential constructions either, it is not presented in Table 15.

[38] As can be seen in (122), YM phase verbs may be either intransitive and impersonal (122a), taking the verbal core in subject function, or they may be transitive and personal (122b), taking the verbal core in direct object function. The personal phase verbs presuppose control of the main participant with respect to the situation expressed by the embedded verb. This construction is taken up in sect. 5.1.2 as a control test for experiencer verbs.

(121) a. *le   k-u   y-il-ik*
           when   IMPF-SBJ.3   0-see-INCMPL
           u   k'uch-ul   wa'pach'   wíinik
           [SBJ.3   arrive-INCMPL   giant   man]$_{VCo}$
           'when he saw the giant arrive' (HK'AN_048.2)

      b. *káa   t-u   y-u'b-ah*
          CNJ   PFV-SBJ.3   0- feel-CMPL
          u   y-a'l-ik   le   ba'l-o': ...
          [SBJ.3   0-say-INCMPL   DEF   thing-D2]$_{VCo}$
          'and he heard the thing say this: (…)' (HLU'M_KÀAB_009.8)

(122) a. *Túun   káah-al   in   meyah/*
          PROG:SBJ.3.SG   begin\DEAG-INCMPL [SBJ.1.SG   work]$_{VCo}$/
          in   meyah-t-ik   in   kòol
          [SBJ.1.SG   work-TRR-INCMPL POSS.1.SG milpa]$_{VCo}$
          'I am starting to work/to make my milpa.' (ACC)

      b. *Tíin   kah-ik   in   meyah/*
          PROG:SBJ.1.SG   begin-INCMPL(ABS:3.SG) [SBJ.1.SG work]$_{VCo}$/
          in   meyah-t-ik   in   kòol.
          [SBJ.1.SG work-TRR-INCMPL   POSS.1.SG milpa]$_{VCo}$
          'I am starting to work/to make my milpa.' (RMC_0596/ACC)

Periphrastic causative constructions also display an incompletive-marked
verbal core as the examples in (123) show.

(123) a. *chéen t-in   bèet-ah*
           just   PFV-SBJ.1   do-CMPL
           a   máans-ik-e'x   óotsil
           [SBJ.2   pass:CAUS-INCMPL-2.PL poor]$_{VCo}$
           'I only made you suffer' (HOSEH_48.03)

      b. *t-in   mèet-ah   u   chíikpah-al*
          PFV-SBJ.1.SG do-CMPL [SBJ.3 appear:SPONT-INCMPL]$_{VCo}$
          'I made it appear' (RMC_2022)

Furthermore, the gerundial construction (124) has an incompletive-marked
verbal core in adjunct function (cf. Bricker 1981[S]:97, Bohnemeyer 1998[T]:
173). It presupposes the co-temporality of the situations referred to in the matrix clause and in the embedded clause.

(124) a. *Le   bin   káa   h   ho'p'   u   tàal*
    when QUOT CNJ PFV begin SBJ.3 come
    u   k'uch-ul   yùum ahaw t-u   kàah-al-o' ...
    [SBJ.3 arrive-INCMPL lord chief LOC-POSS.3 village-REL]$_{VCo}$-D2
    'When the chief began to come (arriving) into his village, (...)'
    (HK'AN_546.1)
   b. *u   hóok'-ol   bin*
    SBJ.3   exit-INCMPL QUOT
    u   y-áalkab-t-ik   u   kan   ti'ts-il   ka'n
    [SBJ.3 0-run-TRR-INCMPL POSS.3 four corner-REL sky]$_{VCo}$
    'it exits running to four corners of the sky' (HAPAIKAN_019.02)

In the second pattern given in Table 15, called 'split' verbal core, transitive and intransitive cores are marked differently. With intransitive cores the subject clitic cross-referencing the subject argument is 'equi-deleted' and the verb is marked for incompletive status. This is referred to as semifinite verbal core (SFVCore) in Table 15. Transitive verbs appear in verbal cores (i.e., they do not show 'equi-deletion' of the subject clitic) and the verb bears the subjunctive status category. A verbal core of the 'split' pattern occurs with some desiderative matrix predicates as their direct object argument (e.g., *k'áat* 'wish' in (119)) as well as in the motion-cum-purpose construction in adjunct function (125).[39] It is restricted to SRef contexts.

(125) a. *Káa   túun   h   bin-o'b   wen-el-i'*...
    CNJ   then PFV go-3.PL [sleep-INCMPL]$_{SFVCo}$ -LOCF
    'And they went to sleep (...)' (MUUCH_299)
   b. *K-u   tàal   in   papah u   chuk-o'n-o'*, ...
    IMPF-SBJ.3 come POSS.1.SG dad [SBJ.3 catch-ABS.1.PL]$_{VCo}$-D2
    'My dad comes to catch us, (...)' (FOTOH_10)

Note that after motion verbs an 'incompletive-marked' pattern vs. a 'split' pattern conveys the semantic distinction between simultaneity vs. purpose reading of the subordinate proposition with respect to the matrix verb (cf. Bricker 1981[S]:97ff., Bohnemeyer 1998[T]:171ff.).

The third construction type given in Table 15 is a verbal clause introduced by the subordinate conjunction *káa*. As is shown in (116a) and (126), *káa* obligatorily triggers subjunctive status on both transitive and intransitive verbs.

---

[39] Note that the prospective marker *muka'h* also takes a split pattern (cf. Table 8), a fact that can be traced back to its origin as a predicate focus construction with the motion verb *bíin* in focus position and the verb *ka'h* 'do' as main verb, i.e., *bíin* SBJ *ka'h* 'going SBJ do'. See Bohnemeyer (1998[T], sect. 6.2.2.1.3.) for an analysis of this development.

(126) a. *In   k'áat*
       SBJ.1.SG   wish

       káa   u   bis-en   Cancun   in   tàatah.
       [that   SBJ.3 take(SUBJ)-ABS.1.SG   Cancun   POSS.1.SG father]$_{VCI}$
       'I want my father to take me to Cancun.' (RMC, ACC, NMP)

   b. *In   k'áat káa   wen-ek-ech.*
       SBJ.1.SG   wish   [that   sleep-SUBJ-ABS.2.SG]$_{VCI}$
       'I want you to sleep.' (ACC, NMP)

The subordinator *káa* is always followed by a dependent verbal core, i.e., there is no 'equi-deletion' of the subject clitic in constellations of the referential identity of a controlling argument in the matrix clause with the subject of the subordinate clause, as can be seen in (127).

(127) a. *Ma'   uts   t-in   t'àan*
       NEG   good   LOC-POSS.1.SG   speech

       káa   in   w-u'y a   tsolxikin   sáansamal-i'.
       [that   SBJ.1.SG   0-feel   POSS.2   advice   every.day]$_{VCI}$-NEGF
       'I don't like to hear your advices every day.' (ACC)

   b. *Mina'n   in   w-óol   káa   xi'k-en   xíimbal.*
       NEG.EXIST POSS.1.SG 0-mind that   go:SUBJ-ABS.1.SG   stroll
       'I don't feel like going for a walk.' (RMC)

As is indicated in Table 15, DRef vs. SRef is one parameter determining construction possibilities in subordination. As has been mentioned above, the 'split' pattern is *per definitionem* restricted to SRef-contexts. The other two construction types are as such not determined by either SRef or DRef. In the previous examples, it was shown that both construction types occur with both reference types. However depending on the matrix predicate, SRef may be a necessary precondition for the incompletive-marked verbal core, e.g., as in (122b) and (124). On the other hand, some matrix predicates, as, e.g., *k'áat* 'wish' that take a 'split' pattern under SRef take a *káa*-clause under DRef.[40] With these, a *káa*-clause is judged as bad under SRef, as is shown in (128).

(128) a. *In   k'áat   in   w-u'y a   tsolxikin.*
       SBJ.1.SG   wish   [SBJ.1.SG   0-feel   POSS.2   advice]$_{VCo}$
       'I want to hear your advice.' (ACC, NMP)

---

[40] Note however that according to Bricker (1981[S]:96) *káa* is optional in subjunctive clauses, whereas my consultants judge elision of *káa* in (126) more acceptable with transitive cores than with intransitive cores, where it is definitely refused.

b.^{??}*In*   *k'áat káa   in   w-u'y a   tsolxikin.*
SBJ.1.SG wish   [that SBJ.1.SG 0-feel POSS.2 advice]_{VCl}
intended 'It is my wish that I hear your advice.' (ACC)

Furthermore, a *káa*-subordination is bound to irrealis situations. A *káa*-clause cannot substitute an incompletive-marked verbal core if the matrix predicate requires a realis reading of the subordinate situation, e.g., with perception verbs or with phasal matrix predicates.[41] Compare (129) with (121) and (130) with (122).

(129) a.*k-u   y-il-ik*
IMPF-SBJ.3 0-see-INCMPL
káa   k'uch-uk   wa'pach' wíinik
[that   arrive-SUBJ giant   man]_{VCl}
intended: 'he saw that the giant arrived' (ACC, NMP)

   b.*t-u   y-u'b-ah   káa   u   y-a'l le   ba'l-o':* ...
PFV-SBJ.3 0-feel-CMPL [that SBJ.3 0-say DEF   thing-D2]_{VCl}
intended: 'he heard that it said this: (…)' (ACC, NMP)

(130) a.*Túun   káah-al*
PROG:SBJ.3.SG begin\DEAG.INCMPL
káa   meyah-nak-en.
[that   work-SUBJ-ABS.1.SG]_{VCl}
intended: 'lit.: It is beginning that I work.' (ACC, NMP)

   b.*Tíin   kah-ik*
PROG:SBJ.1.SG   begin-INCMPL
káa   in   meyah-t   in   kòol.
[that SBJ.1.SG work-TRR   POSS.1.SG   milpa]_{VCl}
intended 'I am starting to make my milpa.' (ACC, NMP)

In cases where there is a choice between an incompletive-marked verbal core vs. a *káa*-subordination, the latter renders the realization of the subordinated situation more 'uncertain' or relates it to a condition. Compare the dialogue contexts in (131) and (132).

(131) a. *Juan: Ko'ten-e'x   way-e'   hats'uts!*
Juan   come:IMP-ABS.2.PL here-D3   very:good
'Juan: Come(pl), here it's nice!'

----

[41] The same holds true as well for other cognitive and emotional matrix predicates such as *tu-kul* etc.; cf. ch. 5 for a detailed description.

b. *Pedro: Ma', màas   ma'lòob*
Pedro: NEG   more   good
k   *ku-tal   y-áanal   le   che'-o'.*
[SBJ.1.PL sit-PROC   0-under   DEF   tree-D2]$_{VC_0}$
'Pedro: No, we better sit down under that tree.' (ACC)

(132)   *In   w-a'l-ik-e'   yan   u   tàal   x-tóos   ha',*
SBJ.1.SG 0-say-INCMPL-CNTR DEB SBJ.3 come   F-drizzle water
màas ma'lòob káa   kul-ak-o'n   y-áanal   le   che'-o'.
more good   [that   sit-SUBJ-ABS.1.PL 0-under   DEF   tree-D2]$_{VCI}$
'I think, it is going to drizzle, it would be better if we sat down under that tree.' (ACC)

Note that the YM *káa*-clause is in no way equivalent to the Engl. *that*-clause
or the German *dass*-clause. The latter convey independent time reference (ITR)
in the sense of Noonan (1985) and correspond to a YM independent "subordinate" clause ('paratactic complement clause' in the sense of Noonan 1985) that
is not marked by a subordinating particle/complementizer (but retains the AM
marker) as exemplified in (116b).

4.3   *Grammatical relations*
4.3.1 *Preliminaries*
The debate of the organization of grammatical relations in YM as well as in
other Mayan languages has not yet been resolved (cf. Bohnemeyer 1998[T]:
154, Van Valin and LaPolla 1997:282ff). In this section, some typologically
valid tests will be conducted in order to discuss a possible subject and object
function for YM. This is meant to be a basis for the discussion of grammatical
properties of YM experiencers in ch. 6.

As is currently widely recognized, subject and object are not conceived of
as primitive but as multi-dimensional concepts. Van Valin and LaPolla (1997)
develops an alternative view of grammatical relations that does not operate
with the traditional notions of subject, direct object and indirect object as
primitive concepts. They propose a theory that operates exclusively with the
notions of syntactic, semantic and pragmatic pivots and controllers. These are
identified per construction.[42] A syntactic pivot presupposes a "restricted neutralization of semantic or pragmatic relations for syntactic purposes" (Van
Valin and LaPolla 1997:274). Thus, if in a given syntactic construction a privileged position (e.g., being the head of a relative clause, being 'equi-deleted' in
a subordinated clause) is only accessible for a reduced number of arguments

---

[42] A construction-specific understanding of the notion of subject is also defended in Croft
(2001:155).

encompassing their semantic or pragmatic functions, this will identify the syntactic pivot of this construction. In the same vein, a syntactic controller may be identified if certain morphosyntactic phenomena are present, like agreement of the verb or cross-reference marking that cover different semantic or pragmatic roles of arguments. The term 'neutralization' refers here to semantic or pragmatic functions that are neutralized for syntactic purposes and the term 'restrictive' points to the fact that the neutralization only applies to a reduced number of arguments. In the latter case, an unrestricted neutralization results.

Only if a language shows the same syntactic pivot over a reasonable number of constructions can this be identified as the subject of the language. For some Mayan languages (Jacaltec and Tzutujil) Van Valin and LaPolla (1997:282ff.) analyzes different variable[43] syntactic pivots in different constructions and conclude that the notion of subject in these languages is not a meaningful concept. Bohnemeyer (2004) follows this view with respect to Yucatec Maya and comes to the conclusion that one cannot reasonably speak of the traditional syntactic relations of subject (and object) in YM.

In the following the question of syntactic relations in YM will be addressed by reviewing syntactic pivothood in a number of constructions. Van Valin and LaPolla (1997) will be observed when identifying syntactic pivots. Since Keenan, (1976) many syntacticians conceive of the subject as a 'multi-factor concept' and distinguish between coding and behavioral properties to identify subjecthood in a language. Coding properties are morphological indicators like uniform case marking and subject-verb agreement, and word order. Behavioral properties manifest themselves in valency changing operations or coreferential constructions such as subject 'equi-deletion' in subordinated clauses, or in the possibility of raising to subject or object.

In the following discussion the commonly used labels S (for the single argument of intransitive verbs and stative predicates), A (for the actor of a transitive verb), U (for the undergoer of a transitive verb) and G (for the goal of a transitive or intransitive verb or a stative predicate) will be taken as polysemous semantic cluster categories. The possessor will be abbreviated as POSS.

4.3.2 *Coding properties*

As was introduced in sect. 4.1.3, YM does not display case marking but rather a cross-reference system indicating A and U of a transitive verb by clitic and suffixal person markers on the verb. The S of an intransitive verb is either cross-referenced like the A (in incompletive status) or like the U (in completive and subjunctive status). Thus, coding properties in YM are not decisive in

---

[43] A syntactic pivot is variable if either the actor or the undergoer of a transitive verb may take this function, i.e., if the language has a passive or antipassive operation. If it does not, it may have an invariable syntactic pivot (cf. Van Valin and LaPolla 1997:281).

identifying a syntactic pivot since displays YM morphologically ergative-absolutive as well as accusative features. Nor is there a difference in markedness between the subject/possessor paradigm and the absolutive paradigm, which would argue for either an ergative/absolutive or a nominative/accusative system (cf. Lehmann 1990[Y], Bohnemeyer 2004). Furthermore, recall from sect. 4.1.3, that the possessor is always marked by the set A paradigm, while the only participant of a stative predicate, which is equated here with an S argument, is always cross-referenced by a set B (absolutive) marker.

Word order does not yield clear results either. Canonical word order in transitive clauses is VUA, in intransitive clauses VS(G). This interacts with the animacy of the participants in such a way that a human participant will generally be interpreted as A in a transitive clause, independent of word order (Skopeteas and Verhoeven 2005). Generally, strings of lexical noun phrases are avoided whenever possible. If the assignment of semantic roles to noun phrases in a transitive clause is ambiguous, or pragmatically unexpected/improbable, other constructions are chosen to clearly identify the semantic structure, i.e, topicalization, focus construction or passivization (Bohnemeyer 1998[T]:163 with reference to Durbin and Ojeda 1978).

4.3.3 *Behavioral (subject) properties*

In this section, pivot behavior in two main syntactic constructions will be reviewed, namely 'equi-deletion' in subordinate clauses/cores and cleft constructions. Other frequently used tests to identify subjecthood such as ellipsis under cross-clause coreference in coordinative clauses, are either not applicable in YM or they do not identify syntactic, but rather pragmatic pivots and are therefore not discussed here.

In sect. 4.2.2, it was shown that YM has one type of embedded verbal core, the semi-finite verbal core that presupposes referential identity of its 'equi-deleted' argument with a controller in the matrix clause. This phenomenon of 'equi-deletion' is generally used as a valuable test for identifying syntactic pivots. In YM, there are at least two construction types that show 'equi-deletion'. One of them is subordination under matrix predicates, e.g., the transitive verb *óot* 'agree', the transitive verboid *k'áat* 'wish', or the stative predicate *sahak* 'afraid' (133). Under referential identity with the A or S argument in the matrix clause, the intransitive S in the dependent core is 'equi-deleted' (133a) (the 'equi-deleted' cross-reference marker being indicated by Ø). This holds true independently of the subclass of intransitive verb, thus is independent of the semantic role of S (i.e., being semantically an actor or an undergoer). (133b) shows that transitive A is not 'equi-deleted'. With transitive embedded cores, the subject cross-reference marker is retained and the verb is marked for subjunctive status. Under referential identity of the S or A argument in the matrix clause and the U argument in the subordinated clause, a construction as in

(133c) with the subjunctive subordinator *káa* introducing the embedded core is chosen. A construction using the passive form of the verb in the subordinate core, as in (133d), is judged ungrammatical by most speakers, both with and without deletion of the set A cross-reference marker. Thus, derived S (in terms of *Role and Reference Grammar*, i.e., U in a passive construction) does not behave like S (i.e. there is no passive construction parallel to (133a)). Instead of (133d), a construction parallel to (133c) is chosen, i.e. a subordinate clause introduced with the subjunctive subordinator *káa* (133e). Thus, derived S ('d-S (passive)' in the notation of Van Valin and LaPolla 1997) behaves like A and P concering 'equi-deletion' in subordinate clauses/cores.

Looking at 'equi-deletion' of the main argument in the subordinate clause/core, it can be concluded that there is a restricted neutralization of S and thus, a syntactic S pivot in this construction. (133f) shows another alternative for the passive construction in (133d) where the verb of the subordinate core is changed into a gerundive form (which is itself based on the passive, cf. sect. 4.1.6). This gerundive form normally takes the cross-reference marker of the absolutive suffixes, which is 'equi-deleted' in (133f). Thus, the d-S(gerundive) argument, has to be grouped with the S argument with relation to a restricted neutralization. 'Equi-deletion' in subordinated clauses/cores thus identifies a [S_A, S_U, d-S(gerundive)] pivot, whereby S_A means 'actor-like S' and S_U means 'undergoer-like S'.

(133) a. *k-in   w-óot-ik/   in   k'áat/ sahak-en*
    IMPF-SBJ.1.SG 0-agree-INCMPL/ SBJ.1.SG wish/ afraid-ABS.1.SG
    Ø   bin Cancun/ Ø   nohoch-tal/
    [SBJ.1.SG go Cancun]$_{SFVCo}$/ [SBJ.1.SG big-PROC]$_{SFVCo}$/
    Ø   meyah /Ø   ku-tal/
    [SBJ.1.SG work]$_{SFVCo}$ /[SBJ.1.SG sit-PROC]$_{SFVCo}$/
    Ø   na'k-al   teh   che'-o'.
    [SBJ.1.SG climb-INCMPL DEF:LOC tree-D2]$_{SFVCo}$
    'I agree/ want/ am afraid to go to Cancun/ to be big/ to work/ to sit down/ to climb on the tree' (ACC, RMC, EMB, FEE, SBM)

  b. *k-in   w-óot-ik/   in   k'áat/ sahak-en*
    IMPF-SBJ.1.SG 0-agree-INCMPL/ SBJ.1.SG wish/ afraid-ABS.1.SG
    in   kan   màaya'
    [SBJ.1.SG learn(SUBJ) Maya]$_{VCo}$
    'I agree/ want/ am afraid to learn Maya'
    (completed after BVS_08.01.18)

c. *k-in   w-óot-ik/   in   k'áat/ sahak-en*
IMPF-SBJ.1.SG 0-agree-INCMPL/ SBJ.1.SG   wish/   afraid-ABS.1.SG
káa u   bis-en   Cancun in   tàatah.
[that SBJ.3 carry(SUBJ)-ABS.1.SG Cancun POSS.1.SG   father]$_{VCt}$
'I agree/ want/ am afraid that my father brings me to Cancun'
(EMB, RMC, ACC)

d. *k-in   w-óot-ik/   in   k'áat/ sahak-en*
IMPF-SBJ.1.SG 0-agree-INCMPL/ SBJ.1.SG wish/   afraid-ABS.1.SG
**Ø/*l'in bis-a'l   Cancun tumen in   tàatah.*
[SBJ.1.SG carry-PASS.INCMPL Cancun by   POSS.1.SG father]$_{VCo}$
'I agree/ want/ am afraid to be taken to Cancun by my father'
(EMB, ACC, RMC)

e. *k-in   w-óot-ik/   in   k'áat/ sahak-en*
IMPF-SBJ.1.SG 0-agree-INCMPL/ SBJ.1.SG   wish/   afraid-ABS.1.SG
káa   bis-a'k-en   Cancun
[that   carry-PASS.SUBJ-ABS.1.SG   Cancun
tumen   in   tàatah.
by   POSS.1.SG   father]$_{VCt}$
'I agree/want/am afraid that I am taken to Cancun by my father.'
(EMB, RMC, ACC)

f. *k-in   w-óot-ik/   in   k'áat/ sahak-en*
IMPF-SBJ.1.SG 0-agree-INCMPL/ SBJ.1.SG wish/   afraid-ABS.1.SG
bis-bil-Ø   Cancun tumen in   tàatah
[carry-GERV-ABS.1.SG Cancun   by   POSS.1.SG father]$_{VCo}$
'I agree/want/am afraid to be taken to Cancun by my father'
(EMB, ACC, RMC)

A further construction, however, seems to give evidence for an [S, A, d-S(gerundive)] pivot: this is a construction with a U-controlled 'equi-deleted' argument in the subordinate core. (134) shows that both S (as in the a-version) and A[44] (as in the b-version) may be 'equi-deleted' in the subordinate core under referential identity with the U argument of the matrix clause. It must, however, be underlined that 'equi-deletion' of A with a transitive verb in the subordinate core is not obligatory. A construction similar to that of (133b) (as in (134c)) is more usual and sometimes preferred to (134b). Furthermore, if the U of the matrix clause is referentially identical with the U of the subordinate clause the passive construction is again judged ungrammatical or questionable (134d). Instead, either a gerundive construction is chosen (134e) or the U may

---

[44] Cf. Bricker (1981[S]:99) for a similar example.

be encoded as a regular absolutive argument in a *káa*-clause (134f) or as a derived S in a passive construction (134g).

(134) a. *Pedro-e'   k-u   túucht-ik   Maria*
Pedro-TOP IMPF-SBJ.3 send-INCMPL Maria
Ø   màanal.
[SBJ.3 buy\INTRV]_{SFVCo}
'Pedro sends Maria to buy.' (ACC, SMB, RMC)

b. *Pedro-e'   k-u   túucht-ik   Maria*
Pedro-TOP IMPF-SBJ.3 send-INCMPL Maria
Ø   man-ik   hun-p'éel   báaxal.
[SBJ.3 buy-INCMPL   one-CL.INAN   toy]_{SFVCo}
'Pedro sends Maria to buy a toy.' (EMB, ACC, RMC)

c. *Pedro-e'   k-u   túucht-ik   María*
Pedro-TOP IMPF-SBJ.3 send-INCMPL Maria
u   man   hun-p'éel   báaxal.
[SBJ.3 buy(SUBJ)one-CL.INAN toy]_{VCo}
'Pedro sends Maria to buy a toy.' (EMB, ACC)

d. *Pedro-e'   t-u   túucht-ah   Maria*
Pedro-TOP PFV-SBJ.3   send-CMPL   Maria
**Ø/*/ʔu y-isíint-a'l*
[SBJ.3   0- bathe:USAT-PASS.INCMPL
mèen u   màamah.
by   POSS.3 mother]_{VCo}
'Pedro sends Maria to be bathed by her mother.' (ACC, RMC)

e. *Pedro-e'   t-u   túucht-ah   Maria*
Pedro-TOP PFV-SBJ.3   send-CMPL   Maria
isíint-bil-Ø   mèen u   màamah.
[bathe:USAT-GERV-ABS.3.SG by   POSS.3 mother]_{VCo}
'Pedro sends Maria to be bathed by her mother.' (ACC, RMC)

f. *Pedro-e'   t-u   túucht-ah   Maria*
Pedro-TOP PFV-SBJ.3   send-CMPL   Maria
káa u   y-isíint   u   màamah.
[that SBJ.3 0- bathe:USAT(SUBJ) POSS.3 mother]_{VCl}
'Pedro sends Maria so that her mother bathes her.' (ACC)

g. *Pedro-e' t-u   túucht-ah   Maria*
Pedro-TOP PFV-SBJ.3 send-CMPL   Maria
káa isíint-a'k   mèen u   màamah.
[that bathe:USAT-SUBJ.PASS by   POSS.3   mother]_{VCl}
'Pedro sends Maria so that she is bathed by her mother.' (ACC, RMC)

Mayan languages often display a special kind of cleft construction. These are often taken to test the behavior of arguments with respect to grammatical relations (cf. Van Valin and LaPolla 1997:283ff.). Yucatec Maya construes argument focus constructions and content questions as clefts (cf. Bricker 1979, Bohnemeyer 1998[T], ch. 4.2.1.5). The focused element, i.e., the focused argument and the interrogative pronoun, behaves as the main predicate while the background information is given in an 'extrafocal' clause, displaying the form of a relative clause.[45] (135) illustrates content questions in the imperfective aspect. If, as in (135a), the actor of a transitive verb is the target of the question, then the subject clitic is 'equi-deleted' after elision of the imperfective aspect marker. (135b-d), on the contrary, retain canonical cross-reference marking as well as aspect marking.[46] This applies to the U argument of a transitive verb (135b), the S argument of an intransitive verb (135c) and the d-S argument of a passive verb (135d).

(135) a. *Máax il-ik-en?*
who   see-INCMPL-ABS.1.SG
'Who sees me?'

b. *Máax k-a   w-il-ik?*
who   IMPF-SBJ.2   0-see-INCMPL
'Whom do you see?'

c. *Máax k-u   bin k'íiwik?*
who   IMPF-SBJ.3   go   market
'Who goes to the market?'

---

[45] An alternative analysis of such constructions is given in Lehmann (1998, sect. 3.2.1.1.1.6), where they are not analyzed as clefts. Instead, a given NP may be in the canonical focus position, which is the position immediately following the left sentence boundary. If it then directly precedes a pronominal (i.e., subject) clitic with which it is coreferential it will replace the latter. Adjacency of focused NP and subject clitic with transitive verbs results from a previous drop of perfective and imperfective markers.

[46] The expression 'canonical' refers to cross-reference marking and aspectual marking in the corresponding non-focused clauses.

d. *Máax k-u   hats'-a'l?*
who   IMPF-SBJ.3   beat-PASS.INCMPL
'Who is beaten?' (ACC)

Such a coding singles out A against S, U and d-S(passive). Since A is the only argument that is 'equi-deleted', a restriction without neutralization in terms of Van Valin and LaPolla (1997, sect. 6.2.1) can be identified. Furthermore note that focusing a G argument (136a) and adjuncts such as a comitative (136b) results in the same construction type as shown for S, U, and d-S(passive). This fact also supports the analysis that the A argument is the pivot in the discussed focus constructions. The results concerning argument marking with the perfective aspect are parallel to those shown for the imperfective aspect (cf. Bricker 1979:133).

(136) a. *Máax ti'   k-u   ts'a'-ik   wàah?*
who   LOC IMPF-SBJ.3 put-INCMPL   tortilla
'To whom does he give tortilla?' (NMP)

b. *Máax yéetel k-u   bin k'íiwik?*
who   with   IMPF-SBJ.3 go   market
'With whom does he go to the market?' (NMP)

Under terminative (and progressive) aspect, argument marking differs from what was shown before. These aspect markers are not deleted in focus constructions, and neither is the A-cross-reference marker. Such constructions display an unrestricted neutralization concerning their focus position. Thus, S, A, P, etc. can be focused in content questions as is shown in (137).[47]

(137) a. *Máax ts'o'k   u   bin k'íiwik?*
who   TERM   SBJ.3   go   market
'Who has gone to the market?

b. *Máax ts'o'k   u   y-il-ik-ech?*
who   TERM   SBJ.3   0-see-INCMPL-ABS.2.SG
'Who has seen you?'

c. *Máax ts'o'k   a   w-il-ik?*
who   TERM   SBJ.2 0-see-INCMPL
'Whom did you see?'

---

[47] Since only a third person argument can be the target of a content question, this is always interpreted as such in a constellation with another non-third-person argument, regardless of their argument function. For argument focus constructions and relative constructions there are comparable disambiguating devices that account for the fact that there is an unrestricted neutralization of the main arguments within this type of construction.

If, however, both arguments of a transitive verb are third person, an ambiguity may arise as to the target of the question. The primary contextless interpretation in a constellation as in (138a), i.e., if a full NP is following the verbal complex, it seems to be that the latter is interpreted as having U function and thus, the A argument is the target of the question.[48] Note, however, that an interpretation with the U argument as the target of the question is not rejected by my consultants. In this latter case, they propose/prefer a passive construction as in (138b). This behavior in YM is opposed to that described by Van Valin and LaPolla (1997:282ff.) for Tzutujil in similar focus constructions. Tzutujil has an ergative variable pivot, using an antipassive construction to focus on the actor. Yucatec Maya, on the contrary, shows a (preferred) [S, A, d-S(passive)] pivot in this construction.[49]

(138) a. *Máax   ts'o'k   u   y-il-ik   hwàan?*
      who   TERM   SBJ.3   0-see-INCMPL   John
      'Who has seen John?' (/ 'Whom has John seen?')

     b. *Máax   ts'o'k   u   y-il-a'l   tumèen   hwàan?*
      who   TERM   SBJ.3   0-see-PASS.INCMPL   by   John
      'Who has been seen by John? (Bricker 1979:121)

Table 16 summarizes the analysis of syntactic pivots and gives a rather heterogeneous picture. Coding alternatives in some cases make the overall picture even more unclear. Nevertheless, some of the constructions investigated show an [S A] syntactic pivot. This is U-controlled 'equi-deletion' of A, S, and d-S(gerundive) in a subordinate clause/core (Construction A2 in Table 16). However, this construction has an alternative construction, which does not show a restricted neutralization of S and A arguments.

A further construction displays a preferred [S, A, d-S(passive)] syntactic pivot, namely, construction B3 in Table 16, which occurs when the extrafocal clause bears the progressive or terminative aspect markers.[50] Note that such a pivot hinges on A/U ambiguity, while in cases where either of those arguments is non-third person there is an unrestricted neutralization with respect to the fo-

---

[48] If there is no full NP following the verbal complex as in *máax ts'o'k u yilik*, the primary contextless interpretation seems to be 'who is it that he has seen', i.e., with U-focus, although as in the above case, an A-focus interpretation is also possible. Note however that in this case my consultants also prefer/propose a passive construction for disambiguation.

[49] According to Bricker (1979), a similar behavior can also be identified with respect to argument focus and relative constructions with A and U in third person. Disambiguation of A and U function is resolved by passive formation.

[50] It can be assumed that constructions with other unbound AM markers that trigger incompletive status on the verb (cf. Table 8) work in the same way.

cused argument (cf. construction B2 in Table 16). The evidence so far points to accusative syntax with respect to these constructions.

Construction	Construction types	
A. Subordinate clauses/cores	[+] 'Equi-deletion'	Plain Construction[51]
1 [S, A]-controlled	S_A, S_U, d-S(gerundive)	A / U, d-S(passive)
2 [U]-controlled	A, S, d-S(gerundive)	A / U d-S(passive)
B. Cleft Constructions	SbjCl. – 'Equi-del.'	Plain Construction
1 Argument Focus, Content Question, Relative Clause, [imperf., perf.][52]	A	S, U, d-S(passive), G, Com., etc.
2 Argument Focus, Content Question, Relative Clause [-]A/UAmbiguity, [progr., term.]		S, A, U, d-S(passive), etc.
3 Argument Focus, Content Question, Relative Clause [+]A/UAmbiguity, [progr., term.]		S, A, preferred d-S(passive)

Table 16. Syntactic pivots

The other two constructions single out only one (type of) argument. Some cleft constructions single out A rather than other participants by a special marking, namely, 'equi-deletion' of the A argument (cf. construction B1 in Table 16). The other participants include all other arguments (namely, S, U, d-S(pas-sive), and G), and adjuncts such as a comitative phrase a.o. This clearly shows that the A argument is the syntactic pivot in these cleft constructions.[53]

---

[51] This includes non-'equi-deletion' of the argument in a question in a verbal core (indicated in front of the backslash) or in a *káa*-clause (indicated behind the backslash).

[52] Cleft constructions with the predictive marker *bíin* display a similar neutralization pattern under A/U ambiguity in content questions and relative clauses. If the U argument however is non-third person, a focused A argument may either appear in a set-A 'equi-deleted' incomple-tive construction as in *Máax bíin il-ik-en*? (who PRDV Ø see-INCMPL-ABS.1.SG) or in a plain construction in subjunctive mood as in *Máax bíin u y-il-en*? (who PRDV SBJ.3 0-see(SUBJ)-ABS.1.SG) 'Who is it that is/was going to see me?'. The corresponding data in Bricker (1979:118) is supported by my consultants. Similarly, my consultants support Bricker (1979:133) in that A focus in a two third person argument constellation can be either conveyed by the A-focus-construction *leti' bíin hats'-ik Juan* (that.one PRDV Ø beat-INCMPL Juan) 'It is he who is/was going to beat Juan' or by the plain subjunctive marked construction *leti' bíin u hats' Juan* (that. one PRDV SBJ.3 beat-(SUBJ) Juan) 'It is he who is/was going to beat Juan'. Contrary to Bricker (1979) however, my consultants judge the latter version as being ambiguous between an A focus and a U focus, i.e 'It is he whom John is/was going to beat.' Passive formation is again an optional means of disambiguation.

[53] Data in Bricker (1979) shows that this special behavior of A is 'weakened' in argument fo-cus constructions with A/P ambiguity. In these constellations, U cannot be focused in a plain construction but passivization is needed to focus on U, thus resulting in d-S(passive). This a-

Furthermore, 'equi-deletion' under A or S control identifies an S pivot including S_A, S_U, and d-S(gerundive) (cf. construction A1 in Table 16).

Altogether it seems justified to assume a rather weakly implemented (accusatively aligned) subject for YM. This is not only supported by those constructions neutralizing [S, A, d-S(passive/gerundive)], but also by the fact that there is no construction neutralizing [S, P, d-S(antipassive)].

4.3.4 *Direct object vs. indirect object*

YM displays a direct vs. indirect object distinction in the way that the patient of a transitive verb and the patient of a ditransitive verb are marked and behave the same way.[54] They are both cross-referenced with the absolutive suffix, *-ech* ABS.2.SG in (139), while a lexical indirect object is marked by the most grammatical preposition *ti'* LOC as in (139b). The form of a pronominal indirect object has already been introduced in sect. 4.1.2 and an example with the first person pronoun is given in (140).

(139) a. *He'   in   bis-ik-ech-e'.*
       ASS   SBJ.1.SG carry-INCMPL-ABS.2.SG-D3
       'I'll take you.' (BVS_16.01.07.02)

   b. *Tíin   w-e's-ik-ech   ti' le   máak-o'b-o'.*
      PROG:SBJ.1.SG 0-show-INCMPL-ABS.2.SG LOC DEF person-PL-D2
      'I am showing you to those people.' (RMC_0418)

Passive formation in YM exclusively targets direct objects as being the new subject; the indirect object cannot be passivized (140).

(140) a. *Pedro-e'   t-u   síih-ah   tèen*
         Pedro-TOP PFV-SBJ.3 give.as.present-CMPL   me
         hun-p'éel   libro.
         one-CL.INAN   book
         'Pedro gave me a book as a present.'

---

gain points to an accusative restricted neutralization. Data from Bohnemeyer (p.c.) does not, however, prove the data given in Bricker (1979), but also accounts for construction B1 in cases of A/P ambiguity. In this case, this last point would be voided.

[54] Cf. Dryer (1986) for a distinction between systems with a direct/indirect object vs. primary/secondary object.

b. *H   síih-a'b   tèen*
  PFV   give.as.present-CMPL.PASS   me
  hun-p'éel   libro   tumen   Pedro.
  one-CL.INAN   book   by   Pedro
  'A book was given to me by Pedro.'

c.**H   tèen-e'   síih-a'b-en*
  PFV   me-TOP   give.as.present-CMPL.PASS-ABS.1.SG
  hun-p'éel   libro   tumen   Pedro.
  one-CL.INAN   book   by   Pedro
  intended: 'I was given a book by Peter.'

In YM, there is no operation similar to dative shift in English. However, non-conservative speakers allow for some variation of direct object assignment with some extraversive verbs. Some verbs of communication may alternatively have the patient or the recipient/addressee cross-referenced by the absolutive suffix (cf. Lehmann and Verhoeven 2006). An oblique argument of an intransitive verb (G) may also be rendered by *ti'* 'LOC' (141).

(141)   *Kensah   ba'x   ts'o'k u   y-úuch-ul*
    who.knows   what   TERM SBJ.3 0-happen-INCMPL
    ti'   in   ts'ùul-il...
    LOC POSS.1.SG   sir-REL
    'Who knows what has happened to my lord (...)' (HA'N_0026.01)

Since prepositional phrases generally appear at the end of the clause, the default word order in intransitive two-place constructions is VSG (142a). However, non-third person pronouns directly follow the verb (142b) and complex S arguments are generally postponed (142c) (cf. Lehmann 1998, ch. 2.4.2).

(142) a. *túun   chéen   k'a'h-al   u   yùum*
      PROG:SBJ.3.SG just   remember-INCMPL POSS.3   father
      ti'   (Pedro)
      LOC Pedro
      'it is simply reminding him (/Peter) of his father' (ACC_0304)

b. *túun   chéen   k'a'h-al   tèen u   yùum*
    PROG:SBJ.3.SG just   remember-INCMPL me   POSS.3   father
    'it is simply reminding me of his father'(ACC_0304)

    c. *h   tu'b   ti'   u   bis-ik*
       PFV   forget LOC SBJ.3 carry-INCMPL
       u   kib-il   le   uk'ul-o'
       POSS.3 candle-REL DEF drink-D2
       'he forgot to bring the candle of the drink' (ACC_0283)

Word order in ditransitive constructions also follows the rules for prepositional phrases and independent pronouns. Since chaining several lexical noun phrases one after another within a clause is generally avoided, default word order in ditransitive clauses is V(U/A)G. Compare (143a) for VAG and (143b) for VUG.

(143) a. *K-u   y-a'l-ik   túun bin   chàak   wíinik*
         IMPF-SBJ.3 0-say-INCMPL then QUOT chàak   man
         ti'   le   chàan   xibpal-e': ...
         LOC DEF little   man:child-D3
         'Then the giant said to the little boy: (...).' (HK'AN_076)

      b. *K-u   ho'p'-ol*
         IMPF-SBJ.3   begin-INCMPL
         u   ts'a'-ik   le   báalche' ti'   u   chi'-o'b-o' ...
         SBJ.3 put-INCMPL DEF   balche   LOC POSS.3 mouth-3.PL-D2
         'He begins to put the balche into their mouths (...)' (CHAAK_072)

In YM, a valency frame with three participants is only weakly developed (cf. Lehmann et al. 2000[D]/[P]). Typical three place verbs that involve a recipient as a third participant also occur naturally in a two participant frame (*ts'a'* 'give, put', *síih* 'give as present', *tàas* 'bring', etc.). This means that the recipient constitutes a part of the semantic valency of these verbs, but its syntactic realization is not obligatory. There are generally three possibilities: it may remain unexpressed (111), it may be marked as the possessor attribute of the NP coding the thing given (144a), or it may be coded as an argument of a subordinate verb which further specifies the relation between the recipient and the main verb (144b). Similar coding options exist with other semantic roles occurring as indirect object as, e.g., the beneficiary. The conditions for these constructions are discussed in Lehmann et al. (2000[D]). Parallel cases of the lack of syntactic coding of an indirect object experiencer will be discussed in sect. 6.4.

(144) a. *He'l   u   páah-tal   in   w-il-ik*
         PRSV SBJ.3 possible-PROC SBJ.1.SG 0-see-INCMPL
         wáah k-in   ts'a-ik   a   sìiya-e'.
         if   IMPF-SBJ.1.SG put-INCMPL POSS.2   seat-D3
         'I will see if I can put your seat on you.' (HNAZ_0067.02)

   b. *t-u*   *tàas-ah*   *u*   *hàan-t*   *u*   *yùumil.*
     PFV-SBJ.3 bring-CMPL SBJ.3 eat-TRR(SUBJ) POSS.3   owner
     'and he brought it for his master to eat.' (PEEK'_035.03, cf.
     Lehmann et al. 2000[D])

On the other hand, prepositional phrases introduced with *ti'* 'LOC' are occasionally added to intransitive and transitive verbs in the semantic roles of source, goal, beneficiary, addressee, stimulus, or experiencer. (145) illustrates peripheral roles introduced by *ti'* with transitive (145a) and intransitive verbs (145b/c) that may even result in a metaphorical meaning (145b). The latter case may well be a calque from Spanish, a hypothesis that may even apply to *ti'* as a marker of indirectly affected participants in general. These examples seem to embody an opposite or reverse development of examples like those in (144).

(145) a. *Buka'h*   *bin*   *h*   *bèet-a'b*   *ti'*
        how.much QUOT PFV do-CMPL.PASS   LOC
        ma' *t-u*   *y-óot-ah*   *y-e's-i'* …
        NEG PFV-SBJ.3 0-agree-CMPL SBJ.3-show-NEGF
        'For how much was done to him, he did not want to show it, (...)'
        (HK'AN_088.1)

      b. *Bèet* *tuláakal* *ba'x* *ken*   *in*   *w-a'l* *tèech*
        do   all   what SR.IRR SBJ.1.SG 0-say you
        k-u   *bin* *tèech* *uts-il.*
        IMPF-SBJ.3 go   you   good:REL
        'Do everything I tell you and you will be fine. (HK'AN_094.02)

      c. *k-u*   *chukpah-al*   *tèen*
        IMPF-SBJ.3 suffice:SPONT-INCMPL me
        'it gets complete for me' (RMC_0318)

4.3.5 *Possessor and absolutive argument of stative predicates*

Finally, something should be said about the arguments of stative predicates, i.e., the possessor and the absolutive argument in stative predications in YM. As has already been shown, possessor and verbal S and A arguments are marked identically in the language. This has been analyzed as an ergative trait of the Mayan languages (e.g., Hofling 1990, Larsen and Norman 1979, Bricker 1981 [S]). Lehmann (1998, sect. 6.2.) underlines not only the morphological but also the grammatical parallelism of the A argument and the possessor in pointing to a parallel behavior of transitive verb and relational noun in relationalizing and derelationalizing processes (causativization and deagentivization). For illustrative reasons, his examples in which a relational noun is derelationalized (146a/a') and a transitive verb is detransitivized (146b/b') are cited here.

(146) a. *in   tàatah-ech*
          POSS.1.SG father-ABS.2.SG
          'you are my father'

      a'.*tàatah-tsil-ech*
          father-ABSOL-ABS.2.SG
          'you are a/the father'

      b. *t-in   p'at-h-ech*
          PFV-SBJ.1.SG   leave-CMPL-ABS.2.SG
          'I left you'

      b'.*h   p'áat-ech*
          PFV   leave\DEAG-ABS.2.SG
          'you stayed'

Furthermore, YM has a larger number of active intransitive verbs that have
a homophonous nominal form. In certain syntactic contexts, an ambiguity
arises between a nominal vs. a verbal analysis of such homophoneous forms,
i.e. identifying the preverbal clitic as having either S or POSS function. Such a
context is given if in a verbal interpretation the item in question is subordinated. Thus, *áalkab* in (147) can be analyzed as being a verb in a subordinate
core (cf. sect. 4.2.2) which depends on the matrix verb *chichkunt* 'make hard'
(with the literal translation '…began to harden to run'), or it may be analyzed
as a possessed noun taking the function of the direct object of the main verb
chichkunt (with the literal translation '…began to harden its running/race').[55] In
such contexts, there is an ambiguity between a subject vs. a possessive interpretation of the preverbal clitic. The currently existing accusative system is assumed to have begun to develop from a former ergative system in such constructions.

(147)   *káa   h   ho'p' u   chich-kunt-ik*
          CNJ   PFV   begin SBJ.3   hard-FACT-INCMPL
          u   y-áalkab le   kéeh-e'.
          SBJ/POSS.3   0-run   DEF   deer-D3
          'And the deer began to run faster.' (AAK_031)

Additionally, the transitive A and the possessor are related in nomen acti
formation, i.e., the transitive A slot is (regularly) converted into the possessor
slot. Morphologically, the introversive formation of the transitive verb marked

---

[55] A parallel example is (122b), while (122)a is a corresponding case with an intransitive matrix verb taking either a subordinate core *in meyah* (in the verbal interpretation) or a possessed
noun *in meyah* (in the nominal interpretation) as its subject.

by low tone on the root vowel is first (cf. sect. 4.1.6). The result of the intro-versive formation becomes part of the class of active intransitive verbs where nominalization is not marked; compare, e.g., *huch'* 'grind' > *hùuch'* dough', *pay* 'owe' > *pàay* 'debt' (cf. Lehmann 1998, ch. 2.5).

A further syntactic context where the transitive A and the possessor of a re-lational noun behave identically is cleft constructions with content questions. (148a) shows that the POSS argument of a relational noun behaves like the A argument of a transitive verb in content questions (135a); i.e., the subject/ pos-sessor cross-reference marker is 'equi-deleted'.[56] Thus a restricted neutraliza-tion that is a syntactic pivot of A and POSS in content questions can be identified. Note however that this does not apply to relative constructions and argument focus constructions which cannot relativize or focus on the posses-sor. Coming back to (148), it can be seen, that the S argument is coded like the U argument of a transitive verb in the same construction type, as a comparison of (148b) with (135b) shows. The only difference between these two examples is that (148b) does not have an aspect marker, which is, as has already been shown in sect. 4.1.3, incompatible with stative predicates.

(148) a. *Máax láak'-il?*
   who other-REL
   'Whose relative is he?' (ACC/RMC)
  b. *Máax u   láak'?*
   who POSS.3 other
   'Who is his relative?' (ACC/RMC)

The noun *láak'* 'other' belongs to the possessive class of inalienable inab-soluble nouns, i.e., those nouns that never occur outside a possessive construc-tion. In (149a/b), nouns from other possessive classes like inalienable absoluble nouns (e.g., *atan* 'wife'), convertible nouns (e.g., *nah* 'house'), clas-sifyable nouns (e.g., *k'áan* 'hammock') and neutral nouns (e.g., *kòol* 'milpa') may occur in the same pattern as the one shown in (148). If the possessor of a non-relational noun is the target of a content question, the dummy possessum *ti'a'l* 'property', which is itself a relational noun, may alternatively take the function of the predicate in the extrafocal part of the construction (149c).

---

[56] Note furthermore that in such a construction the possessed noun is suffixed with the relatio-nal suffix *-il*, irrespective of its possessive class (149). This is explained by Lehmann (1998, sect. 3.2.1.1.1.6) as being based on the model of asking for an object of a specific kind, e.g., *máax ts'ùul-il?* (who stranger-REL) 'what (kind of) stranger'.

(149) a. *Máax atn-il   Isabel?*
      who   wife-REL Isabel
      'Whose wife is Isabel?' (Lehmann 1998:40, ACC, NMP, RMC)

    b. *Máax nah-il/   kòol-il/   k'àan-il   le   he'l-a'?*
      who   house-REL/ milpa-REL/ hammock-REL DEF PRSV-D1
      'Whose house/milpa/hammock is this here?' (ACC, RMC)

    c. *Máax túun ti'a'l-il   le   nah-a'/*
      who   then property-REL DEF house-D1/
      le   kòol-a'/ le   k'àan-a'?
      DEF milpa-D1/ DEF hammock-D1
      'Whose house/milpa/hammock [is this] then?' (ACC)

Furthermore, the subject/possessor argument of perfect participles, which are also stative predicates (cf. sect. 4.1.8), has access to 'equi-deletion' not only in content questions (150a), but also in argument focus constructions (150b) and in relative clauses.

(150) a. *Máax bon-m(ah)-il   le   nah-a'?*
      who   paint-PART.PF-REL   DEF   house-D1
      'Who has painted the house?' (cf. Bohnemeyer 2002:206)

    b. *Leti'   bon-m(ah)-il   le   nah-a'.*
      who   paint- PART.PF-REL   DEF   house-D1
      'It is he who has painted this house.' (ACC)

The S argument of a stative predicate is invariably marked by the absolutive suffix (cf. sect. 4.1.3). For reasons of analogy, it can be equated with the S argument of intransitive verbs with regard to its grammatical relation. For instance, in durative and inchoative derivation, adjectives regularly become intransitive verbs without a change concerning the S argument (cf. sect. 4.1.6).

CHAPTER 5

Experiential constructions

5.1 *General remarks*

5.1.1 *Outline of the chapter*

The aim of this chapter is to give a description of experiential constructions in YM. Every type of construction that represents a pervasive pattern in the domain of experience will be analyzed. This excludes certain rather unique expressions that do not instantiate a constructional pattern. For instance, the collocation of the adverboid *bèey* 'thus' with the person part noun *t'àan* 'speech' renders an experiential expression, as in (151):

> (151) *Bèey   a   t'àan   wáah, nuxib   kéeh?*
>   thus   POSS.2 speech INT   old.man deer
>   'Do you think that, old deer?' (AAK_008)

Since there is no pervasive pattern for the expression of different experiences with a group of adverboids in YM, this unique syntactic collocation is not of interest for a description of the constructional means of encoding experiences in this language.

The presentation of experiential constructions follows a structural outline: construction types are grouped by the word class of the predicative element (be it experiential in meaning, based on metaphor, or a kind of abstract predicator). Following the analysis of word classes in predicate function in sect. 4.1.8, a division will be made between stative constructions (sect. 5.2) and verbal constructions (sect. 5.3).

Before starting the analysis of the specific construction types, some general methodological points have to be addressed. This includes the semantic tests used for the identification of situation type features and role features (sect. 5.1.2) and the way constructions will be represented in YM (sect. 5.1.3).

5.1.2 *Testing situation and role features in YM*

It has been mentioned in sect. 4.1.6 that YM possesses a rich inventory of derivational processes for changing morphosyntactic predicate classes. Experiential predicates belong to most of these classes, and naturally form part of this derivational system. Thus, one point of investigation examines the semantic changes in terms of dynamicity and control that accompany a change in predicate class, especially as regards the transition from a stative class to a dynamic class. First the tests related to dynamicity will be introduced followd by those testing control.

Following from what has been said in sect. 3.2.2.3, the distinction between emotional states and dispositions (i.e., temperaments), is an instance of the general distinction between states and properties. Lehmann (1993[P]:211) proposes the test frame in (152) to distinguish between property and state adjectives. Adjectives that are acceptable in Test 1 are judged as designating properties, those that are not are judged as designating states.

(152) Test 1: Property test frame
     Leti-e',   *hun-túul*   _____   *máak.*
     that.one-TOP   one-CL.AN _____   person
     'That is a ____ person.'

When Test 1 is applied to experiential adjectives which are believed to designate states as, e.g., *su'lak* 'ashamed', it turns out that many of them are compatible with this frame, which points to a property reading. To confirm this result, Test 2 in (153), which is semantically more specific with respect to experiential situations, has been used. Since some of the experiential adjectives may only be ascribed to the person part noun *óol* 'mind', an alternative version is given in brackets in Test 2 (first line). If another body part noun is necessary, it replaces *óol*. Furthermore, negation has to be chosen according to semantic plausibility.

(153) Test 2: Property test frame for experiential adjectives
     Maria-e'   *hach* _____ *(u*   *y-óol),*
     Mary-TOP   really _____ (POSS.3 0-mind)
     (ma') *in*   *k'áat* *ts'o'k-ol*   *in*   *béel*   *yéetel(-i').*
     NEG SBJ.1.SG wish   end-INCMPL POSS.1.SG way with-NEGF
     'Mary is really ___, I (don't) want to marry her.'

Test 2 works on the idea that only properties (i.e., character traits) and not states (i.e momentary emotional situations) are normally taken as a basis of judgment for the long-term decision of marrying another person. Thus, pure states are not semantically compatible with Test 2.

The frame in Test 3 (154) was additionally used to identify experiential state readings. It is based on the fact that states may be located in time[1], but proper-

---

[1] Cf. however Bohnemeyer (1998[T]:239ff.) on the restrictions and interpretations of stative predicates with temporal adverbs of different types.

ties may not. Thus, incompatibility of a given adjective with Test 3 points to a property reading.

(154) Test 3: Stativity test frame for adjectives
       Sàameak-e' /   ho'lyak-e'/   behlak-e'
       a.moment.ago-TOP/   yesterday-TOP/   today-TOP
       hach _____-en//   _____ in   w-óol.
       really _____-ABS.1.SG // _____ POSS.1.SG 0-mind
       'A moment ago/yesterday/today I was very _____.'

Test 4 (155) can be applied to judge the stativity of derived verbs of experience in YM (cf. Van Valin and LaPolla 1997:93). It is necessarily negative with stative predicates, since they cannot function in a construction containing an aspect marker.

(155) Test 4: Stativity test frame for verbs
       Ba'x k-u   y-úuch-ul?
       what   IMPF-SBJ.3   0-happen-INCMPL
       'What is happening/happens?'
       Táan u   _____   Pedro
       PROG SBJ.3   _____   Pedro
       'Pedro is _____.'

The answer in Test 4 contains the progressive aspect marker. The combination of a given verb with the progressive marker can be taken as proof of its dynamic reading (cf. Bohnemeyer 2002:32).

A valuable semantic test to assess the control properties of a given verb is proposed in Bohnemeyer (1998[T]:424ff.). It relies on the fact that transitive phase verbs such as *kah, chun, káahs* all roughly 'begin', *ts'o'ks* 'finish' and *ch'en* 'stop' can only be combined with embedded cores designating controlled situations. Bohnemeyer shows that these transitive phase operators are not compatible (or at least questionable) with verbs whose subject does not control the event (156b) while a combination with action verbs such as *meyah* 'work', *ts'íibt* 'write' is unproblematic (156a). This test examines the "control" properties of the S or A argument of the subordinate verb independent of transitivity. As the examples in (156) show, the subordinate verb may be transitive or intransitive.

(156) a. *Táan   in   kah-ik/   chun-ik/   káah-s-ik/*
          PROG SBJ.1.SG start-INCMPL start-INCMPL start\DEAG-CAUS-INCM
          ts'o'k-s-ik/   *ch'en-ik*   *in*   *meyah/*
          end-CAUS-INCMPL stop-INCMPL SBJ.1.SG   work
          in   *ts'iib-t-ik*   *le*   *kàarta-o'.*
          SBJ.1.SG write-TRR-INCMPL DEF letter-D2
          'I am starting/finishing/stopping working/writing the letter.'

     b. **Táan in   kah-ik/   chun-ik/   káah-s-ik/*
          PROG SBJ.1.SG start-INCMPL start-INCMPL start\DEAG-CAUS-INCMPL
          ts'o'k-s-ik/   *ch'en-ik*   *in*   *ka'n-al/*
          end-CAUS-INCMPL stop-INCMPL SBJ.1.SG   get.tired-INCMPL
          in   *ts'iikil-t-ik[2]*   *Pedro.*
          SBJ.1.SG feel.angry-TRR-INCMPL Pedro
          'I am starting/finishing/stopping to get tired/to be mad at Pedro.'
          (Bohnemeyer 1998[T]:425)

Test 5 (157) will be used as a basis to investigate the control properties of experiential verbs.

(157) Test 5: Control test frame
      Táan   in   kah-ik/   chun-ik/
      PROG SBJ.1.SG start-INCMPL start-INCMPL
      káah-s-ik/   *ts'o'k-s-ik/*   *ch'en-ik*
      start\DEAG-CAUS-INCMPL end-CAUS-INCMPL   stop-INCMPL
      in   ______.
      SBJ.1.SG ______
      'I am starting/finishing/stopping V-ing.'

Numerous control tests which are also applicable to YM have been proposed in the literature (cf. sect. 3.3.2.1, Lehmann 1993[P], 1996[C] for YM). Among these are the formation of a (positive) imperative and subordination under certain control verbs, etc. which will be discussed once they have been used in the analysis of the relevant constructions. In general, Test 5 seems to be the most reliable because it tests the feature indirectly.

A general methodological point concerning the tests introduced in this section is the reliability of acceptability judgments induced by them. As happens frequently with acceptability tests, the judgments by different consultants on a given item were not always identical. In such cases, different readings are assumed for the lexeme in question.

---

[2] Note that my consultants allow for *ts'iikil* in this construction (cf. sect. 5.3.1.1).

5.1.3 *The representation of constructions*

Each construction type is discussed and represented in its structural and functional-semantic properties, as explained in sect. 2.3. In the structural part of a construction (i.e., the layer named 'syntax'), a constituent structure representation with category labels is used as introduced in sect. 4.1.3ff. NPs are given in default word order so that their order in the representation indicates syntactic functions (cf. sect. 4.1.1). Cross-reference markers on the predicates as well as on the possessum noun are not represented in the construction since these are implied by the occurrence of the argument NPs (cf. sect. 4.1.2). The semantic representation uses argument role labels as introduced in sect. 3.3, i.e., the experiential roles Experiencer and Stimulus. More abstract roles such as Actor, Undergoer, Theme, Goal, etc. are used in not specifically experiential constructions or in the immediate semantic representation. At the lexical level, i.e., at the level of instantiation, semantic roles will be indicated in small capitals, as was introduced in sect. 2.1.4.

For reasons of space, motivating superordinate constructions or part constructions are given in an inline representation of the following kind: '$^{(1)}$RELATION <$^{(2)}$Arg. role>' [$^{(1)}$PREP $^{(2)}$NP]$_{PP}$. The first component given in simple quotation marks indicates the semantic layer of the construction while the second component indicates the syntactic layer. The superscript digits are indices which link each item in the semantic representation with its exponent in the syntactic representation.

5.2 *Stative predicate constructions*

Following Table 13, the objects of analysis here are experiential adjectives and verboids. Experiential nouns appear as NPs in certain constructions, but they do not, however, typically occur as predicates by themselves. Stative predicates, in contrast to verbal predicates, encode stative situations.

5.2.1 *Adjectival constructions*

The following subsections are organized according to which one of the participants relevant in a given experiential situation takes the subject function in the adjectival construction. This may be either the experiencer (sect. 5.2.1.2), its person part (sect. 5.2.1.3) or the stimulus (sect. 5.2.1.4). The introductory section (sect. 5.2.1.1) addresses the question of the delimitation between property and state readings of experiential adjectives.

5.2.1.1 *Introduction*

Adjectives in YM denote properties as well as states (Lehmann 1993[P]). As has been mentioned in sect. 4.1.8, they can occur in prenominal as well as in postnominal position when modifying a noun. Some adjectives only occur in prenominal position, some only in postnominal position and a third group oc-curs in both positions.

It is well known that adjectives in many languages may be more or less am-biguous as to whether they denote a property or a state. In Spanish, a given ad-jective may be introduced in a property or a state construction combining with a different copula (*soy* or *estoy*, respectively). German allows adjectives like *ruhig* 'calm, tranquil' or *zufrieden* 'content' to occur both in a property reading (*X ist eine ruhige/zufriedene Person* 'X is a calm, content person') and in a state reading (*das Baby ist nun wieder ruhig/zufrieden* 'The baby is calm/content again'). This also holds true for a number of experiential adjec-tives in YM. On the basis of the test frames introduced in sect. 5.1.2 which dis-tinguish between properties and states, three types of adjectives related to experience can be distinguished: those that designate a state, those that desig-nate a property, and those that are neutral to such a distinction, occurring natu-rally in both readings.

Adjectives denoting bodily sensation, e.g., *wi'h* 'hungry', *uk'ah* 'thirsty' and *na'h* 'full, satisfied', and emotional adjectives as *ts'iibóol* 'eager, longing to', *háak'a'n* 'proud, amazed' belong to the first group. These are generally judged as awkward in Test 1 (158a). (158b) was proposed to be the correct version of (158a). For *ts'iibóol* 'eager, longing to' and *háak'a'n* 'proud, amazed', it can be shown that they are acceptable in Test 3, but not in Test 2.

(158) a.^{??}*Leti'-e'*   *hun-túul*   *wi'h/*   *uk'ah/* *na'h máak.*
that.one-TOP one-CL.AN hungry/ thirsty/ full   person
'That one is a hungry /thirsty /satisfied person.'

    b. *hun-túul*   *óotsil*   *máak,*
one -CL.AN poor   person
wi'h   *k-u*   *y-u'b-ik*
hungry IMPF-SBJ.3 0-feel-INCMPL
'a poor man who suffers hunger'

Included in the second group of experiential adjectives designating a prop-erty are: *ma'na't* 'ignorant', *na't(cha)ha'n* 'intelligent, knowledgeable', *nùun* 'slow-witted', *tu'b(ul)-ìik'* 'forgetful', *tu'b(ul)-óol* 'forgetful', *sàatah-óol* 'con-fused, absent-minded, mad' *mùuk'óol* 'strong, powerful', *nèets* 'fragile, dumb', *ch'óop* 'blind', *tòot* 'mute', *kóok* 'dumb', *ko'* 'obstinate, rebellious, bold, rude'. These adjectives are not compatible with Test 3.

Most of the emotional adjectives belong to the third group. The following adjectives are compatible with a property frame such as Test 2 as well as with a state frame such as Test 3: *ki'mak* 'happy, glad, cheerful', *k'ùux* 'angry, nerv-ous, excitable', *su'lak* 'embarrassed, shy' *ts'íik* 'angry, fierce', *sahak* 'afraid, fearful', *sahlu'm*[3] 'afraid, fearful', *ma'óol* 'weary, listless, lethargic', *ma'k'óol* 'idle, lazy', *sa'k-óol* 'sedulous, active, industrious', *pòoch* 'desirous, greedy', *chi'chnak* 'cross, furious', *p'úuha'n* 'cross, peeved, mad', etc. While some of these adjectives seem to be truly ambiguous between a state reading and a property reading, others seem to be essentially stative, with the property reading being derived. This view is supported by the following observations.

Adjectives occurring in prenominal position prototypically denote properties, while the postnominal position is not restricted to either property or state adjectives. In light of this, it can be seen as meaningful that some of the adjectives in question cannot occur in prenominal position without a morphological change, namely, reduplicating the first part of the monosyllabic base (e.g., *ts'i'ts'iik* 'fierce', *k'u'k'ùux* 'excitable', *po'pòoch* 'greedy'). This operation clearly implies a semantic change to a property and the output of this operation is restricted to the prenominal position. These adjectives can therefore be judged as primarily stative.

In contrast, experiential adjectives as, e.g., *sahak* 'afraid, fearful', *su'lak* 'embarrassed, shy', etc. do not change their form in prenominal position. They really do seem to be ambiguous between a state reading and a property reading in the predicative construction (159a). (159b) clearly has a property reading, which is explicated in the second line of the example.

(159) a. *Maria-e'   sahak.*
     Mary-TOP   afraid
     'Mary feels afraid/is fearful.'

    b. *Maria-e'   hun-túul   sahak   máak,*
     Mary-TOP   one-CL.AN   afraid   person
     u   k'áat   y-a'l-e'   hach   sèeb   u   sahak-tal.
     SBJ.3 wish   SBJ.3-say-TOP really   quickly SBJ.3   afraid-PROC
     'Mary is a fearful person, that means that she gets afraid really quickly.' (RMC)

Finally, note that some of the abovementioned emotion adjectives may be compounded with *óol* 'mind' and then a few will primarily denote a property, e.g., *sahak-óol* 'fearful'. Most of these however, seem to be, in spite of this change, ambiguous as to a property or state reading, e.g., *chi'chnak-óol* 'uneasy, angry', *ki'mak-óol* 'glad, happy, content', *k'ùux-óol* 'bad-tempered, peevish, angry', *ts'iik(il)-óol* 'querulous, peevish, angry', *háak'óol* 'easily scared, nervous, astonished', *náak-óol* 'feel bored, be bored easily'.

---

[3] My consultants' judgments differ as to the register of this expression. Some consider it synonymous with *sahak*, others judge it to be an inferior variant of *sahak*, occurring only in expressions as *sahlu'm kèep* 'cowardly dog, bastard dick'.

5.2.1.2 *Experiencer-oriented constructions*

In three of the experiential subdomains, namely, bodily sensation, emotion, and volition, there are adjectives denoting experiential states. They are listed in Table 17. The subdomains of perception and cognition do not contain adjectives denoting states of the experiencer. Cognitive states expressed by adjectives are rare in YM; some are ascribable to *pòol* 'head' and are discussed in sect. 5.2.1.3. Typical cognitive states such as 'know' belong to the class of transitive verboids (sect. 5.2.2.2.1). Adjectives in the subdomain of cognition denote mainly property concepts (cf. sect. 5.2.1.1).

Table 17 contains a number of basic experiential adjectives (*wi'h, uk'ah, na'h, ke'l, su'lak, pòoch*), as well as a number of adjectives that occur either in their basic forms or in composition with *óol*: *chi'chnak(-óol), k'ùux(-óol), ts'íik(il)(-óol), sahak(-óol)*. These latter may occur in collocation with *óol* as well, as will be shown in sect. 5.2.1.3. Just as the other *óol*-compounds in Table 17, they represent lexicalizations on the basis of collocations with adjectives or intransitive verbs (cf. Table 18, Table 31). Only *sa'k-óol, ma'k'-óol, ma'óol* and *ts'ììbóol* do not have synchronic collocational correspondences. Finally, *k'a'na'n* and *p'ùuha'n* are resultative forms from inactive intransitive verbs (cf. Table 28) and *ni'nich'kil* and *p'ùuhul* are adjectivized forms. Table 17 (and following tables in the current chapter) indicates the constructional properties of the items listed in the rightmost column. These properties are discussed after the table is presented.

The experiential adjectives are stative predicates coding the experiencer in subject function. (160) gives some illustrative examples.

> (160) a. *Míin   ma'   hach   k'oha'n-ech-i'*
>   about   NEG   really   sick-ABS.2.SG-NEGF
>   *chéen   ka'n-a'n-ech.*
>   just   tire-PART.RSLTV-ABS.2.SG
>   'I think you're not really sick, you're just tired.' (BVS_10.01.08)
>
>   b. *Yùum   ahaw   yéetel   u   y-atan-e'   chi'chnak-o'b.*
>   lord   chief   and   POSS.3   0-wife-TOP   infuriated-ABS.3.PL
>   'The chief and his wife were infuriated.' (HK'AN_242)
>
>   c. *Hach   máan   pòoch-ech,   pàal!*
>   really   very   desirous-ABS.2.SG   child
>   'Your are really very greedy, child!' (MPK_049)

subdomain	instance (gloss) 'meaning'	properties	
bodily sensation	*wi'h* 'hungry'	●	-
	uk'ah 'thirsty'	●	-
	na'h 'satified'	●	-
	xul-óol (end-mind) 'exhausted'	●	-
	ke'l 'cold'	○	-
	ka'n-a'n (tire-RSLTV) 'tired'	○	-
	ni'-nich'-kil (RED-bite.off-PAT.ADJR) 'itchy'	○	-
emotion	*lúub(-a'n)-óol* (fall(-RSLTV)-mind) 'sad'	○	-
	hets'(el)-óol (quiet-mind) 'calm'	○	-
	óoyol-óol 'nervous, fearful'	●	-
	háak'óol (scare:mind) 'easily scared, nervous, astonished'	●	■
	ki'mak-óol (happy-mind) 'glad, happy, content'	○	■
	sahak(-óol) 'afraid, fearful'	○	■
	p'úuh-a'n (cross-RSLTV) 'cross, peeved, mad'	●	■
	ts'iik((il)-óol) (furious((DUR)-mind)) 'angry, fierce'	●	■
	chuka'n-óol (suffice-mind) 'patient'	●	■
	k'ùux(-óol) (angry(-mind)) 'angry, nervous, peevish'	●	■□
	su'lak (ashamed) 'embarrassed, shy'	●	■□
	náak-óol (leave.this.way\DEAG-mind) 'feel bored'	●	■□
	péek-óol (move-mind) 'get frightened, troubled'	●	■□
	p'ùuhul (stir:ADJR) 'frightened, bothered angered'	●	■□
	chi'chnak(-óol) (cross(-mind)) 'cross, furious, angry'	○	■□
	ma'k'óol 'idle, lazy'	●	◊
	sa'k-óol 'sedulous, active, industrious'	●	◊
	ma'óol (without:mind) 'weary, listless, lethargic'	●	◊
volition	*pòoch* 'desirous, greedy'	●	■
	ts'iibóol (write:soul) 'eager, longing to'	●	■

properties:

- ●   (exclusively) experiencer-oriented;
- ○   experiencer- or part-oriented;
- ■   adjoins a stimulus complement with *ti*;
- □   adjoins a stimulus complement with *yéetel*;
- ◊   adjoins asyndetic purpose clause as stimulus;
- -   does not adjoin stimulus complement.

Table 17. Experiential adjectives

Construction 5 represents a construction scheme for the items listed in Table 17. Following the format introduced in sect. 2.3, the upper box represents the semantic layer of the construction while the lower box contains the syntactic information in the form of a constituent structure representation. Construction 5 shows that experiential adjectives integrate with the simple adjective construction fusing their EXPERIENCER role with the constructional Theme role.

semantics:	STATE	<Theme>	
instantiation:	PRED	<EXPERIENCER>	
syntax:	[Adj	NP	]$_S$
constraints:	PRED $\in$ {bodily sensation, emotion, volition}		

Construction 5. Simple adj. C. with exp.-oriented adjectives

Some of the items listed in Table 17 exclusively select the experiencer in subject function, while others may additionally select a body part. Then they integrate with Construction 8 or Construction 10, which will be introduced in the following section. Those items identified as "(exclusively) experiencer-oriented" in Table 17 belong to the former group. The members of the latter group are identified as "experiencer- or part-oriented" in Table 17 and will be futher discussed in sect. 5.2.1.3 in their part-oriented construction.

There is further variation among the items listed in Table 17 regarding the adjoining of a stimulus participant. In general, the predicates in Table 17 can be regarded as monovalent since they occur in Construction 5. In addition to this behavior, they may add a nominal stimulus participant adjoined by either *ti'* or *yéetel* (or both), but they differ in whether it is necessary to do so. The group of predicates of bodily sensation is least likely to take a stimulus participant. Generally, sensation adjectives in YM are monovalent. With some of them, a stimulus participant may be added optionally, but with a rather reduced number of potential lexical items as fillers. Thus, *na'h* 'satisfied', *wi'h* 'hungry', and *uk'ah* 'thirsty' might only add nouns referring to food or drink as exemplified in (161a/b).

(161) a. *wi'h-en*   *ti'*   *bak'/uk'ah-en*   *ti'* *síis* *ha'*
        hungry-ABS.1.SG LOC meat/ thirty-ABS.1.SG LOC icy water
        'I am hungry for meat/thirsty for cold water' (ACC)

      b. *na'h-en*   *yéetel bak'*
        satisfied-ABS.1.SG with   meet
        'I am satisfied with meat' (ACC)

Other predicates of bodily sensation, namely, *ka'na'n* 'tired' and *ke'l* 'cold', exclusively add 'nominalized' stimuli referring to situations (162a). These are equivalent to adverbial clauses adding either a cause with, e.g., *tumen* 'because' (162b) or a goal with, e.g., *uti'a'l* 'for' (162c), but not to complement clauses as will be discussed in ch. 7.

(162) a. *ka'na'n-en   ti'   xòok*
     tired-ABS.1.SG   LOC   read\INTRV
     'I am tired of/from reading/I am (too) tired to read' (ACC)

   b. *ka'na'nen   tumen   h   xòok-nah-en*
     tired-ABS.1.SG   because   PFV   read\INTRV-CMPL-ABS.1.SG
     'I am tired because I read' (ACC)

   c. *ka'na'n-en   uti'a'l   xòok*
     tired-ABS.1.SG   for   read\INTRV
     'I am (too) tired to read' (ACC)

While a stimulus participant occurs naturally with adjectives of emotion and volition, it is not obligatory with any of the experiential adjectives. The stimulus is most often added with the grammatical preposition *ti'* 'LOC'. Some adjectives favor *ti'*, but are also possible with *yéetel* 'with' when adjoining a stimulus. The distributions that can be observed are given in Table 17. The adjectives *ma'óol* 'weary, listless, lethargic', *ma'k'óol* 'idle, lazy' and *sa'k-óol* 'sedulous, active, industrious' do not take noun phrases as stimulus arguments but only asyndetic purpose clauses (cf. sect. 7.4.2.3). It can be observed that those adjectives that are ambiguous between a property and a state reading (cf. sect. 5.2.1.1) take the state reading in a construction with a stimulus. Compare the examples in (163).

(163) a. *tumèen   sahak-o'b   ti'   le   ko'lel-o'*
     because   afraid.of-3.PL   LOC   DEF   lady-D2
     'because they were afraid of the woman' (HOSEH_19.2)

   b. *Pedro-e'   hach   pòoch   ti'   tsah-bil   he'.*
     Pedro-TOP   really   desirous   LOC   fry-GERV   egg
     'Peter is really desirous of fried egg.' (NMP_0430)

Thus, experiential adjectives are compatible with the extended adjectival construction as depicted in Construction 6. Here a Location argument is present in the construction frame. The lexical STIMULUS role is mapped onto this constructional role. Construction 6 consists of Construction 5 plus the prepositional phrase resulting from a general syntactic pattern of the type '<Arg. role>' [PREP NP]PP.

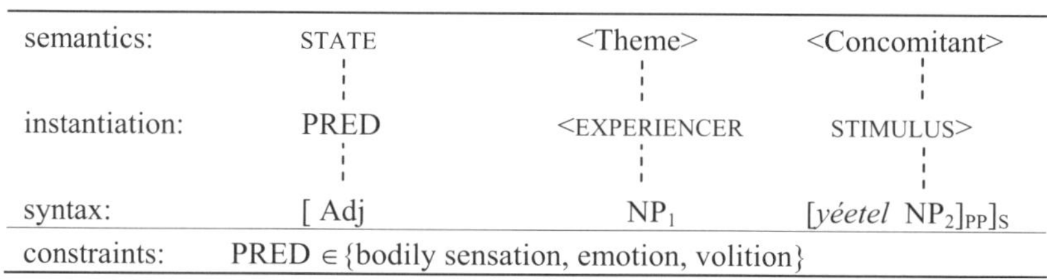

semantics:	STATE	<Theme	Location>
instantiation:	PRED	<EXPERIENCER	STIMULUS>
syntax:	[Adj	NP$_1$	[*ti'* NP$_2$]$_{PP}$]$_S$
constraints:	PRED $\in$ {bodily sensation, emotion, volition}		

Construction 6. Extended adj. C. with exp.-oriented adjectives

Those experiential adjectives taking a prepositional phrase introduced with *yéetel* 'with' are integrated into Construction 7, which is a complex construction consisting of a simple adjectival construction and a concomitant phrase. The STIMULUS role is mapped onto the constructional Concomitant role.

The participant properties of the stimulus generally depend on the nature of the adjectival predicate. The participant properties of the stimulus have already

semantics:	STATE	<Theme>	<Concomitant>
instantiation:	PRED	<EXPERIENCER	STIMULUS>
syntax:	[Adj	NP$_1$	[*yéetel* NP$_2$]$_{PP}$]$_S$
constraints:	PRED $\in$ {bodily sensation, emotion, volition}		

Construction 7. Adj. C. and concomitant phrase with exp.-oriented adjectives

been discussed for adjectives of bodily sensation. With adjectives of emotion and volition, the participant properties of the stimulus depend on the semantics of the adjective. Adjectives like *k'ùux* 'angry', *p'úuha'n* 'cross', *ts'íik* 'angry' exclusively add animate or even human participants in stimulus function. The adjectives *sahak* 'afraid' and *su'lak* 'embarrassed' may select entities as well as propositions as stimulus participant, while *chi'chnak* 'furious' either selects animate participants or propositions. *Pòoch* 'desirous', *ma'óol* 'weary, listless', *ts'íibóol* 'eager' take as stimuli either propositions (cf. sect. 7.4.2), entities (replacing a proposition) or abstract nouns. See (164).

(164) a. *Hach   ma'óol-en   ti'   le   meyah-o'.*
       really   without:mind-ABS.1.SG   LOC   DEF   work-D2
       'I have no energy for that work.' (ACC)

   b. *Ts'íibóol-en   ti'   bak'-el   kéeh.*
      write:soul-ABS.1.SG   LOC   meat-REL   deer
      'I am eager for deer meat.' (Arzápalo 1995, s.v. *ts'íibóol*)

Su'lak 'ashamed, embarrassed' can be combined with two different kinds of stimuli which are differentiated by their subsemantic role. It adds the authority of judgment (generally a person) with *ti'* 'LOC' (164a) and the stimulus with either *ti'* (164b) or *yéetel* 'with' (164c/d). Both stimuli do not generally occur in the same frame since YM does not easily accumulate prepositional phrases (cf. Lehmann et al. 2000[D]).

(165) a. *Tèen-e' hach   su'lak-en   ti'   in   w-íicham*
      me-TOP really ashamed-ABS.1.SG LOC POSS.1.SG 0-spouse
      tumen   t-u   chuk-ah-en,
      because PFV-SBJ.3 catch-CMPL-ABS.1.SG
      táan   in   káal-tal   yéetel hun-túul   máak.
      PROG   SBJ.1.SG drunk-PROC with   one-CL.AN person
      'I am really ashamed in front of my husband, because he caught me (while I was) drinking (alcohol) with a man.' (NMP_0318)

    b. *Su'lak-en   ti'   u   káaltal   in   w-íicham.*
      ashamed-ABS.1.SG LOC SBJ.3 drinking POSS.1.SG 0-spouse
      'I am ashamed of my husband's drinking.' (EMB_0578)

    c. *Ma' su'lak   ti'/   yéetel ba'x t-u   mèent-ah-o'.*
      NEG ashamed LOC/ with   what PFV-SBJ.3 do-CMPL-D2
      'He is not ashamed of what he did!' (ACC_0476)

    d. *Pedro-e' su'lak   ?ti'/   yéetel u   xàanab.*
      Pedro-TOP ashamed LOC/ with   POSS.3 shoe
      'Pedro is ashamed of his shoes.' (ACC)

5.2.1.3 *Part-oriented constructions*

The current section examines all experiential adjectival collocations which take a part of the experiencer in subject function: either a material or immaterial body part or an abstract part. They can be grouped according to their syntactic behavior into several subgroups which instantiate various more specific constructions to be discussed in the following subsections. In sect. 5.2.1.3.1, idiomaticized collocations (mainly containing the person part noun *óol* 'mind') are examined. Sect. 5.2.1.3.2 looks at collocations with *ich* 'eye' related to evidentiality, and sect. 5.2.1.3.3 discussed non-idiomaticized collocations belonging mainly to the subdomain of bodily sensation.

5.2.1.3.1 *Idiomaticized collocations*

Table 18 lists adjectives that occur in collocations with a person part, especially *óol* 'mind' and *pòol* 'head', in subject function. Many of these person part constructions form phrasal compounds which take the experiencer in subject function. These have been discussed in the preceding section as part of

Table 17. Forming phrasal compounds based on collocations is not limited to the adjectival sphere but is a general tendency which also pertains to collocations with intransitive and transitive verbs (cf. sect. 5.3.1.2 and sect. 5.3.2.2.2).[4]

The items listed in Table 18 instantiate two different construction types. The difference is due to the semantics of the adjectival predicate which may either bear experiential semantics itself or not. First, there are a number of experiential predicates from the subdomain of emotion that occur exclusively in construction with *óol* 'mind'. These belong to the non-compositional kind of experiential collocation introduced in sect. 3.5.4. The experiencer is coded as possessive attribute to the immaterial body part noun *óol* which has subject function. *Ki'mak POSS óol* 'happy, glad', *háak'a'n POSS óol* 'proud', *óoya'n POSS óol* 'disheartened' belong to this group. (166) gives some examples.

(166) a. *Leti'-e'*   *chéen*   *ki'mak*   *u*   *y-óol ...*
         that.one-TOP   just   happy   POSS.3   0-mind
         'He was just happy (...)' (HIJO_064)

     b. *Háak'-a'n*   *in*   *w-óol*   *tumen*   *yàan*   *hun-p'éel*
        scare-RSLTV   POSS.1.SG   0-mind   because   EXIST   one-CL.INAN
        túumben   *xanab.*
        new   shoe
        'I am proud because I have a pair of new shoes.' (EMB_0539)

The aforementioned adjectives function in Construction 8. The experiencer is syntactically backgrounded with respect to the person part noun. It is an indirect participant of the predicate because of its possessive relation to the person part noun. Its affectedness as an experiencer is a metonymical inference drawn from the possessive relation expressed.

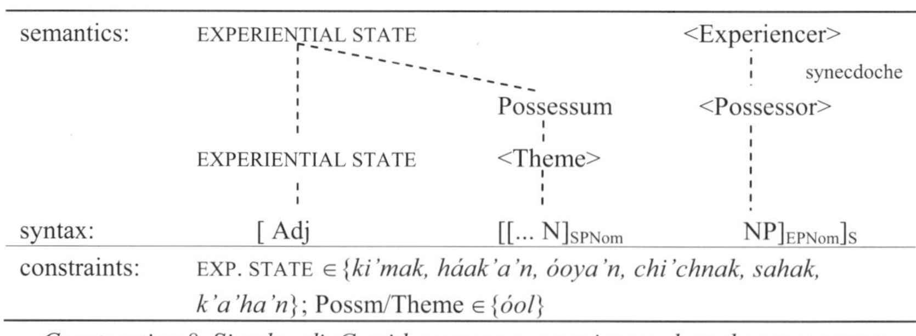

Construction 8. Simple adj. C. with possessor-experiencer, based on metonymy

---

[4] Lexicalization of body part phrasals as compound nouns is also reported in Reh (1998[L]: 392) for Dholuo.

subdo-main	instance (gloss) 'meaning'	properties		
emotion	*ki'(mak) POSS óol* (happy POSS mind) 'happy, glad, cheerful, content'	●	■	□
	háak'-a'n POSS óol (scare-RSLTV POSS mind) 'proud'	●		□
	óoy-a'n POSS óol (lose.nerv-RSLTV mind) 'disheartened'	●	-	
	chi'chnak POSS óol urious POSS mind) 'cross, furious'	●	■	
	sahak POSS óol (afraid POSS mind) 'afraid, fearful'	●	■	
	hets'-a'n POSS óol (quiet-RSLTV POSS mind) 'calm, relaxed; reassured'	○	■	□
	lúub-a'n POSS óol (fall-RSLTV POSS mind) 'sad, depressed, weak'	○	-	
	ala'n POSS óol (heavy POSS mind) 'have a heavy heart'	○	-	
	chuk-a'n POSS óol (suffice-RSLTV POSS mind) 'patient'	○	■	□
	kul-a'n POSS óol (sit-RSLTV POSS mind) 'content'	○	-	
bodily sensation	*uts POSS óol* (good POSS mind) 'feel good'	○	■	
	k'àas POSS óol (bad POSS mind) 'feel bad'	○	■	
	tòoh POSS óol (straight POSS mind) 'fine, well, healthy'	○	-	
	k'oha'n POSS óol (sick POSS mind) 'feel sick, weak'	○	-	
	chokol POSS óol (hot POSS mind) 'feel hot'	○	-	
	síis POSS óol (icy POSS mind) 'feel cool'	○	-	
cognition	*sàatal POSS óol* (lose:ADJR POSS mind) 'lost in thought; unconscious'	○	-	
	chokol POSS pòol (hot POSS head) 'mad'	○	-	
	k'àas POSS pòol (bad POSS head) 'mad'	○	-	
	k'a'h-a'n POSS óol (remember-RSLTV mind) 'remembered to'	●	◊	

properties:

- ● integrates with Construction 8;
- ○ integrates with Construction 9;
- ■ adjoins a stimulus complement with *ti*;
- □ adjoins a stimulus complement with *yéetel*;
- ◊ adjoins asyndetic purpose clause as stimulus;
- - does not adjoin stimulus complement.

Table 18. Person part collocations with adjectives

The fact that Construction 8 is a construction of its own can be deduced from the fact that the person part noun cannot be topicalized in these collocations (cf. (167a)), a property that is normally accessible to the subject argument of an adjectival predicate. This points to the idiomaticization of the collocations under investigation. The person part noun *óol* cannot be topicalized since it is semantically empty. Appropriate topicalization would be as shown in

(167b). The person part noun *óol* is inseparable from the adjective and is part of the larger predicate.

(167) a.*in   w-óol-e'   hach   ki'mak/ háak'-a'n   etc.
       POSS.1.SG   0-mind-TOP   really   happy/   scare-RSLTV
       intended: 'as for my heart, it is really happy/scared etc.' (ACC)
    b. *tèen-e'*   hach ki'mak/ háak'-a'n   in   w-óol
       me-TOP   really happy/   scare-RSLTV   POSS.1.SG   0-mind
       'I am glad / scared'

Construction 8 is a complex construction, consisting of two subconstructions, namely, the simple adjectival construction, as depicted in Construction 5, and the expanded possessed nominal construction, which was introduced in detail in Figure 10 and has the general structure '$^{(1)}$Possessum $^{(2)}$<Possessor>' [[$^{(2)}$PossClit $^{(1)}$N]$_{\text{SPNom}}$ $^{(2)}$NP]$_{\text{EPNom}}$.

Some of the experiential adjectives described in sect. 5.2.1.2 as occurring in Construction 5 can also be ascribed to the immaterial body part *óol*. *Chi'chnak POSS óol* 'cross, furious' and *sahak POSS óol* 'afraid, fearful' as well as *k'a'ha'n POSS óol* 'remember' belong to these. *K'a'ha'n* 'remember, have in mind' alternatively integrates with Construction 13, which will be introduced in sect. 5.2.1.4. Thus, they occur optionally in Construction 8, generally without a change in meaning. In such cases, experiential meaning is conveyed twice (and thus, redundantly), namely, in the predicate adjective and in the immaterial body part noun *óol* which itself has experiential meaning.

Other items from Table 18 constitute more or less clear cases of collocations of an originally non-experiential adjective with *óol*. They represent different types of compositional collocations in the sense introduced in sect. 3.5.4. Most of these collocations are from the subdomain of emotion, others denote bodily sensations or meanings of cognition. Since the predicate does not convey an experiential meaning, the immaterial body part noun *óol* can be analyzed as the indicator of such a meaning. The items *hets'a'n POSS óol* 'calm, relaxed, reassured', *lùuba'n POSS óol* 'sad, depressed, weak', *ala'n POSS óol* 'have a heavy heart', *chuka'n POSS óol* 'patient', *kula'n POSS óol* 'content', *tòoh POSS óol* 'fine, well, healthy', *sàatal POSS óol* 'lost in thought, unconscious' are seemingly based on metaphor, though it must be emphasized that they represent the common way to refer to the respective meanings in the language. (168) gives some illustrative examples and Construction 9 represents the construction.

(168) a. *Don Vicente   hach   chuk-a'n   y-óol   pàax.*
       Don Vicente   really suffice-RSLTV POSS.3-mind   celebrate\INTRV
       'Don   Vicente   is   really   patient   (enough)   to   play   music.'
       (EMB_0529)

 b. *Míin ma' tòoh in w-óol-i'*
  about NEG straight POSS.1.SG 0-mind-NEGF
  k'abéet in xeh.
  necessary SBJ.1.SG vomit
  'I think I'm not well. I need to throw up.' (BVS_16.01.04)

Again, the person part nouns cannot be topicalized in these expressions (169).

(169) **in* *w-óol-e'* *chuk-a'n/* *tòoh* etc.
  POSS.1.SG 0-mind-TOP suffice-RSLTV/ straight
  intended: 'as for my heart, it is patient/fine etc.' (ACC/NMP)

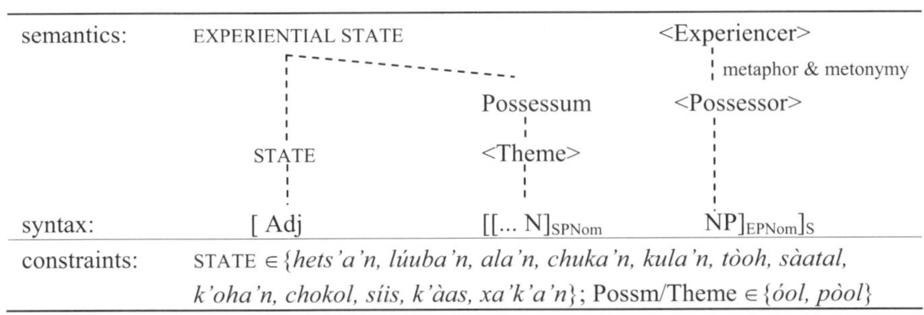

semantics:	EXPERIENTIAL STATE		<Experiencer>
			metaphor & metonymy
		Possessum	<Possessor>
	STATE	<Theme>	
syntax:	[Adj	[[... N]SPNom	NP]EPNom]S
constraints:	STATE ∈ {*hets'a'n, lúuba'n, ala'n, chuka'n, kula'n, tòoh, sàatal,*		
	k'oha'n, chokol, síis, k'àas, xa'k'a'n}; Possm/Theme ∈ {*óol, pòol*}		

Construction 9. Simple adj. C. with possr-expr, based on metaphor + metonymy

In some collocations *óol* signals the meaning of an emotional or a bodily feeling and corresponds to Engl. *feeling X*/Germ. *sich X fühlen*. This holds true for the combination with general evaluative adjectives such as *uts* 'good', *k'àas* 'bad', with adjectives of temperature such as *chokol* 'hot', *síis* 'cool', but also with adjectives denoting bodily conditions or states as, e.g., *k'oha'n* 'ill' in (170). In these collocations, *óol* signals a shift from a non-experiential to an experiential meaning. The adjectives *chokol* 'hot' and *síis* 'cold, icy' have to be combined with *óol* to denote the bodily feeling of temperature, i.e., 'feel hot', 'feel cooled down' as in (171). Thus, these items may be characterized as denoting a state of *óol* which results in the meaning of an experiential state of the experiencer. They fit into Construction 9 as well. In contrast, *ke'l* 'cold' is directly attributable to the experiencer (cf. sect. 5.2.1.1).

(170) *k'oha'n in w-óol*
  sick POSS.1.SG 0-mind
  'I feel weak/sick/weary.' (EMB_0529)

(171)   *Chokol   in   w-óol*
         hot   POSS.1.SG 0-mind
         káa   h   hóok'-en   ch'úul-ul.
         CNJ   PFV   exit-ABS.1.SG   moisten\DEAG-INCMPL
         'I was feeling hot (and/when) I went out to get wet.' (EMB_0520)

The construction with *óol* seems to be at least partly productive. (172) was accepted by a consultant with the meaning given, which fits with the constructional meaning given for Construction 9.

(172)   *nèets   u   y-óol*
         fragile POSS.3 0-mind
         'he is listless/of weak character/mind' (EMB)

The adjectives *chokol* 'hot' and *k'àas* 'bad' are constructed with the body part *pòol* 'head' (173). They also integrate with Construction 9, designating mental states or properties. Similar to *òol* the body part noun *pòol* 'head' cannot be topicalized in these collocations.

(173) a. *le   káal-a'n-o'   chokol u   pòol*
         DEF   drunk-RSLTV-D2   hot   POSS.3 head
         'that drunk person is lost in his mind' (SBM_0299)
     b.**Pedro-e'   u   pòol-e'   chokol*
         Pedro-TOP POSS.3 head-TOP hot
         intended 'as for Pedro, he's mad' (NMP)

Colonial Yucatec Maya had a huge number of examples from the domain of experience that belonged to the kind of construction type represented by Construction 8 and Construction 9, with a number of additional/other body parts (174). Most of these are incomprehensible today.

(174) a. *k'àap-ih   u   kàal   Pedro*[5]
         insert-ABS.3.SG   POSS.3 neck   Pedro
         'Pedro got angry' (Barrera Vásquez et al. eds. 1980, s.v. *k'aap kal*)

---

[5] Since the orthography of the CYM sources hides important phonological information, the CYM examples are represented in the standardized Bielefeld/Erfurt orthography (cf. sect. 1.3.3), with morpheme boundaries added. The reader should note that this entails non-literal quotation from the colonial sources.

b. *xet'-a'n*   *y-óol*
break.off-RSLTV POSS.3-mind
'he is without hope/desperate'
(Barrera Vásquez et al. eds. 1980, s.v. *xet'a'n yol*)

Óol is primarily construed as possessum of an experiencer. Some instances show, however, that it may also be construed as a possessum of a person part (175). *Puksi'k'(al)* 'heart, stomach' may refer either to the material or immaterial body part 'heart' (175a) or to the stomach as a material body part (175b/c). The combinability of *óol* as possessum with respect to another person part suggests its very high degree of desemanticization, and points to the fact that the respective collocations show a high degree of idiomaticization.

(175) a. *Ki'mak* *y-óol*   *in*   *puksi'k'-al.*
     happy   POSS.3-mind POSS.1.SG heart-REL
     'My heart is happy.' (NMP_0402)

    b. *Chokol* *y-óol*   *u*   *puksi'k'al*
     hot   POSS.3-mind POSS.3 heart
     káa *t-u*   *y-uk'ah*   *leche* *le*   *chan* *nèene-o'.*
     CNJ PFV-SBJ.3 0-drink-CMPL milk   DEF little baby-D2
     'The little baby felt hot/sick in its stomach (and/then) it drank milk.' (NMP_0406)

    c. *K'àas-lah-a'n*   *u*   *yóol* *u*   *puksi'k'al*
     bad-PROC.PFV-RSLTV POSS.3 0-mind POSS.3   heart
     la'téen *ma'ch* *u*   *hàan-al.*
     therefore not.ever SBJ.3 eat-INCMPL
     'His stomach is sick, therefore he doesn't eat.' (NMP_0015)

A number of collocations listed in Table 18 may add a stimulus participant; as in (176). Again, some collocations prefer *ti'*, others *yéetel*, others combine naturally with both prepositions to add a stimulus participant, as is indicated in Table 18.[6]

---

[6] *Óoya'n POSS óol* occurs in Dzul Poot (1985) but is not currently used among my consultants. Therefore, stimulus alignment could not be tested.

(176) a. *Yùum ahaw-e' hach ki'   u   y-óol   ti',*
       lord chief-TOP very happy POSS.3 0-mind LOC:ABS.3.SG
       tuméen t'áah.
       because robust
       'The chief was very pleased with him, because he was robust.'
       (HK'AN_220)
   b. *Háak'-a'n   y-óol   yéetel ba'x y-ohel.*
       become.scared-RSLTV POSS.3-mind with   what POSS.3-knowledge
       'He is very proud of what he knows.' (RMC_2194)

Thus, the examples in (176) are compatible with a construction composed of
Construction 8 and a prepositional phrase of the type '<Arg. role>' [PREP
NP]PP, where NP corresponds to the stimulus and PREP to either *ti'* 'LOC' or
yéetel 'with'. This is also true for the items integrating with Construction 9.

5.2.1.3.2 *Evidential collocations*

There are two collocations in the subdomain of emotion conveying an evidential meaning, namely *óotsil Poss ich* (poor POSS eye) 'sad' and *ok'om-óol
Poss ich* (sad:mind POSS eye) 'sad', both of which use the body part noun *ich*
'eye, face'. These collocations are the usual means for referring to the emotion
'sad' (along with *lùuba'n Poss óol* from Table 18). The combination with *ich*
is in both cases idiomaticized. See (177) for illustration.

(177) a. *káa h   ts'o'k le   siihbal-o'   Juan-e' óotsil y-ich*
         CNJ PFV end   DEF present\INTRV-D2 Juan-TOP poor   POSS.3-eye
         tumen ma'   yàan-chah   ti'-i'
         because NEG EXIST-PROC.CMPL   LOC:him-NEGF
         'and/when the gift-giving was over, Juan was sad because there
         was not enough for him' (ACC_0348)
   b. *ok'om-óol u   y-ich Don Vicente*
       sad:mind   POSS.3 0-eye Don Vicente
       tumen h   kim   u   y-atan
       because PFV die(CMPL) POSS.3 0-wife
       'Don Vicente looks sad because his wife died' (RMC_1737/ACC)

The use of *óotsil POSS ich* and *ok'om-óol POSS ich* with a first person possessor is restricted. Most consultants refused it or allowed it only marginally. This
indicates an evidential use of these collocations, based on the idea that the
emotion is not directly accessible by the speaker.[7] Furthermore, the possessed

---

[7] This function is taken to be evidential in the extended sense of the term (cf. sect. 3.3.2.1.1),
referring to the discourse function of qualifying an utterance on the basis of the evidence the

part noun *ich* 'eye' cannot be topicalized in these collocations (178). Moreover the stimulus participant is generally not added to these items.

(178)   **u*   *y-ich -e'*   *ok'om-óol/ óotsil*
        POSS.3 0-eye-TOP   sad:mind/   poor
        intended: 'his eyes look sad'

In addition to the mentioned adjectives, other experiential adjectives (and verbs) can also be combined with *ich* 'eye, face' as, e.g., *chi'chnak* POSS *ich* 'angry/furious looking', *p'úuha'n* POSS *ich* 'furious, peeved looking', *k'ùux* POSS *ich* 'angry, nervous looking, *ts'iik* POSS *ich* 'angry, fierce looking', *[?]sahak/sahlu'm* POSS *ich* 'afraid looking', *su'lak* POSS *ich* 'ashamed looking', *ma'óol* POSS *ich* 'weary, listless looking', *háak'óol* POSS *ich* 'surprised, frightened looking'. However, unlike the evidential collocations, these examples have to be interpreted literally. They are constructed regularly and do not have non-compositional semantics. There is no systematic restriction on the occurrence with the first person apart from plausibility. Thus, in a situation of looking in a mirror or asking a question, combinations with the first person are possible. In contrast to the evidential collocations, in these collocations, *ich* 'eye' can be topicalized (179).

(179)   *u*   *y-ich-e'*   *chi'chnak/ su'lak*   etc.
        POSS.3 0-eye-TOP   cross/   ashamed
        'he looks angry / ashamed'

Some of the examples allow for the adjunction of a prepositional phrase. Note however, how the semantics of the prepositional phrase in this construction (180b) changes in comparison with its semantics in a construction with the experiential adjective alone (180a). In (180a) the prepositional phrase is the stimulus argument of the experiential adjective *ts'iik* 'furious' while in (180b), it is a goal adjunct with respect to *ich* 'eye'. (180c) was proposed as a paraphrase of the first part of (180b).

(180) a. *Pedro-e'*   *ts'iik*   *ti'*   *u*   *xùun.*
         Pedro-TOP   furious LOC   POSS.3   spouse
         'Peter is angry with his wife.' (RMC)

---

^{speaker has for its truth. In this sense, ascribing an emotion to the eyes or the face of a person may be judged as evidential, since the speaker does not ascribe the emotion to the experiencer, but to its eyes/face and marks the utterance in this way as based on his or her perception.}

    b. *Pedro-e' ts'íik   y-ich   (ti'   u   xùun).*
       Pedro-TOP furious POSS.3-eye LOC POSS.3 spouse
       'Peter is looking angrily (at his wife).' (RMC)

    c. *Pedro-e' chíik-a'n   ti',   ts'íik.*
       Peter-TOP appear-RSLTV LOC furious
       'Peter appears (to be) angry.' (EMB, ACC)

Finally, note that some of the complex *óol*-collocations can occur in combination with *ich*, namely, *ki'mak POSS$_i$ óol POSS$_j$ ich$_i$* 'happy looking', *háak'a'n POSS$_i$ óol POSS$_j$ ich$_i$* 'proud looking'. This behavior again points to a high degree of idiomaticization of items 1 and 2 in Table 18 along with a high degree of desemanticization of *óol*.

(181)   *ma' ki'mak y-óol   y-ich-i'*
        NEG happy   POSS.3-mind POSS.3-eye-NEGF
        'he doesn't look very happy' (RMC_1776)

5.2.1.3.3 *Non-idiomaticized collocations*

Finally, some adjectives from the subdomain of bodily sensation are ascribed to appropriate body part nouns without being idiomaticized collocations in the sense of those listed in Table 18. In Table 19 these items are identified as selecting an appropriate body (part) noun in subject function. For instance, the adjectives *sáak* 'itchy', *yah* 'ache, painful', etc. only select an appropriate body part noun as subject (182).

(182)   *Hach sáak/ yah/ cha'yah/ ka'n-a'n   in   w-òok.*
        really itchy/ ache/ let:pain/ tire-RSLTV POSS.1.SG 0-foot
        'My foot is itchy/painful/smarting/tired.' (ACC)

The compounds *síis-óol* and *chokol-óol* select *wíinklil* 'body' as subject (183).

(183)   *Síis-óol in   wíinklil.*
        icy-mind POSS.1.SG body
        'I feel fresh.' (RMC)

Others adjectives of bodily sensation select either the experiencer or a body part. Table 19 presents an overview of relevant items and indicates the selectional restrictions for subject function.

instance	(gloss) 'meaning'	properties
síis-óol	(icy-mind) 'fresh, cool'	■
chokol-óol	(hot-mind) 'hot'	■
si's	'numb'	●[8]
yah	'ache, painful'	●
sáak'[9]	'itchy'	●
tahlak	'tired, fatigued, aching'	●
cha'yah	(let:pain) 'sore, aching, smarting'	●
cha'h	'sensitive (eyes, teeth)'	●
ke'l	'cold'	○
ka'n-a'n	(tire-RSLTV) 'tired'	○
ni'-nich'-kil	(RED-bite.off-PAT.ADJR) 'itchy'	○

properties:
- ● subject selection: body part
- ■ subject selection: body
- ○ subject selection: experiencer/body part

Table 19. Bodily sensation adjectives

Unlike the person part nouns occurring in the collocations integrating with Construction 8 and Construction 9, the body part nouns in bodily sensation collocations can be topicalized (184).

(184)   *In   w-òok-o'b-e'   ka'n-a'n-tak-o'b*
         POSS.1.SG 0-foot-PL-TOP tire-RSLTV-SBSTR.PL-PL
         úuchik   in   bin kòol.
         by.means.of SBJ.1.SG go   milpa
         'As for my feet, they are really tired from going to the milpa.'
         (ACC)

Thus, in contrast to the person part nouns in Construction 8 and Construction 9, the body part nouns discussed here are fully referential. They integrate with the adjectival body part construction as depicted in Construction 10. The specific sensation is only valid for the body part. A general bodily affectedness of the experiencer is necessarily inferred and results from the inherent relation between body part and possessor-experiencer.

---

[8] The concept 'body part' in Table 19 also includes the body as a whole.

[9] With this adjective, consultants do not agree as to its selectional restrictions. At least one allowed for an experiencer subject. The others allowed an experiencer subject only in the figurative meaning of 'bawdy'.

semantics:		Possessum	<Possessor>
	PROPERTY/STATE	<Theme>	
instantiation:	PRED	<THEME>	
syntax:	[Adj	[[... N]$_{SPNom}$	NP]$_{EPNom}$]$_S$
constraints:	PRED ∈ {adjectives of bodily sensation}; Possm/THEME ∈ {body part}		

Construction 10. Simple adj. body part C. with adjectives of bodily sensation

Depending on the nature of the predicative adjective, respective person part constructions can also be used for the expression of physical ability, such as in (185).

(185)   *kóok u   xikin*
        deaf POSS.3 ear
        'he is deaf' (FBC_0036)

In general, it can be observed that YM uses the depicted part-whole constructions not only for conveying experiential meaning, but for all other meanings involving body parts, such as ability, physical properties and states, etc. of a person. This means that Construction 10 is not a genuine experiential construction; rather, experiential collocations such as those formed with the adjectives from Table 19 are instantiations of the more general adjectival body part Construction 10 that ascribes states and properties to a body (or person) part. Depending on the semantics of the adjectival predicate, the possessor of the part may be inferred as being an experiencer, the holder of a property etc.

Finally, note that the expertum noun *tùukul* 'thought' may equally be integrated into Construction 10 in collocation with certain adjectives as in *tòoh POSS tùukul* (straight POSS thought) 'concentrated, relieved; be a sensible person', *xa'k'a'n POSS tùukul* (stirred POSS thought) 'confused'. Comparing (186a) to (186b) shows that *tòoh POSS tùukul* can have a state as well as a property meaning. In the second case, it denotes a characteristic related to the subdomain of cognition. Similarly (186c) can have both a state as well as a property (= permanent) reading.

(186) a. *Ken   ts'o'k-ok   túun bèey-o' pwes*
       SR.FUT finish-SUBJ   then   thus-D2 well
       tòoh   a   tùukul bèey-o' pwes ki'mak a   w-óol ...
       straight POSS.2 thought thus-D2 well   happy   POSS.2 0-mind
       'Then, when it's finished, well, your mind will be clear, now, you
       will be happy (...)' (K'AXBIL_114)

   b. *Le   máak ko'n   ts'a'   ti'   meyah-o'*
       DEF   person SR.FUT:ABS.1.PL   put(SUBJ) LOC   work-D2
       tòoh   u   tùukul.
       straight POSS.3 mind
       'That person to whom we are going to give work is a sensible per-
       son.' (RMC_2235)

   c. *Xa'k'-a'n in   tùukul.*
       stir-RSLTV POSS.1.SG thought
       'I am confused.' (NMP_0063)

These collocations allow the topicalization of *tùukul* 'thought' (187), and
thus, are not idiomaticized as those integrating with Construction 8 and
Construction 9 are.

(187)   *Pedro-e'   u   tùukul-e'   hach tòoh.*
         Pedro-TOP POSS.3 thought-TOP really straight
         'Pedro has a clear mind / is a sensible person.' (NMP)

5.2.1.4 Stimulus-oriented constructions
There are roughly three types of stimulus-oriented constructions to be discussed in this section. Firstly, a number of stimulus-oriented adjectives take the
experiencer as oblique object. Secondly, there are a few bivalent experiential
adjectives which take the experiencer as indirect object. Thirdly, there are
stimulus-oriented collocations coding the experiencer as possessor within a local person part phrase. These will be discussed in the order they were listed
above.

A number of adjectives denote an experiential meaning as a property of the
stimulus, e.g., *ki'* 'delicious, tasty, sweet', *ki'óotsil* 'touching, sentimental',
sah-ben(tsil) (fear-ADJR) 'fearsome, scary', *síis-óol* 'fresh', *ilahben* 'visible',
ch'uhuk 'sweet', *páap* 'piquant, spicy, hot', *chokow* 'hot', *si'h* 'malodorous',
tu' 'stinking', *che'òol* 'raw smell', *ki'-bòok* (delicious-smell) 'fragrant', *tsik-
bentsil* (respect-ADJR) 'dignified', *ni'-nich'-kil* (RED-bite-PAT.ADJR) 'itchy', etc.
(188) gives some illustrative examples.

(188) a. *le   k'iin   behe'l-a' síis-óol*
         DEF   sun   today-D1   icy:mind
         'today it's fresh' (RMC_1118)

     b. *ki'óotsil   u   pàax*
        pleasant   POSS.3   music
        'the music/play is sentimental' (RMC_1656)

     c. *le   ts'ono't-o'   hach   ilahben*
        DEF   cenote-D2   really   visible
        'that cenote is really visible' (FEE_0297)

In their simple construction, they integrate with the simple adjectival construction (Construction 11), fusing the semantic role STIMULUS with the only argument role of the simple adjectival construction. The stimulus' semantics is lexically given, and a general experiencer is understood but does not occur as a valency-dependent argument.

semantics:	STATE	<Theme>	
instantiation:	PRED	<STIMULUS>	
syntax:	[Adj	NP	]$_S$
constraints:	PRED ∈ {perception, bodily sensation, cognition, emotion, volition}		

Construction 11. Simple adj. C. with stimulus-oriented adjectives

The adjectives in question may have causative semantics such as *háak'óol* 'surprising, frightening', *sahbentsil* 'fearsome, scary', *pòoch'il* 'insulting', *xúul-óolal* 'exhausting' or an evaluative character such as *ki'* 'delicious, tasty, sweet', *ki'-óotsil* (delicious-poor) 'touching, sentimental'. This group of adjectives seems to be rather large (and open, being comprised of all the more or less qualifiying and evaluative adjectives), so they are not listed in a table.

Stimulus qualifying adjectives may also be integrated into Construction 12. If the experiencer is added in a prepositional phrase introduced with *ti'*, the respective expressions attain an explicitly experiential meaning and the Experiencer is interpreted as a kind of evaluator. Note that the stimulus-oriented construction in Construction 12 and the experiencer-oriented construction in Construction 6 display the same structure but have a converse alignment regarding experiencer and stimulus.

semantics:	EXPERIENTIAL STATE	<Experiencer	Stimulus>	
	┆			metonymy
	QUALIFIED STATE	<Theme	Location>	
	┆	┆	┆	
syntax:	[Adj	NP$_1$	[*ti'* NP$_2$]$_{PP}$]$_S$	
constraints:	QUALIFIED STATE ∈ {adjectives of emotional, perceptual quality}			

Construction 12. Extended adj. stimulus qualifying C. with experiencer

However, examples such as (189) are quite artificial, though consultants admit their grammaticality. Entities (189a/b) as well as propositions (189c) can function as stimulus participants. A construction with an appropriate perception or evaluation verb which takes the qualifying adjective as secondary predicate is more common (cf. sect. 5.3.2.1.4.)

(189) a. *le   kàan-o'   hach   sahbentsil   ti'   tèen*
      DEF snake-D2 really fear:ADJR:ABSOL LOC me
      'the snake is really scary to me' (EMB)

    b. *le   ha's-o'   hach   ch'uhuk ti'   tèen*
      DEF banana-D2 really sweet LOC me
      'that banana is really sweet to me' (EMB)

    c. *háak'óol/ sahbentsil   tèen u   tàal Pedro way-e'*
      scare:mind/ fear:ADJR:ABSOL me SBJ.3 come Pedro here-D3
      'it is scaring/surprising/scary to me that Pedro comes here' (ACC)

Furthermore, there are a few experiential and modal adjectives that take the stimulus or theme in subject function and the experiencer or modalized participant as indirect object in a prepositional phrase introduced by *ti'*. With these predicates, the prepositional phrase is semantically licensed and the adjectives are bivalent. Among the items relevant here are *k'a'ha'n*[10] 'remembered', *sùuk(a'n)* 'be accustomed' and the modals *k'abéet* and *k'a'náan* both 'necessary, need'. They are listed in Table 20 and exemplified in (190).

---

[10] From *k'a'h* 'remember' which also takes the experiencer in oblique function (with the preposition *ti'*) (cf. sect. 5.3.1.3).

subdomain	instance (gloss) 'meaning'
cognition	*k'a'h-a'n* (remember-RSLTV) 'have in mind'
habituality	*sùuk* (accustomed) 'be accustomed'
necessity	*k'abéet* (necessary) 'necessary, need'
necessity	*k'a'náan* (necessary) 'necessary, need'

Table 20. Bivalent experiential and modal adjectives

(190) a. *K'a'h-a'n*   *tèen tuláakal le*   *ba'x*
remember-RSLTV   me   all   DEF   thing
t-a   *ka'ns-ah*   *tèen-o'*.
PFV-SBJ.2   teach-CMPL   me-D2
'I remember/have in mind everything you taught me.'
(RMC_1532)

     b. *káa*   *t-u*   *ka'h bèet-ah*   *he'bix sùuk*   *ti'-o'* ...
CNJ   PFV-SBJ.3   do   do-CMPL   as   accustomed LOC-D2
'and he did as he was accustomed to do (...)'
(HLU'M_KÀAB_084.3)

     c. *sùuk(-a'n)*   *tèen bey-a'*
accustomed(-RSLTV)   me   thus-D1
'I am accustomed to it this way' (RMC_1144f.)

     d. *le*   *k'ìin k'abéet-ech*   *tèen-e'*
DEF   sun   necessary-ABS.2.SG   me-CNTR
káa   *tàal-ak-en*   *in*   *w-il-ech*
CNJ   come-SUBJ-ABS.1.SG   SBJ.1.SG   0-see-ABS.2.SG
'when I would need you I could come to see you.'
(HK'AN_452.1)

     e. *K'a'náan to'n ka'-p'éel*   *k'áanche'*   *way-e'*.
necessary   us   two-CL.INAN   hammock:wood   here-D3
'We need two chairs here.' (EMB_0824)

The items listed in Table 20 are instances of Construction 13. This construction conveys the meaning of a theme's state which affects a human participant, the latter being called Indirectus. With the experiential adjective *k'a'ha'n* the EXPERIENCER is mapped onto the Indirectus argument of the construction, and the STIMULUS is matched with the Theme argument. If the habitual adjective *sùuk* and the modal adjectives *k'abéet* and *k'a'náan* are integrated into Construction 13, their participant in oblique complement function is interpreted as being affected, as (190d/e) show. (190d) can be interpreted as conveying experiential meaning through a metonymic inference connecting a person's lack or need to an emotional state of missing. Furthermore, note that the items in Table 20 are regularly related to a corresponding intransitive construction, which will be discussed in sect. 5.3.1.3 as Construction 27. These two constructions can be judged as motivating each other.

semantics:	STATE	<Theme	Indirectus>
instantiation:	PRED	<STIMULUS	EXPERIENCER>
syntax:	[Adj	NP$_1$	[*ti'* NP$_2$]$_{PP}$]$_S$
constraints:	PRED $\in$ {*k'a'ha'n, sùuk, k'abéet, k'a'náan*}		

Construction 13. Extended adj. C. with experiential and modal adjectives

Note that under certain circumstances the *ti'*-complement is not syntactically obligatory with the adjectives listed in Table 20. These include their use as matrix predicates or in constructions with certain possessed nominals in subject function. For instance, in (191) the oblique experiencer argument is left unexpressed, a fact having to do with its referential identity with the possessive attribute of the subject NP. This case is discussed in detail in sect. 6.4.

(191) *Hach k'abéet in   tòoh-óolal.*
       really necessary POSS.1.SG straight-mind:ABSTR
       'I desperately need my health.' (Bricker et al. 1998, s.v. *tòoh-óolal*)

Finally, there are stimulus-oriented expressions that code the experiencer as possessive attribute to a person part noun as part of a prepositional phrase The examples in (192) are from Modern YM, while (193) is from Colonial YM.

(192) a. *Pos   wáah uts   t-a   t'àan-e',   he'le'.*
         well if   good LOC-POSS.2   speech-CNTR agreed
         'Well, if you like it, agreed.' (MUUCH_039)

      b. *Téet   máakanmáak uts   t-a   w-ich-i'*
         choose which   good LOC-POSS.2   0-eye-LOCF
         káa   ts'o'k-ok   a   beh-il   yéetel.
         that finish-SUBJ POSS.2 way-REL   with
         'Choose the one you like and you'll get married to him.'
         (HK'AN_282)

(193)   *ki'*   *t-in*   *chi'*
        delicious LOC-POSS.1.SG mouth
        in   *cha'nt-ik*   *ah*   *óok'ot*
        SBJ.1.SG   contemplate-INCMPL   master   dancer
        'I like looking at the dancers' (Barrera Vásquez et al. eds. 1980,
        s.v. *kii' ti' chi'*)

The examples in (192) and (193) convey a positive evaluation of a stimulus which may be an entity or a proposition. A list of collocations of this type is given in Table 21. The subdomain indicates the source domain of evaluation.

subdomain	instance (gloss) 'meaning'	prop.
emotion	*yah ti'* POSS *óol* (ache LOC POSS mind) 'be painful'	●
	uts ti' POSS *óol* (good LOC POSS mind) 'please, like'	○
em./cogn.	*uts ti'* POSS *t'àan* (good LOC POSS speech) 'please, like'	○
perception	*uts ti'* POSS *ich* (good LOC POSS eye) 'look good to, like'	○
	uts ti' POSS *chi'* (good LOC POSS mouth) 'taste good to; like'	○
	ki' ti' POSS *chi'* (delicious LOC POSS mouth) 'taste delicious to, tasty; like'	○
	uts ti' POSS *xikin* (good LOC POSS ear) 'sound good to'	○

properties:
   ○ integrates with Construction 14;
   ● adjoins a propositional stimulus

Table 21. Local person part collocations with adjectives

Construction 14 represents the construction conveying evaluative meaning. It is a complex construction consisting of an extended adjectival construction as depicted in Construction 6 and the expanded possessed nominal construction which itself is part of a prepositional phrase. Like the body part constructions in Construction 8 and Construction 9, Construction 14 represents idiomaticized collocations.

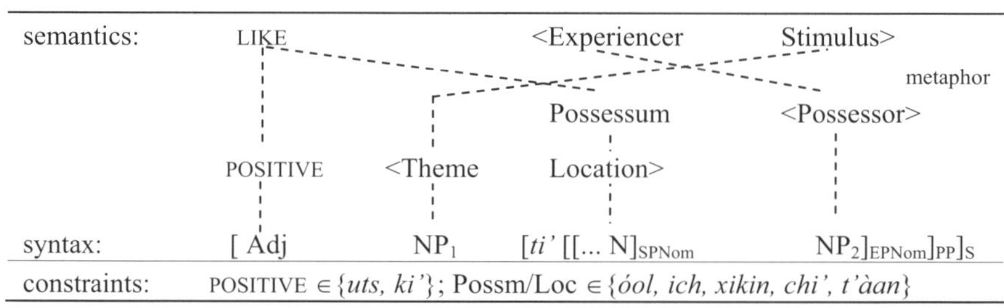

Construction 14. Adj. local C. of positive evaluation with possr-experiencer

While the collocations with *óol* 'mind' and *t'àan* 'speech' convey general evaluation, the collocations featuring body parts of perception are used in contexts where the source of evaluation is immediately linked to the evaluated entity/kind of stimulus. This is true for the collocations with *ich* 'eye', *xikin* 'ear', and *chi'* mouth. However Colonial data shows that at least some of the body parts of perception, e.g. *ich* 'eye' and *chi'* 'mouth' (193) were also used with stimuli unrelated to the perceptual mode they convey (cf. also sect. 8.2.3). The examples in (194) seem to indicate that this kind of construction was more widely used in Colonial Yucatec Maya, i.e., with a greater variety of meanings filling the Adj position in Construction 14 and obviously going beyond the meaning of evaluation.

(194) a. *k'áah-en*   *ti'*   *u*   *chi'*   *Pedro*
    bitter-ABS.1.SG LOC   POSS.3 mouth Peter
    'Peter detests me' (Barrera Vásquez et al. eds. 1980, s.v. *k'a*)

  b. *ma' núuk-a'n*   *t-in*   *xikin*
    NEG answer-RSLTV LOC-POSS.1.SG   ear
    'I do/did not understand'
    (Barrera Vásquez et al. eds. 1980, s.v. *nuukan ti' xikin*)

The same holds true for the collocation *yah ti' POSS óol* 'be painful' from Table 21, which may be supposed to be a relic of this wider use of local body part constructions in the domain of experience. Contrary to (194) however, possible stimuli are restricted to propositions (195).

(195) a. *Hàalibe' yah t-u*   *y-óol*   *le*   *tàatah-tsíil*   *wàal-o'* …
    well.then   ache LOC-POSS.3 0-mind   DEF father-ABSOL perhaps-D2
    'Well then, it may well have been painful to/for the father, (…)'
    (HIJO_061)

  b. *Ma'lòob   kex*   *yah*   *t-in*   *w-óol-e'*,
    good   although ache PFV-POSS.1.SG 0-mind-D3
    sáamal   in   *bis-ik-o'b*   *in*   *p'at-o'b   k'áax.*
    tomorrow SBJ.1.SG   carry-INCMPL-3.PL SBJ.1.SG leave-3.PL jungle
    'O.K., even though it makes me feel bad, tomorrow I will take them to abandon them in the jungle.' (HOSEH_25)

Note that *yah* 'ache' (Table 19) in its supposedly basic meaning (from the subdomain of bodily sensation) can only be integrated into Construction 10, not into a local construction. In this latter use, *yah* does not seem to be part of a pattern. However, see some parallel collocations with intransitive verbs in sect. 5.3.1.3.

182   CHAPTER 5

5.2.2 *Verboid constructions*

As shown in sect. 4.1.8, YM displays a subclass of stative predicates termed
verboids, that occur neither as attributes nor as heads of noun phrases. In contrast to verbal predicates, they do not combine with aspect/mood markers and
auxiliaries. A number of these elements play an important role in the domain of
experience. In the following description, verboids are dealt with according to
the constructions they occur in: intransitive constructions (cf. sect. 5.2.2.1) and
transitive constructions (cf. sect. 5.2.2.2).

5.2.2.1 *Intransitive constructions*

In the following sections, those verboids occurring in intransitive constructions
will be discussed. Modal auxiliaries that function as propositional operators are
examined in sect. 5.2.2.1.1 and the existential predicate *yàan*, which is used in
constructions with body part NPs and expertum NPs to convey experiential
meanings, is dealt with in sect. 5.2.2.1.2.

5.2.2.1.1 *Modal auxiliaries*

In sect. 3.2.2.5, it was noted that modal predicates of volition, including bodily
necessity, take an experiencer in their full verb reading as well as in their participant-oriented modality reading. Table 22 lists those modal auxiliaries that
may be judged as having an experiential meaning when taking a human or
animate entity as modal participant. *K'abéet* and *k'a'náan* have already been
discussed as lexical bivalent adjectives occurring in Construction 13, i.e., taking the stimulus in subject function and the experiencer in indirect object function (cf. sect. 5.2.1.4, (190d/e)).

modal class	instance (gloss) 'meaning'
volition	*tàak* (anxious) 'be anxious, want'
necessity	*k'abéet* (necessary) 'need, necessary'
necessity	*k'a'náan* (necessary) 'need, necessary'

Table 22. Modals related to experience

There are two main distributional criteria distinguishing modal auxiliaries
from lexical stative predicates. Firstly, modal auxiliaries – in contrast to complement-taking lexical predicates – cannot add a subordinate clause introduced
with the subordinator *káa* 'that'. As auxiliaries, *tàak* and *k'abéet/k'a'náan* take
incompletive-marked verbal cores (cf. Table 15) as embedded propositions in
subject function (196). In this use, the experiencer is not a direct dependant of
the predicate but occurs as subject (S, A)[11] in the subordinate core. For *tàak* this
is the only possible construction, i.e., it does not have a lexical variant.

---

[11] There are different judgments among my consultants concerning an embedded passive core.
These vary as to whether the derived S or the oblique A is understood to be referentially iden-

(196) a. *Ba'le'   hach   tàak   bin   u   k'ahóolt-ik*
         however   very   anxious QUOT   [SBJ.3 acquaint-INCMPL
         ba'x-o'b yàan   ichil le   mehen   nah-o'b-o'.
         what-PL [EXIST in   DEF   little house-PL-D2]$_{ReICI}$]$_{VCo}$
         'However he was very anxious to know what was in the rooms.'
         (HK'AN_050)

    b. *K'abéet   a   màas   he'l-s-ik   a   báah.*
        necessary [SBJ.2 more   rest-CAUS-INCMPL   POSS.2 self]$_{VCo}$
        'You need to rest more.' (BVS_10.01.09)

Secondly, modal auxiliaries – in contrast to lexical predicates – cannot take a
personal participant. Thus, in their modal auxiliary use, *k'abéet* and *k'a'náan*
cannot take the experiencer as an oblique complement (197a). This distinguishes them from other lexical matrix predicates that allow for a prepositional
argument in the matrix clause (e.g., *sùuk* 'be accustomed' in (197b), *k'a'h(a'n)*
'have in mind', cf. sect. 5.2.1.4), but may optionally occur without it (197b/c).

(197) a. *K'abéet   (*tèen) in   túuxt-ik   hun-p'éel   kàartah.*
         necessary me   [SBJ.1.SG send-INCMPL   one-CL.INAN   letter]
         'I need to send a letter.' (ACC, RMC, NMP, SME)

    b. *Sùuk   (tèen)   in   w-uk'-ik   kafé.*
        accustomed   me   [SBJ.1.SG 0-drink-INCMPL   coffee]
        'I am accustomed to drinking coffee' (EMB_0832)

    c. *Hach   sùuk   u   bin h   bùul.*
       very   be.accustomed [SBJ.3 go   SS gamble]
       'He had the habit of gambling/was enthusiastic to go gambling.'
       (HK'AN_043)

Construction 15 represents the modal operator construction with the possible experiential fillers *k'abéet*, *k'a'náan* and *tàak*. The EXPERIENCER is mapped
onto the main argument of the subordinate core. The YM modal auxiliaries are
impersonal operators taking the subordinate core as their absolutive argument.
Thus, they differ from the SAE-type that predominantly displays personal modal verbs or auxiliaries. While in the latter languages the experiencer of the
modal verbs is an argument of the modal verb, in YM, the experiencer is coded
as part of the modalized proposition. This difference has already been mentioned in sect. 2.2.3 with respect to examples (6) vs. (8) as a characteristic distinguishing person prominent vs. relation prominent languages.

---

tical to the experiencer. Such control features seem to be a peculiarity of the YM passive construction. This investigation has to be postponed to future research.

semantics:	MODALITY	(PROCESS/EVENT	<Arg.role>)
instantiation:	PRED	<	EXPERIENCER>
syntax:	[Mod	[VP	NP]$_{VCo}$]$_S$
constraints:	PRED $\in$ {$k'abéet, k'a'náan, tàak$}		

Construction 15. Modal operator C.

In addition to conveying a desire, the modal auxiliary *tàak* frequently occurs in contexts of bodily necessity (198.a) as well as in combination with consumption of food/eating (198.b).

(198) a. *le   pàal-o'   túun   kìis,   tàak   u   ta'*
      DEF   child-D2 PROG:SBJ.3   fart\INTRV anxious SBJ.3 defecate
      'that child is farting, it wants to defecate'

   b. *wáah   tuméen   tàak   a   hàan-t-ik-e'* ...
      if   because   anxious SBJ.2   eat-TRR-INCMPL-CNTR
      'if you are craving to eat, (…)' (HLU'M_KÀAB_041.3)

Just as *k'abéet/k'a'náan*, *tàak* may also be related to non-human participants (199); a behavior that points to its being a modal operator (and not a pure experiential predicate).

(199)   *tàak   u   k'áax-al   ha'*
      anxious SBJ.3 rain-INCMPL water
      'it wants to rain' (SBM_0305)

Tàak frequently occurs in the context of weather phenomena if there is indication that a certain meteorological state will come to be, as, e.g., in (199), which was uttered in a situation where the sky had become very cloudy. Bohnemeyer (1998[T]:380) reports that such weather phenomena are ascribed to bodily needs of deities. Smailus (1989:88) identifies bodily needs as the basic meaning of *tàak* in Colonial YM from which the desiderative meaning has developed.

5.2.2.1.2 *The existential predicate*

The existential predicate *yàan* 'be, have' has been introduced as a special kind of stative predicate. Its morphological, syntactic and derivational properties were discussed in sect. 4.1.8.

Yàan combines with a number of nominal(ized) experiential terms, i.e., expertum nouns, and with some person part nouns to express experiential states. In sect. 5.2.2.1.2.1, experiential nouns combining with *yàan* will be characterized, while the remaining sections will be dedicated to the analysis of the possible constructions. There are three main construction types containing existential *yàan*. The first expresses the existence of experience with respect to an experiencer in indirect object function (sect. 5.2.2.1.2.2), the second is an existential possessive construction with the experiencer coded as possessive attribute to the experiential noun. Finally, there is a local existential construction taking the experiencer as possessor of a body part or expertum noun in a local phrase. The latter possessive constructions are dealt with in sect. 5.2.2.1.2.3.

5.2.2.1.2.1 *Experiential nouns*

Nouns of the diverse experiential classes are by default abstract and belong mainly to the possessive class of neutral nouns, i.e., those nouns that are not especially marked outside possessive constructions. They are mainly derived from verbal or adjectival bases. Belonging to the neutral class of nouns means that the noun may be used both in possessive constructions and elsewhere with no morphological or other difference, apart from tone lowering (cf. Lehmann 1998, ch. 3.2.2.2.1). Most abstract nouns belong to this possessive class, which seems to be astonishing at first, at least for experiential nouns. It may be supposed that nouns meaning 'anger', 'sadness', etc. are by default related to the experiencer which seems to be all the more probable if one considers that the YM nouns under consideration are derived from verbal and adjectival bases. According to Lehmann (1998), this is only the first step of development. By nominalization of an experiential verb, e.g., *k'èey* 'scold', a nomen acti (*k'èey* 'scolding') may be formed. The actor/possessor slot of this verbal noun then becomes optional, and the word joins the class of neutral nouns. Many experiential nouns are derived from adjectival bases by the relational suffix *-il*, e.g., *sahak ~ sah(a)kil* 'fear', *su'lak ~ su'lakil, p'ùuha'n ~ p'úuha'nil* 'rancor', *k'ùux ~ k'ùuxil* 'anger', etc. These are originally inabsoluble (i.e., obligatorily possessed), however by changing their meaning to an abstract reading, the suffix *-il* may be reinterpreted as an abstractor and its relationality is lost (cf. Lehmann 1998, ch. 3.2.2.2.2.1).

Furthermore, there are a number of compounds among the experiential nouns. Like the case just discussed, they display corresponding adjectival patterns (*háak'óol ~ háak'óolal* 'fear', *hets'óol ~ hets'(el)-óolal* 'peaceful ~ peace') and the derivation corresponds to the one just described. Only a few nouns in the subdomain of emotion are non-derived. Most do not designate primary emotions but only emotion-related concepts such as *k'eban* 'sin', *síipil* 'remorse, guilt', *su'tsil* 'shame', *yah* 'ache, pain'.

5.2.2.1.2.2 *Experiencer as indirect object*

Table 23 lists experiential collocations containing *yàan*. They are construed with the experiencer in indirect object function.

subdomain	instance (gloss) 'meaning'	prop.
	yàan ts'íikil (EXIST anger) 'be angry'	●
	yàan chi'chnak-óol (EXIST cross-mind) 'be in a bad mood'	●
emotion	*yàan ma'óol(al)* (EXIST without.mind:(ABSTR)) 'be listless'	●
	yàan sahkil (EXIST afraid:ABSTR) 'be afraid'	●
	yàan ya-yah-óolal (EXIST RED-ache-mind:ABSTR) 'be in a depression'	●
	yàan líik'il-óol (EXIST lift\DEAG:INCMPL-mind) 'be in a good mood'	●
	yàan su'lakil (EXIST ashamed:ABSTR) 'be ashamed'	●
	yàan subtal (EXIST shame) 'be ashamed'	○
	yàan chi'chnakil (EXIST cross:ABSTR) 'be cross, weary'	○
	yàan k'ùuxil (EXIST anger) 'be angry'	○
	yàan p'èek(tah)il (EXIST hate:REL) 'feel hatred'	○
	yàan yàabilah (EXIST love) 'feel love'	○
	yàan ki'(mak-)óolal (EXIST pleasure) 'enjoy'	○ ■
	yàan hets'el óolal (EXIST quiet:REL mind:ABSTR) 'be peaceful'	○ ■
	yàan ki'óotsil (EXIST pleasure) 'be delightful, affecting'	○ ■
	yàan náaysah-óol (EXIST entertain-mind) 'be entertaining/diverting'	○ ■
cognition	*yàan k'ahóolal* (EXIST knowledge) 'have knowledge'	○
	yàan tùukul (EXIST thought) 'think, miss, trust'	○
	yàan na't (EXIST knowledge) 'be right'	○
volition	*yàan pòochil* (EXIST desire) 'be greedy'	●
bodily sensation	*yàan k'i'nam (koh, etc.)* (EXIST pain) 'suffer from (tooth, etc.) ache'	●
	yàan muk'yah (EXIST overcome:ache) 'suffer'	●

properties:
- ● integrates only with Construction 16;
- ○ integrates with Construction 16 and Construction 18;
- ■ integrates with 'existence at location' construction.

Table 23. Existential collocations I

As described in the preceding section, most nouns that form part of the collocations are derived from adjectives or verbs with the same meaning. (200) gives some examples.

(200) a. *Hwàan-e' yàan   ya-yah-óolal   ti'*
       H.-TOP   EXIST   RED-ache-mind:ABSTR LOC:3.SG
       'John feels depressed' (EMB_0168)

   b. *Yàan   tèen ki'óolal   in   w-áant-ik-ech...*
      EXIST   me   pleasure   SBJ.1.SG 0-help-INCMPL-ABS.2.SG
      'It is my pleasure to help you (…)' (HK'AN_196.4)

   c. *yàan   yàabilah/ subtal/ k'ùuxil   ti'   Juan*
      EXIST   love/   shame/ anger   LOC   Juan
      'Juan feels love/shame/anger' (NMP, ACC)

   d. *káa yan-ak   tèech hets'el óolal*
      that   EXIST-SUBJ   you   peace
      'so that you have peace' (HNAZ_0020.04)

Construction 16 represents the construction with which the collocations
given in Table 23 integrate. It ascribes an experiential state to the experiencer
in indirect object function.

semantics:	EXPERIENTIAL STATE	<Experiencer>		
	EXIST	<Theme	Indirectus>	metaphor
syntax:	[*yàan*	NP$_1$	[*ti'* NP$_2$]$_{PP}$]$_S$	
constraints:	Theme ∈ {emotion, bodily sensation, cognition}			

Construction 16. Experiential existence C. with indirect object

Construction 16 is a metaphorical extension of an expanded existence construction, which expresses existence of a theme at a location: '$^{(1)}$EXIST
<$^{(2)}$Theme $^{(3)}$Location>' [$^{(1)}$*yàan* $^{(2)}$NP$_1$ [$^{(3)}$NP$_2$]$_{PP}$]$_S$. Thus, an EXPERIENTIAL
STATE X OF Y is identified with an EXISTENCE OF X AT Y. Here, the event struc-
ture metaphor STATES ARE LOCATIONS is involved (Lakoff 1993). Construction
16 is parallel to a further metaphorical extension of the existence-at-location
construction, namely, possession is ascribed to an indirect object (cf. Lehmann
1998:104). This latter construction however is less restricted as to the possible
fillers of Theme and Indirectus.

Localization in time (corresponding to Test 3) is possible with most of the
items which fit into Construction 16 and they are thus judged as denoting states
rather than properties. With those denoting longer lasting states (e.g., *yàabilah*
'love', *p'èek(tah)il* 'hatred', *k'ah-óolal* 'knowledge') Test 3 however is judged
as bad.

As (201) shows, the experiencer in Construction 16 is not replaceable by a
non-sentient entity for most of the items listed in Table 23. If however the

oblique object position can be filled by a non-sentient entity, the latter is interpreted as location. This latter reading is exemplified in (201b). This example is
therefore an instance of the more basic 'existence-at-location construction'
which has been mentioned above.

(201) a.*yàan   k'ùuxil   ti'   le   kàah-o'
        EXIST anger   LOC DEF village-D2
        (ACC, RMC)

      b. yàan   ki'makóolal   ti'   hun-p'éel   fiesta
        EXIST pleasure   LOC one-CL.INAN party
        'there is pleasure at a party' (EMB)

Some of the items integrating with Construction 16 may add a stimulus
coded as possessive attribute to the expertum noun in the manner of a *genitivus
objectivus*. This established possessive relation of the expertum/possessed
nominal to the stimulus is marked by adding the relational suffix *-il*, as in
sahkil-il in (202) (cf. Lehmann 1998, ch. 3.2.2.2.2.2). This way of adding a
stimulus works for only a few of the items listed in Table 23, e.g. *yàan tùukul,
yàan sahkil*.

(202) a. *Yàan   u   sahkil-il   kíimil   ti'   Juan.*
        EXIST POSS.3 fear-REL   dying   LOC Juan
        'Juan is afraid of dying.' (RMC, ACC)

In these cases, NP_1 of Construction 16 is extended to an expanded possessed
nominal of the form '[1]Possessum [2]<Possessor>' [[[2]PossClit [1]N]SPNom
[2]NP]EPNom, where N represents the expertum noun and NP the stimulus.

5.2.2.1.2.3 *Experiencer as possessor*

Lehmann (1998, sect. 4.3.1) describes the functional equivalence of the construction "ascription of possession to indirect object" (i.e., a construction being
parallel to Construction 16) and another existential construction which renders
an "ascription of possession to possessive attribute". It is schematized in
Construction 17. Construction 17 is able to ascribe possession since the possessed nominal in YM is not definite per se, i.e., in this construction, it is understood as indefinite. Furthermore relational nouns generally do not integrate
with the construction.

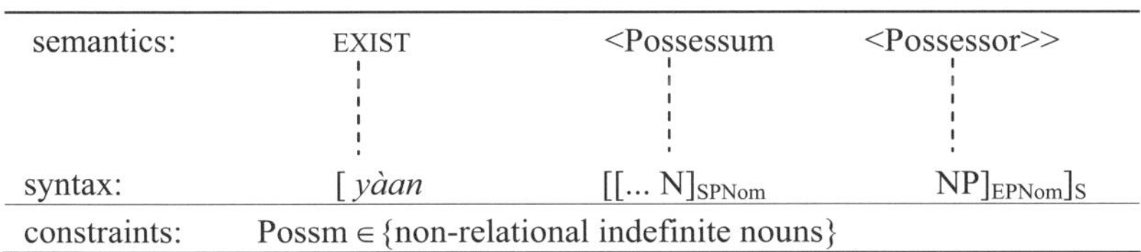

semantics:	EXIST	<Possessum	<Possessor>>
syntax:	[*yàan*	[[... N]_SPNom	NP]_EPNom]_S
constraints:	Possm ∈ {non-relational indefinite nouns}		

Construction 17. Ascription of possession to possessive attribute

Construction 17 inherits its structure from a simple existence construction '[1]EXIST <[2]Theme>' [[1]*yàan* [2]NP]_S and the extended possessed nominal construction '[1]Possessum [2]<Possessor>' [[[2]PossClit [1]N]_SPNom [2]NP]_EPNom.

The structural layer of Construction 17 is accessible for a number of items, as indicated in Table 23. The respective items do in fact integrate with Construction 18 which is motivated by Construction 17 by metaphorical extension. Thus, Construction 18 expresses the existence of experience literally with respect to the possessor-experiencer. This results in the expression of an experiential state (203) or property (204) of the experiencer. Most items in Table 23 render stative situations according to the respective test frame (Test 3) when integrating with Construction 18. Some may additionally refer to a characteristic trait of a person, i.e., a property. These are listed in Table 24 together with a number of other items.

(203) a. *yàan   u   k'ùuxil.*
      EXIST   POSS.3 anger
      'he is angry' (NMP)

    b. *yàan u   chi'chnakil   Juan*
      EXIST POSS.3 cross:ABSTR   Juan
      'Juan feels uncomfortable' (RMC, ACC)

(204)   *Yàan/ mina'n   u   subtal Juan.*
      EXIST/ NEG.EXIST POSS.3 shame Juan
      'Juan has a/no sense of respect.' (RMC, ACC)

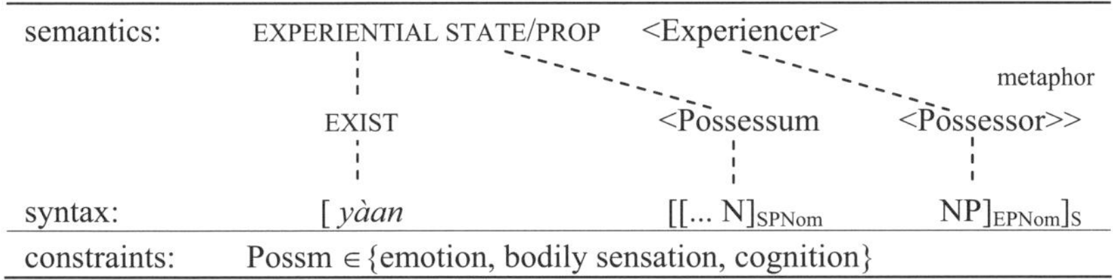

semantics:	EXPERIENTIAL STATE/PROP	<Experiencer>	
	EXIST	<Possessum	<Possessor>>
syntax:	[*yàan*	[[... N]_SPNom	NP]_EPNom]_S
constraints:	Possm ∈ {emotion, bodily sensation, cognition}		

Construction 18. Experiential existence C. with possessive attribute

Note that a number of items listed in Table 23 do not integrate with Construction 18. Instead, these cases are interpreted as combinations of the modal auxiliary *yan* 'DEB' plus an incompletive-marked verbal core (sect. 4.2.2) if the nominal form can be interpreted as a verbal form as well (compare, e.g., (200a) with (205)). In contrast, for most of the items integrating with Construction 18 a verbal interpretation is excluded.

(205)   *Hwàan-e' yan   u   ya-yah-óolal.*
         H.-TOP   DEB POSS.3 RED-ache-mind:ABSTR
         'John will be depressed.' (ACC, NMP)

Construction 18 may be expanded by a prepositional phrase, i.e., by the construction '<Arg. role>' [*ti'* NP]$_{PP}$, which adds a stimulus (206).

(206) a. *Yàan   u   yàabilah Maria ti'   Juan.*
         EXIST POSS.3 love   Maria LOC Juan
         'Maria feels love for Juan.' (NMP, ACC)
      b. *Mina'n   in   k'ahóol-al   ti'   le   ba'l-a'.*
         NEG.EXIST POSS.1.SG know-ABSTR LOC DEF thing-D1
         'I have no knowledge of this (thing).' (Bricker et al. 1998, s.v. *k'ah(2)*)

Thus, Construction 16 as well as Construction 18 can be expanded to add a stimulus. In Construction 16, the expertum noun is relationalized to add the stimulus as its possessor. In Construction 18, the possessor slot of the expertum noun is already occupied by the experiencer, and the stimulus can only be added in a *ti'*-phrase. This is shown in (207) for the expertum noun *tùukul* 'thought'. In (207a), the experiencer is coded as possessor and the stimulus is added in a *ti'*-phrase. In (207b) in contrast, the experiencer appears as an indirect object and the stimulus is coded as a possessive attribute to the expertum noun *tùukul* which is marked by the relationalizing suffix *-il*.

(207) a. *Hach   chéen ti'   leti'   yàan   in   tùukul*
         really just   LOC that.one EXIST POSS.1.SG thought
         tuméen   he'ba'x k'iin k'oha'n-en-e'   leti'   ts'ak-ik.
         because any:what sun   sick-ABS.1.SG-CNTR that.one cure-INCMPL
         'Only in him I have confidence because any day I'm ill he cures (me).' (ICM_0038)

b. *Yàan   u   tùukul-il   ti'   Juan u   k'iinbes-ik*
EXIST POSS.3 thought-REL LOC Juan SBJ.3   sun:CAUS-INCMPL
u   k'àaba'.
POSS.3 name
'Juan has the idea to celebrate his birthday.' (ACC)

Table 23 contains items fitting into Construction 16 and Construction 18. Those items referring to properties when integrating with Construction 18 (e.g., (204)) and some other items which do not integrate with Construction 16 are listed in Table 24. Some examples are given in (208).

subdomain	instance (gloss) 'meaning'
	yàan POSS tsìik (EXIST POSS respect) 'respectful'
	yàan POSS kuxóolal (EXIST POSS compassion) 'sympathetic'
emotion	*yàan POSS subtal* (EXIST POSS shame) 'respectful, know how to behave'
	yàan POSS óol (EXIST POSS mind) 'feel good, feel like ...'
	yàan POSS tùukul (EXIST POSS thought) 'intelligent'
cognition	*yàan POSS na't* (EXIST POSS knowledge) 'intelligent'
	yàan POSS k'ahìik' (EXIST POSS responsibility) 'think responsibly'

Table 24. Existential collocations II

(208) a. *In   suku'n-e'   hach mina'n   u   tùukul*
         POSS.1.SG elder.brother-TOP really NEG.EXIST POSS.3 thought
         chéen bèey u   pul-ik   u   tàak'in-o'.
         just   thus SBJ.3   throw-INCMPL POSS.3 money-D2
         'My older brother, he's not very intelligent! He just throws his money away like that.' (Bricker et al. 1998, s.v. *tùukul*)

     b. *Yàan   u   k'ahìik'.*
        EXIST   POSS.3   responsibility
        'He thinks responsibly.' (Bricker et al. 1998, s.v. *k'ah(2)*)

     c. *X-pìil-e'   hach   mina'n   u   tsìik   u   chi'.*
        F-Phyllis-TOP   really NEG.EXIST POSS.3 respect POSS.3 mouth
        'Phyllis is very rude [lit.: her mouth has no respect at all].'
        (Bricker et al. 1998, s.v. *ts'ik*)

Note that (208c) is a double possessive construction. The expertum is ascribed to the possessor's/experiencer's body part, and thus, only indirectly to the possessor. A comparable double possessive construction has also been exemplified in (175).

Besides the collocations with possessed expertum nouns, Table 24 contains a collocation with the person part noun *óol*. This one does not integrate with Construction 16 because it belongs to the class of inabsoluble nouns that never occur in absolute use (i.e., non-possessed) (cf. Lehmann 1998). (209) gives examples of its positive and negative use.

(209) a. *Chan   yàan   a   w-óol   behe'l-a'*?
        a.bit   EXIST POSS.2 0-mind today-D1
        'Are you better today?' (NMP_0056)

   b. *mina'n   u   y-óol*
      NEG.EXIST   POSS.3   0-mind
      'he/she/it is listless/apathetic/dispirited'
      (Bricker et al. 1998, s.v. *óol*)

   c. *yàan/   mina'n   in   w-óol   (ti')   meyah*
      EXIST/ NEG.EXIST   POSS.1.SG   0-mind (LOC)   work
      'I do (not) feel like working' (RMC_1734)

This collocation renders a positive state of mind, which may be directed towards a controllable activity, as shown in (209c). Thus, only propositions can be added as stimuli to this collocation, either in the form of a 'split' pattern core (cf. sect. 7.4.2.3) or introduced by the preposition *ti'*.

There are further existential collocations containing person part nouns as subject arguments which do not however, express experiential states but rather physical ability or disposition such as *mina'n POSS t'àan* (NEG.EXIST POSS speech) 'mute', *yàan POSS xikin* (EXIST POSS ear) 'have a good hearing', etc. The latter conveys a 'par excellence'-reading. However, in contrast to the experiential instance of Construction 17, i.e., Construction 18, these do not take a prepositional object phrase.

Finally, there are some local existential person part collocations rendering experiential meanings (Table 25).

subdomain	instance (gloss) 'meaning'
emotion	*yàan ti' POSS puksi'k'al* (EXIST LOC POSS heart) 'be in one's heart'
cognition	*yàan ti' POSS pòol/ho'l* (EXIST LOC POSS head) 'be/have in one's head'
	yàan ti' POSS tùukul (EXIST LOC POSS thought) 'be keen on'

Table 25. Local existential person part collocations

The instances listed in Table 25 code the stimulus in subject function and the experiencer as possessive attribute to the person part noun as part of a prepositional phrase. It is a complex construction consisting of the abovementioned 'existence-at-location construction' and the expanded possessed nominal construction which itself is part of a prepositional phrase (cf. Construction 19). (210) gives examples from Modern YM, (211) from Colonial YM. Furthermore, see Construction 14, which schematizes a parallel construction with an adjectival predicate.

(210) a. *Leti'-e'*   *chen ti'   yàan   t-u   tùukul*
         that.one-TOP   just   there EXIST LOC-POSS.3 thought
         u   bin u   kan xòok-e'
         SBJ.3 go   SBJ.3 learn studies-D3
         t-u   pàach u   láak-o'b.
         LOC-POSS.3 back   POSS.3 other-PL
         'He thinks that he wants to study (go to school) with his brothers.'
         (ICM_0037)

      b. *Tèech-e'   ti'   yàan-ech   ti'   in   puksi'k'al-e'*
         you-TOP   there EXIST-ABS.2   LOC   POSS.1.SG heart-D3
         kex   náach yàan-ech   ti'   tèen-e'.
         although far   EXIST-ABS.2   LOC me-D3
         'You are in my heart, although you are far away from me.'
         (RMC_1726)

(211)   *yàan   ti'   xikin*
         EXIST LOC ear
         'know something' (Barrera Vásquez et al. eds. 1980, s.v. *yan*)

Since Barrera Vásquez et al. eds. (1980) mentions further local existential person part collocations of the 'stimulus=subject' kind for Colonial Yucatec Maya (e.g., *yan ti' ol* 'have decided, intend, inner agreement' etc.) one can assume that the semantic scheme is not calqued from the superstratum Spanish (which has equivalent expressions) but existed in the language before.

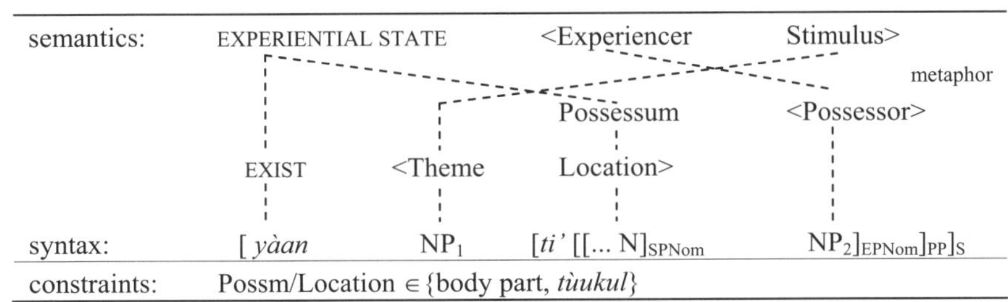

Construction 19. Local existential person part C. with stimulus

5.2.2.2 *Transitive constructions*
5.2.2.2.1 *Transitive verboids*

Another subclass of items belonging to the class of stative predicates used in the domain of experience is transitive verboids. They are characterized, as the label suggests, by being on the one hand bi-relational/transitive and stative on the other hand, since they never combine with members of the class of aspect/mood markers and auxiliaries. The members of this class are exclusively experiential in meaning (Table 26). The experiencer is cross-referenced by the subject clitic and the stimulus by the absolutive suffix.

subdomain	instance (gloss) 'meaning'
volition	*k'áat* 'wish, want; love'
emotion	*p'èek* 'hate, dislike'
	yàa(ku)mah 'love, fond of'
cognition	*ohel* 'know'
	k'ahóol 'acquaint'
	òoksmah POSS óol ti' 'believe in, trust in'

Table 26. Transitive verboids

(212) shows that *k'áat* and *ohel* preferably take propositional/abstract stimuli while *p'èek* and *k'ah-óol* take non-propositional stimuli. While *ohel* and *k'ah-óol* seem to be in complementary distribution as to this feature of participant properties of the stimulus, both *p'èek* and *k'áat* occur with both non-propositional and propositional stimuli (213).

(212) a. *wáah t-u   hàah-il   a   k'áat a   man-e'* ...
     if   LOC-POSS.3 true-ABSTR SBJ.2 wish SBJ.2 buy(SUBJ)-D3
     'if you really want to buy it, (...)' (HA'N_0023.08)

   b. *Te'x-e'   tuláakal-e'x a   w-ohel-e'x wáah màaya' t'àan?*
     you.all-TOP all-2.PL   SBJ.2 0-know-2.PL INT   Maya   speech
     'Do you all know Maya?' (BVS_02.01.11)

   c. *U   p'èek-en   in   láak'-o'b-o'.*
     SBJ.3   hate-ABS.1.SG POSS.1.SG equal-PL-D2
     'My brothers envy me.' (MUUCH_273)

   d. *Máax-ech,   ma' in   k'ahóol-ech-i'.*
     who-ABS.2.SG NEG SBJ.1.SG   acquaint-ABS.2.SG-NEGF
     'Who are you, I do not know you.' (HNAZ_0028.03)

(213) a. *in   k'áat u   si'n-el*
     SBJ.1.SG wish   POSS.3 back-REL
     'I want its back'

b. *u   p'èek   u   tusbèel-t-a'l*
   SBJ.3 hate   SBJ.3 send:way:REL-TRR-PASS.INCMPL
   'she hates to be sent around/to get orders' (AEF_0012)

Construction 20 represents the transitive verboid construction.

semantics:	EXPERIENTIAL STATE	<Experiencer	Stimulus>
	¦	¦	¦
syntax:	[Trvd	NP$_1$	NP$_2$]$_S$
constraints:	EXP. STATE ∈ {emotion, volition, cognition}		

Construction 20. Transitive verboid C.

Some of the items listed in Table 26 have also been referred to as relational nouns (cf. Lehmann 1998, Bohnemeyer 1998[T], 2002), since they obligatorily fill the subject/possessor slot and the absolutive slot, as do relational nouns. They would then belong to the class of inabsoluble nouns, i.e., to those nouns that never occur in absolute use. In contrast to nouns, however, the items in Table 26 do not occur as heads of an NP. Rather, their functional locus is in predication. Moreover, some of them can be derived in order to become nouns (cf. Table 23, i.e., *p'èek(tah)il* 'hatred, animosity', *k'ah-óolal* 'knowledge', *yàabilah* 'love').[12]

In fact, the transitive verboids listed in Table 26 do have nominal as well as verbal properties. They share the property that they cannot be combined with the aspect/mood markers and auxiliaries with nouns. They share the property that they cannot be the head of an NP with verbs. Further evidence for their syntactic behavior can be taken from focus constructions. For instance, in contrast to relational nouns (214c), but similar to verbs (214a), transitive verboids (214b) can appear in argument focus constructions focusing on the subject/possessor argument.

(214) a. *Leti'   bon   le   nah-a'*?
         who   paint DEF   house-D1
         'It is he who painted this house?' (ACC)

      b. *Leti'   u   k'áat/ p'èek   káa xi'k-en.*
         that.one SBJ.3 wish/ hate   that go:SUBJ-ABS.1.SG
         'It is he who wants me to go/who hates that I go.' (RMC/ACC)

---

[12] Andrade (1955:75) calls them 'defective verbs' since they do not show the verbal inflectional suffixes. Tozzer (1921:60ff.) mentiones *k'áat* and *p'èek* as part of a larger group of irregular and defective verbs containing moreover members of the class of modal auxiliaries such as *tàak* and *k'abéet*.

c.**Leti'   láak'-il.*
    that.one other-REL
    intended: 'It is he whose relative he is.' (ACC/NMP)

Concerning the properties discussed so far, transitive verboids behave identically to perfect participles (cf. sect. 4.1.8.1 for A/M combination, (150b) for the argument focus construction). There is, however, one property that distinguishes transitive verboids from all the three other classes, namely, that they do not allow for the elision of the subject/possessor clitic. Thus, in contrast to transitive verboids (215), relational nouns (148), perfect participles (150a) and transitive verbs (135a) 'equi-delete' the subject/possessor clitic in content questions.

(215)   **Máax k'ahòol(-ih)*?
        who   know(-ABS.3.SG)
        intended: 'Who knows him?' (ACC)

Table 27 summarizes the evidence as to the noun-like vs. verb-like behavior of transitive verboids. It can be concluded that transitive verboids display both nominal and verbal properties and that they are most similar to perfect participles.

	relational nouns	perfect participles	transitive verboids	verbs
A/M combination	no	no	no	yes
Arg. focus	no	yes	yes	yes
NP formation	yes	no	no	no
Subj./Poss. clitic	also without	also without	only with	also without

Table 27. Syntactic properties of transitive verboids

Two items mentioned in Table 26 are obviously derived with the perfect form *-mah*, namely *yàa(ku)mah* 'love, to be fond of' and *òoksmah POSS óol ti'* 'believe in, to trust in'. Compare the illustrative examples in (216).

(216) a. *kex   wàal yah   t-a   w-óol-e'*
         although DUB   ache LOC-POSS.2 0-mind-CNTR
         yan   a   kìins-ik-en   wáah a   yàakumah-en ...
         DEB   SBJ.2 kill-INCMPL-ABS.1.SG   if   SBJ.2 love-ABS.1.SG
         'even if it pains you, you have to kill me if you love me, (...)'
         (HK'AN_613.2)

b. *a   w-òoksmah   a   w-óol-e'x*
SBJ.2 0-enter:CAUS:PART.PF POSS.2 0-mind-2.PL
'you (pl.) believe(d)'

Perfect participles and transitive verboids are not only similar in the behavior mentioned in Table 27; they also display a similar argument structure in taking the experiencer/agent in subject function and the stimulus/patient in direct object function (cf. sect. 4.1.6, (112)). *Yàakumah* 'love, be fond of', but not *òoksmah* POSS *óol ti'* 'believe in, trust in', behaves like a canonical perfect participle in focus constructions such as content questions and argument focus constructions. For *yàakumah* compare (217) with the perfect form in focus constructions in (150).

(217) a. *Máax yàakum-il   Pedro?*
      who   love:PART.PF-REL Pedro
      'Who loves Pedro?' (ACC/NMP)

      b. *Leti'   yàakum-il   Pedro.*
      that.one love:PART.PF-REL Pedro
      'It is he who loves Pedro.' (ACC/NMP)

Òoksmah POSS *óol* 'believe' in contrast, behaves like the basic transitive verboids in not allowing for 'equi-deletion' of the subject clitic in content questions (218).

(218) **Máax òoksm(ah)-il   u   y-óol?*
       who   believe:PART.PF-REL POSS.3 0-mind
       intended:'Who believes?' (ACC/NMP)

Instead, subject focus in a content question and in an argument focus construction is constructed in the same way as with the transitive verboids (cf. (219) in comparison to (214b)). Note however, that *òoksmah* POSS *óol* has a special argument structure in that it does not adjoin the stimulus in direct object function but rather as a *ti'*-complement; a behavior that is explained by the fact that the direct object function is occupied by *óol*.

(219) a. *Máax u   y-òoksmah   u   y-óol ti'   Kristo?*
      who   SBJ.3 0-believe:PART.PF POSS.3 0-mind LOC Christ
      'Who believes in Christ?' (ACC/NMP)

      b. *Leti'   u   y-òoksmah   u   y-óol   ti'   Kristo.*
      that.one SBJ.3 0-believe:PART.PF POSS.3 0-mind LOC Christ
      'It is he who believes in Christ.' (ACC/NMP)

In general, it can be argued that the class of perfect participles is a suitable source of transitive verboids because of their common argument structure and their common internal temporal structure. The motivation for integrating 'new' members into the class of transitive verboids seems to be semantic since it exclusively contains experiential concepts.

To conclude this section, the derivational behavior of transitive verboids will be briefly addressed. Unlike adjectives and modals (which have been shown to create intransitive and transitive verbs in *-tal* 'PROC' and in *-kint/s/ -kunt/s* 'FACT' respectively), but like intransitive verbs and some nouns, all transitive verboids can be formed with *-t*, which enables them to function as full transitive verbs. Resultative derivation in *-a'n* (220) and perfect derivation in *-mah* (310) are assumed to operate (at least semantically) on the transitivized/verbalized verboids (recall from sect. 4.1.6 that YM seems to avoid multiple derivational suffixes).

(220)   *Ma', ma' hach   k'ahóol(-t)-a'n   radyos-i'*,
         NEG NEG really   acquaint(-TRR)-RSLTV radio-NEG
         ma' k'ahóol(-t)-a'n   kareteras-i'.
         NEG acquaint(-TRR)-RSLTV streets-NEG
         'Radios were not very well known, streets were not known.'
         (EMB & AME 200/ACC)

5.2.2.2.2 *Perfect participles*

Perfect formation has already been introduced in sect. 4.1.6 as a dynamicity reducing operation. Perfect participles are regularly derived from transitive verbs resulting in stative bivalent predicates. They keep the relational structure and valency frame of their bases. Both features mentionend, birelationality and stativity, have been identified as characteristic of the class of transitive verboids in the preceding section. These are the features that support the analysis that the goal category of the perfect derivation is the class of transitive verboids.

As regards the domain of experience, perfect forms are used to refer to a resultant state of a usually dynamic situation, such as in (221a/c). In (221b), the perfect form *yàabiltmah* is based on the transitive base verb *yàabilt*, which has itself a stative (note that it is itself derived from a noun *yàabil(ah)* 'love') or a dynamic reading depending on the combination with an aspect auxiliary (cf. sect. 5.3.2.1.1.1). The perfect participle is preferred in contexts where the speaker wants to underline the stative and permanent reading (compare German: *lieb haben*). Thus with respect to (221b), the transitive form *k-u yàabil-t-ik* (IMPF-SBJ.3 love-TRR-INCMPL) was judged as bad.instead of the perfect form *u yàabil-t-mah* (SBJ.3 love-TRR-PART.PF).

(221) a. *A   kan-mah   t-a   tùukul,   k'a'h-a'n   tèech?*
SBJ.2 learn-PART.PF LOC-POSS.2 thought remember-RSLTV you
'You know it by heart, do you remember it/have it in mind?'
(RMC_0053)

   b. *In   nohoch chìich-e'*
POSS.1.SG big   grandmother-TOP
yàan   ti'   hun-p'éel   ka';
EXIST LOC:ABS.3.SG one-CL.INAN   mill
chen   ba'l-e'   hach   u   yàabil-t-mah,
just   thing-TOP   really SBJ.3 love-TRR-PART.PF
ma'ch u   y-óot-ik   u   mahant-eh.
not.ever SBJ.3   0-agree-INCMPL SBJ.3   borrow-SUBJ
'My grandmother has a handmill, but she loves it so much that she
never wants to lend it.' (ACC_0080)

   c. *A   na't-mah?*
SBJ.2   understand-PART.PF
literally: 'Do you have/take it understood?' (ACC)

There is a frozen perfect participle, namely, *nahmah* 'deserve, be necessary
to'. It occurs in texts by Dzul Poot (1985), but seems to be obsolete in the dialect investigated, at least in verboid use. At present, there is a cognate full verb
náahal(t) 'earn'. *Nahmah* in its modal use has been replaced by the modal auxiliaries *k'a'na'n/k'abéet* 'need, necessary' (cf. sect. 5.2.2.1.1).

5.3   *Verbal constructions*
Verbal predicates, in contrast to stative predicates, generally encode dynamic
situations.[13] Following the outline of predicate classes in sect. 4.1.8, intransitive, transitive and ditransitive verbal constructions are distinguished.

5.3.1 *Intransitive constructions*
The following sections examine verbal experiential construction types of different intransitive classes, which are again organized by the orientation of the
construction towards the experiencer (sect. 5.3.1.1), its part (sect. 5.3.1.2), and
the stimulus (sect. 5.3.1.3).

---

[13] This holds true with the exception of the modal verbs *páahtal*and *beytal*, both meaning 'be
possible' which commonly occur with a reduced number of aspect markers/auxiliaries. Other
possible exceptions among the derived experiential verbs will be discussed later in this chapter.

5.3.1.1 *Experiencer-oriented constructions*

There are experiencer-oriented verbs in each of the intransitive verb classes, apart from the positional class (cf. Table 3). First those verbs belonging to the intransitive subclasses denoting state changes (i.e., inactive and inchoative intransitive verbs) will be discussed, followed by verbs of the active class. It will become obvious that there is a certain clustering of semantic subdomains according to formal verb class. While inactive and inchoative intransitive experiential verbs are predominantly from the subdomains of bodily sensation and emotion, active intransitive experiential verbs are mostly from the subdomains of cognition and emotion. The subdomain of volition is represented only marginally in both subclasses. The subdomain of perception is marginally represented by verbs of active perception.

Both inactive and inchoative experiential verbs encode state changes (sect. 4.1.8.2). Experiencer-oriented inactive intransitive verbs are listed in Table 28. These belong to the subdomains of bodily sensation and emotion. See (222) for some illustrative examples.

subdomain	instance (gloss) 'meaning'	properties		
bodily	*he'l* 'rest'	◊	●	-
sensation	*búuy* (pervade) 'get extremely tired'	◊	○	-
	ka'n 'tire, get tired'	◊	○	-
	hets'k'ah (quiet:SPONT) 'calm by itself'	◊	○	-
emotion	*buy* (get.amused) 'get amused'	◊	?	?
	p'u'h (get.mad) 'get annoyed, angry'	◊	●	■

properties:
- ◊   integrates with Construction 21;
- ○   non-controllable;
- ●   controllable;
- ■   adjoins a stimulus argument with *ti'*;
- -   does not adjoin a stimulus complement.

Table 28. Inactive intransitive experiential verbs

(222) a. *Káa   h   ho'p'   u   ka'n-al   le   óotsil   kéeh-e'.*
       CNJ   PFV begin   SBJ.3   tire-INCMPL DEF   poor   deer-D3
       'And the poor deer started to get tired.' (AAK_032)

    b. *ti'   y-o'lal   a   chàan   he'l-el.*
       LOC   POSS.3-reason   SBJ.2   little   rest-INCMPL
       'in order for you to rest a little. (BVS_16.01.11)

The items in Table 28 integrate with the simple intransitive construction represented in Construction 21. The EXPERIENCER is mapped onto the constructional Theme argument. One item in Table 28, *ka'n*, selects either the experiencer or an appropriate body part in subject function. In the latter case, it integrates with the construction represented in Construction 25.

As regards control properties of the items in Table 28, *he'l* 'rest' and *p'u'h* 'get annoyed, angry' are judged as being compatible with Test 5, while *búuy* 'get extremely tired' and *ka'n* 'tire, get tired' were negative in this test.[14] *He'l* and *p'u'h* however are not necessarily understood as being controlled. If they are subordinated to an impersonal phase verb, the experiencer is understood as having no control (223).

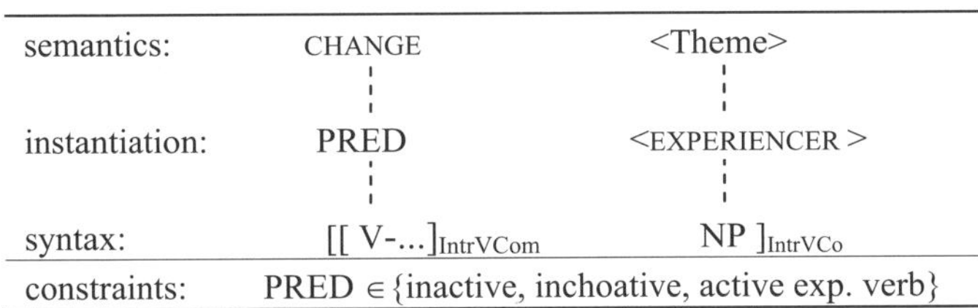

semantics:	CHANGE	<Theme>
instantiation:	PRED	<EXPERIENCER >
syntax:	[[V-...]IntrVCom	NP]IntrVCo
constraints:	PRED ∈ {inactive, inchoative, active exp. verb}	

Construction 21. Simple intr. C. with experiencer-oriented verbs

(223)   *túun   káah-al*
        PROG:SBJ.3   begin\DEAG-INCMPL
        in   p'u'h-ul/   in   he'l-el
        SBJ.1.SG   get.mad-INCMPL/ SBJ.1.SG   rest-INCMPL
        lit.: 'it started that I got angry / that I rested' (ACC)

While most of the items given in Table 28 do not adjoin a stimulus in complement function, emotional verbs such as *p'u'h* 'get annoyed, angry' do. See (224) for an example and Construction 22 for the construction. It consists of Construction 21 plus a prepositional phrase introducing a Goal argument. The STIMULUS is mapped onto the constructional Goal argument.

(224)   *káa   h   ho'p'   u   p'u'h-ul   ti'   u   y-atan*
        CNJ   PFV   begin   SBJ.3   get.mad-INCMPL   LOC   POSS.3   0-wife
        '(and/then) he started to get angry with his wife' (HNAZ_0001)

---

[14] Since *buy* 'get amused' is only present in Owen (1968) and not known in the dialect of my consultants, it could not be tested.

semantics:	CHANGE	<Theme	Goal>
instantiation:	PRED	<EXPERIENCER	STIMULUS>
syntax:	[[V-...]$_{\text{IntrVCom}}$	NP$_1$	[*ti'* NP$_2$]$_{\text{PP}}$]$_{\text{IntrVCo}}$
constraints:	PRED $\in$ {inactive, inchoative, active exp. verb}		

Construction 22. Extended intr. C. with experiencer-oriented verbs

Table 29 lists experiential verbs from the inchoative class of intransitive verbs. Most items in Table 29 are derivations from stative predicates, which are enumerated in Table 17. Since inchoative derivation is productive, further items derived from items of Table 17 could be added. Thus, Table 29 is not complete, but contains the more recurrent inchoative experiential verbs.

subdo-main	instance (gloss) 'meaning'	properties		
	wi'h-tal (hungry-PROC) 'get hungry'	◊	○	-
bodily	*uts-tal* (good-PROC) 'recover, become well'	◊	○	-
sensation	*ke'l-tal* (cold-PROC) 'freeze, be cold'	◊	○	-
	lúub-óol-tal (sad-mind-PROC) 'get sad, depressed'	◊	○	-
	chi'chnak-tal (cross-PROC) 'get angry, get annoyed; be bored'	◊	○	■□
	k'ùux-tal (angry-PROC) 'get angry'	◊	○	■□
emotion	*su'lak-tal* (ashamed-PROC) 'get ashamed'	◊	○	■□
	péek-óol-tal (move-mind-PROC) 'get nervous'	◊	○	■□
	sahak-tal (afraid.of-PROC) 'get frightened'	◊	○	■
	háak'óol-tal (scare:mind-PROC) 'get (easily) scared, nervous'	◊	○	■
	ts'íik-tal (furious-PROC) 'get furious, angry'	◊	○	■
volition	*pòoch-tal* (desirous-PROC) 'desirous, greedy'	◊	○	■
	ts'íibóol-tal (write:soul-PROC) 'get eager'	◊	○	■

properties:

  ◊   integrates with Construction 21;
  ○   non-controllable;
  ■   adjoins a stimulus complement introduced by *ti*;
  □   adjoins a stimulus complement introduced by *yeetel*;
  -    does not adjoin a stimulus complement.

Table 29. Inchoative experiential verbs

Like their base forms, the derived items belong to the subdomains of emotion, volition and bodily sensation. The derivation yields a shift from a state reading to a change of state reading. The items in Table 29 thus integrate with the aforementioned Construction 21. Furthermore, note that *utstal* and *ke'ltal* may also be used in a part-oriented construction (cf. Construction 25).

As regards control properties, none of the items in Table 29 is acceptable in Test 5. This also fits with the lack of an imperative form for the class of inchoative intransitives (cf. sect. 4.1.6). See (225) for some examples.

(225) a. *K-in*   *w-u'y-ik*   *in*   *su'lak-tal*
        IMPF-SBJ.1.SG 0-feel-INCMPL SBJ.1.SG ashamed-PROC
        chen   *k'uch-uk-en*   *t-u*   *nah-il*
        SR.FUT arrive-SUBJ-ABS.1.SG LOC-POSS.3 house-REL
        le   *máak-o'b-o'*.
        DEF   person-PL-D2
        'I feel embarrassed when I arrive at those men's house.'(RMC_2200)

      b. *Ma',* *ts'o'k* *u*   *y-uts-tal*.
        NEG   TERM SBJ.3 0-good-PROC
        'No, she's recovered.' (BVS_10.01.24)

The option of adjoining a stimulus participant is lexically determined and can be derived from the options indicated for the base forms (cf. sect. 5.2.1.2). Thus, those items in Table 29 adding a stimulus with the preposition *ti'* 'LOC' integrate with Construction 22; those adding it with *yéetel* integrate with a complex construction consisting of Construction 21 plus the concomitant phrase construction '<Concomitant>' [*yèetel* NP]_{PP.} (cf. Construction 7 for the corresponding adjectival construction).

Table 30 lists experiential verbs belonging to the active intransitive class. There are only a few basic verbs in this class; all of them coming from the subdomain of cognition. Some members of the subdomain of emotion are derived from adjectives by a durative derivation in *-(lank)il*. Furthermore, there are a number of compound and incorporative verbs from different subdomains, most containing the person part noun *óol* 'mind'. These also occur as transitive verbs bearing the transitivizing suffix *-t* (cf. sect. 5.3.2.1.1). Some of these items listed in Table 30 occur more naturally as transitive verbs (e.g., *ts'iibóolt* 'desire, wish', *alabóolt* 'wait, hope, trust', *òoksah-óolt* 'believe, honor'). Finally, Table 30 contains some introversive derivations of transitive verbs (mentioned below in Table 36, sect. 5.3.2.1.1). Note that only those introversives that frequently and naturally occur are listed. Introversives such as, e.g., *ch'a'k'ùux* 'be angry', *ch'a'p'èek* 'hate', *nàa't* 'understand, guess' are seldom or even non-existent.

The verbs in Table 30 also integrate with the simple intransitive construction frame as given in Construction 21. The EXPERIENCER is mapped onto the constructional Theme argument. According to what has been said about the aspectual character of the class of active intransitive verbs in sect. 4.1.8, these verbs denote activities and processes.

All the verbs in Table 30 are compatible with the 'happening' frame in Test 4. This behavior is, in principle, not worth mentioning for the items of verbal origin. It should, however, be discussed for those items in Table 30 which are derived from adjectives, namely, *ts'íikil* 'feel angry', *k'ùuxil* 'feel angry', and *su'lankil* 'feel ashamed', in order to observe a possible change in dynamicity, i.e., from a state reading to a dynamic reading. (226a) was allowed as an answer in Test 4 with the translation 'Pedro está regañando' which clearly points to an activity reading, i.e., the activity which is accompanying the feeling of *ts'íik* 'furious, angry'. Similarly in (226b), the dog is taught to show wild behavior (in an appropriate situation).

subdomain	instance (gloss) 'meaning'	verb class	properties		
cognition	*náay* 'dream'	basic	◊	●	-
	kàan/kàambal (learn\INTRV) 'study'	introversive	◊	●	-
	òoksah-óol 'believe, honor'	incorporative	◊	●	-
	alab-óol(al) 'wait, hope, trust'	comp/incorp	◊	●	-
	wayáak' 'dream, imagine'	basic	◊	○	-
	tùukul 'think; worry, long'	introversive	◊	○	-
emotion	*k'ùuxil* 'feel angry'	durative	◊	●	■□
	su'lankil (ashamed:DUR) 'feel ashamed'	durative	◊	○	■□
	ts'íikil 'feel angry'	durative	◊	●	■
	nich'bal (bite:INTRV) 'become angry'	introversive	◊	○	-
volition	*ts'íibóol* (write:soul) 'desire, wish'	comp/incorp	◊	○	-
bodily	*muk'yah* (overcome:ache) 'suffer'	incorporative	◊	○	-
sensation	*nich'bal* (bite:INTRV) 'feel itchy'	introversive	◊	○	-

properties:

◊   integrates with Construction 21;

○   non-controllable;

●   controllable;

■   adjoins stimulus complement with *ti'*;

□   adjoins a stimulus complement introduced by *yeetel*;

-   does not adjoin stimulus complement.

Table 30. Active intransitive experiential verbs

(226) a. *Táan   u   ts'íikil   Pedro.*
      PROG   SBJ.3 feel.angry Pedro
      'Pedro is scolding.' (ACC)

b. *tàak   u   ka'ns-ik   ts'iikil/   chi'bal   le pèek'-o'*
anxious SBJ.3.SG teach-INCMPL feel.angry/ bite\INTRV DEF dog-D2
'he wants to teach the dog to be brave / to bite'

However, adjective-based intransitive verbs do not necessarily refer to actions accompanying the feeling coded in the base adjective when they occur in a dynamic frame. For instance in (227), which is part of a story, the feeling of *ts'iik* seems to be profiled. Due to the combination of *ts'iikil* with the progressive auxiliary, the feeling is conceptualized as ongoing.

(227)   *Táan   u   ts'iikil   ti'   u   na',*
PROG SBJ.3 feel.angry LOC POSS.3   mother
k-u   y-a'l-a'l   ti'   tumen yùum hesus-e':
IMPF-SBJ.3 0-say-PASS.INCMPL LOC by   lord Jesus-CNTR
ma'   a   ts'iikil   ti'   a   na',
NEG SBJ.2 feel.angry LOC POSS.2 mother
xèen   a   bo't a   p'àax-o'.
go:IMP SBJ.2 pay   POSS.2 debt-D2
'He was angry with his mother, (and) it was said to him by Lord Jesus: Don't get excited about your mother, go to pay your debt.' (HNAZ_0019)

According to Test 5, nearly half of the items in Table 30 are judged as having a control reading.[15] The fact that *tsíikil* 'feel angry' implies control is made explicit in (228a) by the adverbial clause following the main clause. Furthermore, note that in (227) – third line – *tsíikil* appears in the imperative, which also points to a control reading. *Tùukul* in (228b) was judged differently by my consultants. One consultant argued that it is compatible with Test 5 only in the corresponding transitive form *tukul(t)* (cf. Table 36) with the meaning of 'plan', while the intransitive form is always uncontrolled.

(228) a. *ts'o'k   in   chúuns-ik   in   ts'iikil*
TERM SBJ.1.SG start:CAUS-INCMPL SBJ.1.SG feel.angry(INCMPL)
tumen   túun   tratar-t-ik-en   k'àas-il
because PROG:SBJ.3 treat-TRR-INCMPL-ABS.1.SG bad-ADVR
'I have started to get worked up since they treat me badly' (RMC)

---

[15] Note that this distribution of control behavior (as well as the one discussed for inactive intransitive verbs) supports the claim made in Bohnemeyer (2002, sect. 5.1.2.9) that predicate classes are not motivated by control.

b.ʔ*ts'iin*   *chúuns-ik*   *in*   *tùukul*
 TERM:SBJ.1 start:CAUS-INCMPL SBJ.1.SG think
 int.: 'I have started to think' (RMC)

Only a few of the items mentioned in Table 30 add a stimulus in complement function. *Ts'íikil* 'feel angry', *k'ùuxil* 'feel angry', and *su'lankil* 'feel ashamed' are some of these. Again, these items add their stimulus argument in the same way as the base form does (cf. sect. 5.2.1.2). Thus, all three items integrate with Construction 22 and map their STIMULUS argument onto the constructional Goal argument. *K'ùuxil* 'feel angry' and *su'lankil* 'feel ashamed' may also add their stimulus with *yéetel* and are compatible with a complex construction consisting of Construction 21 plus the concomitant phrase construction '<Concomitant>' [*yèetel* NP]ₚₚ. Thus it can be observed that stimulus adjoinment for active intransitive experiencer verbs is parallel to that of inactive and inchoative experiencer verbs. The other items in Table 30, which are either basic, compounds, incorporatives, or introversives only add a stimulus argument to the transitive or transitivized form, not to the intransitive verb (cf. Lehmann and Verhoeven 2005).

Table 30 contains lexemes from all experiential subdomains, apart from the subdomain of perception. Most perception verbs are basic transitive verbs (cf. Table 36) and they do not regularly form introversive derivations, at least in the dialect investigated.[16] Furthermore, a number of active perception verbs are morphologically basic in the class of active intransitive verbs: *kanáan* 'guard, watch', *cha'n* 'enjoy seeing', *ch'éeneb* 'peek, look after', *ch'úuk* 'watch, observe, spy'. Despite being basic active intransitive verbs, these verbs occur more naturally as derived transitive, i.e., extraversive verbs (cf. Table 38). The same is true for the compound and incorporative active perception verbs listed in Table 38. Only a few active intransitive perception verbs, namely, *ta-talòok* (RED-feel:foot) 'grope around with foot', *ta-talk'ab* (RED-feel:hand) 'feel around, pat down', *u'sni'* (blow:nose) 'sniff around' occur exclusively or primarily as intransitive verbs.

Finally, note that the class of active intransitives hosts many concepts that have been identified in sect. 3.2.2 as being related to experience, but do not themselves belong to the domain (or are at best marginal). These are, e.g., verbs denoting bodily action or function, e.g., *he'síin* 'sneeze', *síin* 'blow one's nose', *xèeh* 'vomit', etc., or verbs indicating the expression of emotion, e.g., *che'h* 'laugh', *òok'ol* 'weep', *hak'ìik'* 'sigh, suspire', *ki'kilankil* 'quiver, tremble', *tíitbal* 'tremble, shake', *ki'ki't'àan* 'praise', *k'èey* 'scold', *áakan* 'groan,

---

[16] However compare Bricker et al. (1998) which lists introversive forms of *il* 'see' and *u'y* 'hear, feel', namely, *ilah* 'see, be careful', *u'yah* 'hear, feel, understand, listen'. In the dialect of my consultants, both forms occur only as part of fixed expressions.

complain'. A number of incorporatives which often literally denote motion/action of a body part (the latter generally representing the incorporated noun) have come to denote emotional meanings as well: *chinpòol* (tilt:head) 'bow, nod; show respect' and some of the above mentioned perception verbs.[17]

5.3.1.2 *Part-oriented constructions*

Part-oriented intransitive verbs form collocations that are of the same types as those collocations based on adjectives (cf. sect. 5.2.1.3), i.e. there are idiomaticized collocations (cf. sect. 5.3.1.2.1) and non-idiomaticized collocations (cf. sect. 5.3.1.2.2).

5.3.1.2.1 *Idiomaticized collocations*

A great majority of part-oriented intransitive verbs are from those classes that lexicalize state changes, i.e., from the inactive and inchoative classes. Furthermore, there are some irregular verbs which also lexicalize state changes, namely, verbs of inherently directed motion (cf. Table 31). Only one frequently used collocation, i.e., *péek* POSS *óol* (move POSS mind) 'get frightened, appal(led), shocked; be ill at ease, worry, trouble' displays a verb from the active class. However, in contrast to most other verbs from this class, *péek* 'move' patterns with the inactive verbs in its transitivization behavior, i.e., like most verbs of the inactive intransitive class, it causativizes (cf. Table 6, sect. 4.1.6). This may be a hint that its main argument is semantically an undergoer, just like the main argument of inactive and inchoative intransitive verbs.

As concerns the items given in Table 31, they form either non-compositional or compositional collocations in a way parallel to idiomaticized collocations with experiential adjectives (cf. sect. 5.2.1.3.1). Because of this parallelism the description of the intransitive constructions will not be as detailed as that given for the adjectival constructions; rather it can be deduced from the analysis given there.

The first four items in Table 31 are unique collocations in the sense that the verbs *háak'* 'scare', *óoy* 'loose.nerve', *náay* 'calm.down' and *ki'mak-tal* 'happy-PROC' only occur in collocation with *óol* 'mind', i.e., these collocations are non-compositional in the sense introduced in sect. 3.5.4. Thus the verbs themselves have experiential meaning. The representation in Construction 23 shows this fact at the semantic level. Literally, the person part *óol* undergoes a change of an experiential state and, by metonymic inference based on the part – whole relation, the experiencer undergoes a change of state. Construction 23 is parallel to the adjectival experiential construction with possessor-experiencer in Construction 8. Refer to (229) for some illustrative examples.

---

[17] For a comprehensive analysis of incorporation in YM cf. Lehmann and Verhoeven 2005.

subdomain	instance (gloss) 'meaning'	prop.	
	óoy POSS óol (lose.nerve POSS mind) 'get disheartened; give up hope'	●	-
	háak' POSS óol (scare POSS mind) 'become/get scared/impressed'	●	■
	ki'mak-tal POSS óol (happy-PROC POSS mind) 'get happy'	●	■□
	náak POSS óol (leave.this.way\DEAG POSS mind) 'get bored (with), tired (of), weary of'	○	■□
emotion	*péek POSS óol* (move POSS mind) 'get frightened, shocked; ill at ease, worry, trouble; distrust(ful)'	○	■□
	lúub POSS óol (fall POSS mind) 'get disappointed, resign'	○	-
	bin POSS óol (go POSS mind) 'lose interest'	○	◊
	tàal POSS óol (come POSS mind) 'feel like'	○	◊
	máan POSS óol (pass POSS mind) 'lose heart; lose interest, be rather bored (with)'	○	■
	chukpah POSS óol (suffice:SPONT POSS mind) 'be patient, with stamina'	○	■
	náay POSS óol (calm.down POSS mind) 'calm down, be diverted, relaxed'	●	■□
cognition	*tu'b POSS óol/ìik'* (forget POSS mind/air) 'lose one's mind'	●	◊
	k'a'h POSS ìik (remember POSS air) 'cross one's mind (moral duties)'	●	◊
	chokow-tal POSS pòol/ho'l (hot-PROC POSS head) 'lose one's head'	○	-
	k'àas-tal POSS pòol (bad-PROC POSS head) 'get mad'	○	-
	sa't POSS óol (lose\PASS POSS mind) 'lose consciousness; forget'	○	-
bodily	*hòom POSS óol* (break POSS mind) 'recover, regain lucidity'	○	-
sensation	*líik' POSS óol* (get.up POSS mind) 'recover'	○	-
	xúul POSS óol (end\DEAG POSS mind) 'get exhausted'	○	-
	uts-tal POSS óol (good-PROC POSS mind) 'recover, become well'	○	-
	tòohtal POSS óol (straight:POSS mind) 'recover'	○	-

properties:

- ● integrates with Construction 23;
- ○ integrates with Construction 24;
- ■ adjoins stimulus complement with *ti'*;
- □ adjoins stimulus complement with *yéetel*;
- ◊ adjoins asyndetic purpose clause as stimulus;
- - does not adjoin stimulus complement.

Table 31. Person part collocations with intransitive verbs

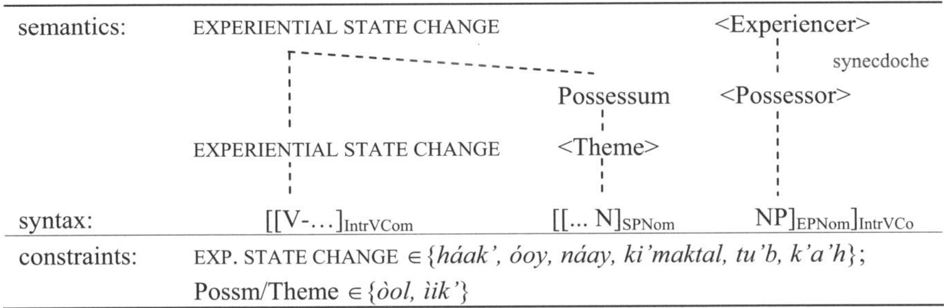

semantics:	EXPERIENTIAL STATE CHANGE		<Experiencer>
			synecdoche
		Possessum	<Possessor>
	EXPERIENTIAL STATE CHANGE	<Theme>	
syntax:	[[V-...]IntrVCom	[[... N]SPNom	NP]EPNom]IntrVCo
constraints:	EXP. STATE CHANGE ∈ {háak', óoy, náay, ki'maktal, tu'b, k'a'h};		
	Possm/Theme ∈ {òol, ìik'}		

Construction 23. Simple intr. C. with possessor-experiencer, based on metonymy

(229) a. *ts'o'k   bin   u   óoyol   u   y-óol*
       TERM   QUOT   SBJ.3   lose.nerve   POSS.3   0-mind
       'he had already lost his nerves' (HK'AN_155.1)

   b. *ts'o'k u   náay-al   y-óol   le   pàal-o'*
       TERM POSS.3   calm.down-INCMPL   POSS.3-mind   DEF   child-D2
       'the child already calmed down' (RMC_1861)

Construction 23 is a complex construction consisting of two subconstructions, namely, the intransitive state change construction, as depicted in
Construction 21, and the expanded possessed nominal construction
'[(1)]Possessum [(2)]<Possessor>' [[[(2)]PossClit [(1)]N]SPNom [(2)]NP]EPNom.

Again, as has been shown for the parallel adjectival construction in
Construction 8, the person part noun cannot be topicalized (230a). Appropriate
topicalization would be as shown in (230b). The person part noun *óol* is inseparable from the verb and constitutes part of the larger predicate.

(230) a.*in   w-óol-e'*
       POSS.1.SG   0-mind-TOP
       ts'o'k   u   náay-al/   háak'-al
       TERM   SBJ.3   calm.down-INCMPL/   become.scared-INCMPL
       intended: 'as for my heart, it has calmed down / has become
       scared' (ACC)

   b. *tèen-e'   ts'o'k   u   náay-al/*
       me-TOP   TERM   SBJ.3   calm.down-INCMPL/
       háak'-al   in   w-óol
       become.scared-INCMPL   POSS.1.SG   0-mind
       'as for me, I have calmed down / I have become scared' (ACC)

The items *tu'b* 'forget' and *k'a'h* 'remember' in Table 31 can be optionally
collocated with *òol* or *ìik'* 'air; life, breath, memory' and the meaning of the
collocation is similar to their simple use (cf. sect. 5.3.1.3). In these collocations

the person part noun takes subject function, as can be seen in (231). These collocations integrate with Construction 23 as well.

(231) a. *yàan   súutuk-o'b*
        EXIST   moment-PL
        k-u   tu'b-ul   in   w-ìik'/ in   w-óol
        IMPF-SBJ.3 forget-INCMPL POSS.1.SG 0-air / POSS.1.SG 0-mind
        'there are moments when my memory is going' (ACC_0290)

   b. *h   k'a'h   u   y-ìik' Israel yan u   bin sáamal*
      PFV remember POSS.3 0-air   Israel DEB SBJ.3 go tomorrow
      'Israel rememberd that he had to go tomorrow' (NMP_0417)

The remaining verbs in Table 31 form compositional collocations with *óol*, which may generally be understood as metaphorical combinations. These verbs are from several domains, e.g., phase verbs (*xúul* 'end\DEAG', *náak* 'leave.this.way\DEAG'), motion verbs (*máan* 'pass', *bin* 'go', *tàal* 'come', *lúub* 'fall', *líik'* 'get up, rise') and some other verbs from the domains of material processes, possession, etc. (*hòom* 'break through', *chukpah* 'suffice:SPONT', *sáat* 'lose\DEAG'). See (232) and (233) for some illustrative examples.

(232) a. *ti'   le   kàah-o'   k-u   náak-al*
        LOC DEF village-D2 IMPF-SBJ.3 leave.this.way\DEAG-IMPF
        y-óol   máak   yàan-tal-i'
        POSS.3-mind person EXIST-PROC-LOC
        'in the village, people living there get bored' (RMC_1744)

   b. *k-u   chukpah-al   in   w-óol*
      IMPF-SBJ.3 suffice:SPONT-INCMPL POSS.1.SG   0-mind
      in   kan-eh
      SBJ.1.SG learn-SUBJ
      'I am patient (enough) to learn it' (SME_0013)

(233) a. *h   lúub in   w-óol káa t-in   w-il-ah*
        PST fall   POSS.1.SG 0-mind CNJ PFV-SBJ.1.SG 0-see-CMPL
        ba'x ts'o'k u   mèet-ik   tèen x-Màaria
        what TERM SBJ.3 do-INCMPL me   F-Maria
        'I lost interest when I saw what Maria had done to me'
        (NMP_0024)

   b. *táan u   máan u   y-óol   le   t'ùup-o'*
      PROG SBJ.3 pass   POSS.3 0-mind DEF youngest.sibling-D2
      'the youngest brother was losing heart' (T'UUP_264)

Construction 24 indicates that the meaning of the construction is a result of a combined metaphorical and metonymic process, equivalent to that analyzed for Construction 9. Again, as has been shown for the collocations integrating with Construction 9 and those discussed above with respect to Construction 23, the person part noun *óol* 'mind' cannot be topicalized. This again indicates the high degree of idiomaticization of these collocations.

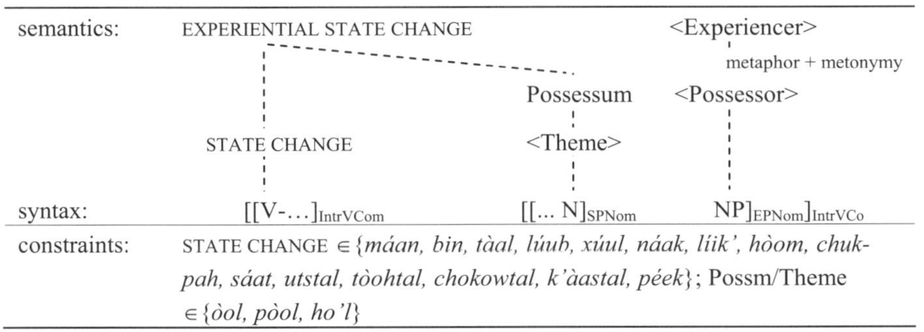

Construction 24. Simple intr. C. with possr-expr, based on metaphor + metonymy

Items from both types of collocations examined above may add a stimulus in complement function, either with *ti'* 'LOC' and/or with *yéetel* 'with'. Preposition choice is indicated in the first column of Table 31. The resulting complex constructions are compositionally formed from Construction 23 or Construction 24 plus the prepositional constructions, which have already been mentioned (cf. sect. 5.2.1.2). The complex construction taking a *ti'*-introduced stimulus is motivated by Construction 22. Note again that items from the subdomain of bodily sensation generally do not take a stimulus as a complement.

Finally, as regards control properties, all items given in Table 31 are negative in Test 5. Thus, in contrast to experiencer-oriented intransitive verbs which may be either controlled or non-controlled, body part-oriented intransitive verbs always designate uncontrolled situations.

5.3.1.2.2 *Non-idiomaticized collocations*

Along with idiomaticized person part collocations, there are non-idiomaticized collocations based on intransitive verbs and body part nouns that convey bodily sensation. Table 32 lists intransitive verbs of bodily sensation which take a body part noun in subject function. There are verbs from all three classes, i.e., inchoative derivations based on adjectives from Table 19, inactive verbs like *k'íil* 'hurt (a wound(ed) body part))' and *èel* 'burn (eye, stomach)', and active/introversive verbs (*k'i'nam* 'hurt, ache', *nich'bal* 'bite, ache', *chi'bal* 'feel itchy').

instance (gloss) 'meaning'	verb class
yah-tal (ache-PROC) 'become painful, infected'	inchoative
si's-tal (numb-PROC) 'become numb'	inchoative
cha'yah-tal (let:ache-PROC) 'ache, smart'	inchoative
cha'htal (become.sensitive) 'be blinded, become sensitive (teeth)'	inchoative
sáak'-tal (itchy-PROC) 'itch'	inchoative
èel (burn) 'burn (eye, stomach)'	inactive
k'íil (hurt\DEAG) 'hurt (a wound(ed body part))'	deagentive
k'i'nam 'hurt, ache'	active
chi'bal (bite\INTRV) 'bite, ache'	introversive
nich'bal (bite:INTRV) 'feel itchy'	introversive

Table 32. Intransitive verbs of bodily sensation (body part-oriented)

These verbs combine with a semantically appropriate body part noun in a compositional way and designate a process or state change with respect to the body part (234). Note that *k'íil* only selects a wounded part in subject function.

(234) a. *h   k'íil   in   w-òok   yah-a'*
          PFV   hurt\DEAG POSS.1.SG 0-foot   ache-D1
          'I hurt my sore foot' (FEE_0259)

     b. *táan   u   nich'bal   u   bàak-el   in   w-òok*
        PROG SBJ.3   bite:INTRV   POSS.3   bone-REL   POSS.1.SG 0-foot
        'the foot bone is aching' (RMC_1740)

These collocations instantiate an intransitive body part construction fully parallel to the adjectival body part construction with a possessor-experiencer of bodily sensation, as depicted in Construction 10. The properties of the intransitive construction are analogous to those mentioned for Construction 10, for instance, the body part nouns in these collocations can be topicalized. The specific sensation only affects the body part while a general bodily affectedness of the experiencer is necessarily inferred due to the inherent relation between body part and possessor-experiencer. This latter point becomes obvious in the question – answer pair in (235). Construction 25 is a constructional representation.

(235) a. *Ba'x k-u   y-úuch-ul   tèech?*
        what IMPF-SBJ.3   0-happen-INCMPL   you
        'What is happening to you?'

     b. *Túun   k'i'nam   in   w-òok.*
        PROG:SBJ.3 hurt   POSS.1.SG 0-foot
        'My foot is aching.' (ACC)

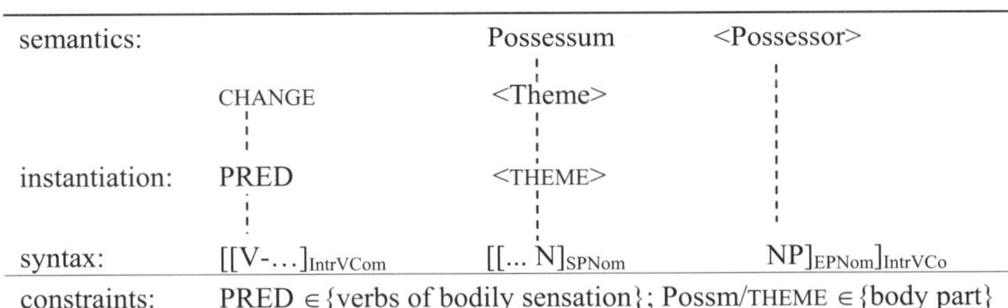

Construction 25. Simple intr. body part C. with verbs of bodily sensation

Analoguous to Construction 10, Construction 25 has further instantiations from other semantic subdomains, for example, from the subdomain of bodily processes or bodily functions, as in (236).

(236) *túun   k'iilkab in   w-òok*
       PROG:SBJ.3 sweat   POSS.1.SG 0-foot
       'my feet are sweating' (FEE)

5.3.1.3 *Stimulus-oriented constructions*

Stimulus-oriented intransitive constructions are largely analogous in terms of alignment possibilities to the stimulus-oriented adjectival constructions discussed in sect. 5.2.1.4. They can be further split up according to the syntactic coding of the experiencer. First, one group of stimulus-oriented intransitive verbs cannot accommodate an experiencer argument in their construction frame. A second group of stimulus-oriented intransitive verbs takes the experiencer as an indirect object. Third, there is one group of stimulus-oriented experiential collocations coding the experiencer as a possessor in a local person part phrase. These construction types will be discussed in the mentioned order.

Intransitive stimulus-oriented experiential verbs which cannot accommodate the experiencer in their construction frame will be addressed first. These verbs are generally from the subdomain of perception and they belong to the active as well as the inactive and inchoative classes of intransitive verbs (Table 33). They are converse to experiencer oriented (inactive) perception verbs (e.g., *smell*: *the flowers are smelling* vs. *I can smell the flowers*). (237) shows that with such stimulus-oriented perception verbs, the experiencer cannot be added in a *ti'*-phrase. It remains implicit and is interpreted from the context as being a generalized experiencer.

(237) **túun   bòoklankil/ t'iip-il/   tu'-tal   ti'   tèen*
       PROG:SBJ.3 odor:DUR/ become.visible/ stinking-PROC LOC   me
       intended: 'it is smelly/becomes visible/is stinking to/for me' (ACC)

subdomain	instance (gloss) 'meaning'	verb class
auditory	*hùum* 'make noise'	active
olfactory	*bòoklankil* (odor:DUR) 'smell'	durative/active
	pàah-tal (acid-PROC) 'lose flavor'	inchoative
	tu'-tal (stinking-PROC) 'stink'	inchoative
visual	*léembal* (shine\INTRV) 'shine'	introversive
	tíip' 'become visible; come out over'	deagentive
	chíik 'appear'	inactive

Table 33. Stimulus-oriented verbs of perception

The items given in Table 33 integrate with the simple intransitive construction and the lexical STIMULUS role is mapped onto the constructional Theme argument as shown in Construction 26. The STIMULUS is generally a concrete entity (cf. Figure 2).

In contrast to some Indo-European languages, YM does not exploit the deagentive derivation to form stimulus-oriented perception verbs (cf., e.g., German *sehen* 'see' ~ *aussehen* 'look', *hören* 'hear' ~ *sich anhören* 'sound', etc.; or Modern Greek passive/medium forms of inactive perception verbs, e.g., *akúi* (hear:3.SG) 'he hears' ~ *akújete* (hear:MEDP:3SG) 'it sounds').

semantics:	CHANGE	<Theme>
instantiation:	PRED	<STIMULUS>
syntax:	[[V-...]_{IntrVCom}	NP]_{IntrVCo}
constraints:	PRED ∈ {inactive, inchoative, active exp.	
	verb}; STIMULUS ∈ {concrete entity}	

Construction 26. Simple intr. C. with stimulus-oriented verbs

Next, those stimulus-oriented intransitive verbs that take the experiencer as an indirect object introduced by the preposition *ti'* will be discussed. Table 34 contains basic experiential verbs and full verbs with modal meanings expressing habituality, volition, and necessity or a lack of something. The modal verbs are inchoative derivations of modal auxiliaries (cf. Table 22) or modal adjectives (cf. Table 20), and the pseudo-transitive verb *bíinèet ti'* 'lack'.

subdomain	instance (gloss) 'meaning'	verb class	prop.	
b. sensation	*tsa'y* (strike LOC) 'strike (disease)'	inactive	●	
emotion	*náak* (grieve LOC) 'feel, grieve, be moved'	inactive	●	
	kóoh (have.feeling LOC) 'have a feeling/sense'	inactive	●	
cognition	*k'a'h* (remember LOC) 'cross one's mind'	inactive	●	□
	tu'b (forget LOC) 'get forgotten, escape'	inactive	●	□
habitual	*sùuk-tal* (custom-PROC LOC) 'become accustomed'	inchoative	●	□
volition	*tàak-tal* (anxious-PROC (LOC)) 'feel like, be keen on'	inchoative	●	□
	k'abéet-tal (necessary-PROC LOC) 'become necessary'	inchoative	●	□
need	*k'a'náan-tal* (necessary-PROC LOC) 'become necessary'	inchoative	●	□
	bíinèet (lack LOC) 'need, lack'	pseudo-tr.	●	

properties:
- ● integrates with Construction 27;
- □ integrates with Construction 28.

Table 34. Bivalent intransitive experiential and modal verbs

The basic experiential verbs belong to the inactive subclass. They are among the few intransitive verbs that take an argument in indirect object function. They differ as to the prototypical participant properties of their stimulus. *Náak'* 'feel, grieve, be moved' and *kóoh* 'have a feeling/senses' select only propositional stimuli, while *k'a'h* 'cross one's mind' and *tu'b* 'get forgotten, escape' prefer propositional stimuli but are possible with concrete stimuli as well. *Tsa'y* 'strike (disease)' takes the disease in subject function. For illustration compare (142), (238), and (351).

(238) a. *hach   ts'o'k   u   náak'-al   tèen*
       really TERM   SBJ.3   grieve-INCMPL   me
       ba'x   k-u   bèet-ik   to'n   le   ko'lel-a' ...
       what   IMPF-SBJ.3 do-INCMPL   us   DEF   lady-D1
       'what this woman is doing to us really hurts me (...).
       (HOSEH_20.1)

   b. *tuméen   wa'pach'-e'   táan   u*
      because   giant-TOP   PROG   SBJ.3
      kóoh-ol   ti'   ba'x   k-a   mèent-ik
      have.feeling-INCMPL   LOC   what   IMPF-SBJ.2 do-INCMPL
      'because the giant feels what you are doing' (HK'AN_064.2)

   c. *h   tsa'y   ta'   ti'   le   pàal-o'*
      PFV   strike   shit   LOC   DEF   child-D2
      'the child got diarrhea' (EMB&RMC_0131)

The experiential verbs in Table 34 integrate with Construction 27. It features an Indirectus argument role, bearing the meaning of an animate argument that is indirectly affected by the state change conveyed by the predicate meaning. The lexical EXPERIENCER role is matched with the Indirectus argument role and the STIMULUS role is matched with the constructional Theme role. The argument structure is identical to the one given in Construction 13 and both constructions motivate each other.

semantics:	STATE CHANGE	<Theme	Indirectus>
instantiation:	PRED	<STIMULUS	EXPERIENCER>
syntax:	[[V-...]$_{IntrVCom}$	NP$_1$	[*ti'* NP$_2$]$_{PP}$]$_{IntrVCo}$
constraints:	PRED ∈ {*náak', kóoh, k'a'h, tu'b, tsa'y, tàaktal, sùuktal, k'abéettal, k'a'náantal, bíinèet*}		

Construction 27. Extended intr. C. with stimulus-oriented verbs

If the modal verbs listed in Table 34 take an animate participant in oblique complement function, it is understood to be indirectly affected by the verbal meaning (cf. (239), (240)). In certain contexts, *k'abéettal/k'a'náantal* and *bíinèet* seem to convey emotional meaning, presumably based on a metonymic inference (cf. (239a), (240b)). Note that the modal *bíinèet ti'* 'lack, need' is morphologically transitive but it lacks a direct object argument. Instead, it takes a goal argument adjoined by the preposition *ti'*. Its irregularity is also manifested in a reduced status marking, since it appears only with incompletive and completive status and not with subjunctive status.

(239) a. *le   k'ìin k-in   k'abéet-tal   ti'   tèech-e'*
      DEF   sun   IMPF-SBJ.1.SG   necessary-PROC   LOC   you-CNTR
      káa   tàal-ak-ech   a   ch'a'-en
      CNJ   come-SUBJ-ABS.2.SG   SBJ.2   take-ABS.2
      'the day you need me, you come to see me' (HK'AN_198.2)

   b. *k-u   tàak-tal   ti'   tèen*
      IMPF-SBJ.3   anxious-PROC   LOC   me
      'I fancy it' (ACC)

(240) a. *Yàan   k-u   bíinèet-ik   tèen*
       EXIST-ABS.3.SG IMPF-SBJ.3   lack-INCMPL me
       káa   xi'k-en   Cancun.
       that   go:SUBJ-ABS.1.SG   Cancun
       'I am still missing something to go to Cancun.' (ACC_0494)

   b. *Táan   bíinèet-ik   ti'   tèen.*
       PROG:SBJ.2   lack-INCMPL LOC   me
       'I am missing you' (RMC_0194)

In their construction with an animate participant in oblique complement
function the modal verbs in Table 34 also instantiate Construction 27. Due to
their stimulus-orientation, the verbs in Table 34 are not acceptable in Test 5.

As was mentioned above for some adjectives which take an indirect object
experiencer (cf. Table 20), some items in Table 34 optionally or obligatorily do
not add the experiencer as an indirect object if the verb functions as a matrix
predicate. Compare (241) from Modern YM and (242) from Colonial YM.

(241) a. *Le   kiik-tsil-o'b-e'   tak   bin   xeh*
       DEF   elder.sister-PL-TOP   as.far.as QUOT vomit
       k-u   tàak-tal   u   mèent-ik-o'b
       IMPF-SBJ.3   anxious-PROC   SBJ.3   do-INCMPL-3.PL
       ken   u   y-il-o'b
       SR.FUT   SBJ.3   0-see-3.PL
       bix u   ki'makóolt-a'l   h-p'óokinah   tsùuk.
       how SBJ.3   delight-PASS.INCMPL   M-hat:USAT:NR paunch
       'The elder sisters even felt like vomiting when they saw how
       Paunchhat was fondled.' (HK'AN_382)

   b. *hach k-u   tàak-tal*
       really IMPF-SBJ.3 anxious-PROC
       in   hàan-t-ik   ìib
       SBJ.1.SG   eat-TRR-INCMPL   fresh.beans
       'I really fancy eating fresh beans' (ACC_0524)

   c. *h   tu'b   (tèen) in   bin Cancun*
       PFV   forget   me   [SBJ.1.SG go   Cancun]
       'I forgot to go to Cancun' (EMB, ACC)

(242)   *tu'b-ih   in   xok-ik   in   kwentas*
        forget-ABS.3.SG [SBJ.1.SG count-INCMPL POSS.1.SG counts]
        'I forgot to tell my beads' (Barrera Vásquez et al. eds. 1980, s.v. *xok*)

In these cases, the experiencer is understood to be the main participant in the subordinate clause. The resulting construction is depicted in Construction 28; it is inherited from the impersonal construction of the modal auxiliaries (cf. Construction 15 in sect. 5.2.2.1.1). The inheritance relation will be explained in detail in sect. 6.4.

semantics:	EXP. STATE CHANGE	<PROCESS/EVENT	<Arg.role>>
instantiation:	PRED	<	EXPERIENCER>
syntax:	[V	[VP	NP]$_{VCo}$]$_S$
constraints:	PRED ∈ {k'a'h, tu'b, tàaktal, sùuktal, k'abéettal, k'a'náantal}		

Construction 28. Backward indirect object control C.

Finally, some local person part collocations with intransitive verbs coding the experiencer as the possessor of a person part noun will be examined (Table 35). These are compositional metaphorical collocations which either include a motion verb (*tàal* 'come', *máan* 'pass') or other verbs like *p'áat* 'stay'. Furthermore, there is a regular inchoative derivation of *yah* (cf. sect. 5.2.1.4), namely, *yahtal* 'ache'.

subdomain	instance (gloss) 'meaning'	verb class
emotion	*yah-tal ti' POSS óol* (ache-PROC LOC POSS mind) 'ache, feel'	inchoative
cognition	*tàal ti' POSS óol* (come LOC POSS mind) 'have the idea'	irregular
	máan ti' POSS tùukul (pass LOC POSS thought) 'pass through one's mind'	irregular
	p'áat ti' POSS pòol (stay LOC POSS head) 'keep in mind'	deagentive

Table 35. Local person part collocations with intransitive verbs

The stimulus participant, which is generally a proposition, takes subject function in this construction type, while the person part noun occurs as part of a local phrase introduced by *ti'* 'LOC'. The stimulus is metaphorically located in the person part. This construction, which is represented in Construction 29, de-signates mental state changes (with the motion verb collocations as well as *p'áat* 'stay', (243)) and an emotional change of state (244). Like the body part constructions in Construction 23 and Construction 24, Construction 29 repre-sents idiomaticized collocations. Due to their stimulus-orientation, these collo-cations are not acceptable in the control frame in Test 5.

(243) a. *káa h máan t-u tùukul-e'*
CNJ PFV pass LOC-POSS.3 thought-CNTR
hach ta'itak u sùut wa'pach' wíinik
very almost SBJ.3 turn\INTRV giant man
'and the thought came into his mind that the giant would return soon' (HK'AN_0056.2)

b. *hach h p'áat t-in pòol*
really PFV stay(CMPL) LOC- POSS.1.SG head
'I kept it in my mind' (CPP_0021)

c. *K-u tàal t-in w-óol xíimbal.*
IMPF-SBJ.3 come(INCMPL) LOC-POSS.1.SG 0-mind stroll(INCMPL)
'It comes into my mind to go for a walk.' (ACC_0003)

(244) *K-u yah-tal tin w-óol ba'x*
IMPF-SBJ.3.SG ache-PROC LOC:POSS.1.SG 0-mind what
k-in w-il-ik u beet-ik le máak-o'b-o'.
IMPF-SBJ.1.SG 0-see-INCMPL SBJ.3 do-INCMPL DEF person-PL-D2
'It hurts me what I see those people doing to me.' (RMC_1791)

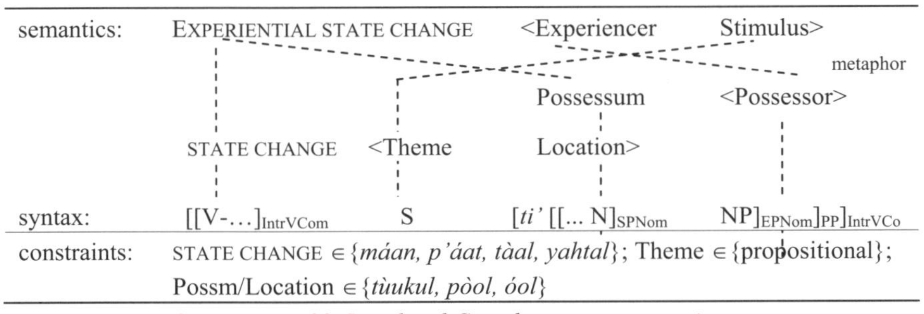

semantics:	EXPERIENTIAL STATE CHANGE	<Experiencer	Stimulus>	
				metaphor
		Possessum	<Possessor>	
	STATE CHANGE <Theme	Location>		
syntax:	[[V-...]IntrVCom S	[*ti'* [[... N]SPNom	NP]EPNom]PP]IntrVCo	
constraints:	STATE CHANGE ∈ {*máan, p'áat, tàal, yahtal*}; Theme ∈ {propositional};			
	Possm/Location ∈ {*tùukul, pòol, óol*}			

Construction 29. Intr. local C. with possessor-experiencer

5.3.2 *Transitive constructions*

YM transitive experiential constructions have to be distinguished as to whether or not they are oriented towards the experiencer (sect. 5.3.2.1) or towards the stimulus or an agent (sect. 5.3.2.2). YM does not provide for a transitive pattern that is part- or expertum-oriented, similar to those patterns featuring adjectives and intransitive verbs as predicates.[18] This is consistent with observations made in Bohnemeyer (1998[T]:242), according to which there are no transitive verbs in YM that would restrict their subject argument to inanimate or abstract participants. Indeed many transitive verbs only take animate subjects. Thus, the

---

[18] Part- and expertum-oriented transitive patterns are, in contrast, recurrent in many other languages, including African languages (cf. sect. 3.4.3.3.3).

prototypical actor is clearly animate in YM. This does not mean that there are
no inanimate or abstract Actor arguments. Instead the language prefers topicalization or passive constructions if a non-human actor acts on a human undergoer.

5.3.2.1 *Experiencer-oriented constructions*
The discussion of transitive experiencer-oriented constructions will proceed as
follows: Sect. 5.3.2.1.1 deals with the default transitive constructions taking
experiential non-reflexive verbs. Sect. 5.3.2.1.2 is devoted to reflexive experiential verbs. Sect. 5.3.2.1.3. examines non-congruent experiential expressions
that use a transitive verb as 'metaphorical predicator'. Finally, sect. 5.3.2.1.4
examines constructions in which a perception verb as the main predicate takes
an adjectival secondary predicate, generally with an evaluative meaning.

5.3.2.1.1 *Transitive experiential verbs*
The current chapter discusses the construction options of transitive experiential
verbs that take the experiencer in subject function. The direct object function is
taken by the stimulus in most cases. Some verbs designate a rather general experiential meaning and may then take an expertum noun in direct object function. The discussion will start with those transitive verbs that express proper
experience (sect. 5.3.2.1.1.1), followed by verbs designating the expression of
experience (sect. 5.3.2.1.1.2) and conclude with verbs of active perception
(sect. 5.3.2.1.1.3).

5.3.2.1.1.1 *Experiential verbs proper*
As mentioned before, experiencer-oriented transitive verbs may take either the
stimulus in direct object function or an expertum noun, as some experiential
verbs with a rather general meaning do. These cases will be discussed in the
mentioned order.

Stimulus as direct object
Table 36 lists transitive experiential verbs from all subdomains. First, there is a
group of basic experiencer-oriented transitive verbs. It contains the basic perception verbs *il* 'see' and *u'y* 'hear, feel' (245a), the latter being at the same
time a general verb of experience (related to sensation as well as emotion, as
will be explained further down in more detail). The table also includes a number of cognition verbs (*tukul*[19] 'think' (245b), *kan* 'learn', *na't* 'understand'
(245a)), and two items from the subdomain of volition (*óot*[20] 'agree', *pa't*

---

[19] *tukul* is fully equivalent in constructional options and meaning to the derived extraversive
verb *tùukult*, the latter being formally based on the introversive form *tùukul* 'think'

[20] Historically *óot* is an extraversive derivation from *óol* 'mind', i.e., *óol-t* 'mind-TRR', which
may no longer be transparent.

'wait, hope'). The basic verb *chuk* (246) primarily has the concrete meaning 'catch, grasp', but is metaphorically used with the meaning 'comprehend'. Note that the subdomains of emotion and bodily sensation are not represented by basic transitive verbs.

(245) a. *Ma' k-k   na't-ik.*
       NEG IMPF-SBJ.1.PL   understand-INCMPL
       Ma' k-k   il-ik.
       NEG IMPF-SBJ.1.PL   see-INCMPL
       Ma' k-k   u'y-ik.
       NEG IMPF-SBJ.1.PL   feel-INCMPL
       'We don't understand. We don't see [it]. We don't hear [it].'
       (BVS_03.01.38ff.)

   b. *Le bin   k-u   chéen tukul-ik   chàan xi'pàal-e'* ...
      that QUOT IMPF-SBJ.3 just think-INCMPL little man:child-D3
      'This is what the little boy was just thinking, (...).' (HK'AN_048.1)

(246)   *T-in   chuk-ah/ na't-ah*
         PFV-SBJ.1.SG catch-CMPL/ understand-CMPL
         bix   mèeta'b-ih.
         how do-PASS.CMPL-ABS.3.SG
         'I understood how it was made.' (RMC_0317)

A second group of transitive experiencer verbs consists of those items derived from transitive verboids (i.e., *ohelt* 'know', *(ka')k'ah-óolt* 'acquaint, recognize', *p'èekt* 'dislike, hate', *yàabilt/yàakunt*[21] 'love, like').[22]

subdomain	instance (gloss) 'meaning'	prop.
perception	*u'y* 'hear, taste, smell, sense, feel; pay willful attention to'	●○ ■□◊
	il 'see, look at'	●○ ■□◊
	tukul(-t) (think(-TRR)) 'think; long for, miss, worry about, plan'	●○ ■□
	na't 'understand, guess'	● □

[21] *Yàabilt* and *yàakun* are not in an immediate morphological derivational relation to *yàa(ku)mah*; rather all items seem to be derivationally related to a form *ya(h)* 'love', which is in this meaning extinct in the dialect discussed here. Furthermore note that *yàabilt* and *yàakun(t)* are used rather synonymously in the dialect investigated here. The apparently factitive (-*kun*) and gerundive (-*bil*) morphemes are frozen. Andrade and Máas Collí (1991) mentions a further form *yàabikunt* 'love, appreciate'.

[22] Note that the transitive verboid *k'áat* 'wish' can be verbalized resulting in *k'áat* 'ask, solicit' which has developed into a full communication verb. The compound *k'áat-óolt* 'solicit, ask for, wish' represented in Table 37 is closer to the experiential meaning of the base and may be regarded as the active counterpart of stative *k'áat*.

	kan 'learn'	●	□
	chuk 'catch, comprehend'	●	□
cognition	*xot'óol-t* (cut:mind-TRR) 'decide, define'	●	□
	péek-óol-t (move-mind-TRR) 'plan'	●	□
	òoksah-óol-t (enter:CAUS:INTRV-mind-TRR) 'believe, honor'	●	■□
	tu'bs (forget:CAUS) 'forget'	●	◊
	k'a'hs (remember:CAUS) 'remind; commemorate'	●	◊
	alabóol-t (hope.for-TRR) 'hope for, be concerned over, rely on'	●	■
	ch'a'nu'k-t (fetch:advice-TRR) 'understand, pay attention to'	●	■□
	u'ynu'k-t (feel:advice-TRR) 'listen and obey, pay attention to'	●	■□
	náa'tukul(-t) (very:think(-TRR)) 'worry about, think intensely'	○	■□
	sèentukul(-t) (very:think(-TRR)) 'worry about, think intensely'	○	■□
	ohel-t (know-TRR) 'know; learn, come to know, experience'[23]	○	□
	k'ahóol-t (acquaint-TRR) 'acquaint, recognize'	○	■
	ka'-k'ahóolt (RED-acquaint-TRR) 'recognize'	○	■
	nay-t (dream-TRR) 'dream'	○	◊
	wayáak'-t (dream-TRR) 'dream'	○	◊
	ts'íibóol-t (write:soul-TRR) 'wish, desire'	○	◊
volition	*pa't* 'wait, hope'	●	◊
	óot (mind:TRR) 'agree; want, wish'	●	□
	ich-t (eye-TRR) 'fall in love, adore'	●	■
	yàabil-t (love-TRR) 'love, like; care for, tend'	●	■
	yàa-kunt (love-FACT) 'love, appreciate, care for, tend'	●	■
emotion	*ts'íikil-t* (feel.angry-TRR) 'be furious at sb., be annoyed with/at'	●	■
	k'ùuxil-t (get.angry-TRR) 'get angry about, scold'	●	■
	ch'a'k'ùux-t (fetch:anger-TRR) 'be angry at, hate; quarrel'	●	■
	p'èek-t (hate-TRR) 'dislike, hate, envy; quarrel'	●	■□
	ch'a'p'èek-t (fetch:hate-TRR) 'hate, be hostile to, quarrel'	●	■□
	p'èek-óol-t[24] (hate-mind-TRR) 'hate'	●	□
	yah-óol-t (ache-mind-TRR) 'be depressed /sad because of; regret'	○	■□
b. sens.	*muk'yah-t* (overcome:ache-TRR) 'suffer, feel'	○	□

properties:

- ● controllable;
- ○ non-controllable;
- ■ adjoins human (or entity) stimuli as direct object;
- □ adjoins abstract/propositional stimuli as direct object;
- ◊ no restriction as to participant properties of stimulus direct object.

Table 36. Transitive verbs of experience

---

[23] Andrade (1955:102f.) provides the more specific meaning 'find out by being told about'.

[24] This item is used rarely by only a few of my consultants.

The largest group of experiencer-oriented transitive verbs in Table 36 consists of those verbs that are derivations of active intransitive verbs (cf. subgroups below) or nouns (e.g., *icht*). The active intransitive base verbs may themselves be basic (*náayt* 'dream', *wayáak't* 'dream, imagine'), derived (*ts'íikilt* 'be furious at sb., be annoyed with/at, scold', *k'ùuxilt* 'be angry about, scold'), composed or incorporative verbs (*náa'tukul* 'worry about, think intensely', *sèentukult* 'worry about, think intensely', *yah-óolt* 'regret', *muk'yaht* 'suffer, feel', *ch'a'k'ùuxt* 'be angry/envious at, hate; quarrel', *ch'a'p'èekt* 'hate, be hostile to, quarrel', *p'èek-óolt* 'hate', *ts'íibóolt* 'wish, desire', *alabóolt* 'hope for, be concerned over, take confidence, rely on', *òoksah-óolt* 'believe, honor', *xot'óolt* 'decide, define', *ch'a'nu'kt* 'understand, pay attention to', *u'ynu'kt* 'listen and obey, pay attention to'). These verbs are from the subdomns of bodily sensation, emotion, cognition, and volition. Transitivization assigns these verbs another participant in direct object function which in most cases is the stimulus. Consider (247) for illustration.

(247) a. *T-in   náay-t-ah   in   chàan   xibpal.*
        PFV-SBJ.1.SG dream-TRR-CMPL POSS.1.SG little   man:child
        'I dreamed of my little boy.' (EMB_0767)

    b. *Táan   in   ts'íikil-t-ik   in   màama.*
        PROG SBJ.1.SG feel.angry-TRR-INCMPL POSS.1.SG mother
        'I am scolding my mother.' (NMP_0362)

    c. *le   ken   òok-ok   k'ìin-e'   k-u*
        when SR.FUT enter-SUBJ sun-TOP IMPF-SBJ.3
        ts'íibóol-t-ik   káa   háahan sáas-ak
        write:soul-TRR-INCMPL that   hurriedly light-SUBJ
        'when night was falling, she wished that it would soon dawn again'
        (HK'AN_261.3)

The occurrence of the causative forms *tu'bs* 'forget' and *k'a'hs* 'remember, commemorate' among the experiencer-oriented transitive verbs shown in Table 36 appears to be exceptional and unexpected (causative derivations are commonly found among the causer/stimulus-oriented verbs (cf. sect. 5.3.2.2)). Indeed, *k'a'hs* can also be constructed taking an 'external' causer in subject function (cf. sect. 5.3.3.1). Both *tu'bs* and *k'a'hs* however, take an experiencer subject argument in the construction instantiated by the items listed in Table 36. They constitute an exceptional pattern in that they code the oblique argument of the base inactive intransitive verbs as subject argument of the transitivized verb (cf. (248) in comparison to (241c), (242) and (326c)).

(248) a. *Xump'at   a   tsikbal yéetel le   we'ch   máak-o'*
      stop(IMP) SBJ.2   chat   with   DEF   scabies   person-D2
      káa   tu'bs-eh!
      that:SBJ.2   forget:CAUS-SUBJ
      'Stop chatting with that mangy man and forget him!'
      (HK'AN_266.2)

     b. *T-in   k'a'hs-ah   u   k'àaba'   in*
      PFV-SBJ.1.SG   remember:CAUS-CMPL POSS.3   name   POSS.1.SG
      x-ka'na'   t-u   k'ìin-il   pixan-o'b.
      F-two:mother LOC-POSS.3   sun-REL soul-PL
      'I commemorated the name of my stepmother on the day of the
      souls.' (RMC_2220)

The items listed in Table 36 differ as to their restrictions on selecting participant properties of the stimulus. Some verbs only (or at least preferably) take human participants as their stimulus argument: *yàabilt/yàakunt* 'love', *ts'íikilt* 'be furious at', *k'ùuxilt* 'be angry about', *ch'a'k'ùuxt* 'be angry/envious at, hate', *alabóolt* 'hope for, be concerned over, take confidence, rely on'; *k'ah-óolt* 'acquaint, recognize' takes an entity as direct object. Most others take human participants or propositional/abstract participants as their stimulus: *p'èekt* 'dislike, hate, envy', *ch'a'p'èekt* 'hate, be hostile to', *yah-óolt* 'regret', *ts'íibóolt* 'wish, desire', *ch'a'nu'kt* 'understand, pay attention to', *u'ynu'kt* 'listen and obey, pay attention to', *náa'tukul(t)* 'worry about, think intensely', *sèentukul(t)* 'worry about, think intensely', *òoksah-óolt* 'believe, honor', *p'èek-óolt* 'hate'. Some of these, including *k'a'hs* 'remember, commemorate', *tu'bs* 'forget', *pa't* 'wait, hope', *náayt* 'dream', and *wayáak't* 'dream, imagine' may also take inanimate entities in stimulus function. Verbs of cognition such as *kan* 'learn', *na't* 'understand, guess', *tukult* 'think; long for, miss, worry about, plan', *ohelt* 'know; learn, come to know', *xot'óolt* 'decide, define', *il* 'see' and *u'y* 'feel' (the latter two in their cognition senses) and volitional *óot* 'agree' exclusively take propositional or abstract stimuli. *K'ah-óolt* 'acquaint, recognize' and *ohelt* 'know; learn, come to know' are primarily distinguished by the participant properties of their stimulus arguments (cf. sect. 5.2.2.2.1).

Construction 30 shows that transitive experiencer-oriented verbs integrate with the general transitive construction. The lexical EXPERIENCER is matched with the constructional Actor while the lexical STIMULUS is matched with the constructional Undergoer.

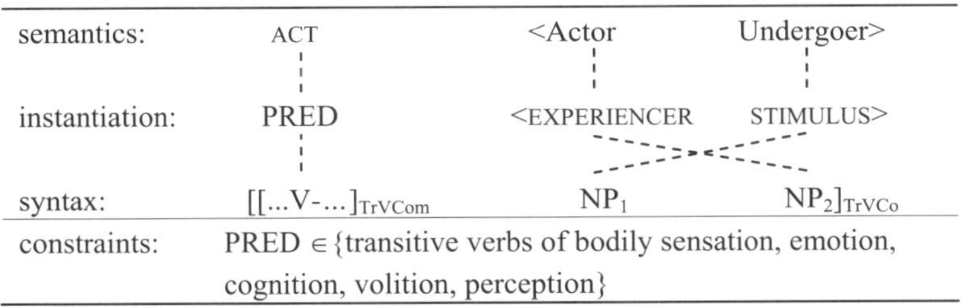

semantics:	ACT	<Actor	Undergoer>
instantiation:	PRED	<EXPERIENCER	STIMULUS>
syntax:	[[...V-...]$_{\text{TrVCom}}$	NP$_1$	NP$_2$]$_{\text{TrVCo}}$
constraints:	PRED ∈ {transitive verbs of bodily sensation, emotion, cognition, volition, perception}		

Construction 30. General transitive C. with experiencer-oriented verbs

Some items in Table 36 belong to several experiential subdomains. A change of the subdomain often accompanies a change of stimulus properties, e.g., *tukul* as an emotional verb with the meaning 'long for, miss, worry' requires animate participants in stimulus function, while in its basic cognitive sense 'think', it takes a propositional stimulus. Similarly, in their perception sense *il* 'see' and *u'y* 'hear, feel' take concrete entities as stimuli while in their cognition sense they take propositions as stimuli (cf. 7.2 for a discussion of a patterning of this behavior for different subordination types).

Finally note that passive formation is fully regular with all items mentioned in Table 36. See (249) for some illustrative examples.

(249) a. *k-a   p'èek-t-a'l-e'x*
     IMPF-SBJ.2   hate-TRR-INCMPL.PASS-2.PL
     'you are hated' (CPP_0022)

    b. *káa   h   il-a'b   tuméen hun-túul   kéeh.*
      CNJ   PFV   see-CMPL.PASS   by   one-CL.AN   deer
      'when it was seen by a deer.' (AAK_001.2)

As has been show above, the class of transitive experiential verbs which take the stimulus as direct object includes members of different origins, i.e., nouns, transitive verboids, and intransitive verbs of different subclasses. This may be a reason for a class-internally diverging behavior concerning semantic properties such as dynamicity and control. These issues will be discussed in the following paragraphs.

Dynamicity of derived transitive verbs
For the transitive verboids, it has been argued in sect. 5.2.2.2.1 that they are formally/constructionally as well as semantically stative. Now the question arises as to whether the aspectual character changes with verbalization, i.e., whether the derived transitive verbs adopt the aspectual character commonly associated with the class of transitive verbs. Thus the question is if transitive verboids assume a dynamic reading or if they retain the semantic feature of stativity even when integrating with a transitive construction.

Verbalization in YM endows stative predicates with two main syntactic options that are only accessible by verbs: the option of combining with aspectual and modal markers and auxiliaries and the option of occurring in embedded clauses of complement taking predicates. It may be argued that from a functional point of view, both characteristics do not prototypically co-occur with stativity, though, on the other hand, stative concepts do not seem to be excluded theoretically from such co-occurrence. One semantic test that has often been used to detect stativity (especially with respect to English) is co-occurrence with the progressive, which fails with statives (cf. Lehmann 1993[G]: 198, Van Valin and LaPolla 1997:94 among many others). Furthermore, modal meanings like obligation (*you have to be thin*) or volition (*I want to be thin*), complement-taking predicates like 'see' (**I see him being thin*) etc. often presuppose either dynamicity or control on the subordinate situation. Generally speaking, stative concepts do not seem to be prototypically modified by aspectual or modal categories or be subordinated to control concepts, since they are themselves generally conceived of as non-controllable. YM has grammaticalized this prototypical co-occurrence.[25]

The following discussion will show that verbalization of transitive verboids provides for a possible dynamic interpretation of a clause containing a transitivized verboid, though the preservation of a stative reading is not excluded. The specific reading is a result of the larger construction into which the item in question is integrated and of pragmatic inferences. *K'ah-óolt* 'acquaint' (250) and *ohelt* '(get to) know' (251) may have an ingressive meaning.

<pre>
(250)   mix   hun-téen   òok-ok-en
        nor   one-time   enter-SUBJ-ABS.1.SG
        in   k'ahóolt   le   mehen   nah-o'b-a'
        SBJ.1.SG   acquaint   DEF   small   house-PL-D1
        'but not even once I entered to get to know the rooms'
        (HK'AN_047.1)

(251)   t-y-o'lal   in   w-ohel-t-ik
        LOC-POSS.3-reason   SBJ.1.SG   0-know-TRR-INCMPL
        hach   bix   t-u   bèet-ah-il-e'
        really how   PFV-SBJ.3 do-CMPL-ADVR-CNTR
        pos   káa   h   ho'p' in   viajar tèen Mexico xàan
        well   CNJ   PFV begin SBJ.1.SG travel me   Mexico also
        'in order to learn how he really had done it, well, I also traveled to
        Mexico' (FCP_205)
</pre>

---

[25] Many languages show traces of a grammaticalization of the distinction between stativity vs. dynamicity, e.g., Korean where the so-called stative verbs show a reduced pattern of tense/aspect marking (cf. (18a) vs. (18b)).

Note that in (250) and (251) *k'ah-óolt* and *ohelt* occur in subordinate clauses without aspect marking. Thus, the dynamicity interpretation is not due to co-occurrence with a special aspectual marker. Rather, it seems to be induced by the context, more specifically, by the semantics of the matrix predicates. In (250), *k'ah-óolt* appears in an SRef purpose clause after a motion verb, where a stative situation is unlikely to appear.

The examples in (252)ff concern cases where the items in question are combined with aspect markers. The mere fact that an item occurs with an aspect marker presupposes an internally complex structure with respect to dynamicity. Thus, the terminative marker *ts'o'k* conveys a post-state reading of the situations referred to by *ohelt* '(come to) know', *p'èekt* 'dislike, hate', and *yàabilt* 'love, like' in (252) (cf. Bohnemeyer 2002, sect. 6.2.2.1.2). If these verbs had a stative reading, combination with the terminative auxiliary *ts'o'k* would lead to the interpretation that the respective states were at their end, which is surely not what is intended. (252c) is appropriate in a situation where the speaker did not love his wife when he got married. This implies that a change of state must have occurred to yield the post-state reading of 'love'.

(252) a. *Maria-e'   teh   t-u   nah-il*
      Maria-TOP LOC:DEF   LOC-POSS.3 house-REL
      tu'x   k-u   xòok
      where IMPF-SBJ.3 read\INTRV
      ts'o'k   u   y-ohel-t-ik
      TERM   SBJ.3 0-knowledge-TRR-INCMPL
      wáah ba'x pektsil-il-o'b   ti'   Estados   Unidos.
      any   what news-REL-PL   LOC States   United
      'In school, Mary has learned/has come to know some news about the United States.' (ICM_19)

    b. *To'n   le   k-u   y-a'l-ik   in   swèegróo,*
      us   DEF   IMPF-SBJ.3 0-say-INCMPL POSS.1.SG father.in.law
      ts'o'k u   hach p'èek-t-ik-o'n.
      TERM SBJ.3   really hate-TRR-INCMPL-ABS.1. PL
      'It was for/about us that my father-in-law said it, he already dislikes us.' (HA'N_0003)

    c. *Behla'k-e' ts'o'k in   yàabilt-ik   in   xùun.*
      today-TOP TERM SBJ.1.SG love-INCMPL POSS.1.SG wife
      'Today I love my wife.' (ACC)

The examples in (253) show combinations of derived verboids with the perfective marker, which also points to their dynamic interpretation. Here, the (possibly initiated) states referred to by the transitive verboids are pragmatically (253a) or literally/lexically (253b) closed and identified as being terminated by the use of the perfective marker (cf. the analysis in Bickel 1997[A], sect. 4 of ingressive-stative predicates). (253a) was uttered in a situation where the speaker's father was already dead.

(253) a. *T-a*   *k'ahóol-t-ah*   *in*   *tàatah ...?*
       PFV-SBJ.2 acquaint-TRR-CMPL POSS.1.SG   father
       'Did you (get to) know my father (…)?' (Bohnemeyer 1998[T]:319)

      b. *T-in*   *yàa-kunt-ah*   *Pedro*
       PFV-SBJ.1.SG love-FACT-CMPL   Pedro
       h   *úuch*   *kux-a'n-ih.*
       PFV   happen be.alive-RSLTV-ABS.3.SG
       'I loved Peter when he was (still) alive.' (RMC)

Combination with *úuch* 'happen' seems to be similar to combinations with the progressive in that both are confined to dynamic situations. In (254), the matrix predicate *úuch* 'happen' underlines the change reading of the subordinate verbs *k'ah-óolt* 'acquaint', *yàabilt* 'love, like', and *p'èekt* 'hate, dislike'.

(254)   *Bix h*   *úuch*   *a*   *k'ahóol-t-ik/*   *yàabil-t-ik/*
      how PFV   happen SBJ.2 acquaint-TRR-INCMPL/ love-TRR-INCMPL/
      p'èek-t-ik   *le*   *xibpal-o'?*
      hate-TRR-INCMPL DEF man:child-D2
      'How did you happen to (come to) know / (fall in) love with / hate that boy?' (ACC_0294)

Furthermore, the fact that the transitivized verboids regularly form perfects and resultatives points to a dynamic reading of their bases (cf. (221), (255)). The perfect form conveys a stative reading, but it is implied that it is a state after having undergone the situation denoted by the base verb (= the derived transitive). If the base verb had a stative reading, a further stative derivation would be superfluous.

(255)   *xèen*   *iknal*   *a*   *nohoch* *chìich-o'*
      go:IMP at   POSS.2 big   grandmother-D2
      leti'-e'   *u*   *y-ohel-t-mah*
      that.one-TOP SBJ.3 0-know-TRR-PART.PF
      bix   *u*   *ts'a'k-al*
      how   SBJ.3 cure:PASS-INCMPL
      'go to your grandmother, she knows (=has learned) how it is cured'
      (ACC_0281)

So far, the evidence from the combination with aspect auxiliaries and the derivational potential of verboid-based transitive verbs has shown that they take dynamic readings. The examples in (256) and (257) show the options for combination with the progressive auxiliary *táan*. This is unproblematic for *k'ah-óolt* 'acquaint' (256a) and *ohelt* 'come to know' (256b), but more difficult for *yàabilt* 'love, like' and *p'èekt* 'hate, dislike' (257). This suggests that *yàabilt* and *p'èekt* are more strongly associated with a stative reading.

(256) a. *Pedro-e'   hach   táan   u   k'ahóolt-ik   Juana-e',* ...
Pedro-TOP   really   PROG   SBJ.3   acquaint-INCMPL   Juana-D3,
'While Pedro was about to get to know Juana, (...)' (ACC)

b. *Hach   táan   u   y-ohel-t-ik*
really   PROG   SBJ.3   0-know-TRR-INCMPL
ba'x   h   ùuch   ti'   u   yùum-o'.
what   PFV   happen   LOC   POSS.3   lord-D2
'She is learning what happend to her father.' (ACC)

(257)   *ʔtáan   in   yàabil-t/   yàa-kunt-ik*
PROG   SBJ.1.SG   love-TRR/   love-FACT-INCMPL
p'èek-t-ik   in   x-ka'na'
hate-TRR-INCMPL   POSS.3   F-stepmother
intended: 'I am loving / hating my stepmother' (RMC/ACC)

Examples in texts/natural discourse show that a stative meaning is expressed either by the transitive verboids *p'èek/yàamah* or by the various stativized forms, i.e., the perfect *p'èek(t)mah/yàabil(t)mah/yàakumah* or the resultative *p'èekta'n/yàabilta'n/yàakunta'n*. The transitivized form occurs if there is a grammatical need, for example, formation of the imperative (258) or occurrence in a subordinate clause such as, e.g., in the extrafocal clause of a manner adverb (259).[26] In these contexts, a more concrete meaning (associated with the feeling) may be articulated as, e.g., in (259) for *p'èekt*. Here *p'èekt* implies not only the feeling of dislike but also actions associated with or demonstrating the respective feeling, e.g., 'quarrel', 'dispute', 'fight', etc. The latter meanings are expressed by the compound *ch'a'p'èekt*, too (cf. below). *Yàabilt/yàakunt* in (258) is associated with the meaning 'care for', 'tend', etc.

---

[26] For manner focus constructions see also sect. 5.3.2.1.4.

(258) a. *tuméen   in   yàamah-ech,   ba'le'   ma'   a*
         because   SBJ.1.SG   love-ABS.2.SG   however   NEG   SBJ.2
         p'èek-t -ik   a   na' ...
         hate-TRR-INCMPL   POSS.2   mother
         'because I love you, but do not hate your mother (…)'
         (HNAZ_0016.03)

    b. *Yàabil-t-eh /   yàa-kunt-eh!*
       love-TRR-IMP/ love-FACT-IMPF
       'Treat him well/care for him!' (RMC)

(259)   *hach   ya'b   u   p'èek-t-ik   u   báah-o'b*
         really   much   SBJ.3   hate-TRR-INCMPL   POSS.3   self-PL
         'they quarrel a lot with each other' (RMC_1868)

Having discussed the dynamicity of transitive verboid-based verbs, I will briefly comment on those transitivized verbs that are based on intransitive verbs which are themselves based on adjectives. In sect. 5.3.1.1, it was shown that these intransitive verbs (e.g., *ts'iikil* 'feel angry', *k'ùuxil* 'feel angry' etc.) may have a stative or a dynamic reading depending on the context. This also holds true for their respective transitivized verbs. Verbs such as *ts'iikilt* 'feel angry about', *k'ùuxilt* 'feel angry about' denote either emotional states as directed towards a stimulus (260b) or actions that are related to the respective emotion (260a). Furthermore, the compound forms *ch'a'k'ùuxt, ch'a'p'èekt* also can have a dynamic reading (260c).

(260) a. *Pedro   tàah-a'n   u   ts'íikil-t/*
         Pedro   come-RSLTV   SBJ.3   feel.angry-TRR(SUBJ)/
         k'ùuxil-t   Pablo.
         get.angry-TRR(SUBJ)   Pablo
         'Pedro has come to scold Pablo.' (ACC)

    b. *Ba'x   t-a   ts'íikil-t-ah-e'x/*
       what   PFV-SBJ.2   feel.angry-TRR-CMPL-ABS.2.PL/
       k'ùuxil-t-ah-e'x?
       get.angry-TRR-CMPL-ABS.2.PL
       'What are you (pl.) angry about?' (ACC_0029)

    c. *Le   máak-o'   chéen   k-u   bin*
       DEF   person-D2   just   IMPF-SBJ.3   go
       u   ch'a'k'ùux-t   u   y-éet   wíinkil.
       SBJ.3   fetch:anger-TRR(SUBJ)   POSS.3   0-companion   body
       'That man only goes to quarrel with his colleagues.' (NMP_0139)

Control of transitive experiential verbs
The transitive experiential verbs listed in Table 36 differ as to their behavior regarding control. Three groups of verbs can be identified in this respect: one group of verbs is acceptable in Test 5, one group of verbs is not compatible with Test 5, and one group of verbs is acceptable in Test 5 only in one of its meaning variants. The specific results are as follows.

While the basic transitive verbs *kan* 'learn', *na't* 'guess', *óot* 'agree', *pa't* 'wait, hope', and *chuk* 'comprehend' are judged as being controlled according to Test 5, the perception verbs *il* and *u'y* both have two readings, one non-controlled (i.e., the inactive perception meaning) and one controlled (i.e., the active perception meaning, cf. Table *38* below). Thus, (261) implies that the A argument is actively directing its attention to the U argument.

(261)　　*Ts'in*　　　　　*chúuns-ik*　　　　　*in*　　　*w-il-ik*
　　　　　TERM-SBJ.1.SG　start:CAUS-INCMPL　SBJ.1.SG 0-see-INCMPL
　　　　　ba'x k-u　　　*y-ùuch-ul*　　　　*ti'*　*le*　*noticia-o'.*
　　　　　what IMPF-SBJ.3　0-happen-INCMPL LOC DEF　news-D2
　　　　　'I have started watching what is going on in the news.' (RMC)

As regards *tu'bs* 'forget' and *k'a'hs* 'remember, commemorate', the examples in (248) suggest control of their subject arguments, which is confirmed by their behavior in Test 5. Concerning this property, *tu'bs* and *k'a'hs* differ from their bases which have been shown to not integrate felicitously with Test 5 (cf. sect. 5.3.1.3).

The intransitive-base extraversives of Table 36 split up into two groups regarding control. The verbs *muk'yaht* 'suffer, feel', *náayt*[27] 'dream', *wayáak't* 'dream', *yah-óolt* 'regret', *ts'iibóolt* 'wish, desire', *náa'tukul(t)* 'worry about', *sèentukul(t)* 'worry about' are uncontrolled according to Test 5. The verbs *ts'iikilt* 'scold', *k'ùuxilt* 'scold', *icht* 'adore', *ch'a'k'ùuxt* 'quarrel', *ch'a'p'èekt* 'quarrel', *p'èek-óolt* 'get annoyed', *alabóolt* 'take confidence in, rely on', *òoksah-óolt* 'believe', *xot'óolt* 'decide', *ch'a'nu'kt* understand, pay attention to', *u'ynu'kt* 'listen and obey, pay attention to' take a controlling participant in subject function, as is consistent with their felicitous insertion in Test 5. *Tukul(t)* has a number of readings (given in Table 36) most of which are non-controlled. Only with the meaning 'plan' do consultants allow its insertion in Test 5 (262).

---

[27] This holds true at least with respect to a night dream, a day dream may be judged as controlled.

(262) a.*_ts'-in_   _chúuns-ik_
      TERM-SBJ.1.SG   start:CAUS-INCMPL
      _in_   _tukl-ik_   _in_   _ìiho_
      SBJ.1.SG   think-INCMPL POSS.1.SG son
      intended: 'I have started to long for my son' (RMC)

    b. _ts'-in_   _chúuns-ik_
      TERM-SBJ.1.SG   start:CAUS-INCMPL
      _in_   _tukl-ik_
      SBJ.1.SG   think-INCMPL
      'I have started planning it' (RMC)

Finally, the transitive verboid-based items in Table 36 also split up into two groups concerning the control frame in Test 5. While _yàabilt_ 'love, like; care for, tend', _yàakunt_ 'love, appreciate, care for, tend', and _p'èekt_ 'dislike, hate' are judged as being able to function in Test 5, this at least disputable for _ohelt_ 'know; learn, come to know' and _(ka')k'ah-óolt_ 'acquaint, recognize'. _(Ka')k'ah-óolt_ is clearly preferred with impersonal phasal matrix predicates. Note however, that contexts such as (250) for _k'ah-óolt_ and (251) for _ohelt_ suggest a control reading due to their occurrence in purpose clauses. Thus, it might be concluded that consultants' judgments of the compatibility of a given item with Test 5 is based on a default reading, while certain contexts may cancel such a reading.

Expertum as direct object
Two verbs mentioned in Table 36, i.e., _u'y_ 'feel' (263) and _muk'yaht_ 'suffer, feel' (264), may take an expertum noun in direct object function. Both verbs are generalized sensation verbs and, thus, may take a noun designating a specific sensation or pain as their direct object. In general only a limited and narrowly defined set of participants may occur in direct object function. Sensation verbs are distinguished by this behavior from verbs of the other subdomains which clearly take the stimulus in U function. This behavior correlates with the fact earlier stated that bodily sensation is generally not directed towards a stimulus. Rather it is thought of as either occurring on its own or as being induced by another situation. Note that it had already been seen in sect. 5.2.1.2 that sensation adjectives are the only predicates that do not have an oblique stimulus argument; possible stimulus participants are analyzed as adjuncts.

(263) a. *h   háak'   y-óol*
PFV   become.scared   POSS.3-mind
tumen   t-u   y-u'b-ah   u   sáak'il u   wíinklal ...
because PFV-SBJ.3 0-feel-CMPL POSS.3 itching POSS.3 body
'he felt scared because he felt his body itching (…)'
(HNAZ_0004.02)

   b. *Tèen-e' ma'tech in   w-u'y-ik   in   ka'nal.*
me-TOP never   SBJ.1.SG 0-feel-INCMPL SBJ.1.SG tire
'I don't feel (that I am) tired.' (HK'AN_171)

(264)   *táan in   muk'yah-t-ik*
PROG SBJ.1.SG overcome:ache-TRR-INCMPL
uk'ah/ wi'h/ u   k'i'nam
thirsty/ hungry/ POSS.3   pain
'I am suffering thirst/hunger/pain' (RMC_1698)

Construction 31 represents a transitive construction with a generalized experiential verb in predicate function. The direct object function is taken by an expertum noun. Although coded as a noun phrase, it is a part of the predicate, and the overall meaning of the construction is to express a specific experiential state of an experiencer.

semantics:	EXPERIENTIAL STATE	<Experiencer>	
			specification
	SENSE	<Experiencer	Theme>
syntax:	[[...V-...]_{TrVCom}	NP$_1$	NP$_2$]_{TrVCo}
constraints:	SENSE ∈ {*muk'yaht, u'y*}; Theme ∈ {expertum}		

Construction 31. Transitive C. with generalized experiential verb

As with all items in Table 36, passive formation is regular with the generalized sensation verbs. Note that *ke'lil* 'coldness' is thought of as the subject in the passive clause (265).

(265)   *Ken   u   mèent   ke'lil-e'   hach k-u*
SR.FUT SBJ.3 do(SUBJ) cold:ABSTR-D3 really IMPF-SBJ.3
muk'yah-t-a'l   ti' le   mehen kàah-o'b-o'.
overcome:ache-TRR-PASS.INCMPL LOC DEF small   village-PL-D2
'When it is cold, the people in the small villages really suffer.'
(ACC_0605)

5.3.2.1.1.2 *Transitive verbs of the expression of experience*
As has been noted above, all experiencer-oriented transitive verbs from the
subdomains of emotion and bodily sensation are non-basic. There are however,
some basic transitive verbs in the subdomain of emotion that designate expression of emotion (Table 37), which will be discussed in this section.

subdomain	instance (gloss) 'meaning'
gesture	*tsik* 'respect, honor; obey'
	xil 'fluff up'
	yach-ich-t (frown:eye-TRR) 'frown'
	k'úuychi'-t (twist:mouth-TRR) 'grimace at; scorn'
	ts'úuyni'-t (bend:nose-TRR) 'wrinkle nose (at bad odor)'
	muts'ich-t (close.eyes:eye-TRR) 'blink, wink at s.b.; scowl at'
	chinpòol-t (tilt:head-TRR) 'nod, bow before, acknowledge'
communi-cation	*poch'* 'insult'
	ki'-ki'a'l-t (RED-delicious:say-TRR) 'praise, flatter'
	ts'iikt'àan-t (furious:speak-TRR) 'scold'
	sáalt'àan-t (light:speak-TRR) 'speak reassuringly'
	tu-tukchi'-t (RED-pile.up:mouth-TRR) 'scold and mutter; argue'
	ki'-ki't'àan-t (RED-delicious:speak-TRR) 'praise, commend'
	lo'-lòobt'àan-t (RED-evil:speak-TRR) 'curse'
	níib-óolt 'thank'
	òok'olk'áat (weep:ask) 'solicit, beg'
	k'áat-óol-t (wish:mind-TRR) 'solicit, ask for, wish'
	sáas-t (light-TRR) 'foretell, prophecy, divine'
	pulya'h-t (throw:ache-TRR) 'bewitch'
	payalchi't 'adore'
perception	*k'áa-k'àas-pàakat* (RED-bad-look) 'look badly at'
	ts'iikpàakat (angry:look) 'look angrily at'
	lek'pàakat (open:look) 'glare fixedly, angrily at'
	ts'e'pàakat (side:look) 'look angrily at from the side'
	k'éel-ich-t (squint-eye-TRR) 'look scornfully, despisingly at'
action	*ki'ki'óolt/ki'mak-óol-t* (happy-mind-TRR) 'delight, caress, fe-licitate'
	k'ult 'worship'
	táan-óol-t (front:mind-TRR) 'attend, look after'

Table 37. Transitive verbs of emotional, volitive, and cognitive expression

Table 37 lists items designating the expression of experience. These are
verbs that code different sorts of acting out emotional and volitive, and more
seldomly, cognitive states. There are only a few basic transitive verbs referring
to the expression of an emotion, namely, *tsik* 'respect, honor; obey', *poch'* 'in-

sult', *xil* 'fluff up', and *k'ult* 'worship'. A larger number are compounds and incorporatives that refer to a gesture or a communicative act which is accompanied by an emotional state or serves to express such a state. The meaning of emotion is secondary here, although it is clearly present. The mentioned verbs are composed of a usually transitive verb and a body part noun, which is used to perform the gesture (266) (cf. Lehmann and Verhoeven 2005).

(266) a. *u   kìik   h-Pèedroh-e'*
      POSS.3 elder.sister M-Peter-TOP
      t-u   muts'ich-t-en
      PFV-SBJ.3 close.eyes:eye-TRR(CMPL)-ABS.1.SG
      'Peter's older sister scowled at me' (Bricker et al. 1998, s.v. *muts'*)

     b. *t-u   k'úuychi'-t-ah-en*
      PFV-SBJ.3 twist:mouth-TRR-CMPL-ABS.1.SG
      'he looked at me scornfully' (RMC_1679)

Another group which is obviously related to emotion but is primarily part of another semantic domain is the verbs of communication which transmit an emotional attitude. These are again either incorporatives, incorporating a person part noun such as *chi'* 'mouth' or *óol* 'mind', or they are compounds, usually taking a modifying adjective (sometimes reduplicated) as the first part of the compound verb (e.g., the compounds with *t'àan* 'speak', *a'l* 'say'). Note that some of these communication verbs take the message in direct object function while the addressee is coded as indirect object (267a). Others are bivalent, taking the addressee in direct object function (267b).

(267) a. *Kìins-en-i'*
      kill-ABS.1.SG-LOCF
      hach k-in   k'áat-óot-ik   tèech
      really IMPF-SBJ.1.SG ask-soul:TRR-INCMPL you
      'Kill me, I really adjure you.' (HK'AN_613.4)

     b. *ts'íikt'àan-t   le   pàal-o'*
      angry:speak-TRR DEF child-D2
      yo'sal   u   bey-tal   u   y-u'b-ik
      in.order SBJ.3 possible-PROC SBJ.3 0-feel-INCMPL
      ba'x k-a   w-a'l-ik
      what IMPF-SBJ.2 0-say-INCMPL
      'speak with fury to that child so that it can understand what you say' (RMC_2053)

A third group contains verbs of perception which are either compounds with
pàakat 'look' or an incorporative with *ich* 'eye'. These take the stimulus in direct object function.

Most of the verbs given in Table 37 integrate with the general transitive
construction as depicted in Construction 30. They match their AGENT with the
constructional Actor argument and their GOAL or ADDRESSEE with the constructional Undergoer argument. Some communication verbs (e.g., (267a)) integrate
with a ditransitive construction (cf. Construction 40 below) and map the lexical
ADDRESSEE on the constructional Indirectus argument while the MESSAGE is
matched with the Undergoer argument.

The expression of emotion through complex lexemes that are based on incorporation or compounding with a body or person part noun can also be found
in other languages, e.g., in Guarani (cf. Velázquez Castillo 1996). Such a strategy can be seen as being functionally similar to the evidential marking of the
linguistic rendering of non-Ego situations of emotion (cf. discussion of (18) in
sect. 3.3.2.1.1).

5.3.2.1.1.3 *Transitive verbs of active perception*

In addition to the verbs of the expression of experience, transitive verbs of active perception also integrate with the general transitive construction (cf.
Construction 30). Table 38 lists a number of active perception verbs. The active perceiver is viewed as an AGENT corresponding to the experiencer of inactive perception verbs and the object/target of perception, i.e., the PATIENT
corresponds to the stimulus of inactive perception verbs (cf. *il* 'see', *u'y* 'hear,
taste, smell, sense, feel' in Table 36). Thus, the verbs in Table 38 match their
AGENT with the constructional Actor argument and their PATIENT with the constructional Undergoer argument in Construction 30. (268) shows some examples.

(268) a. *t-in*   *ch'éenxikin-t-ah*
       PFV-SBJ.1.SG   eavesdrop-TRR-CMPL
       le   ba'x   k-a   *w-a'l-ik-e'x-o'*
       DEF   what   IMPF-SBJ.2   0-say-INCMPL-2.PL-D2
       'I eavesdropped on / listened to what you said' (VEC_0006)

     b. *Nip'chi'-t*   *a*   *w-u'y-eh*!
        taste:mouth-TRR(IMP)   SBJ.2   0-feel-SUBJ
        'Try it so that you taste it!' (RMC_1673)

Glosses in Table 38 show that most of the items are non-basic and thus (at
least morphologically) are derived from intransitive verbs. Note however, that
with most of these verbs, intransitive variants are rarely (if at all) used. Thus,

from a usage-based point of view, the transitive verbs have to be considered as more basic (and they are therefore only listed here and not in Table 30).

It has already been noted in sect. 5.3.2.1.1.1 that the basic perception verbs *il* 'see' and *u'y* 'hear, feel, etc.' also occur as active perception verbs. In this reading they are controlled, just as the complex active perception verbs are. Sect. 7.2 will discuss the issue of active perception verbs as matrix predicates.

subdomain	instance (gloss) 'meaning'
non-visual	*u'y* (feel) 'feel, hear, taste, smell, sense'
visual	*il* (see) 'see, look at'
	cha'n-t (enjoy-TRR) 'contemplate, look at; enjoy seeing'
	pàakat/pakt (look:TRR) 'look (at); see, gaze'
	ch'éeneb-t (peek-TRR) 'examine, peek, spy'
	ch'úuk-t (watch-TRR) 'watch for, hunt up'
	kanáan-t (guard-TRR) 'guard, watch over'
	pakapakt (RED:look:TRR) 'look face to face'
	ts'e'pàakat (side:look:TRR) 'see from the corner of the eye at'
	nunulpakt 'look up and down, side to side at'
	háaych'èeneb-t (extend:peek-TRR) 'watch at'
	manak'il-t (unclear:see-TRR) 'see unclearly, scarcely'
auditory	*ch'ehxikin-t* (strengthen:ear-TRR) 'cock one's ear, listening attentively'
	ch'éenxikint 'listen attentively to'
	núuk(-t) (answer(-TRR)) 'answer, listen'
olfactory	*úuts'(bent)* (smell.at) 'smell at'
	úuts'ni'-t (smell:nose-TRR) 'sniff, suffle'
	k'ok'obni'-t (RED:punch:nose-TRR) 'sniff around'
	(ch'a')-ch'a'bòok-t ((RED-)fetch:smell-TRR) 'sniff at'
gustatory	*nip'chi'-t* (taste:mouth-TRR) 'try, taste'

Table 38. Transitive verbs of active perception

5.3.2.1.2 *Reflexive constructions*

Reflexive constructions in YM are identical to transitive constructions, but take the possessed relational noun *báah* 'self' in direct object function. This is obligatorily possessed and its possessor is referentially identical to the subject argument of the transitive verb.

Reflexive verbs are rather rare in the domain of experience in YM, in contrast to many other languages, including SAE languages, which use reflexive verbs to express emotional states (cf. sect. 3.4.2.3). Thus, it might be the case that some of the reflexive verbs listed in Table 39 are calqued from Spanish.

subdomain	instance (gloss) 'meaning'
bodily	*he'ls POSS báah* (rest:CAUS POSS self) 'rest'
sensation	*óolint POSS báah* (mind:USAT POSS self) 'recover, recuperate'
emotion	*wo'l-t POSS báah* (round.off-TRR POSS self) 'despair'
cognition	*mèet POSS báah* (do POSS self) 'think a great deal of oneself, think very highly of oneself'

Table 39. Reflexive verbs and collocations of experience

The first two items in Table 39 are causative and usative derivations, respectively. The inactive intransitive base verb *he'l* has itself experiential meaning and is judged as controlled (cf. sect. 5.3.1.1, Table 28) just as the reflexive derivation *he'ls POSS báah* is (269a). Both integrate felitiously with Test 5 and form positive imperatives. *Óolint* (269b) only occurs in a reflexive construction and is judged as non-controlled with respect to Test 5.

(269) a. *Le   k'iin he'l-o'*
     DEF   sun   PRSV-D2
     h   p'áat chital   u   he'ls   u   báah.
     PFV   stay   lie:PROC SBJ.3   rest:CAUS POSS.3   self
     'That day he kept lying to recover.' (HK'AN_158)

    b. *Ma'   papah, pa't-eh;   pa'tik*
     NEG   father await-IMP   be.going.to
     in   chan   óolint-ik   in   báah …
     SBJ.1.SG a.bit   mind:USAT-INCMPL   POSS.1.SG   self
     'No, father, wait, I am going to recover a bit (…)' (HA'N_0022.01)

The last two items in Table 39 are based on metaphor (270). These are rather singular collocations that are not part of a general pattern. Note that *mèet POSS báah* has the variant *mèet POSS óol* (270b). The latter construction type will be examined in sect. 5.3.2.2.2.1. The items in Table 39 do not take a stimulus in complement function.

(270) a. *Táan u   wo'lt-ik   u   báah*
     PROG SBJ.3   round.off-INCMPL POSS.3   self
     tumen ma'   u   y-ohel   ba'x ken   u   mèet-i'.
     because NEG SBJ.3   0-know   what SR.FUT   SBJ.3   do(SUBJ)-NEGF
     'He despairs because he does not know what to do.' (ACC_0404)

    b. *hach k-u   mèet-ik   u   báah-a'/ y-óol-a'*
     really IMPF-SBJ.3 do-INCMPL   POSS.3   self-D1/ 0-mind-D1
     'he thinks a great deal of himself' (RMC_1780)

Table 39 only lists those verbs that are necessarily reflexive, i.e. that do not allow for a non-referentially identical direct object. Note that a number of verbs listed in Table 36 may also occur in a reflexive construction, i.e. they may take the possessed relational noun *báah* 'self' in direct object function, e.g., *(ch'a')p'èekt, yàabilt/yàakunt, ts'íikilt, etc.*, which results in an explicitly reflexive meaning. Furthermore, with these items a plural A argument leads to a possibly ambiguous interpretation as to reflexivity or reciprocity, as is shown in (271). Note that a reciprocity meaning is not possible for the items listed in Table 39.

(271) a. *Yàabil-t   a   báah-e'x!*
         love-TRR(IMP) POSS.2   self-2.PL
         'Love (pl.) yourselves/each other!' (EMB_0747)

      b. *Yàan máak-o'b-e' u   ch'a'p'èek-t-mah   u   báah-o'b.*
         EXIST person-PL-D3 SBJ.3 take:hate-TRR-PART.PF POSS.3 self-PL
         'There are people that hate themselves/each other.' (EMB_0718)

Finally, it has to be noted that the general sensation verb *u'y* 'feel' may also be constructed with the reflexive *POSS báah*. However, it is always accompanied by a secondary predicate (cf. sect. 5.3.2.1.4).

5.3.2.1.3 *Transitive verbs as metaphorical predicators*

A number of experiential constructions are based on metaphors consisting of a transitive verb which takes an expertum noun or a person part noun in direct object function.

First, there is a pattern in which the transitive verb *ch'a'* 'take' functions as the predicator taking a nominalized experiential term, i.e., the expertum, in direct object function. The nouns are mostly derived from the emotion adjectives in Table 17. Refer to (272) for illustration. Table 40 lists the most common collocations.

(272) a. *Le   óotsil kéeh-e' t-u   ch'a'-ah   subtal*
         DEF poor   deer-D3 PFV-SBJ.3 take-CMPL   shame
         káa h   hóok' y-áalkab.
         CNJ PFV   exit   SBJ.3-run
         'The poor deer became ashamed and ran away.' (AAK_036)

      b. *ba'le'   ma' a   ch'a'-ik   sahak-il*
         however NEG SBJ.2 take-INCMPL afraid-ABSTR
         'but don't get afraid' (HNAZ_0023)

Most of the items listed in Table 40 have corresponding intransitives in the class of inchoative verbs (cf. Table 29). While the *ch'a'*-collocations are generally judged as taking a controlling experiencer in subject function according to Test 5, the inchoative counterparts tested as consistently uncontrolled. Note however, that the *ch'a'*-collocations are not necessarily interpreted as controlled. Combination with an impersonal phase predicate results in an uncontrolled meaning.

subdomain	instance (gloss) 'meaning'
	ch'a' k'ùuxil (take anger) 'get annoyed'
	ch'a' sahkil(il) (take fear(-ABSTR)) 'get afraid'
emotion	*ch'a' su'lakil* (take ashamed:ABSTR) 'get ashamed'
	ch'a' subtal (take shame LOC) 'get ashamed'
	ch'a' óotsilil ti' (take poor:ABSTR LOC) 'take pity on'

Table 40. ch'a'-collocations with expertum noun

Construction 32 represents the construction scheme of the *ch'a'*-collocations. Their analysis is similar to that given for the German *Funktionsverbgefüge* discussed in sect. 2.3. Note that the generalized function of the syntactic predicate is similar to that in Construction 31.

semantics:	INCH (EMOTIONAL STATE <Experiencer >)		metaphor
	TAKE	<Actor	Undergoer>
syntax:	[[... *ch'a'*-...]$_{TrVCom}$	NP$_1$	NP$_2$]$_{TrVCo}$
constraints:	Undergoer ∈ {emotion}		

Construction 32. Inchoative C. with ch'a' and emotional expertum nouns

Like their simple adjectival and verbal counterparts, the collocations in Table 40 may add a stimulus as an oblique complement. The choice of the preposition is identical to that given for the base adjectives (cf. sect. 5.2.1.2), i.e., all may adjoin their stimulus with *ti'*. *Ch'a' k'ùuxil* 'get annoyed' and *ch'a' su'lakil/subtal* also allow *yéetel* to adjoin a stimulus argument. *Ch'a' óotsilil* differs from the others in obligatorily adjoining a stimulus argument in a *ti'* phrase.

Construction 32 has limited productivity. Thus, *ch'a' p'èektahil* lit.: 'take hate' is accepted by most consultants but the more idiomatic *ch'a'p'èekt* 'hate, be hostile to, quarrel' is clearly preferred (cf. Table 36); acceptability of further collocations is as follows: *ch'a' yahóolal ti'* 'feel (compassion, pity) for somebody', *ch'a' chi'chnakil ti'* 'feel furious with s.o.', *?ch'a' yàabilah/ yàakunah ti'* 'feel love for somebody', *?ch'a' ki'mak-óolal ti'* 'feel happy about'. Other expertum nouns, e.g., *péek-óolal* 'doubt, distrust', *ma'óolal* 'sadness, depression', *òok'ol-óolal* 'sadness, despair', *etc.* do not fit into Construction 32.

While the items listed in Table 40 take non-possessed expertum noun phrases in direct object function, those in Table 41 obligatorily take possessed noun phrases in direct object function. These are collocations with *óol* 'mind', *tùukul* 'thought' and *ìik'* 'air; life, breath' as heads of the direct object noun phrases. Most of the collocations belong to the subdomain of cognition and refer to cognitive activities. The subject argument is necessarily coreferential with the possessor attribute of the direct object argument, which results in a kind of reflexive construction. (273), (274), and (276b) are examples from Modern YM and (275) and (276a) illustrate Colonial YM cases. Nowadays the Colonial collocation *lèep' POSS óol* 'take courage, cheer up' (275) has lost its experiential sense, instead meaning roughly 'hurry (up)'. Construction 33 gives the construction scheme. All items of Table 41 are controlled according to Test 5.

subdomain	instance (gloss) 'meaning'
	ch'a' POSS ìik' (take POSS air) 'inhale; concentrate'
cognition	*tòoh-kint POSS tùukul* (straight-FACT POSS thought) 'concentrate'
	máans POSS tùukul (pass:CAUS POSS thought) 'think, reflect, ponder'
emotion	*mèet POSS óol* (do POSS mind) 'think a great deal of oneself'
b. sensation	*ch'a' POSS óol* (take POSS mind) 'recover from illness'

Table 41. Reflexive collocations with person part noun/expertum noun

(273)   *k-u*   *máans-ik*   *u*   *tùukul Pedro*
         IMPF- SBJ.3 pass:CAUS-INCMPL POSS.3   thought Pedro
         'Pedro is thinking/reflecting ' (NMP_0041)

(274) a. *Sáam*   *in*   *ch'a'*   *in*   *w-óol*
         some.time.ago SBJ.1.SG fetch(SUBJ) POSS.3 0-mind
         úuchik   *in*   *w-íichint-ik*   *síis ha'.*
         by.means.of SBJ.1.SG 0-bathe:USAT-INCMPL   icy water
         'I just feel better after having taken a cold shower.' (NMP_0025)

     b. *Pedro-e'* *k-u*   *mèet-ik*   *u*   *y-óol*
         Pedro-TOP IMPF-SBJ.3 do-INCMPL POSS.3 0-mind
         ti'   *le*   *ba'x y-ohel*   *u*   *mèet-o'.*
         LOC DEF thing SBJ.3-know SBJ.3 do(SUBJ)-D2
         'Pedro thinks a great deal of himself for the things he can do.'
         (AME_0065)

(275)   *lèep'*   *a*   *w-óol!*
         scrape(IMP) POSS.2   0-mind
         'Cheer up/take courage!' (Barrera Vásquez et al. eds. 1980, s.v. *lep' ol*)

(276) a. *t-in*   *ch'a'-ah*   *w-ìik'*
         PFV- SBJ.1.SG   fetch-CMPL   POSS.1.SG-air
         'I turned inside myself; I caught my breath' (Barrera Vásquez et al.
         eds. 1980, s.v. *ik'*)[28]

      b. *Káa   túun   bin   tu   ch'a'-ah   u   y-ìik'al*
         CNJ   then   QUOT PFV   fetch-CMPL   POSS.3   0-air:ABSTR
         u   y-áalkab   uti'a'l   u   síit't-ik
         SBJ.3   0-run   for   SBJ.3   jump-INCMPL
         'And then he gathered the strength to run and jump over it.'
         (HK'AN_182.1)

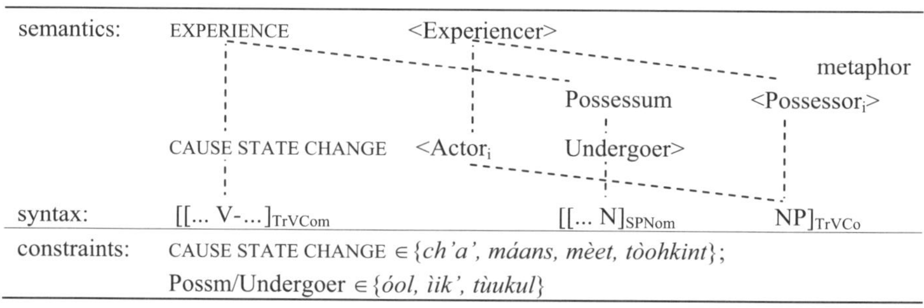

Construction 33. Reflexive experiential C. with possessor-experiencer

Note that all items integrating with Construction 33 (with the exception of
ch'a' POSS *óol* 'recover from illness') may also fit into an extended construction which takes an oblique stimulus argument introduced by *ti'* 'LOC'.

5.3.2.1.4 *Secondary predicates*
In sect. 5.2.1.4 Construction 14 was examined as a specialized construction for
the expression of an evaluation. Another common way of expressing an
evaluation with respect to a stimulus participant consists of using a transitive

---

[28] The expression *ch'a' Poss ìik'* with the given meaning seems to no longer exist in the dialect
of Yaxley. However a contemporary narration contains a similar meaning as in the following
example. Cf. also (276b) from the same story, which is interpreted literally by one of my consultants as taking breath for running, contrary to the Spanish translation of the original text.

u mùuk' óolal-il yéetel u ch'a'ìik'-il

POSS.3 strength desire-REL and POSS.3 take:breath-REL

'his mental strength and his inspiration' (HK'AN_0515)

perception/sensation verb (or a transitive verb metonymically related to perception, as, e.g., *hàant* 'eat') as main predicate in a construction with an evaluative adjective as secondary predicate, the latter being 'attributed' to the direct object argument of the perception/sensation verb. Though, the respective construction type is quite productive, some instances that constitute frequent collocations are listed in Table 42.

subdomain[29]	instance (gloss) 'meaning'
emotion/cognition	*yah Sbj il X* (ache SBJ see X) 'find X difficult'
	uts Sbj il X (good SBJ see X) 'like X'
perception	*hela'n Sbj u'y X* (different SBJ feel X) 'X sounds strange to'
	ki' Sbj u'y X (delicious SBJ feel X) 'taste good to X'
	ki' Sbj hàan-t X (delicious SBJ eat-TRR X) 'enjoy eating X'
bodily sensation	*yah Sbj u'y X* (ache SBJ feel X) 'feel X painful'

Table 42. Perception/evaluation collocations with adjectival secondary predicate

To express an evaluation with this type of collocation, the secondary predicate is preferentially focused. In (277a), the focus construction is judged as good by all consultants while the non-focused version in (277b) is highly disfavored or even judged as bad by some. This is indicated by the question mark accompanying the abbreviations for the consultants following the translation in (277b). Furthermore, note that the text base used here only contains instances parallel to (277a), and none parallel to (277b). (277a) shows that the auxiliary is dropped in the focus construction if the verb has incompletive status marking.

(277) a. *Hela'n   in   w-u'y-ik   le   máasewáal t'àan-a'.*
different SBJ.1.SG 0-feel-INCMPL DEF Indian   speech-D1
'This Indian tongue sounds strange to me.'
(RMC, SME, ACC, EMB, FEE, SBM)

   b. *K-in   w-u'y-ik   hela'n le   máasewáal t'àan-a'.*
IMPF-SBJ.1.SG 0-feel-INCMPL different DEF Indian   speech-D1
'This Indian tongue sounds strange to me.'
([?]RMC, [?]SME, [?]ACC, EMB, FEE, SBM)

The pair of examples in (278) shows that the focused adjective refers to the direct object noun phrase of the perception/sensation verb. (278a) is parallel to (277a), while (278b) shows two independent clauses, the first of which is a focused nominal clause with *ka'na'n* 'tired' as a nominal predicate of the subject

---

[29] source domain of evaluation

in wòoko'b 'my feet'. The direct object of the verb *u'y* 'feel' in the second clause is identical to the first clause as a whole. The examples are judged as being synonymous by my consultants. Construction 34 represents the perception/evaluation focus construction. It covers the incompletive case.

(278) a. *Ka'n-a'n   in   w-u'y-ik   in   w-òok-o'b.*
tire-RSLTV SBJ.1.SG 0-feel-INCMPL POSS.1.SG 0-foot-PL
'I am feeling (that) my feet (are) tired.' (ACC)

b. *Ka'n-a'n   in   w-òok-o'b k-in   w-u'y-ik.*
tire-RSLTV POSS.1.SG 0-foot-PL   IMPF-SBJ.1.SG 0-feel-INCMPL
'My feet are tired, (as) I feel.' (BVS_15.01.17)

semantics:	EVALUATION/SENSATION	<Experiencer	Stimulus>
			metonymy
	SENSE	<Experiencer QUALITY	<Stimulus>>
syntax:	[Adj [[... V-...]$_{TrVCom}$	NP$_1$	NP$_2$]$_{TrVCo}$]$_S$
constraints:	SENSE ∈ {perception}		

Construction 34. Evaluation/perception C. with focused secondary predicate

Note that reflexive constructions with *báah* 'self' or the person part nouns *óol* 'mind' or *wíinklal* 'body' in direct object function are compatible with Construction 34 as well, provided that NP₁ is a possessed NP with a person part noun as its head and provided that the respective referential identity restrictions between subject and possessor hold true (279). However, such 'reflexive' constructions differ from canonical transitive constructions in that they do not allow for a passive, since the latter always presupposes that actor and undergoer be referentially disjunct.

(279) a. *Hela'n   in   w-u'y-ik   in   wíinkil-al*
different SBJ.1.SG 0-feel-INCMPL POSS.1.SG body-REL
tumen   tíin   chokwil.
because PROG:SBJ.1.SG fever
'I feel strange since I have a fever.' (SBM_0206)

b. *Pedro-e'   hach   nohoch y-u'b-ik   u   báah.*
Pedro-TOP really big   SBJ.3-feel-INCMPL POSS.3 self
'Pedro thinks the world of himself.' (EMB_0806)

Construction 34 is an instance of a more general focus construction, called manner focus construction in Bohnemeyer (1998[T]:196). (280) shows that an adverb in focus position triggers the same form of the transitive verb complex, i.e., the auxiliary is dropped if the verb has incompletive status marking.

(280)   *Hwàan-e' uts   u   balak'òok-t-ik   le   bòola-o'.*
           Juan-TOP   good SBJ.3 roll:foot-TRR-INCMPL DEF ball-D2
           'Juan plays the ball well.' (EMB_0280, ACC, RMC, SME)

Furthermore, the auxiliary is preserved with completive status marking in both cases (281).

(281) a. *Hela'n t-a   w-u'y-ah   le   máasewáal t'àan-a'?*
           different PFV-SBJ.2 0-feel-CMPL DEF Indian   speech-D1
           'Did this Indian tongue sound strange to you? (ACC)
      b. *Uts   t-u   balak'òok-t-ah   le   bòola-o'?*
           good PFV-SBJ.3 roll:foot-TRR-CMPL DEF ball-D2
           'Did he play the ball well?' (NMP)

Construction 35 illustrates the manner focus construction represented with an incompletive-marked verbal core.

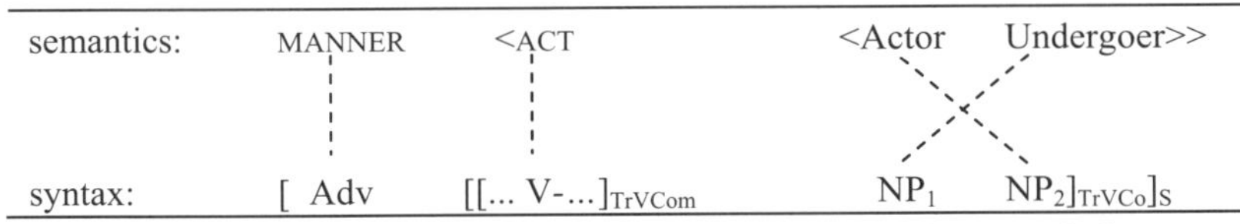

Construction 35. Manner focus C. with transitive incompletive verbal core

The evaluation/perception construction with a focused secondary predicate (Construction 34) is regularly related to a passive construction with a secondary predicate. (282) shows examples with incomplete marking which are parallel to the transitive construction in (277a) as concerns the 'deletion' of the aspect marker. (283) is an example with completive status on the passive verb. This construction type does not have the perfective aspect marker either (contrary to the active counterpart in (281)), and the verb is additionally marked by the extrafocal suffix *-ik* for intransitive verbs (cf. Table 4 in sect. 4.1.6). This construction allows for the option of leaving the experiencer implicit, and it is in this respect functionally equivalent to the stimulus qualifying adjectival construction examined in sect. 5.2.1.4. The focus position is generally taken by stimulus-oriented or evaluative adjectives such as those mentioned in that section.

(282) a. *le   pinya   yéetel le   mango,*
      DEF pineapple and   DEF mango

      hach   máan-óol   u   hàan-t-a'l
      really pass-mind SBJ.3 eat-TRR-PASS.INCMPL
      'the pineapple and the mango are really very satisfactory/filling
      up/boring to eat' (EMB_0843)

   b. *hun-p'éel   sìirko, háak'óol   u   cha'nt-a'l*
      one-CL.INAN circus scare:mind SBJ.3 contemplate-PASS.INCMPL
      'a circus scary to observe' (RMC_2222)

(283)   *Káa h   yáax máan   sìirko úuchil-e'*
         CNJ PFV first pass(CMPL) circus formerly-TOP
         háak'óol   il-a'b-ik   tumen le   hèente-o'.
         scare:mind see-CMPL.PASS-EF   by   DEF people-D2
         'When a circus passed for the first time, it was scary to the poeple
         watching it.' (EMB_0067/ACC)

As has been explained in sect. 4.1.6, passives are constructed in the same
way as intransitives and, thus, their behavior in focus constructions is identical
to that of intransitive verbs. Compare the examples in (282) with (284a) for the
incompletive construction and (283) with (284b) for the completive construction with focused manner adverbs.

(284) a. *séeban   in   w-áalkab*
      fast   SBJ.1.SG   0-run
      'fast is how I run' (ACC)

   b. *séeban   áalkab-nah-ik-en*
      fast   run-CMPL-EF-ABS.1.SG
      'fast was how I ran' (RMC)

It can thus be seen that focused secondary predicates are constructed in the
same way as focused manner adverbs in intransitive/passive and in transitive
constructions.

5.3.2.2 *Stimulus and agent-oriented constructions*

Stimulus- and agent-oriented experiential constructions are classified according to the syntactic coding of the experiencer which may be a direct object
(sect. 5.3.2.2.1) or a possessor of a body part or expertum noun in direct object
function (sect. 5.3.2.2.2).

5.3.2.2.1 *Experiencer as object*

Table 43 lists derived transitive verbs in all of which a stimulus or an agent takes subject function and the experiencer is coded as direct object. The verbs in Table 43 are either causatives derived from inactive intransitives (Table 28) or factitives from adjectival (Table 17) or modal bases (Table 22). The processes of causativization and factitivization are highly productive and regular in their semantics (cf. Table 6). The S argument receives U function within the frame of the transitivized verb, a new A is introduced bringing about the state of U. (285) gives some illustrative examples.

subdomain	instance (gloss) 'meaning'
emotion	*k'ùux-kin*[30] (be.angry-FACT) 'bother'
	ts'íik-kun (furious-FACT) 'bother, make fierce'
	chi'chnak-kun (cross-FACT) 'disturb, bother'
	p'úuh-a'n-kun (cross-RSLTV-FACT) 'make cross, peeved, mad'
	su'lak-kun/kin (ashamed-FACT) 'shame, abash, embarrass'
	sahak-kun (afraid-FACT) 'frighten'
	hets'-kun[31] (quiet-FACT) 'appease, calm'
	chokoh-kin (hot-FACT) 'heat, make fall in love'
	lúubóol-kin (fall:mind-FACT) 'make feel sad, depressed'
	ma'k'óol-kin (idle-FACT) 'make idle, lazy'
	sa'k-óol-kin (sedulous-FACT) 'make sedulous, active, industrious'
	ma'óol-kin (without:mind-FACT) 'make listless'
	sahbes (fear:CAUS) 'frighten'
	p'u'hs (get.mad:CAUS) 'bother, scare, make angry'
bodily sensation	*ka'ns* (tire:CAUS) 'tire, make tired'
	wi'h-kun (hungry-FACT) 'make hungry/appetite'
	uk'ah-kun (thirsty-FACT) 'make thirsty'
	na'h-kun (satified-FACT) 'make full, satisfied'
	nich'ban-kun (bite:INTRV-FACT) 'pick, cause to itch'
volition	*pooch-kin* (desirous-FACT) 'make desirous'
	tàak-kun (anxious-FACT) 'animate, incite'
cognition	*ka'ns* (learn\PASS:CAUS) 'teach'

Table 43. Causative experiential verbs taking the experiencer as direct object

---

[30] This form is not very common in the dialect of my consultants, they prefer the periphrastic causative with *mèet* 'do', i.e., *mèet u k'ùuxil* do SBJ.3 get.angry 'make hin/her angry'.

[31] According to Bricker et. al. (1998, s.v. *hets'*) *hets'* is a transitive as well as a positional root; *hets'kun* is based on the positional root *hets'*.

(285) shows that the stimulus may be located in different positions in the hierarchy of participant properties (Figure 2). (373) and (374) demonstrate that propositions are also allowed to function as subjects with causative experiential verbs.[32]

(285) a. *U   bòok le   hàanal-o'*
POSS.3 smell DEF   food-D2
k-u   wi'h-kúuns-ik   máak.
IMPF-SBJ.3 hungry-FACT-INCMPL person
'The smell of food makes a man hungry.' (ACC)

   b. *Le   káan-o' hach   k-u   sah-bes-ik.*
DEF   snake-D2 really   IMPF-SBJ.3   fear-CAUS-INCMPL
'The snake scares him a lot.' (PLC_006)

The causative experiential verbs integrate with the general transitive construction depicted in Construction 36. The causing AGENT or STIMULUS is mapped onto the Actor argument of the construction, while the lexical EXPERIENCER is mapped onto the Undergoer argument. This alignment is converse to the alignment of the experiencer-oriented verbs in Construction 30.

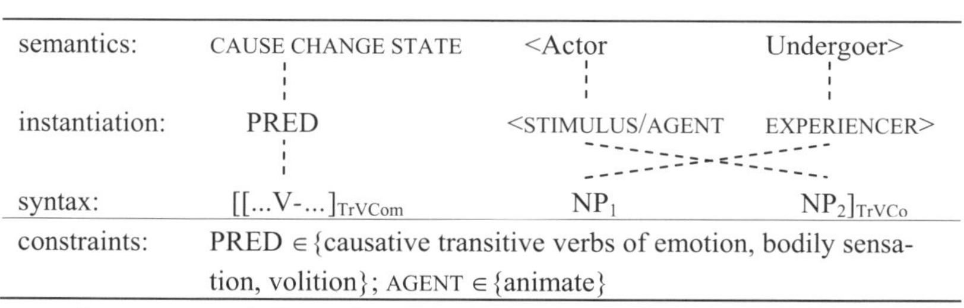

Construction 36. General transitive C. with causative experiential verbs

There is a further constructional frame with YM causative verbs. If the subject position is occupied by a causing AGENT, a STIMULUS may be adjoined in an instrument phrase, as in (286).

---

[32] Bohnemeyer (1998[T]:242) states that inanimate participants are often bad A arguments with transitive verbs, and he even claims that "there are no transitive verbs in YM that would select for an abstract or propositional A-argument". This restriction does not hold true with examples like (373) and (374), which take a propositional A argument. Such examples however may indeed be quite artificial. In transitive clauses, where non-human A arguments act on human U arguments, YM seems to prefer passivization or topicalization, as in (285).

(286) a. *Pedro-e'   t-u   sahak-kuns-ah   x-Maria*
      Pedro-TOP PFV-SBJ.3 afraid-FACT-CMPL F-Maria
      yéetel hun-p'éel   sùum
      with   one-CL.INAN   rope
      'Pedro frightened Maria with a rope' (NMP_0432)

   b. *Pedro-e'   t-u   hets'-kuns-ah-en*
      Pedro-TOP PFV-SBJ.3 quiet-FACT-CMPL-ABS.1.SG
      yèetel le   ba'x t-u   y-a'l-ah-o'.
      with   DEF what PFV-SBJ.3 0-say-CMPL-D2
      'Pedro annoyed/provoked/appeased me with what he said.' (ACC)

These expressions integrate with a complex construction composed of the general transitive construction (Construction 36) together with a concomitant phrase in adjunct function: '<Concomitant>' [*yèetel* NP]ₚₚ.

Passive formation is regular with all causative experiential verbs and it occurs regularly with both AGENT as well as with STIMULUS Actors (287).

(287) a. *Le   máak-o' h   wi'h-kuns-a'b/*
      DEF   person-D2 PFV hungry-FACT-CMPL.PASS/
      táan   u   wi'h-kuns-a'l
      PROG   SBJ.3 hungry-FACT-INCMPL.PASS
      tumen   u   bòok le   hàanal-o'.
      by   POSS.3.SG smell DEF   food-D2
      'That person was made/is being made hungry by the smell of that food.' (ACC)

   b. *Pedro-e'   h   sahbes-a'b*
      Pedro-TOP PFV fear:CAUS-CMPL.PASS
      tumen   le   libro/ u   y-iits'in.
      by   DEF book/ POSS.3 0-younger.sibling
      'Pedro got/was frightened by the book/his younger sibling.' (ACC)

In this, YM differs from those languages that display restrictions on passive formation with a certain group of transitive experiential verbs, namely, those verbs that have been referred to as the *frighten/preoccupare*-class following Belletti and Rizzi (1988). In a number of SAE-languages, these verbs do not form a verbal passive in their non-agentive realization (cf. sect. 3.4.2.3). Passive formation in these languages seems to depend on the agentivity of the actor and/or the dynamicity of the active verb.

In YM however, the nature of the actor (e.g., his animacy etc.) does not seem to play a role in passive formation. Furthermore, the passive in YM has a dynamic reading. There is no stative passive as, e.g. in German (cf. (40c)). The distinction between a dynamic vs. stative undergoer-oriented form is coded in YM by the passive vs. resultative distinction. For instance, a dynamic reading is obvious in (288a), while the resultative form in (288b) has a stative reading.

(288) a. *X-ch'úuppal,   míin   táan   t'àan-a'l*
        F-woman:child about   PROG:SBJ.2 call-PASS.INCMPL
        tumen le   xibpal-o'?
        by   DEF   man:child-D2
        'Girl, are you being talked to by that boy/is that boy flirting with you?' (ACC_0328)

   b. *U   y-íits'in   Juan-e'   t'àan-a'n   tumen Carlos.*
        POSS.3 0-younger.sibling Juan-TOP call-RSLTV   by   Carlos
        'Juan's younger sister is engaged to Carlos.' (ACC_0330)

In light of these differences in passive and resultative formation between YM and some SAE languages it can be concluded that the semantics of the causative transitive experiential verbs in YM differs from that of their SAE counterparts. First, in YM the verbs do not show any difference in grammatical behavior with respect to agentivity. Passive and resultative formation is fully regular with animate as well as with non-animate (mostly propositional) causers. Furthermore, there are differences in dynamicity between the YM and the SAE-type of causative experiential verbs (of the *frighten*-type and the *please*-type). While members of the SAE-type are clearly stative (cf. sect. 3.3.3), the YM transitive verbs are by default dynamic due to their compatibility with the progressive. The overtly derived causative verbs represent caused state changes and, thus regularly form a passive.

There is a further difference between the SAE-type of causative experiential verbs and the YM type. While in the SAE-type, the causative transitive verbs are basic (cf., e.g., Germ. *entsetzen, (ver)ärgern, aufregen, nerven*, etc.) and the stative passive or adjectival form is morphologically derived (e.g., *entsetzt, verärgert, aufgeregt, genervt*, etc.), this is opposite in YM. As has been shown above, stative adjectives and intransitive verbs are the bases of most causative transitive experiential verbs. This type of causative experiencer-object verb is also present in a number of other languages. Languages such as Korean and Tamil display direct object experiencers exclusively or mainly with causative verbs that are overtly derived from basic experiencer-oriented adjectives or verbs (cf. sect. 3.4.3.3.2).

5.3.2.2.2 *Person part noun as object*

Transitive experiential verbs which take a person part noun in direct object function are parallel to the adjectival and intransitive verbs taking a person part of the experiencer in subject function (cf. sect. 5.2.1.3 and sect. 5.3.1.2), while the experiencer is coded as its possessive attribute. The transitive verbs form collocations that are of the same types as those collocations based on adjectives and intransitive verbs, i.e., there are idiomaticized collocations (cf. sect. 5.3.2.2.2.1) and non-idiomaticized collocations (cf. sect. 5.3.2.2.2.2).

5.3.2.2.2.1 *Idiomaticized collocations*
In Table 44, idiomaticized collocations which take a person part noun in direct object function are listed. These are formed with semantically causative verbs, too, taking an agent or a stimulus participant in subject function. There are a small number of basic transitive verbs which are used in collocation with *óol* 'mind', namely, *hets' POSS óol* 'quiet, calm, ease, appease', *nay POSS óol* 'entertain', and *bèet POSS óol* 'provoke, spoof, hoax' (289).

(289) a. *He'l   hun-p'éel   lìibro*
      PRSV   one-CL.INAN book
      utia'l   a   nay-ik   u   y-óol.
      for   SBJ.2   divert-INCMPL SBJ.3   0-mind
      'Here is a book for you to divert him with.' (after HNAZ_0008)

    b. *k-u   bèet-ik   in   w-óol*
      IMPF-SBJ.3   do-INCMPL   POSS.1.SG   0-mind
      '(s)he does my "óol" (kids me)' (Hanks 1990:87)

Similar to Table 43, most items in Table 44 are causative or factitive derivations of intransitive verbs (cf. Table 31) or adjectives (cf. Table 18, Table 19). Like their base forms *háak's/ha's* 'scare, frighten; cause admiration/ impression', *ki'makkun* 'delight', *nay/náays* 'console; entertain, distract' are exclusively constructed with *óol*. These form non-compositional collocations as illustrated in (290) and represented in Construction 37.

(290) a. *Le   máak k-u   hòoch-a'*
      DEF   person IMPF-SBJ.3   harvest\INTRV-D1
      yàan in   háak's-ik   y- óol.
      DEB   SBJ.1.SG become.scared:CAUS-INCMPL POSS.3- mind
      'I will scare the man who is harvesting.' (HLU'M_KÀAB_016.1)

    b. *Le   chàan x-ch'úuppal-o'*
      DEF   little   F-woman:child-D2
      hach k-u   ki'mak-kunt-ik   in   w-óol,
      really IMPF-SBJ.3 happy-FACT-INCMPL POSS.1.SG 0-mind
      chéen ho'p' u   y-óok'ot.
      just   begin   SBJ.3   0-dance(INCMPL)   (NMP_0159)
      'That little girl really makes me happy when she starts to dance.'

subdomain	instance (gloss) 'meaning'	prop.	
emotion	*hets' POSS óol* (quiet POSS mind) 'quiet, calm, ease, appease'	○	
	bèet/mèet POSS óol (do POSS mind) 'provoke, spoof, hoax'	○	
	ha's/háak's POSS óol (become.scared:CAUS) 'scare, frighten; cause admiration/impression'	●	□
	náaks POSS óol (reach:CAUS POSS mind) 'bore, annoy, bother'	○	
	péeks POSS óol (move:CAUS POSS mind) 'disturb, trouble, worry, frighten, scare'	○	□
	lúubs POSS óol (fall:CAUS POSS mind) 'disappoint, make feel sad, depressed'	○	
	ki'(mak)-kun POSS óol (happy-FACT) 'delight	●	□
	lúub-a'n-kun POSS óol (fall-RSLTV-FACT POSS mind) 'make sad, depressed'	○	
	tòoh-kin POSS óol (straight-FACT POSS mind) 'calm down'	○	
	nich'ban-kun POSS óol (bite:INTRV-FACT POSS mind) 'make angry, bother'	○	
cognition	*k'a'hs POSS iik'* (remember:CAUS POSS air) 'remind, remember (sth. promised/a moral duty))'	●	□
	líik's POSS óol (get.up:CAUS POSS mind) 'encourage'	○	□
	nay[33] POSS óol (divert POSS mind) 'entertain'	●	□
	náays POSS óol (calm.down:CAUS) 'console; entertain, neglect'	●	□
	uts-kin POSS óol (good-FACT POSS mind/thought) 'calm down'	○	
	chokoh-kin POSS pòol (hot-FACT POSS head) 'drive mad, make furious'	○	
bodily sensation	*k'àas-kun POSS óol* (bad-FACT POSS mind) 'make feel bad'	○	
	chokoh-kin POSS óol (hot-FACT POSS mind) 'make feel hot'	○	
	síis-kun POSS óol (icy-FACT POSS mind) 'make feel cool'	○	
	k'oha'n-kun POSS óol (sick-FACT POSS mind) 'make feel sickly, weak'	○	

properties:

- ● integrates with Construction 37;
- ○ integrates with Construction 38;
- □ plus SRef

Table 44. Person part collocations with transitive 'causative' verbs

---

[33] This form is documented in Andrade and Máas Collí (1991) but seems to have been mainly replaced by *náays Poss óol* in the dialect investigated here.

Construction 37 is the causative version of the adjectival and intransitive constructions in Construction 8 and Construction 23, respectively. What has been said concerning the lack of referentiality of *óol* with respect to these constructions, is also true for Construction 37. The direct object NP with *óol* as its head cannot be topicalized. Therefore it is a part of the larger predicate.

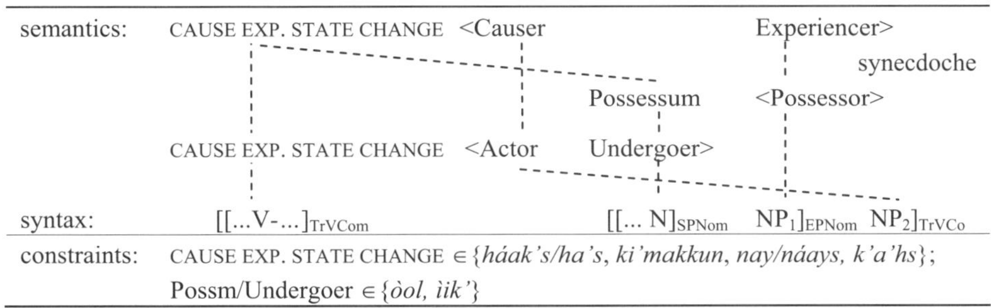

Construction 37. Causative C. with possessor-experiencer, based on metonymy

Construction 37 is a complex construction consisting of two subconstructions, namely, the general transitive construction as depicted in Construction 36, and the expanded possessed nominal construction '$^{(1)}$Possessum $^{(2)}$<Possessor>' [[$^{(2)}$PossClit $^{(1)}$N]$_{SPNom}$ $^{(2)}$NP]$_{EPNom}$.

K'a'hs optionally occurs in collocation with *ìik'* (291a). This collocation is the causative derivation of the collocation *k'a'h POSS ìik'* (cf. Table 31). Both the verb form alone (cf. Table 36) and the collocation convey the meaning 'remember, remind'. Note that within the collocation, the stimulus, i.e., the 'thing remembered' may be optionally coded as an adjunct (291b), while if the transitive verb is alone the stimulus is in direct object function and the experiencer can take either subject function (248b) or indirect object function.

(291) a. *In   na'-e'*
         POSS.1.SG mother-TOP
         k-u   k'a'hs-ik   in   w-ìik'.
         IMPF-SBJ.3 remember:CAUS-INCMPL POSS.1.SG 0-air
         'My mother makes me think.' (ACC_0301)

      b. *Maria, k'a'hs   a   w-ìik'-e'*
         Maria, remember:CAUS(IMP) POSS.2 0-air-CNTR
         tu'x   t-in   lìik's-ah   le   wàah-o'.
         where PFV-SBJ.3 guard-CMPL   DEF   tortilla-D2
         'Maria, try to remember where I put the tortillas.' (NMP_0169)

In the above examples, only human participants occur as causers. However non-human participants may also be causers or stimuli in Construction 37, such as *sìirkoh* 'circus' in (292a) and *ch'a'n* 'spectacle' in (292b).

(292) a. *Káa yáax máan sìirkoh úuchil-e', t-u*
CNJ first pass circus formerly-CNTR PFV-SBJ.3
háak's-ah y-óol le hèente-o'.
become.scared:CAUS-CMPL POSS.3-mind DEF people-D2
'When/and the circus passed by the first time, it surprised/astonished the people.' (EMB_0069)

b. *le cha'n-o' t-u náays-ah a w-óol*
DEF spectacle-D2 PFV-SBJ.3 calm.down:CAUS-CMPL POSS.2 0-mind
'the spectacle/dance distracted you' (NMP)

Furthermore, abstract entities (293) and propositions (374) occur naturally as causing stimuli with causative verbs of emotion and cognition.

(293) *Le pàax-o' k-u ki'makkuns-ik in w-óol.*
DEF music-D2 IMPF-SBJ.3 delight-INCMPL POSS.1.SG 0-mind
'That music delights me.' (EMB_0803)

Other verbs mentioned in Table 44 form compositional collocations with *óol* 'mind' (294) or *pòol* 'head' and can be analyzed as being based on metaphor, since these verbs also occur outside of collocations and with a concrete meaning (cf., e.g., *bèet* 'do', *náaks* 'take to its destination', *péeks* 'move', *líik's* 'lift, raise', *utskin* 'repair', *tòohkin* 'straighten', *k'àaskun* 'make bad', etc.). These collocations are represented in Construction 38.

(294) a. *U mehen kisin,*
POSS.3 small devil
ts'o'k a náaks-ik in w-óol.
TERM SBJ.2 reach:CAUS-INCMPL POSS.1 0-mind
'The hell with it, you have bothered me.' (HOSEH_42.01)

b. *Juan-e' k-u péeks-ik u y-óol Maria*
Juan-TOP IMPF-SBJ.3 move:CAUS-INCMPL POSS.3 0-mind Maria
chen tàak wáah káal-a'n.
just come:SUBJ if drunk-RSLTV
'Juan frightens Maria if he comes drunk.' (RMC_2183)

Construction 38 represents the causative version of the adjectival and intransitive constructions in Construction 9 and Construction 24. The structural layer is identical to that of Construction 37. Like causative verbs which take the experiencer in direct object function, the verbs discussed here (295) have a regular passive formation. The *tumen*-phrase adjoins the Causer, which may be a STIMULUS or an AGENT.

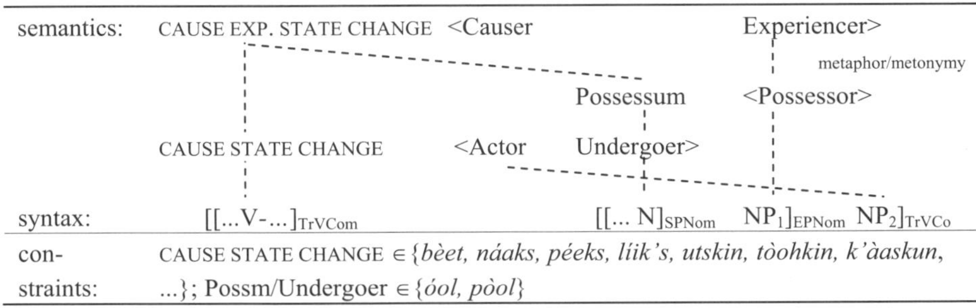

Construction 38. Causative C. with possr-expr, based on metaphor + metonymy

(295) a. *tuméen   leti'-o'b*
          because   that.one-PL
          h   háak's-a'b   y-óol-o'b
          PFV   become.scared:CAUS-CMPL.PASS   0- mind-PL
          'because they became scared' (UTSTS'_031.2)

      b. *Juana-e'   h   péeks-a'b   y-óol*
          Juana-TOP   PFV   move:CAUS-CMPL.PASS   POSS.3-mind
          tumen le   ba'te'l   h   úuch-o'.
          by   DEF   fight   PFV   happen-D2
          'Juana got scared by the fight that happened.' (ACC_0421)

If the subject participant is human or animate, it can be interpreted as the causer and a stimulus may be adjoined to it in a *yéetel*-phrase (296). Thus, Construction 37 and Construction 38 may both be combined with the comitative construction '<Concomitant>' [*yèetel* NP]PP.

(296)   *t-in   náay-s-ah   u   y-óol in   iiho*
          PFV-SBJ.1.SG calm.down:CAUS-CMPL POSS.3 0-mind POSS.3 son
          yéetel hun-p'éel   báaxal
          with   one-CL.INAN   toy
          'I calmed my son down with a toy' (RMC_1864)

In (297a) the experiencer is coded twice (i.e., as subject and as possessive attribute of *óol*) resulting in a reflexive meaning. Such a construction is possible with those items in Table 44 that are listed with 'plus SRef' (same reference).

(297) a. *yan   in   bin   in   náays   in   w-óol*
DEB SBJ.1.SG go   SBJ.1.SG good.mood:CAUS POSS.1.SG 0-mind
'I have to go and comfort my soul' (HIJO_056/ACC)

b. *Te'x-e'   lòoko-tak-e'x,   tèen-e'*
you.all-TOP mad-SBSTR.PL-ABS.2.PL   me-TOP
chéen táan   in   ki'mak-kuns-ik   in   w-óol.
just   PROG SBJ.1.SG happy-FACT-INCMPL POSS.1.SG 0-mind
'You are mad, I am just diverting/entertaining myself.'
(HA'N_0027.01)

Similarly, some items in Table 43 may take the possessed NP *POSS báah*
'POSS self' in direct object function resulting in an (explicitly) reflexive or reciprocal construction (298). This is true for *su'lakkun* 'shame, embarrass',
chi'chnakkun 'disturb, bother', and *ts'íikkun* 'bother', *hets'kun* 'appease,
calm'. Reflexivity requires referential identity between the subject and the possessive pronoun (298a/b), while reciprocity requires a plural subject, in addition (298c).

(298) a. *Juan-e'   k-u   p'u'hs-ik   u   báah.*
Juan-TOP IMPF-SBJ.3ᵢ get.mad:CAUS-INCMPL POSS.3ᵢ   self
'Juan gets excited.' (RMC)

b. *Su'lak-kuns   a   báah!*
ashamed-FACT(IMP)   POSS.2   self
'Be ashamed! (EMB_0582/ACC)

c. *Juan   yéetel   Pedro*
Juan   and   Pedro
k-u   p'u'hs-ik   u   báah-o'b.
IMPF-SBJ.3ᵢ get.mad:CAUS-INCMPL POSS.3ᵢ   self-PL
'Juan and Pedro annoy each other.' (RMC)

These items resemble those listed in Table 39, but differ from the latter in
that the reflexive construction is just a more specific construction option. The
same holds true for the reciprocal construction, which is not possible for those
items listed in Table 39.

5.3.2.2.2.2 *Non-idiomaticized collocations*

Finally, those verbs listed in Table 45 combine with an appropriate body part
noun in direct object function to convey the causation of bodily sensation.
Apart from *k'il* all of these verbs are factitive derivations from basic adjectives
(cf. Table 19). Compare (299) for some illustrative examples.

(299) a. *t-u   yah-kunt-ah   in   k'ab*
       PFV-SBJ.3 ache-FACT-CMPL POSS.1.SG hand
       'he hurt my hand' (Bricker et. al. 1998, s.v. *yah*)

   b. *Le   chàan   pàal-o'*
      DEF   little   child-D2
      t-u   k'il-ah   in   w-òok   yah-a'.
      PFV-SBJ.3 hurt-CMPL POSS.1.SG 0-foot   ache-D1
      'That little child hurt my aching foot.' (FEE_0258)

instance	(gloss) 'meaning'
k'il	'hurt, reopen /wound'
cha'yah-kun	(let:ache-FACT) 'cause, ache'
yah-kun	(ache-FACT) 'hurt'
sáak'-kun	(itchy-FACT) 'make feel itchy'
si's-kun	(numb-FACT) 'make numb'
ke'l-kun	(cold-FACT) 'make feel cold'

Table 45. Transitive 'causative' verbs of bodily sensation

The verbs in Table 45 integrate with Construction 39, which is the causative version of the adjectival construction in Construction 10. The properties of the causative construction are analogous to those mentioned for this construction, i.e., the body part nouns in these collocations are fully referential and can, for instance, be topicalized. The specific sensation only affects the body part while a general bodily affectedness of the experiencer is necessarily inferred due to the inherent relation between body part and possessor-experiencer.

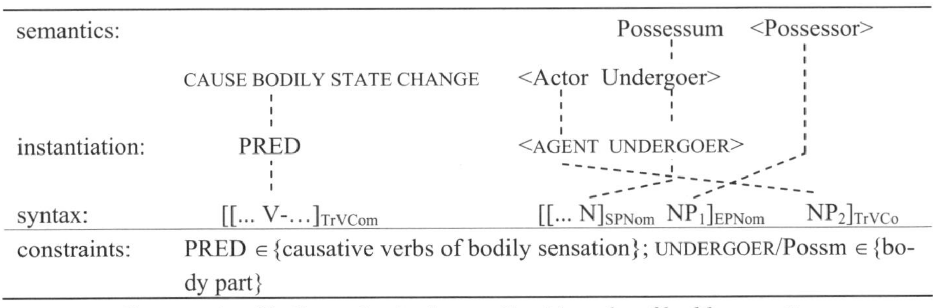

semantics:		Possessum	<Possessor>
	CAUSE BODILY STATE CHANGE	<Actor Undergoer>	
instantiation:	PRED	<AGENT UNDERGOER>	
syntax:	[[... V-...]TrVCom	[[... N]SPNom NP₁]EPNom	NP₂]TrVCo
constraints:	PRED ∈ {causative verbs of bodily sensation}; UNDERGOER/Possm ∈ {body part}		

Construction 39. Causative body part C. with verbs of bodily sensation

5.3.3 *Ditransitive constructions*

Ditransitive constructions are not used very frequently in the domain of experience in YM. In the following discussion a distinction is made between constructions with a ditransitive experiential verb (sect. 5.3.3.1) and constructions with a ditransitive metaphorical predicate (sect. 5.3.3.2). In the latter construction one argument slot is taken by an expertum nominal.

5.3.3.1 *Experiential verbs proper*

YM has a few ditransitive verbs which take an experiencer as indirect object. These are listed in Table 46 and exemplified in (300). *Ka'ns* 'teach' is used in two different valency frames, either with the experiencer in direct object function (cf. Table 43) or with the experiencer in indirect object function (190a). Other 'candidates' such as *chíikbes* '(open up and) show, point out' do not take the experiencer 'naturally'.

subdomain	instance (gloss) 'meaning'
perception	*e's ti'* (show LOC) 'show'
cognition	*k'a'hs ti'* (remember:CAUS LOC) 'remind'
	ka'ns ti' (learn\PASS:CAUS LOC) 'teach'

Table 46. Ditransitive verbs of experience

(300) a. *E's   ti'   to'n bix a   ts'íib-t-ik   x-ch'úuppal!*
       show LOC us   how SBJ.2 write-TRR-INCMPL F-woman:child
       'Show us how you write "x-ch'úupal"!' (BVS_05.01.10)

    b. *Lel-o' k-u   k'a'h-s-ik   tèen*
       it-D2   IMPF-SBJ.3 remember-CAUS-INCMPL me
       k'abéet   in   túuxt-ik   hun-p'éel   kàartah.
       necessary SBJ.1.SG send-INCMPL one-CL.INAN letter
       'That reminds me, I need to send a letter.' (BVS_10.01.18)

Construction 40 represents the ditransitive construction with experiential verbs. The lexical EXPERIENCER is matched with the constructional Indirectus argument. The Actor may be either an animate AGENT (300a) or a STIMULUS (300b). The latter is not restricted as to its participant properties. The constructional Undergoer argument is filled by a lexical STIMULUS/THEME role. The latter may be called either THEME or STIMULUS since the situation designated has agentive as well as experiential aspects. If the Actor argument is a lexical STIMULUS, a distinction between source stimulus and goal stimulus, as introduced in sect. 3.3.2.2 can be applied. Thus in (300b), the subject can be identified as a source stimulus and the direct object argument, represented by a semantically subordinate clause, as a goal stimulus.

semantics:	CAUSE CHANGE STATE	<Actor	Undergoer	Indirectus>
instantiation:	PRED	<AGENT /STIMULUS	STIMULUS /THEME	EXPERIENCER>
syntax:	[[...V-...]ₜᵣVCom	NP₁	NP₂	[*ti'* NP₂]ₚₚ]ₜᵣVCo
constraints:	PRED ∈ {*e's, k'a'hs, ka'ns*}			

Construction 40. Ditransitive C. with experiential verbs

5.3.3.2 *Ditransitive verbs as metaphorical predicators*

YM uses a number of verbs denoting a general causative change-of-location within metaphorical collocations in the domain of experience. These collocations take the experiencer in subject function and either the expertum/person part noun or the stimulus in direct object function.

Stimulus as prepositional object

The collocations *ts'a POSS óol ti'* 'concentrate on' and *òoks POSS óol ti'* 'believe in' (Table 47) from the subdomain of cognition preserve the trivalent structure of their verbs *ts'a* 'put' and *òok's* 'enter', by adjoining the stimulus as a prepositional phrase introduced by *ti'*. The latter is preferably an abstract noun or a proposition. The experiencer takes subject function and at the same time is coded as the possessor of the person part noun *óol*, which takes direct object function. Both collocations are controlled according to Test 5.

subdomain	instance (gloss) 'meaning'
	òoks POSS óol ti' (enter:CAUS POSS óol LOC) 'believe in'
	ts'a POSS óol ti' (put POSS mind LOC) 'concentrate on, pay attention to, do with enthusiasm'
cognition	*ts'a ti' POSS tùukul* (put LOC POSS thought) 'think about'
	ch'a' ti' POSS tùukul (take LOC POSS thought) 'take into account'
	òoks ti' POSS tùukul (enter:CAUS LOC POSS óol) 'plan, think of'

Table 47. Transitive local collocations

(301) illustrates the use of these collocations. They fit into a construction composed of Construction 33 and the prepositional phrase construction '<Arg. role>' [*ti'* NP]ₚₚ.

(301) a. *K-u   y-òoks-ik   u   y-óol*
　　　　　IMPF-SBJ.3 0-enter:CAUS-INCMPL POSS.3 0-mind
　　　　　ti'   ba'x k-u   y-u'b-ik   y-a'l-a'l.
　　　　　LOC   what IMPF-SBJ.3 0-feel-INCMPL SBJ.3-say-PASS.INCMPL
　　　　　'He believes in what he hears being said.' (NMP_0023)

b. *K-u   hach   ts'a-ik   y-óol   ti'   meyah.*
IMPF-SBJ.3   really   put-INCMPL POSS.3-mind LOC   work
'He really concentrates on working.' (MPK_002)

Expertum noun as prepositional object
Finally, there are some collocations that show a reverse alignment of stimulus
and expertum/person part noun, i.e., they take the stimulus as a direct object
and the possessed expertum noun *tùukul* 'thought', occurring in a prepositional
phrase, as an oblique argument of a ditransitive verb (Table 47, (302)). These
collocations are also characterized by a general causative change-of-location
verb (*ts'a* 'put', *ch'a'* 'take' and *òok's* 'enter'). They manifest a causative version of Construction 29. While in Construction 29 the stimulus is the subject,
here the experiencer is the subject. At the same time, it is coded as the possessor of the expertum noun, thus forming another kind of reflexive construction.
The expertum noun *tùukul* is conceptualized as goal in these collocations.
Again, all three collocations are from the subdomain of cognition due to the
presence of the expertum noun *tùukul*. The stimulus is preferably an abstract
noun or a proposition. All three items are controlled according to Test 5.

(302) a. *ma'   a   sen   ts'a-ik   ti'   a   tùukul*
NEG SBJ.2 very put-INCMPL   LOC POSS.2   thought
'don't think so much about it' (EMB_0707)

b. *káa   t-in   ch'a'-ah   tuláakal t-in   tùukul*
CNJ PFV-SBJ.1.SG fetch-CMPL all   LOC-POSS.1.SG thought
'then I took everything into consideration' (CHAN_090)

c. *Ts'o'k in   w-óoks-ik   t-in   tùukul*
TERM SBJ.1.SG 0-enter:CAUS-INCMPL LOC-POSS.1.SG thought
ba'x ken   in   mèet-eh
what SR.FUT SBJ.1.SG do-SUBJ
ti'   le   ha'b k-u   tàal-o'.
LOC DEF year IMPF-SBJ.3   come-D2
'I have already planned/thought of what I am going to do next
year.' (RMC_2218)

5.4 *Summary: Evaluation of coding strategies*
5.4.1 *Word classes in experience*
The YM data presented in this chapter shows that there are several correlations
between the experiential subdomains (cf. sect. 3.2.2) and the formal predicate
types (i.e., word classes). In fact, there is a rather striking iconicity in the lexicalization of the experiential subdomains in formal predicate classes. Meanings
of bodily sensation and emotion are mainly lexicalized as predicative adjec-

tives (e.g. *wi'h* 'hungry', *ke'l* 'cold', *su'lak* 'ashamed', *sahak* 'afraid', etc.) and intransitive verbs (e.g., *ka'n* 'get tired', *k'i'nam* 'hurt', *p'u'h* 'get annoyed, angry', *háak'* POSS *óol* 'become/get scared/impressed', etc.). Furthermore, the subdomain of cognition has some basic intransitive verbs such as *tu'b* 'forget', *náay* 'dream', etc. Only for the expression of cognition and perception can basic transitive verbs such as *na't* 'understand', *kan* 'learn', *il* 'see', *u'y* 'feel, hear', etc. be found. The subdomain of volition can be seen as being located between these two groups, as regards the word classes representing this subdomain. There might be a tendency towards stativity in volition, since YM has two basic items among the stative predicates (*tàak* 'be anxious, want', *k'àat* 'wish') as opposed to the transitive verb *ts'íibóolt* 'wish'.

A fine-grained analysis of these correlations results in the pattern shown in Table 48, which is based on recognizing the basic lexicalization of the main concepts of the subdomains. Predicate-types of all orientations, i.e., experiencer-oriented, person part oriented and stimulus-oriented predicates are equally considered. The distribution of the word classes in the experiential subdomains mirrors a rather iconic lexicalization of the semantic properties relationality and dynamicity, which identifies the subdomains bodily sensation, emotion, volition, cognition and perception in that order as increasingly relational and increasingly dynamic.

word class	bod. sensation	emotion	volition	cognition	perception
pred. adj./modal	✓	✓	✓		
intr. verbs	✓	✓	(✓)	✓	
tr. verboids		✓	✓	✓	
tr. verbs			(✓)	✓	✓

Table 48. Basic lexicalization of experiential concepts in YM

Note that the subdomain of volition conforms only to some extent to the pattern of basic lexicalization in word classes. This may be due to the fact that its members are fewer and more strongly grammaticalized compared to the other subdomains. Basic lexemes of volition are the modal *tàak* 'be anxious, want' and the transitive verboid *k'àat* 'wish'. The brackets for intransitive and transitive verbs in the second and last line of Table 48 are due to the (etymologically) complex but very frequently occurring volitive verb *ts'íibóol(t)* 'wish', which is morphologically adjective/intransitive-based but generally used in its transitive form.

Table 48 represents lexicalization in basic lexical items. The above treatment of experiential constructions has shown that the language makes full use of its derivational apparatus to change dynamicity as well as relationality of basic and derived lexemes. Additionally, a given lexeme may be integrated into a certain collocation or construction type with a similar effect. This holds true, e.g., for the integration of experiential lexemes in the reflexive construction, the existential constructions (Construction 16, Construction 18) or the *ch'a'*-collocation (Construction 32). Ch. 6 will discuss the function of the highly regular derivational system against the background of the syntactic prominence of the experiencer.

Transitive verboids as a genuinely experiential class cover the middle part of Table 48. These subdomains can be identified as covering the core or prototypical subdomains of experience in that they are both stative and relational (i.e., involving an experiencer and a stimulus). This is different than what is found in SAE. German and related languages generally code relational experiential concepts as transitive verbs, i.e., they express them as prototypical dynamic actions that are related to an undergoer. YM, in contrast, needs the overt formation of a transitive verb to allow a transitive verboid to be integrated into the general transitive construction (cf. Construction 30).

Other languages such as, e.g., Korean and Japanese, are more comparable to YM in that they differentiate systematically between basic stative and derived dynamic experiential concepts. (303a) (repeated from (73b)) in comparison to (303b) from Korean shows this derivational relationship between the basic stative experiential verbs and the derived dynamic verbs. The latter method of construction implies an emotional behavior, that makes the emotion accessible for non-first persons (cf. sect. 3.3.2.1).

(303) a. *Na-nɨn   paem-i   musəp/coh-ta.*
     1.SG-TOP snake-NOM   terrible/good-DECL
     'I am afraid of snakes/I like snakes.' (Jo 1988:13)

  b. *Uli   ai-nɨn   paem-ɨl   musə-wə-ha-n-ta/*
     1.PL child-TOP snake-ACC terrible-GER-do-PRS-DECL/
     coh-a-ha-n-ta.
     good-GER-do-PRS-DECL
     'Our child is afraid of snakes/our child likes snakes.' (MCK)

5.4.2 *Subdomain-specific assessment*

The YM linguistic means for expressing bodily sensation are to a large extent cross-linguistically unremarkable; determined by the semantic structure of the subdomain which has been characterized as prototypically stative and monovalent in sect. 3.2.2.2. YM most frequently uses predicative adjectives (cf. sect. 5.2.1.2, 5.2.1.3) and to a lesser degree intransitive verbs (cf. sect. 5.3.1.1, 5.3.1.2) to convey experiencer-oriented or body part-oriented bodily sensation. Regularly derived transitive verbs code the causation of the respective bodily sensation states (cf. sect. 5.3.2.2.1, sect. 5.3.2.2.2).

The most conspicuous YM trait in the subdomain of bodily sensation seems to be the recurrent use of body and person part constructions. Thus, not only body part constructions involving physical body parts are frequently used (e.g., Construction 10, Construction 25), but *óol*-constructions may express bodily sensations of the person as a whole (e.g., Construction 9, Construction 24). Contrary to person prominent languages, the experiencer of bodily sensation is obligatorily coded as possessive attribute of the body/person part in person part constructions. The language does not provide for the option of 'raising' a possessor-experiencer to indirect or oblique object function, i.e., to have an external possessor.

As has already been mentioned in sect. 3.2.2.2, YM uses *óol*-collocations not only to render bodily sensation but also to express some bodily conditions. Thus, 'pregnant' is expressed as *ma' tòoh POSS óol (ti' chàampal)-i'*, 'give birth (to a baby)' as *tòohtal POSS óol ti' chàampal*. Given that the lexeme *óol* signals an experiential state, the notions of pregnancy and birth are categorized as experiential in YM.

The subdomain of emotion, like the subdomain of bodily sensation, is characterized by basic adjectival predicates and basic intransitive verbs. Additionally, the emotional concepts 'love' and 'hate' are expressed by transitive verboids. Transitive experiencer-oriented verbs are all overtly derived from the mentioned adjectives, intransitive verbs and transitive verboids. The same is true for most causative (stimulus- or agent-oriented) experiential verbs.

The subdomain of emotion is also characterized by person part collocations in YM. The predominant person part noun occurring as psycho-noun in the sense of Matisoff (1986, sect. 3.5.4) in emotional collocations is *óol* 'mind'. It forms non-compositional, semantically experiential (cf. Construction 8, Construction 23) as well as compositional collocations when combined with a metaphorical predicate (cf. Construction 9, Construction 24). Furthermore *puksi'k'* 'heart' occurs marginally in emotional collocations, and is possibly calqued from Spanish in this function.

As regards emotional concepts lexicalized in YM, there are a great many basic concepts corresponding to those familiar to European languages. All 'basic' emotion terms that have been identified in the literature (cf. sect. 3.2.2.3) have a correlation in YM emotional terms, among them 'happy', 'sad', 'afraid', 'angry', 'ashamed', 'love', 'hate'. Some more specific emotions present in European languages are subsumed under more general ones in YM. Thus, 'envy' is conveyed by *p'èek* 'dislike, hate' or *yah-óolal* 'pain of sentiments', 'worry', 'miss' are conveyed by *tùukul*, the main meaning of which is 'think'. The concept of 'jealous' seems not to be lexicalized in Modern YM. It is not listed in the current dictionaries (e.g., Bricker et al. 1998, Academia de la lengua maya de Yucatán s.d.) and most of my consultants did not understand the concept connected to the Spanish word *celos*.

As has been addressed at several points before, the subdomain of volition is more 'grammatical' than the other subdomains, exhibiting, not only in YM but also in many other languages, grammaticalized modal verbs or auxiliaries or even affixes. YM has the modal auxiliary *tàak* 'be anxious, want' which is cross-linguistically conspicuous in that it is impersonal and takes a subordinate clause as its only participant.[34] Semantically, however, it controls the subject of the subordinate clause as a volitive experiencer, a point that will be discussed in comparison to the behavior of some stimulus-oriented intransitive verbs in matrix contructions in sect. 6.4.

Along with the modal *tàak*, the transitive verboid *k'áat* 'wish' and two compound/derived lexemes *ts'íibóol(t)* 'wish, desire' and *óot* 'agree' are the most frequent representatives of the volitive subdomain. Other volitive lexemes have more specific meanings such as *pòoch* 'desirous, greedy' etc. Experiential collocations are nearly absent from the subdomain of volition. Rather, *óol* is conserved in the morphological structure of two of the mentioned volitive items, namely, in *ts'íibóol(t)* 'wish, desire' and *óot* 'agree'.

In contrast to the aforementioned subdomains of emotion, volition and bodily sensation, the subdomain of cognition does not have basic adjectival lexemes. There are only some metaphorical collocations with adjectival predicates, conveying either a cognitive property or a cognitive state (cf. Table 18). Rather, the locus of cognitive experience seems to be in the verbal sphere. Thus, there are intransitive and transitive basic cognition verbs as well as transitive verboids. Furthermore, the few ditransitive verbs which take an indirect object experiencer are mostly of a cognitive nature (cf. Table 46). This conforms to the cross-linguistic tendencies in the subdomain of cognition that have been outlined in sect. 3.2.2.4 and 3.3.2.1.

The cognitive subdomain is also characterized by person part collocations that can be distinguished from the emotional ones by being less related to *óol* (though there are some cognitive *óol*-collocations), and also by being related to *pòol* 'head', *iik'* 'air; life, breath', *tùukul* 'thought', and marginally, *ho'l* 'head' (cf. Table 18, Table 25, Table 31, Table 35). The cognitive person part collocations are all compositional and based on metaphor, in contrast to some of the emotional ones. Furthermore, it can be noted that most local person part collocations are of a cognitive nature, which seems to be due to the conceptualization of cognitive states and activities that take the respective person part as location or goal with respect to which the state (cf. Table 25) or activity (cf. Table 35, Table 47) is predicated.

Finally, the subdomain of perception has basic transitive verbs. For inactive perception YM does not distinguish between the perception of auditory, olfactory and gustatory modes. On the contrary, for active perception in all of these

---

[34] In a cross-linguistic study involving 9 languages (cf. Lehmann et al 2000[P]), YM could be identified (along with Tamil) as one of two languages that have impersonal volitive/desiderative predicates as opposed to the other languages that all feature personal operators in the domain.

modes there are multiple expressions or verbs denoting different kinds of active controlled perception.

Contrary to many SAE languages YM uses its perception verbs to express evaluation in an experiencer-oriented construction (cf. Construction 34) where the former languages often use stimulus-oriented verbs like *look, please, etc.* This strategy of expressing evaluation may be a common Mayan trait since, e.g., Colonial Tzotzil (304a) and Modern Tzotzil (304b) display the same construction type.

(304) a. *Mu   x-k-a'i.*
        tasty NEUT-ERG.1.SG-feel
        'It tastes good.'   (Haviland 1988:117)

     b. *Toj   lek   x-k-a'i*   *li   manko-e.*
        very good NEUT-ERG.1.SG-feel DET mango-DETF
        'I like mangos.' (Lehmann et al. 2000[P]:123)

Alternatively YM uses a stimulus-oriented strategy with a local person part construction (cf. Construction 14). This construction type may be functionally equivalent to the stimulus-oriented perception verbs mentioned before.

Finally, some words should be said about the control behavior of experiential lexemes and expressions and a possible correlation with the experiential subdomains. The systematic investigation of control shows a rough correlation with the distribution of the subdomains given in Table 48. Thus, most items from the subdomain of bodily sensation are non-controlled. They mostly belong to the word classes that are always non-controlled, i.e. adjectives and inchoative verbs. Most of the items coding bodily sensation are also non-controlled. The subdomain of emotion also has many non-controlled items. It was shown above that a large percentage of emotional concepts are lexicalized in the stative classes. Furthermore the subdomain of emotion also possesses a great many person part-oriented items that are non-controlled, too. Among the intransitive and transitive emotion verbs however, there are a number of controlled items. The subdomain of volition displays an equal number of non-controlled and controlled members. Finally, in the subdomains of cognition and perception the number of controllable items is greater than that of the non-controllable ones. This holds true for the active perception verbs and for cognition verbs from different classes, i.e. there are larger percentages of controlled cognition verbs among the active intransitive and the transitive experiencer-oriented verbs. Furthermore, the frequent metaphorical collocations in the subdomain of cognition are also controlled.

5.4.3 *Congruent vs. non-congruent expressions*

The above description of experiential constructions has shown that YM uses non-congruent experiential expressions to roughly the same degree as congruent expressions (cf. sect. 3.5.1). Experiential adjectives, intransitive and transitive verbs are congruent expressions. In YM, most of them are directly related to the experiencer and some of these are related to the person part noun *óol* 'mind'. Non-congruent expressions are either those that use a non-experiential predicator and combine it with an experiential term (cf. sect. 5.2.2.1.2 and sect. 5.3.2.1.3) or those metaphor-based person part collocations, that combine a non-experiential predicate with a person part expression.

In this respect, it is important to note that non-congruent expressions are not just figurative expressions of what could otherwise be rendered by a congruent expression, but that they constitute a usual way of expressing experience in the language.

5.4.4 *Person part constructions*

In the preceding analysis of person part constructions, a distinction was made between idiomaticized and non-idiomaticized person part collocations. The former are predominantly constructed with the person part noun *óol* 'mind', while the latter occur with any person or body part noun. It has been shown that the *óol*-collocations differ in their constructional potential from the non-idomaticized person part collocations due to the fact that *óol* is semantically rather empty. These constructions can be identified as genuine experiential constructions with *óol* as experience marker (cf. sect. 5.2.1.3.1, sect. 5.3.1.2.1, and sect. 5.3.2.2.2.1). They have developed from non-idiomaticized person part collocations to express specifically experiential meanings from the subdomains of emotion, cognition, and bodily sensation.

At different points it has been shown that a person's physiological, physiognomical and behavioral characteristics involving a body part are also expressed in body part constructions that are otherwise exploited to express experience (cf., e.g., the non-idiomaticized collocations discussed in sect. 5.2.1.3.3, sect. 5.3.1.2.2, and sect. 5.3.2.2.2.2). Barrera Vásquez et al. (eds., 1980) lists a large number of such constructions with experiential as well as other meanings. This construction type is a reflection of a underlying principle, that the language follows in other subdomains as well. It has been introduced as relation-prominence in sect. 2.2.3, following Lehmann et al. (2000[P]). This principle materializes, e.g., in the preponderance of the coding of possessive relations which the language renders meticulously. For example, a property that would be ascribed to the person as a whole in other languages (cf., e.g., the Spanish translation of (305a), is generally ascribed to a person part in YM.

(305) a. *tich-a'n*   *u*   *nak' Juan*
       reach.up-RSLTV   POSS.3   belly   Juan
       'Juan is very fat' (Barrera Vásquez et al. eds. 1980, s.v. *ticha'n*)

      b. *benel u*   *ka'h y-ìik'*   *Pedro*
        go   SBJ.3   do   POSS.3-air   Pedro
        'Pedro is dying' (Barrera Vásquez et al. eds. 1980, s.v. *benel*)

      c. *ya'b yits'atil u*   *pòol Juan*
        many   wisdom   POSS.3   head   Juan
        'Juan is very wise'
        (Barrera Vásquez et al. eds. 1980, s.v. *its'atil pol*)

      d. *ak-a'n*   *u*   *t'àan*   *Pedro yéetel Juan*
        fix-RSLTV   POSS.3   speech   Pedro   with   Juan
        'Pedro agrees with Juan'
        (Barrera Vásquez et al. eds. 1980, s.v. *aka'n*)

Idiomaticized possessive person part collocations such as *ki'mak POSS óol* 'happy' etc. may themselves be attributed to a person part noun, as in examples such as (175), resulting in double possessive constructions.

While experiential person part constructions were supposedly the predominant coding strategy in stages prior to Contemporary YM, namely, Colonial YM (cf. Barrera Vásquez et al. eds. 1980), nowadays this construction type is simply one among many, as has been shown in detail in the empirical part of this investigation.

The existence of psycho-collocations and -compounds leads to a greater semantic transparency of the lexical inventory in the domain of experience. Thus, the presence of *óol* 'mind', which occurs in most of these collocations and compounds, classifies the expressions as experiential.[35] More specifically, *óol* signals bodily sensation, emotion or cognition.[36] This classifying function can be the reason why some adjectives that primarily select the experiencer in absolutive function may alternatively be ascribed to *óol* 'mind' (cf. Table 18) or form compounds with it (cf. Table 17).

---

[35] Cf. Matisoff (1986) for a similar view with respect to South-east Asian languages.

[36] Cf. sect. 8 for a detailed analysis of person parts in experiential collocations.

CHAPTER 6

Grammatical properties of experiencers

On the basis of the discussion of grammatical relations set out in sect. 4.3, this chapter addresses the issue of the grammatical properties of experiencers in YM. It has been mentioned at several points in sect. 3.4 that it is not rare in the world's languages for experiencers to attain higher syntactic (i.e., pivotal) functions than would be expected based on their morphological marking. This has been discussed as 'non-canonical marking' (cf. Aikhenvald et al. eds. 2001) or 'morphological downgrading' (Bickel 2004) for a number of languages. In light of this, the present chapter will focus on how YM organizes grammatical coding of experiencers by balancing the functional requirements of pragmatic prominence (in terms of topicality) and semantic affectedness.

6.1 *Coding properties*

As has been extensively demonstrated in the preceding chapter, the experiencer appears in all possible grammatical relations: as subject of a transitive verb or verboid, as direct object of a causative transitive verb, as subject of an intransitive or stative (adjectival) predicate, as indirect object of an adjectival, intransitive or transitive predicate, and as possessor of a person part or expertum noun. Morphological marking for all of these functions is regular. For convenience, examples are given in (306) and (307). (306a) and (306b) show subject marking with an intransitive and a transitive experiential verb, respectively. (306c) shows absolute marking for a direct object experiencer. (307a) shows an indirect object experiencer, (307b) absolutive marking of the experiencer of a stative predicate, (307c) possessor marking, and (307d) subject marking with a transitive verboid.

    (306) a. *Táan u   tùukul   don Vicente.*
            PROG SBJ.3 think(INCMPL) don Vicente
            'Don Vicente is worrying.' (NMP_0071)

         b. *Le bin   k-u   chéen tukul-ik   chàan xi'pàal-e'* ...
           that QUOT IMPF-SBJ.3 just   think-INCMPL little   man:child-D3
           'This is what the little boy was just thinking, (…)' (HK'AN_048.1)

    c. *Le   káan-o'*
       DEF   snake-D2
       hach k-u   sah-bes-ik-Ø   Pedro.
       really IMPF-SBJ.3   fear:CAUS-INCMPL-ABS.3.SG Pedro
       'The snake scares Pedro a lot.' (after PLC_006)

(307) a. *Hach ts'o'k u   náak'-al   tèen*
       really TERM SBJ.3   grieve-INCMPL me
       ba'x k-u   bèet-ik   to'n le   ko'lel-a' ...
       what IMPF-SBJ.3   do-INCMPL   us   DEF   lady-D1
       'What this woman is doing to us really hurts me, (...)'
       (HOSEH_20.1)

    b. *Su'lak-en.*
       ashamed-ABS.1.SG
       'I am ashamed.'

    c. *Ki'mak   in   w-óol.*
       happy(ABS.3) POSS.1.SG 0-mind
       'I am happy.'

    d. *In   p'èek-ech.*
       SBJ.3   hate-ABS.1.SG
       'I hate you.'

6.2   *Behavioral properties*

Similarly, the experiencer behaves canonically to a large extent with regard to
its syntactic behavior in the diverse functions it may take. Some minor exceptions are discussed below. The following subsections will briefly review the
experiencer in its diverse grammatical relations in a number of constructions
that have been discussed in sect. 4.3.3 as identifying subject or pivotal function
in YM.

6.2.1 *Cleft constructions*

A agent and A experiencer behave identically in focus constructions. This is illustrated in (308). It can be noted that the subject cross-reference marker (referring to the experiencer) is canonically deleted if it is the target of question-
formation (cf. sect. 4.3.3).

(308)   *Máax ts'íikil-t-ik   Pedro?*
      who   feel.angry-TRR-INCMPL Pedro
      'Who is angry with Pedro?' (EMB)

If however, the experiencer of a transitive verboid is the target of a content question, it cannot be deleted, as (309a) shows. A construction preserving the subject cross-reference marker generally implies U focus (309b/c).[1] Regarding this construction type, transitive verboids differ not only from transitive verbs, but also from relational nouns since the latter form a construction with an 'equi-deleted' possessor argument in a content question (cf. (148)).

(309) a.*_Máax k'ahòol(-ih)_?
     who   know(-ABS.3.SG)
     intended: 'Who knows him?' (ACC/NMP)

    b. _Máax u   k'ahóol_?
     who   SBJ.3 acquaint
     'whom does he know? (not for 'who knows him')
     (RMC, EMB, ACC, NMP)

    c.*_Leti' u   p'èek-en_.
     that.one POSS.3 hate-ABS.1.SG
     intended: 'It is he who hates me.' (RMC/NMP)

To form an A focus construction, a derived perfect participle form is used, as in (310). This is the result of a complex process which consists of verbalizing the transitive verboid and subsequently forming a perfect participle which (again) joins the class of stative predicates.

(310) a. _Máax k'ahóol(-t)-mah-il_?
     who   acquaint(-TRR)-PART.PF-REL
     'Who knows him?' (ACC/NMP)

---

[1] There seem to be some exceptions for at least some consultants. For instance, if there is a clear difference in animacy between the A and the U argument, the mentioned construction may also focus on the A argument. Thus, (i) is judged as impossible but (ii) not.

(i)   *_Leti' u   k'áat_.
     that.one SBJ.3 wish(ABS.3.SG)
     intended: 'It is he who wants it'

(ii) _Leti' u   k'áat   káa   xi'k-en_.
     that.one SBJ.3 wish(ABS.3.SG) that   go:SUBJ(ABS.1.SG)
     'It is he who wants me to go.' (RMC/ACC/NMP)

Similarly, contrast (309b) with the following example in (iii)

(iii) _Máax u   k'ahóol le   ba'x-a'_?
     who   SBJ.3 know   DEF   what-D1
     'Who knows this thing?' (NMP)

   b. *Leti'   p'èek(-t)-mah-il-en.*
     that.one hate(-TRR)-PART.PF-REL-ABS.1.SG
     'It is he who hates me.' (ACC/NMP)

Like transitive verboids and relational nouns, perfect participles are two-place and take subject and absolutive cross-reference marking (cf. sect. 4.1.6). In cleft sentences, they behave like transitive verbs (and relational nouns): If the question or argument focus is on the A experiencer, its cross-reference marker is 'equi-deleted', and the verb takes the relational suffix *-il*. This is shown in (310).

Furthermore, a manner focus construction (cf. sect. 5.3.2.1.4) is not possible with a transitive verboid in the extrafocal part. Again, verbalization is the operation to render the construction possible (311).

(311) a.**hach   ya'b   u   p'èek   u   báah-o'b*
       really   much SBJ.3 hate   POSS.3 self-PL
       intended: 'they hate each other a lot' (ACC)

     b. *hach   ya'b u   p'èek-t-ik   u   báah-o'b*
       really   much SBJ.3   hate-TRR-INCMPL POSS.3 self-PL
       'they hate each other/quarrel with each other a lot'
       (RMC_1868, ACC)

It can thus be concluded that the A experiencer of a transitive verboid does not have regular access to the pivot in cleft constructions. Instead, a complex derivation, i.e., verbalization with subsequent stativization, is carried out so that the A experiencer may be integrated into a focus construction.

6.2.2 *'Equi-deletion' in subordinate clause/core*
'Equi-deletion' occurs regularly with S experiencers in embedded verbal cores as is shown in (312a) with the matrix predicate *k'áat* 'wish'. Similarly, the A experiencers may be 'equi-deleted' under undergoer-control as is exemplified by (312b).

(312) a. *In   k'áat Ø   ts'íikil   ti'   in   w-iícham.*
       POSS.1 wish [SBJ.1 feel.angry LOC POSS.1.SG 0-spouse]SFVCo
       'I want to feel angry about my husband' (ACC)

     b. *Pedro-e'   t-u   túucht-ah   Maria*
       Pedro-TOP PFV-SBJ.3 send-CMPL Maria
       Ø   ohel-t-ik   le   péektsil-o'b.
       [SBJ.3   know-TRR-INCMPL DEF news-PL]SFVCo
       'Peter sent Maria to learn the news.' (ACC)

When applied to G experiencers of an intransitive verb, the same test gives the results shown in (313). (313a) shows that the embedding of an oblique experiencer verb is ungrammatical because the criterion of referential identity is not fulfilled for the possessor of *k'áat* 'wish' and the S of the embedded core verb *k'a'h* 'remember'. (313b) shows the construction chosen by the language if the S or A argument of the embedded core is not identical to the possessor of *k'áat*: the subjunctive subordinator *káa* is chosen to introduce the embedded core which is itself marked by the subjunctive mood on the verb. (313c) shows another strategy for making (313a) grammatical, namely, the causative derivation of the intransitive *k'a'h* 'remember', resulting in *k'a'hs* 'remind'. The derived causative verb takes the experiencer in A function and a regular embedding (retaining the A cross-reference marker) results (compare (133b).

(313) a.*In   k'áat   u   k'a'h-al   tèen.
        SBJ.1.SG wish   [SBJ.3   remember-INCMPL me]$_{VCo}$
        intended: 'I want to recall it.' (ACC)

     b. In   k'áat káa k'a'h-ak   tèen.
        SBJ.1.SG wish   [that remember-SUBJ me]$_{VCl}$
        'I wish that it would occur to me.' (ACC)

     c. In   k'áat in   k'a'hs-eh.
        SBJ.1.SG wish   [SBJ.1.SG remember:CAUS-SUBJ]$_{VCo}$
        'I want to recall it.' (ACC)

Section 4.2 has shown that stative clauses cannot be embedded in YM. Therefore, (314a) is ungrammatical and the stative predicate *ohel* 'know' has to be verbalized in order to be embedded under the desiderative matrix predicate *k'áat* (314b).

(314) a.*In   k'áat in   w-ohel
        SBJ.1.SG wish   [SBJ.1.SG 0-knowledge
        ba'n k'ìin a   súut.
        what sun   SBJ.2   turn\DEAG]$_{VCo}$
        intended: 'I want to know which day you will return.' (RMC)

     b. In   k'áat in   w-ohel-t-eh ...
        SBJ.1.SG wish   [SBJ.1.SG 0-know-TRR-SUBJ]$_{VCo}$
        'I want to learn (...).' (RMC)

Similarly, the S argument of an adjectival predicate does not have access to the pivot position in the subordinate clause because stative clauses cannot be embedded. Thus, there is no adjectival correspondence to the embedded verbal clause in (312a), replacing the intransitive verb *ts'íikil* 'feel angry' with the basic adjectival form *ts'íik* 'furious'.

Turning to possessive constructions, those possessive constructions that collocate with stative predicates have to be distinguished from those that collocate with dynamic verbal predicates. One would expect to find the construction in (315a) if the experiential possessor is the possessive attribute of an NP in subject function and if the subject of *k'áat* and the subject of the subordinate clause are referentially disjunctive. This is indeed the case. Again, a causative derivation is available which results in the construction shown in (315b).

(315) a. *In   k'áat   káa náay-ak   in   w-óol*
SBJ.1.SG$_i$ wish   [that calm.down-SUBJ$_j$ POSS.1.SG$_i$ 0-mind$_j$]$_{VCl}$
'I want to relax/calm down.' (ACC)

b. *In   k'áat*
SBJ.1.SG$_i$ wish

in   náays   in   w-óol.
[SBJ.1.SG$_i$ calm.down:CAUS(SUBJ) POSS.1.SG$_i$ 0-mind]$_{VCo}$
'I want to relax/calm down.' (ACC)

Interestingly however, there seems to be yet another possible construction that is unexpected given the rules of control in subordination (cf. sect. 4.2), i.e., S or A may be 'equi-deleted' under object control. In (316a), S of the subordinate core which is cross-referencing *óol* 'mind' is 'equi-deleted' although it lacks referential identity with the U argument of the matrix clause. The same situation arises in (316b) with subordination under the desiderative matrix predicate *k'áat* 'wish'. Such a construction seems to be based on the referential identity of the subject of the matrix predicate *k'áat* and the possessor of *bèel* and *óol* in the subordinate cores. This is because the example would be ungrammatical if the subject of *k'áat* and the possessor of *bèel* 'way' referred to different persons, as is illustrated in (316c). The behavior in question however seems not to be restricted to experiential cases, as (316b) shows, but seems to be a general characteristic of idiomaticized possessive collocations containing an animate possessor.

(316) a. *Pedro-e'   t-u   túucht-ah   Maria*
Pedro-TOP PFV-SBJ.3 send-CMPL   Maria$_i$
Ø   náay-al   u   y-óol.
[SBJ.3$_j$ calm.down-INCMPL POSS.3$_i$ 0-mind$_j$]$_{SFVCo}$
'Peter sent Mary away to calm down.' (ACC/NMP)

   b. *Ko'lel,   in   k'áat*
      lady   SBJ.1.SG$_i$ wish
     Ø   *ts'o'k-ol*   *in*   *bèel t-a*   *w-éetel* ....
     [SBJ.3$_j$ finish-INCMPL POSS.1$_i$ way$_j$ LOC-POSS.2 0-with]$_{SFVCo}$
     'Woman, I wish to marry you (...)' (HOSEH_05.1)
   c.**In*   *k'áat*
     SBJ.1.SG$_i$ wish
     Ø   *ts'o'k-ol*   *a*   *bèel t-in*   *w-éetel.*
     [SBJ.3$_j$ finish-INCMPL POSS.2$_k$ way$_j$ LOC-POSS.1$_i$ 0-with]$_{SFVCo}$
     intended: 'I want you to marry me.'

6.2.3 *Imperative formation*

Imperative formation is possible with all basic and derived transitive experiential verbs (cf., e.g., (317a)). Intransitive verbs only form an imperative if this is felt to be semantically appropriate. In some cases consultants answered that it is possible to give the form, but that it does not make sense, e.g., (317c). Other cases are possible without restrictions, e.g., (317b).

(317) a. *Yàabil-t-eh!*
        love-TRR-IMP
        'Love him!' (EMB_0747)
     b. *He'l-en!*
        rest-IMP
        'Take a rest!' (SBM)
     c.$^{??}$*Ka'n-en!*
        tire-IMP
        'Be tired!' (SBM)

As has been mentioned in sect. 4.1.6, intransitives of the inchoative class do not form an imperative, thus, its experiential members are excluded from imperative formation. This correlates with the semantics of its members because they all have non-agentive S arguments, e.g., *sahaktal, su'laktal*, etc. These may form, if semantically appropriate, negative commands (318a) which however, are not true imperatives. Compare the formation with third person S arguments below. Furthermore, intransitive verbs with an indirect object experiencer and those with a possessive experiencer cannot form an imperative. Instead they form a jussive, (either by means of a negated incompletive core (318b), (319a) or a subjunctive (319b)), seemingly with the same communicative goal.

(318) a. *Ma' a   sahak-tal/   háak'óol-tal!*
         NEG SBJ.2 afraid-PROC/ become.scared:mind-PROC
         'Don't get scared!" (RMC_2085)

     b. *Ma' u   tu'b-ul   tèech!*
         NEG SBJ.3 forget-INCMPL you
         'Do not forget it!' (NMP)

(319) a. *Ma' u   háak'-al   a   w-óol!*
         NEG SBJ.3 become.scared-INCMPL POSS.2 0-mind
         'Don't be amazed!' (EMB_0744)

     b. *Ki'mak-chak   a   w-óol!*
         happy-PROC.SUBJ   POSS.2   0-mind
         Way yàan   a   w-atan-e', ts'o'k   u   k'uch-ul!
         here EXIST POSS.2 0-wife-D3   TERM SBJ.3   arrive-INCMPL
         'Be happy! Here is your wife, she is back!' (RMC_2182)

For a 'true' imperative construction, a derived causative verb is chosen in both
cases, as (320) and (321) show.

(320)   *Háak's   a   w-óol-e'x,*
         become.scared:CAUS(IMP) POSS.2   0-mind-2.PL
         yàan   ba'l u   tàal u   k'iin.
         EXIST thing SBJ.3.SG come POSS.3   sun
         'Be amazed, there will happen something today.' (EMB_0745)

(321)   *Tu'bs   le   ba'l h   úuch-o'!*
         forget:CAUS(IMP) DEF thing PFV happen(CMPL)-D2
         'Forget what has happened!' (ACC_0287)

Finally, transitive verboids have to be verbalized before they can form an
imperative (322), (cf. (258a) for a negative imperative).

(322) a. *P'èek-t-eh!*
         hate-TRR-IMP
         'Hate him/scold him!' (NMP_0290)

     b. *K'ahóol-t-eh!*
         acquaint-TRR-IMP
         'Come to know him/recognize him!' (NMP)

     c. *Ohel-t-eh!   Yan in   lah-ik-ech.*
         know-TRR-IMP DEB SBJ.1.SG slap-INCMPL-ABS.2.SG
         'You have to know, I will slap you.' (NMP)

6.2.4 *Passivization*

All transitive experiential verbs can be passivized regularly. This includes basic experiencer-oriented verbs (e.g., *na't* 'understand', *kan* 'learn', *il* 'see', etc.) and complex experiencer-oriented verbs (e.g., *ts'iikilt* 'be furious at sb.', *yàakunt* 'love, care for', *ts'iibóolt* 'wish, desire', etc.) as well as stimulus-oriented verbs (e.g., *sahbes* 'frighten', *ts'iikkunt* 'bother, make fierce', etc.). With experiencer-oriented verbs, the stimulus takes subject function after passivization (323a), while with causer- or stimulus-oriented verbs, the experiencer takes subject function in the passive construction (323b).

(323) a. *Le   o'lal   h   ch'a'p'èek-t-a'b-ih ...*
      DEF   reason   PFV   take:hate-TRR-PASS.CMPL-ABS.3.SG
      'That is why he was hated, (...)' (FCP_191)

    b. *Pedro-e'   h   p'u'hs-a'b-ih.*
      Pedro-TOP   PFV   get.mad:CAUS-CMPL.PASS-ABS.3.SG
      'Pedro was bothered/they bothered Pedro.' (AME)

This is in accordance with what has been reported for the passivization of experiencer-oriented verbs in German and English in sect. 3.4.2.3. YM stimulus-oriented transitive verbs, however, differ in this point from the corresponding group of transitive experiencer verbs in languages which impose restrictions on the possibility of passive formation with this group (cf. sect. 3.4.2.3). The only restrictions on passive formation in YM are for 'reflexive' constructions, as has been addressed in sect. 5.3.2.1.4.

6.2.5 *Summary: Syntactic prominence of experiencer*

In ch. 5 it was shown that in a significant number of experiential constructions the experiencer is coded as a possessive attribute of a person part noun or of an expertum noun. Furthermore, the experiencer is coded as an indirect object with some verbs and stative predicates. In both functions, the experiencer does not have access to the pivotal positions in a number of constructions, namely, focus constructions, control constructions and imperative formation.

As has become obvious at several points in the preceding sections, regular derivational operations such as extraversion and causativization (sometimes combined with reflexive formation) enable the experiencer to have access to the pivot position in these constructions. For instance, transitive verboids have to be verbalized by extraversion and then subsequently stativized by the perfect participle marker in order to be integrated into the A focus construction (310). Similarly, transitive verboids have to be verbalized to occur in a control construction, as is shown in (314), and imperative formation is only possible after verbalization (322). Intransitive verbs with indirect object experiencers such as *tu'b ti'* 'forget', *k'a'h ti'* 'remember' regularly causativize, coding the experiencer in subject function. This process is then used to allow these experiencers to be integrated into control constructions (313c) and form an imperative (321).

Finally, constructions with possessor-experiencers such as *háak' POSS óol* 'become/get scared/impressed', *náay POSS óol* 'calm down, be diverted, relaxed', *ki'mak POSS óol* 'happy, glad', etc. possess regular causative and factitive derivations, namely, *háaks POSS óol* 'scare, impress', *náays POSS óol* 'entertain, console', *ki'makkuns POSS óol* 'delight', as has been described in sect. 5.3.2.2.2. In these causative constructions the experiencer may take subject function and at the same time be the possessor of the person part noun in direct object function. In this case, the experiencer may attain the pivot position in control constructions (315b), or be the addressee of an imperative (320). In this way causative/factitive reflexive constructions which take not only the person part *óol* 'mind' (cf. furthermore (297)) but also relational self referring nouns such as *báah* 'self' (298), *wíinklal* 'body' or a more specific body part noun in direct object function are regularly exploited to allow the experiencer to attain pivot function in certain constructions.

In all three cases of experiencer foregrounding to subject function, the operation (potentially) comes along with the acquisition of volitionality and control of the experiencer (cf. sect. 5.2.2.2.1 and sect. 5.3.2.1.1.1 for transitive verboids and their transitivized derivations, sect. 5.3.1.3 and sect. 5.3.2.1.1.1 for indirect object experiencer verbs and their causative derivations, and sect. 5.2.1.3, sect. 5.3.1.2 and sect. 5.3.2.2.2 for possessor-experiencer predicates and their causative-reflexive derivations). Thus there is no full equality in meaning between the backgrounded coding and the foregrounded coding of the experiencer. At the same time, the derived constructions are clearly more complex and, thus, secondary vis-à-vis the basic constructions. This especially holds true with respect to the possessive construction and its causative-reflexive derivation.

In general, however, it can be concluded that the discussed transitivizing operations can be viewed as a regular alternative in YM to a syntactically prominent marking of morphologically downgraded experiencers (such as those dative or possessor subjects that have been described for other languages in sect. 3.4.3). While in YM syntactic foregrounding of the experiencer is just a functionally based alternative to syntactic backgrounding[2], in languages with dative subjects, the non-canonical, syntactically higher coding is generally grammaticalized and there is no alternative.

---

[2] This seems to be equally true for the possessor subject construction in Belhare which is reported to be conditioned by transitivization of the experiential verb and specificity of the stimulus (cf. sect. 3.4.3.6.1).

6.3   *Experiencer coding in collocations vs. phrasal compounds*

It was shown at several points in ch. 5 that there are regular relations between collocations containing person part nouns (mostly *óol* 'mind') and compound and incorporative verbs and adjectives. These are discussed here because these variants display different grammatical codings of the experiencer. Table 17 contains adjectival lexicalizations, e.g., *ki'mak-óol* 'glad, happy, content', *háak'óol* '(easily) frightened/scared, nervous, astonished', *chi'chnak(-óol)* 'cross, furious, angry', *k'ùux(-óol)* 'angry, nervous, peevish', *ts'íik(il)(-óol)* 'angry, fierce', *sahak(-óol)* 'afraid, fearful', etc. from collocations given in Table 18 and Table 31. Table 36 contains some compound and incorporative verbs, e.g., *yah-óolt* 'be depressed /sad because of; regret' from a local person part collocations (Table 21).

The examples in (324) and (325) contrast the syntactically low prominence of the possessor-experiencer in (324a) and (325a) with the syntactically more prominent coding of the subject experiencer of the compound verb in (324b) or the absolutive experiencer of the adjectival compound in (325b).

(324) a. *Yah   t-in   w-óol*
        ache   LOC-POSS.1.SG 0-mind
        u   tóok-a'l   le   k'áax-o'.
        SBJ.3 burn-PASS.INCMPL DEF jungle-D2
        'It hurts me that they burn down the forest.' (ACC, NMP)

    b. *K-in   yah-óolt-ik*
       IMPF-SBJ.1.SG   ache-mind:TRR-INCMPL
       u   tóok-a'l   le   k'áax-o'.
       SBJ.3 burn-PASS.INCMPL DEF jungle-D2
       'I regret / suffer very much that the jungle is being burned down.'
       (EMB_0690, NMP)

(325) a. *Hach   h   háak'-a'n   in   w-óol*
        really PFV   scare-RSLTV POSS.3 0-mind
        le   k-in   w-il-ik
        DEF   IMPF-SBJ.1.SG 0-see-INCMPL
        u   k'áax-al   ha',   ma' u   tyèempo-il-i'.
        SBJ.3 rain-INCMPL water   NEG POSS.3 time-REL-NEGF
        'I am really astonished to see that it is raining, this is not the right season.' (ACC, NMP)

    b. *Hach háak'óol-en*   *in*   *w-il-ik*
      really   scare:mind-ABS.1.SG SBJ.1.SG 0-see-INCMPL
      u   *k'áax-al*   *ha',*   *ma' u*   *tyèempo-il-i'.*
      SBJ.3   rain-INCMPL water   NEG POSS.3   time-REL-NEGF
      'I am really astonished to see that it is raining, this is not the right
      season.' (FEE_0251, NMP)

The use of the compound form displays a more prominent syntactic coding of the experiencer as an immediate argument of the experiential predicate as opposed to a syntactically lower coding when it is a possessive attribute to the person part noun *óol*.

These compounds generally preserve their phrasal nature, as they are mostly transparent in meaning. Nevertheless there is no regular syntactic operation between the phrasal construction and the compound item, rather the compounds are subject to lexicalization and idiomaticization. Thus, the compound adjectives differ as to whether they are stimulus-oriented (e.g., *máan-óol* 'boring, sating', *síis-óol* 'cool', etc.) or experiencer-oriented (e.g., *chuka'n-óol* 'patient', *xul-óol* 'exhausted', etc.), cf. sect. 5.2.1.1. Furthermore, not all items from Table 21 form verbal compounds, and similarly, not all items from Table 18 and Table 31 form adjectival compounds, though the latter process seems to be more frequent. Through this analysis, variation, as shown in (324) and (325), is lexically determined and the varying allocation of the experiencer on the hierarchy of grammatical relation is a matter of lexical choice.

Other compounds and incorporatives from Table 36, e.g., *ts'íibóolt* 'wish, desire', *alabóolt* 'hope for, be concerned over, take confidence, rely on', *muk'yaht* 'suffer, feel', etc. are no longer fully transparent. They do not have corresponding phrasal expressions in contemporary YM, and thus there is no variation in the syntactic level of the experiencer coding.

6.4 *Experiencer in indirect object function*

As has already been mentioned in sect. 4.3.4 for G participants such as beneficiary and recipient in indirect object function, an indirect object experiencer may also remain syntactically unexpressed under certain conditions. Experiential adjectives and verbs that take an indirect object experiencer (cf. Table 20, Table 34) provide for variation, as shown in (326). In (326a/b/c) the experiencer is coded as an indirect object pronoun, while in the primed versions of these examples it is coded as the possessor of the subject, which expresses the stimulus argument. Thus, in the primed versions the relation as an indirect object remains unexpressed, but is inferred in these examples from the possessive relation expressed. This holds true with different kinds of 'possessive' relations between the experiencer and the stimulus, i.e., they may be in an actual possessive relation (326c) as well as in a future possessive relation (326b).

(326) a. *Hach k'abéet   tèen tòoh-óolal.*
      really   necessary   me   straight-mind:ABSTR
      'I really need health.' (ACC)

   a'.*Hach k'abéet   in   tòoh-óolal.*
      really   necessary POSS.1.SG straight-mind:ABSTR
      'I desperately need my health.'
      (Bricker et al. 1998, s.v. *tòoh-óolal*)[3]

   b. *K'abéet   tèen túumben   xanab.*
      necessary me   new   shoe
      'I need new shoes. (NMP)

   b'.*K'abéet   in   túumben   xanab.*
      necessary POSS.1.SG new   shoe
      'I need new shoes' (NMP)

   c. *H   tu'b tèen le   kib-o'.*
      PFV forget me   DEF   candle-D2
      'I forgot the candle.' (ACC, RMC, NMP)

   c'.*H   tu'b in   kib.*
      PFV forget POSS.3.SG candle
      'I forgot the/my candle.' (ACC, RMC, NMP)

Similarly, in matrix constructions with G experiencers, there is the option of leaving the G experiencer argument implicit within the matrix clause. This is again true for adjectival stative predicates such as *sùuk* in (327a), as well as for some intransitive verbs with indirect object experiencers (327b/c). The examples in (327) show that the oblique pronoun *tèen* in the matrix clause is optional under referential identity with the subject of the subordinate clause.[4, 5]

(327) a. *Sùuk   (tèen) in   w-uk'-ik   kafe.*
      accustomed   me   [SBJ.1.SG 0-drink-INCMPL   coffee]$_{VCo}$
      'I am accustomed to drinking coffee.' (EMB_0832, NMP)

---

[3] repeated from (191)

[4] Also Andrade (1955:176) mentions *tu'b* 'forget' in this construction type.

[5] This phenomenon is reminiscent of data from Caucasian languages (e.g., Tsez) that has been analyzed as 'backward (subject) control' in Polinsky and Potsdam (2002). The YM data however, differs from these data in several points, among them the fact that the controlled function is that of an indirect complement and that the elision is optional. Common to both cases however, is that under referential identity, one actant of the superordinate clause is not syntactically coded.

   b. *H   tu'b   (tèen) in   bin   Cancun.*
     PFV forget me   [SBJ.1.SG go   Cancun]$_{VCo}$
     'I forgot to go to Cancun.' (EMB, ACC)

   c. *H   k'a'h   (tèen) in   bis-ik   le   kib-o'.*
     PFV remember me   [SBJ.1.SG carry-INCMPL DEF candle-D2]$_{VCo}$
     'I remembered taking the candle with me.'
     (EMB, RMC, SME, FEE, NMP)

(197c) above and (328) below show examples from natural texts which lack an indirect object experiencer in the matrix clause. (329), repeated from (242), is an example from Colonial Yucatec Maya (from the Diccionario de Motul II (17th century)) and illustrates that such a construction was already possible in the language stage prior to present day Modern Yucatec Maya. At this stage the verb *tu'b* was already used with an oblique experiencer in full verb use/non-matrix use (cf. sect. 5.3.1.3).

  (328)   *Sùuk   y-il-ik*
          accustomed SBJ.3-see-INCMPL
          bey u   bèet-ik   u   ts'ùul-il-o',...
          thus SBJ.3 do-INCMPL POSS.3   sir-REL-D2
          'He was accustomed to seeing that his master was doing it that way, (...)' (XTUUCHAH_021.1)
  (329)   *tu'b-ih   in   xok-ik   in   kwentas*
          forget-ABS.3.SG [SBJ.1.SG count-INCMPL POSS.1.SG counts]$_{VCo}$
          I forgot to tell my beads'
          (Barrera Vásquez et al. eds. 1980, s.v. *xok*)

The fact that there has to be presupposed referential identity between the experiencer in the matrix clause and the subject of the subordinate clause can be deduced from the ill-formed nature of the examples in (330). Under referential distinctness between the indirect object of the matrix predicate and the subject of the subordinate verb an incompletive-marked verbal core is not possible. This is not only true for personal participants but also for non-personal participants as in (330d).

  (330) a.**Sùuk   tèen a   ts'u'ts'.*
        accustomed me   [SBJ.2.SG smoke]
        intended: 'I am accustomed to your smoking.' (EMB, RMC, NMP)

     b.**H   tu'b tèen a   bin   Cancun.*
        PFV forget me   [SBJ.2.SG go Cancun]
        intended: 'I forgot that you go to Cancun.' (EMB, NMP)

c.*_H   k'a'h   tèech_
   PFV   remember(CMPL) you
   in   bis-ik   le   kib-o'.
   [SBJ.1.SG carry-INCMPL DEF candle-D2]
   intended: 'You remembered that I bring the candle.' (SME, NMP)

d.*_H   k'a'h/   tu'b   tèen   u   k'áax-al   ha'._
   PFV   remember/ forget me   SBJ.3 rain-INCMPL water
   intended: 'I remembered/forgot that is was raining.' (EMB, NMP)

Instead, the construction with _sùuk_ requires the insertion of the perception verb _il_ 'see' in order to attain referential identity with the indirect object of the matrix clause (331a). The intransitive verbs _tu'b_ 'forget' and _k'a'h_ 'remember' require a non-embedded semantically dependent clause as matrix predicates under DRef, as shown in (331b/c/d).

(331) a. _Sùuk   tèen   in   w-il-ik   a   ts'u'ts'._
         accustomed me   [SBJ.1.SG 0-see-INCMPL [SBJ.2.SG smoke]]
         'I am accustomed to seeing you smoking.' (SBM, EMB, NMP)

      b. _H   tu'b   tèen wáah tàak   a   bin   Cancun._
         PFV forget me   [if   anxious SBJ.2 go   Cancun]
         'I forgot that you wanted to go to Cancun.' (EMB, NMP)

      c. _H   k'a'h   tèech_
         PFV remember(CMPL) you
         yan   in   bis-ik   le   kib-o'.
         [DEB SBJ.1.SG carry-INCMPL DEF candle-D2]
         'You remembered that I have to/will bring the candle.' (ACC)

      d. _H   tu'b   tèen wáah yan   u   k'áax-al   ha'._
         PFV forget me   if   DEB SBJ.3 rain-INCMPL water
         'I forgot if/that it was going to rain.' (EMB)

At the same time, 'reverse' control, i.e., forward control in the sense of 'equi-deletion' of the subject of the subordinate clause with the indirect object experiencer as a controller, is excluded (332). Thus the experiencer is obligatorily coded in the subordinate clause. Insofar as it is also coded as indirect object in the matrix clause, there is a redundancy which may contribute to the optionality of the indirect object experiencer in the matrix clause.

(332)   *Sùuk/*   *h*   *tu'b/*   *h*   *k'a'h*   *tèen*
        accustomed/ PFV forget/ PFV remember me
        **(in)*   *bin*   *Cancun.*
        [SBJ.1.SG   go   Cancun]
        'I am accustomed/forgot/remembered to going/go to Cancun.'
        (ACC, EMB, NMP)

Both constructions, the possessive one exemplified in (326) and the 'backward indirect object control construction' exemplified in (327), are alternative constructions to a construction that codes the experiencer as an indirect object. In sect. 4.3.4, it was shown that constructions with participants such as the recipient or the beneficiary possess parallel alternative constructions. Those with an experiencer however, prototypically differ from those with a recipient or a beneficiary with respect to the transitivity of the predicate. This leads to systematic differences concerning the grammatical relation of the other participant that is coded in relation to the experiencer. The experiencer is coded as a possessive attribute of the stimulus in subject function (Construction A2 in Figure 15). The recipient is coded as a possessive attribute to the trajector in direct object function (Construction B2 in Figure 15). The experiencer can be coded as the subject of a subject clause of an experiential matrix verb (Construction A3 in Figure 15), the recipient can be coded as actant in a purpose clause (Construction B3 in Figure 15). For reasons of space a simplified representation of these constructions is presented in Figure 15.

experience	EXPERIENCER		transfer	RECIPIENT
stat. PRED/intr. V	indirect object		ditransitive V	indirect object
STIMULUS gets_forgotten to			EMITTER gives TRAJECTOR to	
EXPERIENCER (326c)			RECIPIENT (140a)	
Construction A1			*Construction B1*	

experience	EXPERIENCER		transfer	RECIPIENT
stat. PRED/intr. V	attribute of SBJ		transitive V	attribute of DO
STIMULUS of EXPERIENCER			EMITTER gives TRAJECTOR of	
gets_forgotten (326c')			RECIPIENT (144a)	
Construction A2			*Construction B2*	

experience	EXPERIENCER		transfer	RECIPIENT
stat. PRED/intr. V	actant of sub. V		transitive V	actant of sub. V
gets_forgotten, EXPERIENCER acts			EMITTER gives TRAJECTOR, so that	
(327b)			RECIPIENT acts (144b)	
Construction A3			*Construction B3*	

Figure 15. Parallel constructions

Thus in these cases, YM provides for the option of not coding the participant relation (of recipient and experiencer) to the main predicate syntactically, but instead coding another relation the participant in question holds in the situation. Given however, that both recipient and experiencer are generally inherent in the valency and semantics of the respective predicates, these alternative coding strategies are not functionally motivated. Instead, the language uses coding strategies that have their functional locus in other grammatical domains, e.g., in the inherence in the possessum (333) or in the subordinate verb (to be addressed further down), and overgeneralizes them. The result is an unusually low syntactic prominence of the participants in question.

In terms of a constructional approach, examples like those given in (326) are structurally identical to examples like (333a), which were represented in Construction 10, and its verbal counterpart (333b), which was represented in Construction 25.

(333) a. *yah   in   nak'*
      ache   POSS.1.SG belly
      'my stomach aches' (BVS_16.01.03)

   b. *Túun   k'i'nam   in   w-òok.*
      PROG:SBJ.3   hurt   POSS.1.SG   0-foot
      'My foot is aching.' (ACC)

Similarly, examples coding the recipient as the possessor of the trajector (cf. (144.a)) are structurally identical to examples designating the affectedness of a body part (334).

(334)   *T-a   ya'-chek'-t-ah   in   w-òok.*
         PFV-SBJ.2   step-foot-TRR-CMPL   [POSS.1.SG   Ø-foot]
         'You stepped on my foot.' (EMB 047)

Examples like (333) and (334) (and their respective constructions) feature an inherent possessive relation and the (experiential or sympathetic) affectedness of the possessor in the situation can be deduced from this intimate part-whole relation (cf. for this analysis Construction 10 and Construction 25 and explanations there). This however is not the case in examples such as those in (326). They inherit the structural layer from the aforementioned constructions; their semantics however, is different. The experiential interpretation of the possessor results from the predicate meaning. The adjectives and verbs integrating with the construction under consideration are canonically bivalent adjectives such as *k'abéet/k'a'náan* 'necessary', *sùuk* 'accustomed to' and canonically bivalent intransitive verbs such as *tu'b* 'forget' and *k'a'h* 'remember, occur to'. They integrate with such constructions which implies that their EXPERIENCER is mapped onto the constructional Possessor argument. This is represented in Construction 41, which generalizes over the predicate type (being either an adjective or an intransitive verb). Thus, Construction 41 is an alternative to Construction 13 and Construction 27, as represented in Figure 15.

Correspondingly, the 'backward indirect object control construction' (Construction 28) can be analyzed as an instance of the modal operator construction that was outlined in Construction 15. Volitive *tàak* 'be anxious, want' and the modal auxiliaries of necessity such as *k'abéet* and *k'a'náan*, both meaning 'necessary' integrate with Construction 15. As has been reported in sect. 5.2.2.1.1, these code the participant to whom the modality applies as the subject (S, A) of the subordinate core. Experiencer marking in the 'backward indirect object control construction' is identical to this, i.e., the experiencer is understood to be the subject (S, A) of the subordinate clause.

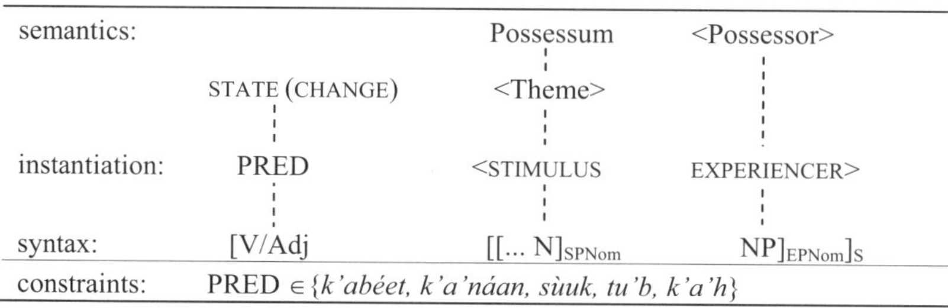

Construction 41. Possessive C. with experiencer and stimulus

The constructions analyzed in this section again show the similarity between the possessor and the subject (S, A) of a subordinate core, a fact that has already been highlighted in sect. 4.3.5. For the constructions under investigation it has been shown that the possessor as well as the subordinate subject may take functions otherwise fulfilled by the indirect object. Given the analysis that the subject of the subordinate core is a former possessive attribute of a nominalized verb, 'backward control' of the indirect object is then just a variant of the possessor – indirect object alternation shown in (326). (335) illustrates the ambiguity between analyzing the part in square brackets as a nominal element and analyzing it as a verbal element.

(335)   *Sùuk   u   xíimbal.*
         accustomed   [SBJ/POSS.3   stroll/journey]
         'He is accustomed to strolling.' (RMC)

The fact that the possessor may take functions of the indirect object reflects the YM dominance of (bi)relationality that is true not only for the verbal but also for the nominal sphere. Thus, irrespective of the hierarchy of grammatical relations in Figure 3, those arguments reflected by the cross-reference morphology are more indispensable than arguments that are not coded in this way, such as the indirect object. Thus, in YM a possessor argument, though taking adnominal function according to Figure 3, may dominate a verb dependent argument (i.e. the indirect object) since it is not cross-referenced on the verb.

6.5   *Pragmatic prominence of experiencers*
Topicalization is a very frequently used method of pragmatically foregrounding the experiencer in natural texts. There is no restriction on the lower grammatical relations the experiencer may take to occur in the topic position. This holds true not only for possessor-experiencers as in (166a), but also for regular (336) as well as 'implicit' indirect object experiencers that only surface in the subordinate clause (337).

(336)   *tuméen   wa'pach'-e' táan   u   kóoh-ol*
        because   giant-TOP   PROG SBJ.3   have.a.feeling-INCMPL
        ti'   ba'x k-a   mèent-ik
        LOC   what IMPF-SBJ.2 do-INCMPL
        'because the giant can feel what you are doing' (HK'AN_064.2)

(337)   *Le<bin> ti'-e'   hach sùuk   u   bin h bùul.*
        <QUOT>that.one-TOP very be.accustomed [SBJ.3 go SS gamble]vCo
        'As for him, he had a gambling habit.' (HK'AN_043)

In (338), the implicit experiencer of the matrix predicate *tu'bbanak* 'forget' is not only expressed in the subordinate clause, but is also the subject of the preceding clauses.

(338)   *Le   bin   káa   h   hóok' u   bin-bal-e',*
        when   QUOT   CNJ PFV exit   SBJ.3   go-INTRV-CNTR
        tu'b-banak   [u   bis-ik   u   nu'kul
        forget-PART.PRS SBJ.3 carry-INCMPL POSS.3 instrument
        [u   ch'ot-ik   u   y-otoch]vCo]vCo.
        SBJ.3 wind.up-INCMPL POSS.3 0-home
        'But when the giant left, he forgot to take his house keys with him.'
        (HK'AN_092)

6.6   *Summary*
It can be concluded from the above investigation of grammatical properties of experiencers that YM consistently draws on existing grammatical resources and integrates experiencer coding with these (i.e., the language does not show

(at least not to a noteworthy degree) non-canonical experiencer-special marking, as has been reported for other languages (cf. sect. 3.4.3).

There are two main typological characteristics that influence the grammatical structure of the domain of experience. This is, on the one hand, the weak implementation of the indirect object, and on the other hand, the elaborated system of the grammar of possession, which takes functions which are fulfilled in other languages by verbal dependency.

YM displays a strikingly low syntactic prominence of the experiencer for a number of basic experiential lexemes. Given the weak implementation of the indirect object, only a few predicates code the experiencer in this function. If these predicates occur as matrix predicates, the syntactic realization of the experiencer in the matrix clause is optional, and it may be exclusively coded as part of the subordinate clause. Its experiential role in these constructions can only be inferred. This type of construction is inherited from constructions with grammaticalized (experiential) matrix operators such as *tàak* 'be anxious, want', *k'abéet/k'a'náan* 'necessary', etc. These latter matrix operators do not have a slot for the experiencer, but realize it exclusively as the subject of the subordinate verb (at the detriment of coding the experiencer-role).

Furthermore, YM uses possessive constructions in coding the experiencer. Frequently, the experiencer is coded as the possessor of a person part noun. In person part constructions only the possessive role is coded, while the experiential role is not. This construction type contrasts with external possessor constructions, that are used in other languages in similar situations (cf. sect. 3.4.3.1 and sect. 3.4.3.2.2). Furthermore, it has been shown that the experiencer may even be coded as the possessor of a stimulus subject with some experiential stative predicates and intransitive verbs (cf. (326), sect. 6.4). In these cases the experiential role is not coded either, but can be inferred from the experiential meaning of the predicate. Such a construction seems to be the true converse of an external possessor construction. While the external possessor construction codes a possessor as a verb dependant, the YM construction under investigation codes a verb dependant as the possessor of another argument. A parallel example has only been found in Samoan (cf. (83)).

In both strategies characteristic for YM, the experiencer has a low syntactic prominence which is in contrast to its topic properties. It has been discussed before (sect. 3.4) that many languages that display morphologically downgraded experiencers possess at the same time options of syntactic foregrounding such as attributing subject properties to dative experiencers. In YM on the contrary, the rich derivational possibilities (especially transitivization) are exploited to foreground the experiencer in a syntactically regular way. At the same time, as has been shown in sect. 6.5, a syntactically backgrounded experiencer that takes indirect object or possessor function or occurs in a subordinate clause can always attain pragmatic prominence through topicalization.

Both factors, the regular derivation of subject-experiencers as well as the strong topic position of YM seem to make a change to subject-experiencers, such as the one that has taken place in SAE-languages (sect. 3.6) superfluous.

CHAPTER 7

Complementation with experiential predicates

7.1 *Introduction*

The groups of experiential predicates established above exhibit characteristic behavior with respect to subordination. Each group employs a given type of subordinative construction, according to its specific semantics, as introduced in sect. 4.2. The groups relevant here are perception verbs, predicates of (the acquisition of) knowledge, predicates of propositional attitude, emotional and evaluative 'commentative' predicates, and volition and volitive emotion predicates such as desiderative or 'fear' predicates. The following subsections will introduce the formal and functional prerequisites needed to investigate constructions with propositional predicates, while the following parallel sections will analyze subordinative constructions involving experiential propositional predicates according to the abovementioned semantic classes.

7.1.1 *Syntactic relation of subordinate clause*

Propositional predicates take their stimulus argument in a subject- or object-relation. Objects may be either direct objects or prepositional objects that are governed by the matrix predicate. Complement clauses in subject- or direct object-function can be identified by the valency and argument-structure properties of the matrix predicate. Thus, transitive experiencer-oriented matrix predicates (e.g., *il* 'see', *ohelt* '(get) to know', *tùukult* 'think') take their propositional stimulus in direct object function and transitive verboids (e.g., *ohel* 'know', *p'èek* 'dislike, hate') take their propositional stimulus in object function. With stimulus-oriented causative verbs (e.g., *ki'makkuns* POSS *óol* 'delight', *náays* POSS *óol* 'console, to entertain', etc.), the propositional stimulus takes subject function. In addition, with intransitive stimulus-oriented verbs (e.g., *k'a'h* 'remember', *tu'b* 'forget', *tàal ti'* POSS *tùukul* 'come into one's mind') as well as stative stimulus-oriented predicates (e.g., *k'a'ha'n* 'be in one's mind', *sahbentsil* 'scary', *háak'óol* 'surprising, frightening'), the propositional stimulus is in subject function, as well, while with experiencer- or body part-oriented intransitive verbs (e.g., *máan/tàal* POSS *óol* 'lose/take interest', *su'laktal* 'get ashamed', *ts'íikil* 'feel angry', etc.) and stative predicates (e.g., *ki'mak* POSS *óol* 'happy', *uts ti'* POSS *t'àan* 'please, like', *chi'chnak* 'furious', *su'lak* 'ashamed', etc.) the propositional stimulus phrase may be equiva-

lent to a prepositional complement (i.e., if it is governed by the predicate) or to
an adjunct (i.e., if it is modifying the predicate).

We have to acknowledge that on the surface clauses or cores in complement
function do not differ from those in adjunct function if the latter are not introduced by a conjunction. This has been shown in sect. 4.2. Thus, motion verbs
may take an incompletive-marked verbal core (cf. (124)) or a 'split' verbal core
(cf. (125)) in adjunct function. Moreover, the same pattern is used for propositional predicates. For instance, *k'áat* 'wish' takes a 'split' verbal core in complement function (cf. (119)) while perception predicates take an incompletive-
marked verbal core in complement function (cf. (121)). Correspondingly, *káa*-
clauses may not only introduce complements (e.g., with *k'áat* 'wish' in (126))
but also purpose clauses in adjunct function, as in (339).

(339)   *Túun   y-òok'ol-t-ik   káa u   ma't-eh.*
        PROG:SBJ.3 0-weep-TRR-INCMPL that SBJ.3   get.present-SUBJ
        'He is weeping for it so that he will get it as a present.'
        (RMC_2213)

Furthermore, it has been shown in sect. 4.2, that semantically subordinated
independent clauses may be in a 'complement-relation' to a matrix predicate.
In this case, the two clauses are only in an adjacent position without a formal
marking of the dependency relation (cf. (116b) and (345)). At the same time,
semantic relations of cause or temporal simultaneity may also be in effect between two clauses in cases where they are simply adjacent to each other. This
point will be dicussed in more detail in sect. 7.4.1.

These cases show that the structure of the subordinate clause/core itself does
not identify complement vs. adjunct clauses or cores. Rather, their syntactic
status may be deduced from the valency and associated argument structure of
the main predicate. Thus, propositional stimuli are conceived of as being
equivalent to nominal or prepositional phrases in stimulus function.

7.1.2 *Semantic criteria*

There are a number of semantic criteria that play a role in types of subordination; these concern the number and interrelation of the situations involved. The
crucial distinction is if there are two different situations referred to by the matrix clause and the subordinate clause, or if the 'subordinate' situation is integrated into or part of the 'superordinate' situation, i.e., if there is only one
situation (cf., e.g., Givón 1980, 1990, Lehmann 1988). This distinction correlates to a number of other factors, most importantly the difference of independent time reference (ITR) vs. dependent/determined time reference (DTR) of the
subordinate proposition as introduced in Noonan (1985:92). A further criterion
that prototypically correlates with the above distinction is the question of DRef

vs. SRef, as introduced in sect. 4.2.2. Finally, the subordinate proposition receives a value which reflects its discourse status and its truth, i.e., its relation to reality. Some predicates 'presuppose' the reality/factivity of the subordinate proposition while others convey 'new' information (Kiparsky and Kiparsky 1970, cf. Noonan 1985). While presupposed/factive complements are real per se, those complements conveying 'new' information may be either real/actual or unreal/potential. This latter distinction may coincide with the (implicit) assertion vs. non-assertion of the truth of the subordinate proposition. The mentioned parameters are summarized in Table 49.

Parameter	Values
Number of situations	1 vs. 2
Time reference	ITR vs. DTR
Person reference	DRef/SRef vs. SRef
Discourse status	presupposed vs. asserted vs. non-asserted
Reality/Truth status of subordinate proposition[1]	factive (presupposed) vs. real/actual (asserted) vs. unreal/potential (non-asserted)

Table 49. Semantic parameters determining subordinate propositions

The most basic criterion used to partition experiential predicates seems to be the question of whether a given expression is able to function as propositional or complement taking predicate. Following the subject nature of the current chapter, only propositional predicates are dealt with. Some predicates only marginally allow for propositional stimuli as complement clauses. In such cases, consultants suggest placing other interpropositional relations such as temporal, causal, manner, etc. between the experiential matrix predicate and the subordinate proposition. These cases are discussed in the following paragraphs as cases of delimitation. As has been mentioned above, propositional stimuli in adverbial function are not discussed here, since their occurrence is assumed to be independent of experiential meaning following the general rules of adverbial subordination in the language.

7.2 *Perception*

A situation of immediate perception is characterized by the fact that the perceiver directly perceives the situation expressed in the subordinate proposition. Situations of direct perception prototypically consist of two subsituations, one expressed in the main clause and one in the subordinate clause. If these subsituations occur simultaneously it is an immediate (sensory) perception (cf. Givón 1990). Cross-linguistically, complex perception constructions generally display DTR due to the restriction of the simultaneity of both situations (cf.

---

[1] with generally associated discourse status given in brackets

Noonan 1985:130). Furthermore, perception seems to be prototypically directed towards other entities (thus involving DRef), though self-perception is assumed to be possible in all perceptual modalities. Cases of internal perception in the sense of a feeling are relevant here (cf. (340) repeated from (225))

(340)   *K-in*   *w-u'y-ik*   *in*   *su'lak-tal*
        IMPF-SBJ.1.SG 0-feel-INCMPL [SBJ.1.SG ashamed-PROC]$_{VC_0}$
        chen   *k'uch-uk-en*   *t-u*   *nah-il*
        SR.FUT   arrive-SUBJ-ABS.1.SG   LOC-POSS.3   house-REL
        le   máak-o'b-o'.
        DEF   person-PL-D2
        'I feel that I am getting embarrassed when I arrive at the house of
        those men.' (RMC_2200)

Furthermore, SRef does not seem to be excluded in contexts of imagined 'self'-perception as in cases like Germ. *ich sah mich schon durch die Prüfung fallen* 'I already saw myself failing the examination'. Note that Noonan (loc. cit.) includes predicates like 'imagine' "where the event and its perception are entirely mental" within the group of perception predicates for their cross-linguistically asserted identical behavior as complement-taking predicates. Perception predicates indirectly assert the truth of the subordinate proposition.

In YM, perception verbs in their immediate perception sense take an incompletive-marked verbal core in direct object function, as has been explained and exemplified in sect. 4.2.2 with reference to (121) (cf. also Bohnemeyer 1998[T]:165). Further examples are given in (341) with *il* 'see' as matrix predicate and in (342) with *u'y* 'hear, feel' as matrix predicate. (342b) shows that an incompletive-marked verbal core is also used in the sensation sense of *u'y*.

(341) a. *T-u*   *y-il-ah*   *in*   *tàal.*
         PFV-SBJ.3 0-see-CMPL   [SBJ.1.SG   come]$_{VC_0}$
         'he saw me coming' (ACC)

      b. *T-u*   *y-il-ah*   *in*   *hàan-t-ik.*
         PFV-SBJ.3 0-see-CMPL   [SBJ.1.SG   eat-TRR-INCMPL]$_{VC_0}$
         'he saw me eating it' (ACC)

(342) a. *Wáah k-in*   *w-u'y-ik*
         if   IMPF-SBJ.1.SG 0-feel-INCMPL
         u   *k'àay*   *hun-túul*   *ninya*   *be'òoráah-a'* ...
         [SBJ.3 sing\INTRV one-CL.AN   girl   now-D1]$_{VC_0}$
         'If I hear a girl singing now, (...)' (MUUCH_061)

b. *Mix   sah-en-i'*   *pero   yàan   ba'x*
NEG   fear-ABS.1.SG-NEGF   but   EXIST   thing
k-in   *w-u'y-ik*   *y-ùuch-ul*   *tèen.*
IMPF-SBJ.3.SG   0-feel-INCMPL   [SBJ.3-happen-INCMPL   me]$_{VCo}$
'I am not afraid but there is something I feel happening to me.'
(NMP_0305)

With most of the active perception verbs, consultants were able to add an incompletive-marked verbal core, as is shown in (343a) for *ch'ehxikint* and in (343b) for *ch'úukt*. Further examples have been given for *pàak(a)t* 'look (at)', *kanáant* 'guard, watch over', *cha'nt* 'contemplate, to look at', *ch'a'ch'a'bòokt* 'sniff at', *úuts'bent* 'smell at' among others. However *ch'éenebt* (344b) and *úuts'ni't*, at least, seem to prefer an entity as direct object.

(343) a. *K-u*   *ch'ehxikin-t-ik*
        IMPF-SBJ.3   strengthen:ear-TRR-INCMPL
        u   *y-a'l-a'l.*
        [SBJ.3   0-say-PASS.INCMPL]$_{VCo}$
        'He listens carefully to what is being said.' (ACC)
     b. *Tíin*   *ch'úukt-ik*   *u*   *máan*
        PROG:SBJ.1.SG   hunt.up-INCMPL   [SBJ.3   pass]$_{VCo}$
        káa   in   t'àan-eh.
        [that   SBJ.1.SG call-SUBJ]$_{VCI}$
        'I am watching for him to pass so that I can call him.' (RMC_2108)

(344) a. *$^{?}$K-u*   *ch'éeneb-t-ik*   *in*   *wichkíil.*
        IMPF-SBJ.3   peek-TRR-INCMPL   [SBJ.1.SG   bathe]$_{VCo}$
     b. *K-u*   *ch'éeneb-t-ik-en,*   *táan   in   wichkíil.*
        IMPF-SBJ.3   peek-TRR-INCMPL-ABS.1.SG   PROG   SBJ.1.SG   bathe
        'He spies me, (while) I am bathing.' (ACC)

Perception verbs in YM may also be constructed with independent subordinate clauses, bearing the AM marker and thus displaying ITR (345). Such a construction does not convey immediate perception of the situation expressed in the subordinate clause, but may refer to an inference made from perception (cf. Bohnemeyer 1998[T]:165). In (345b) for example, the 'perceiver' may infer the fact that 'I ate it' from something caused by this event that he has perceived, e.g., an empty plate etc. Following Noonan (1985:118f.), a perception predicate that is combined with an independent subordinate clause behaves like a predicate of knowledge (cf. sect. 7.3.1). In this construction type the subordinate proposition is generally presupposed to be true, similar to propositions of complements of knowledge predicates.

(345) a. *T-u*   *y-il-ah*   *h*   *tàal-en.*
         PFV-SBJ.3   0-see-CMPL   [PFV   come-ABS.1.SG]$_{VCl}$
         'He saw that I came.'

      b. *T-u*   *y-il-ah*   *t-in*   *hàan-t-ah.*
         PFV-SBJ.3   0-see-CMPL   [PFV-SBJ.1.SG   eat-TRR-CMPL]$_{VCl}$
         'He saw that I ate it.' (Bricker 1981[S]:99/ACC)

In the text examples in (346), a reading of inference is evident. The propositions coded in the independent subordinate clauses are interpreted as facts and not as simultaneously occurring events.

(346) a. *Ma'* *t-a*   *w-il-ik-e'*
         NEG PROG-SBJ.2 0-see-INCMPL-CNTR
         t-in   *xot-ah?*
         [PFV-SBJ.1.SG saw-CMPL]$_{VCl}$
         'Don't you see that I cut it?' (HK'AN_079.2)

      b. *a'le'*   *k-u*   *y-il-ik-o'b-e'*
         however   IMPF-SBJ.3   0-see-INCMPL-3.PL-TOP
         ts'o'k   *u*   *y-áak'abtal*
         [TERM   SBJ.3   0-night:PROC]$_{VCl}$
         'but they saw that it had become night' (HOSEH_35.2)

      c. *le*   *káa*   *t-u*   *y-il-ah-o'b*
         DEF   CNJ   PFV-SBJ.3   0-see-CMPL-3.PL
         h   *bin*   *u*   *ka'*   *nóokhàats'-bil u*   *tàatah-o'b-o'*
         [PFV   go   SBJ.3   again hit-GERV   POSS.3 father-3.PL-D2]$_{VCl}$
         'and when they saw that she was going to beat their father again'
         (HOSEH_46.02)

In the examples in (347) however, the context suggests a meaning of immediate perception with an independent subordinate clause. This reading seems to be based on the use of the progressive in the second clause. Following Bohnemeyer (1998[T]:344) the progressive may be interpreted as being simultaneous to a situation in adjacent discourse. In (347a/b) these simultaneous situations are represented by the predicates of perception.

(347) a. *chéen   t-in*   *w-u'y-ah*   *t-u*
        just   PFV-SBJ.1.SG   0-feel-CMPL [PROG-SBJ.3
        y-a'l-a'l   *ti'*   *tumen hun-túul*   *u*   *meyah*
        0-say-PASS.INCMPL LOC by   one-CL.AN POSS.3 worker]ᵥcɪ
        'this, I heard it being said to him by one of his workers'
        (HALA'CH_08)
    b. *T-in*   *w-u'y-ah*   *túun*   *tàal*
        PFV-SBJ.1.SG 0-feel-CMPL   [PROG:SBJ.3 come
        le   *huhux*   *òok*   *máak-o'.*
        DEF   scuffle   foot   person-D2]ᵥcɪ
        'I heard the man come scuffling.' (RMC_1603)

I propose a three-fold distinction in the construction possibilities of the perception verbs just addressed, which can be made following Dik and Hengeveld 1991:239f. Thus, a distinction first has to be made between immediate perception and knowledge based on perception. The choice between an incompletive-marked verbal core and an independent subordinate clause as complement clauses to a perception verb corresponds to this distinction (cf. (341), (342) vs. (345) and following examples). Knowledge based on perception may be called mental perception. Here, a second distinction can be made concerning the source of mental perception. If immediate perception is the basis, then it can be called primary mental perception, which applies to cases such as (347a/b), i.e., if the independent subordinate clause is in the progressive. If the acquisition of knowledge is based on perception plus further knowledge, it can be called secondary mental perception based on inference. This applies to cases such as (345) and (346).

Perception verbs are further used with evaluating/judgment or experiential adjectives to express an evaluation of a proposition, e.g., with *yah*/*uts* SBJ *il*, *ki'*/*yah* SBJ *u'y*, etc. The respective simple construction has been introduced as Construction 34. As complement taking predicates they belong to the group of commentative emotion predicates and will be discussed in sect. 7.4.1.

7.3 *Cognition*

Propositional predicates of the subdomain of cognition are further divided into predicates of knowledge and of propositional attitude according to their behavior in subordination.

7.3.1 *Knowledge*

Predicates of (the acquisition of) knowledge typically occur with propositions that are taken as facts by the speaker and that involve ITR according to Noonan (1985). Complements of knowledge predicates (contrary to commentative predicates, cf. sect. 7.4.1) are often part of the new information and are thus asserted along with the matrix predicate. Similarly to situations of perception, situations of knowledge may show DRef or SRef.

Ohel 'know', *k'a'h(s)* 'remember', *tu'b(s)* 'forget', *náayt* 'dream', and *wayáak't* 'dream' belong to the YM predicates of knowledge. Predicates of the acquisition of knowledge such as Engl. *discover*, *realize*, etc. seem to be less frequent in YM; one YM example is the verbalized form of *ohel* which is used with the meaning 'find out, come to know, learn'. YM combines predicates of knowledge with independent clauses as 'semantic' complements conveying ITR (348).

(348) a. *A   w-ohel   yàan   u   xikin   túunich ...*
         SBJ.2 0-knowledge [EXIST POSS.3 ear   rock]$_{VCl}$
         'You know that the stones have ears (= can hear), (...)'
         (HTS'ON_008)

      b. *T-in   wayáak't-ah*
         PFV-SBJ.1.SG   dream-CMPL
         tíin   na'k-al   teh   ka'n-o'.
         [PROG:SBJ.1.SG climb-INCMPL   LOC:DEF   sky-D2]$_{VCl}$
         'I dreamt I was going up to the sky.' (RMC_1398)

      c. *H   tu'b   tèen   k'abéet   in*
         PFV   forget me   [necessary   SBJ.1.SG
         man-ik   hun-p'éel   ch'óoy ...
         buy-INCMPL one-CL.INAN   bucket]$_{VCl}$
         'I forgot that I have to buy a bucket (...)' (BVS_07.01.12.01)

If the knowledge predicate is negated the complementizer *wáah* must be inserted, introducing the independent complement clause (349) (cf. also (120b)).

(349)   *Maria-e'   ma' y-ohel   wáah ts'o'k   u*
        Maria-TOP NEG SBJ.3-knowledge [if   TERM   SBJ.3
        y-u'l-ul   u   y-íicham-i'.
        0-come.home-INCMPL   POSS.3   0-spouse-NEGF]$_{VCl}$
        'Maria does not know that her husband has already come home.'
        (AEF_0049)

Some of the knowledge predicates occur in other construction types as well which may lead to a change in meaning. Some of the predicates of (the acquisition of) knowledge such as *náayt* 'dream', *wayáak't* 'dream' also occur with an incompletive-marked verbal core under SRef and DRef. In (350a) *náayt* refers to the world of an actual dream that has taken place within this reality, conveyed by an independent clause with ITR. (350b) shows that *náayt* may also refer to a figurative sense of dream related to a wish. In this sense the proposition refers to an imagined 'reality', similar to propositions related to volitive emotion predicates (cf. sect. 7.4.2). In this sense *náayt* takes an incompletive-marked subordinate core in direct object function. Finally, (350c) shows that an incompletive-marked verbal core is possible with actual dreams as well, similar to (350a). Since it conveys DTR, the temporal reference of the subordinate proposition in this case is inferred from the matrix predicate.

(350) a. *T-in   náay-t-ah   tíin   bis-ik*
       PFV-SBJ.1.SG dream-TRR-CMPL [PROG:SBJ.1.SG carry-INCMPL
      in   chan   xibpal.
      POSS.1.SG   little   man:child]$_{VCl}$
      'I dreamt that I took my little boy with me.' (EMB)

    b. *K-in   náay-t-ik*
      IMPF-SBJ.1.SG dream-TRR-INCMPL
      in   bis-ik   in   chan   xibpal.
      [SBJ.1.SG carry-INCMPL POSS.1.SG   little   man:child]$_{VCo}$
      'I dream taking/to take my little boy with me.' (EMB)

    c. *T-in   náay-t-ah   u   k'áax-al   ha'.*
      PFV-SBJ.1.SG dream-TRR-CMPL [SBJ.3   rain-INCMPL water]$_{VCo}$
      'I dreamt it rained.' (EMB)

Thus, it may be concluded that for some knowledge predicates an incompletive-marked verbal core may substitute an independent clause if time reference is identical with that established by the matrix predicate. Some items, such as, e.g., *ohel(t)* 'know', are, however, not compatible with an incompletive-marked verbal core. Furthermore, a *káa*-clause is generally incompatible with the knowledge predicates introduced here.

Other verbs, like intransitive *tu'b* 'forget' and *k'a'h* 'remember', take an incompletive-marked verbal core only under SRef (351). In this construction type they behave like implicative predicates[2] in the sense of Karttunen (1971), and refer to the manner or reason of realization (or failure of realization) of the complement proposition, which therefore has DTR.

---

[2] Noonan (1985:129) classifies these as achievement predicates (together with *dare, manage, try, fail, avoid* etc.).

(351) a. *H   tu'b/   k'a'h   ti'*
           PFV   forget/ remember LOC
       u   bis-ik   u   kib-il   le   uk'ul-o'.
       [SBJ.3   carry-INCMPL   SBJ.3   candle-REL   DEF   drink-D2]$_{VCl}$
       'He forgot/ remembered to bring the candle of the drink.'
       (ACC_0283)

    b. *K'a'náan a   k'a'hs-ik   a   bis-ik*
       necessary SBJ.2   remember:CAUS-INCMPL   [SBJ.2   carry-INCMPL
       a   màanal-o'.
       SBJ.2   buy\INTRV-D2]$_{VCo}$
       'It is necessary that you remember to take your purchase with you.'
       (ACC_0300)

Causative *k'a'hs* 'remind' takes an incompletive-marked verbal core as does
(352). Here the indirect object is referentially identical with the subject of the
subordinate clause. This construction contrasts with that of control verbs which
take a 'split' pattern core under SRef (cf., e.g., the construction of *túucht* 'send'
in (134)). *K'a'hs* 'remind' may alternatively take a *káa*-clause, a behavior that
seems to be due to its purpose semantics.

(352)   *K-in   k'a'h-s-ik   ti'   Pedro*
         IMPF-SBJ.1.SG   remember-CAUS-INCMPL   LOC   Pedro
         u   bin   u   xíimba-t-eh   Maria.
         [SBJ.3   go   [SBJ.3   walk-TRR-SUBJ   Maria]$_{VCo}$]$_{VCo}$
         /káa   xi'k   u   xíimba-t   Maria.
         [that   go:SUBJ   [SBJ.3   walk-TRR(SUBJ)   Maria]$_{VCo}$]$_{VCl}$
         'I remind Pedro to go to visit Maria.' (ACC)

There are at least two propositional predicates of the knowledge type, that
take a 'split' pattern core (under SRef, DRef necessarily involves an independent clause), namely, *ohel(t)* 'know'(353) and *kan* 'learn'. In the case of *ohel*,
the modal meaning of ability ('can', 'be able') or habituality 'be used to' is
conveyed.[3]

(353) a. *Le   nohoch màak-o'   u   y-ohel   páats'.*
           DEF   big   person-D2   SBJ.3   0-know   [massage]$_{SFVCo}$
       'That old man knows to massage.' (SBM_0278)

---

[3] The development of the meaning of ability from the source 'know' is rather widespread in the
languages of the world and instantiates a case where a modal meaning develops from an experiential meaning. In the specific case of *ohel* it may well be a hispanism.

    b. *u   y-ohel   u   páats'-t   u*
       SBJ.3 0-know [SBJ.3 massage-TRR(SUBJ) POSS.3
       k'ab màak
       hand person]$_{VCo}$
       'he knows to massage people's hands' (SBM_0279)

(354) a. *Ts'-in   kan-ik   xòok.*
        TERM-SBJ.1.SG learn-INCMPL [read\INTRV]$_{SFVCo}$
        'I've learned to read.' (EMB)

      b. *Ts'in   kan-ik*
        TERM-SBJ.1.SG learn-INCMPL
        in   xok   lìibro/tàak'in.
        [SBJ.1.SG read(SUBJ) book/money]$_{VCo}$
        'I've learned to read books/count money.' (EMB)

Summarizing the behavior of knowledge predicates in subordination, it can be concluded that in their basic meaning they generally take an independent clause as their complement. Time reference and person reference are then independent. Combination with one of the 'reduced' patterns results in different kinds of meaning shifts, such as volitive or purposive meaning (350b), implicative meaning (351), (352) or modal meaning (353), (354). The 'reduced' patterns always show SRef.

7.3.2 *Propositional attitude*

A propositional attitude communicates a commitment of the experiencer towards the truth of the complement proposition. YM complement clauses of these predicates may be independent clauses conveying ITR (355) or incompletive-marked verbal cores with DTR (356). Construction options depend partly on the matrix predicate. While *tukul/tùukult* 'think' is possible with both types, *bèey POSS óol/t'àan* 'think, be of the opinion' only occurs with independent subordinate clauses as propositional stimulus. If the complement is an incompletive-marked verbal core, its time reference is necessarily dependent on the matrix predicate and understood to be simultaneous or following the reference point given in it.

(355) a. *Yùum Nasàario-e'   t-u   tukul-t-ah*
        lord   Nasario-TOP   PFV-SBJ.3 think-TRR-CMPL
        ts'o'k   u   k'am-ik   u   meyah ...
        [TERM SBJ.3 receive-INCMPL POSS.3 work]$_{VCI}$
        'Nasario thought that he (already) had got his work (...)'
        (HNAZ_0034.01)

   b. *Sahak hóok'ol,   bèey   y-óol-e'*
      afraid exit-INCMPL thus   POSS.3-mind-TOP
      he'l   u   y-il-ik   u   y-iicham-e'.
      [DEF.FUT SBJ.3   0-see-INCMPL POSS.3 0-spouse-D3]ᵥCᵢ
      'she is afraid of going out (because) she thinks that she will meet
      her husband' (ACC_0428)

(356)   *Bix   kan   a   tukult*
        how   SR.FUT:SBJ.2   SBJ.2   think(SUBJ)
        in   p'at-ik-ech?
        [SBJ.1.SG   leave-INCMPL-ABS.2.SG]ᵥCₒ
        'How is it (possible) that you think that I (will) leave you?'
        (HNAZ_0069.02)

In YM there seem to be only one verb of propositional attitude: *tu-
kul/tùukult* 'think', used interchangeably in the basic and transitivized form.
Along with *tukul/tùukult*, which is by itself very polysemous (also conveying
'imagination', 'plan', 'concern', etc., cf. below), the primary communication
verb *a'l* 'say' is used to convey propositional attitude in a fixed first person expression.[4] As an expression of propositional attitude it always combines with
independent clauses (357).

(357)   *Tahlak yah-il   in   wiinklal,*
        aching   ache-ADVR POSS.1.SG body
        in   w-a'l-ik-e'   muka'h-en   x-chokwil.
        SBJ.1.SG   0-say-INCMPL-CNTR [PROSP-ABS.1.SG F-fever]ᵥCᵢ
        'My body feels really painful, I think I am going to have a fever.'
        (RMC_2267)

Unlike other languages, YM does not use the incompletive/subjunctive distinction to indicate positive vs. negative propositional attitude (cf. Noonan
1985:95, 115). YM can use an incompletive-marked verbal core in both cases
(358).

(358) a. *K-in   tukl-ik   u   tàal.*
         IMPF-SBJ.1.SG   think-INCMPL [SBJ.3 come]ᵥCₒ
         'I think he comes/he'll come.' (ACC)

---

[4] This phenomenon of displaying just one predicate of propositional attitude also seems to be
recurrent in other languages (cf. Noonan 1985:114). Further nuances of commitment are then
expressed by adverbs or sentence particles.

    b. *Mi'n*   *tukl-ik*   *u*   *tàal.*
       NEG.PROG:SBJ.1.SG think-INCMPL [SBJ.3 come]$_{VCo}$
       'I don't think he comes/he'll come.' (ACC)

Instead, it is the choice of an incompletive-marked verbal core vs. a *káa*-clause which indicates the different degrees of commitment to the truth/occurrence of the subordinate proposition. In (359a), the experiencer (identical to the speaker) is more sure about the actual occurrence (which may be simultaneous or in the near future with respect to the time of utterance) of the situation denoted in the subordinate core than in (359b). In (358) and (359) *tukul* can also have the reading 'fear, be concerned'. However, note that it does not show the typical pattern of volitive emotion predicates (cf. sect. 7.4.2). Even with this meaning, *tukul* cannot be combined with a 'split' pattern core. Primary *fear*-predicates, on the contrary, cannot be combined with an incompletive-marked verbal core under DRef, but instead need a *káa*-clause under this condition, which will be described in sect. 7.4.2.2.

  (359) a. *K-in*   *tukl-ik*   *u*   *k'áax-al*   *ha'.*
        IMPF-SBJ.1.SG think-INCMPL [SBJ.3 rain-INCMPL water]$_{VCo}$
        'I think/fear it is raining/going to rain.' (ACC, NMP, EMB)
      b. *K-in*   *tukl-ik*   *káa* *k'áax-ak* *ha'.*
        IMPF-SBJ.1.SG think-INCMPL [that rain-SUBJ water]$_{VCI}$
        'I think/fear it could rain.' (ACC, NMP, EMB)

When *tukul/tùukult* is combined with an incompletive-marked verbal core under SRef, its meaning shifts from 'propositional attitude' to 'plan'. This meaning is dealt with in sect. 7.4.2.1. For an example see (383a).

    As has been said above, *tukul/tùukult* is used in contexts of imagination as well. Despite referring to a non-real world, it does not take a subjunctive *káa*-clause with this meaning, but rather an independent clause conveying ITR (360). This behavior fits Noonan's observations for Russian and Spanish: neither uses the subjunctive mood in complement clauses after predicates meaning 'pretend' or similar meanings but rather take indicative complement clauses (cf. Noonan 1985:116).

  (360)   *K-in*   *tukl-ik-e'*   *túun*   *tàal.*
        IMPF-SBJ.1.SG think-INCMPL-CNTR [PROG:SBJ.3come]$_{VCI}$
        'I imagine that he comes.' (ACC)

To summarize the subordination patterns of predicates of propositional attitude, it can be seen that the respective predicates combine primarily with an independent subordinate clause. The most frequent verb conveying propositional attitude *tùukul(t)* 'think' may take in addition an incompletive-marked verbal core without changing its basic meaning, whereas *bèey Poss óol* 'think, be of the opinion' and the aforementioned fixed expression with *a'l* 'say' combine exclusively with independent subordinate clauses.

7.4   *Emotion and Volition*

Emotion and volition predicates are treated here together in their function as complement taking predicates, since a group of the emotion predicates clusters with volition predicates in their subordination behavior. The main distinction in the present section is between commentative[5] emotion predicates on the one hand and volition and volitive emotion predicates on the other hand. The first group contains predicates that are comments on presupposed or factive situations in the sense of Kiparsky and Kiparsky 1970. Predicates of the second group do not allow for such a reading. Rather they typically impose the truth status unreal/potential on the subordinate proposition.

This distinction can be related to Bolinger's distinction between "emotions caused and emotions projected" which goes back to his investigation of English emotion predicates as propositional predicates (cf. Bolinger 1984:52) and the refinements concering projective emotions made in Wierzbicka (1988:98ff.). "Emotions caused" are reactions to propositional stimuli while "emotions projected" express an attitude towards a situation. This can be seen in (361) where (361a/b) exemplify emotional reactions to a fact while (361c/d) exemplify attitudes towards situations.

> (361) a. *I am glad that I heard the news.*
>   b. *I am sorry that Peter is not here.*
>   c. *I am sorry/glad to hear the news.*
>   d. *I am afraid to fall asleep.*

Wierzbicka (1988:98) accounts for the difference between cases like (361c) and (361d) by introducing the distinction between "emotions based on awareness" and "emotions based on wanting", for the mentioned examples respectively.

The following investigation of YM complementation patterns with emotion and volition predicates will show this distinction to be crucial: commentative emotion predicates on the one hand (cf. sect. 7.4.1) are either reactions to factive propositions or they express an attitude towards a proposition. This distinction is then reflected in different subordination patterns. Volition and volitive emotion predicates, on the other hand, (cf. sect. 7.4.2) convey an atti-

---

[5] This term is introduced for this group of propositional predicates in Noonan 1985.

tude concerning the realization of the subordinate proposition based on positive or negative will. These predicates show yet another prevailing subordination pattern distinct from those patterns prevalent with commentative emotion predicates.

7.4.1 *Commentative emotion*

Emotional predicates classified here as commentative include predicates conveying either an emotional reaction, or an emotional judgment or evaluation with respect to the subordinate proposition. Following the semantic nature of a commentative predicate, the truth status of the subordinate proposition is prototypically real and presupposed. The type of time reference is prototypically ITR and there is no specification or default for the DRef or SRef value. Furthermore, commentative emotion predicates may combine with reduced complement clauses such as nominalizations, infinitives, etc., which involve DTR. In such constructions the comment may pertain to 'any potential occurrence' of the proposition embodied in the subordinate clause (cf. Noonan 1985:117). In the following paragraphs, the subordinative patterns occurring with YM commentative emotion predicates and the semantics associated with each pattern will be discussed.

In YM commentative emotion predicates combine with independent subordinate clauses conveying ITR (362).

(362) a. *Ki'mak u   y-óol*
        happy   POSS.3 0-mind
        ts'-u   k'uch-ul   a   w-íits'in.
        [TERM-SBJ.3 arrive-INCMPL POSS.2 0-younger.sibling]$_{VCI}$
        'He is happy that your younger brother has arrived.' (HIJO_145)

    b. *Táan   in   yahóol-t-ik   ma'   táan   u*
        PROG   SBJ.1.SG ache:mind-TRR-INCMPL [NEG   PROG SBJ.3.SG
        páah-tal   in   bin   báaxal   sáamal.
        possible-PROC [SBJ.1.SG   go   play   tomorrow]$_{VCo}$]$_{VCI}$
        'I regret that I cannot go playing tomorrow.' (ACC)

    c. *Su'lak-en   ts'o'k   in   tus-ik-ech.*
        ashamed-ABS.1.SG [TERM SBJ.1.SG lie-INCMPL-ABS.2.SG]$_{VCI}$
        'I am ashamed that I have betrayed you.' (ACC)

As an alternative to the method of construction shown in (362), consultants propose introducing the second clause with the conjunction *úuch(ik)* 'by (the fact that)', which is a possibly grammaticalized form of the verb *úuch* 'happen', either in its incompletive or in its completive form (363).

(363) a. *Hach   uts'   t-in   t'àan*
      really   good   LOC-POSS.1.SG   speech
      úuch   in   kan-ik.
      [by.means.of   SBJ.1.SG   learn-INCMPL]$_{VCI}$
      'I was really glad having learned it. (UUCHUL_24)

    b. *T-in   yahóol-t-ah   úuch   u*
      PFV-SBJ.1.SG   ache:mind-TRR-CMPL   [by.means.of   SBJ.3
      p'at-ik-en   in   nobia.
      leave-INCMPL-ABS.1.SG   POSS.1.SG   girlfriend]$_{VCI}$
      'It hurt me very much that my girlfriend left me.' (EMB_0509)

    c. *In   p'èek   úuchik   a   tus-ik   a   tàatah.*
      SBJ.1.SG dislike [by.means.of SBJ.1.SG lie-CMPL   POSS.2   father]$_{VCI}$
      'I dislike that you have betrayed your father.' (ACC)

Alongside the mentioned subordinate constructions, commentative emotion predicates can also be combined with incompletive-marked verbal cores in complement function. This applies to the transitive verbs and verboids *yah-óolt* 'regret', *p'èek(t)* 'hate, dislike', *ch'a'p'èekt* 'hate', *muk'yaht* 'suffer, feel'. It also holds true for the intransitive verb *náak' ti'* 'feel, grieve', for the adjective *chi'chnak* 'cross, furious', and for the adjective based collocations *ki'(mak) POSS óol* 'happy', *yah ti' POSS óol* 'sorry, sad', *uts' ti' POSS t'àan/ich* 'like, please'.

(364) a. *Hach   ki'mak   in   w-óol*
      really   happy   POSS.1.SG   0-mind
      in   w-il-ik-ech!
      [SBJ.1.SG   0-see-INCMPL- ABS.2.SG]$_{VCo}$
      'I am very happy to see you!' (BVS_01.01.06)

    b. *K-in   yah-óol-t-ik*
      IMPF-SBJ.1.SG   ache-mind-TRR-INCMPL
      u   tóok-a'l   le   k'áax-o'.
      [SBJ.3   burn-PASS.INCMPL   DEF   jungle-D2]$_{VCo}$
      'I regret very much for the jungle to be burned down.'
      (EMB_0690)

    c. *Chi'chnak-en*
      cross-ABS.1.SG
      in/u   w/y-il-ik   in/u   x-ka'na'.
      [SBJ.1/3.SG   0/0-see-INCMPL POSS.1/3.SG   F-two:mother]$_{VCo}$
      'I am feeling uneasy/bad seeing my stepmother/that he sees his stepmother.' (ACC)

The examples in (364b/c) show that this construction is possible with DRef as well as with SRef. However, some matrix predicates are semantically restricted in that they do not add an incompletive-marked verbal core under DRef (cf. e.g. *ki'(mak)* POSS *óol* 'happy'in (365) and *su'lak* in (366)). These may insert the perception verb *il* 'see' to account for the SRef demand. In such a way these matrix predicates can be related to the DRef situation indirectly via the perception verb.

(365)   *Ki'mak in   w-óol *(in   w-il-ik)*
        happy   POSS.1.SG 0-mind [SBJ.1.SG   0-see-INCMPL
        u   k'áaxal   ha'.
        [SBJ.3.SG   rain-INCMPL   water]$_{VCo}$]$_{VCo}$
        'I am happy to see that it is raining.' (ACC, RMC)

(366) a.*Su'lak-en   u   káal-tal   in   ìihóoh.*
        ashamed-ABS.1.SG [SBJ.3   drunk-PROC POSS.1.SG   son]$_{VCo}$
        intended: 'I feel ashamed that my son is drinking' (ACC, NMP)
   b. *Su'lak-en   in   w-il-ik*
        ashamed-ABS.1.SG [SBJ.1.SG 0-see-INCMPL
        u   káal-tal   in   ìihóoh
        [SBJ.3 drunk-PROC POSS.1.SG   son]$_{VCo}$]$_{VCo}$
        'I am feeling ashamed seeing that my son is drinking' (NMP)

Using perception verbs in this function has an evidential basis. However, the perception verb is not only a semantic 'bridge' to the subordinated situation, but also a syntactic one. Perception verbs in their immediate perception sense only/always take incompletive-marked verbal cores. Remember the analysis of *sùuk ti'* 'accustomed to' in sect. 6.4 with respect to (330) and (331) 'bridging' the DRef situation in the subordinate clause.

Another group of experiential predicates takes an incompletive-marked verbal core in direct object function. These are perception/sensation verbs taking an evaluative secondary predicate (cf. Construction 34). They inherit the subordination construction with an incompletive-marked verbal core from the immediate perception construction that was introduced in sect. 7.2 with respect to (340)ff. (367) gives some examples.[6]

---

[6] Note that the structure in (367b) is ambiguous between a nominal and a verbal analysis given that a number of intransitive verbs of the active class have the same shape in their incompletive aspect as the respective nouns (cf. Lehmann 1993[P]).

(367) a. *Yàan   bin   u   mùuk',   ma'   yah   y-il-ik*
         EXIST QUOT POSS.3   strength   NEG   ache   SBJ.3-see-INCMPL
         u   kach-la'n-t-ik   che'-o'b-i' ...
         [SBJ.3   break.apart-DISTR-TRR-INCMPL   tree-PL]$_{VCo}$-NEGF
         'He had strength, it did not hurt him/he did not find it difficult to
         break apart all the wood, (...)' (HK'AN_143.1)
      b. *Ki'óotsil   in   w-u'y-ik*
         pleasant   SBJ.1.SG   0-feel-INCMPL
         u   pàax   le   konhùunto-a'.
         [SBJ/POSS.3 play   DEF   group-D1]$_{VCo}$
         'I find it very moving to listen to the music/play of this group'.
         (RMC_1794)

Now the question arises as to what difference in meaning is associated with
the choice of an incompletive-marked verbal clause as opposed to an independent subordinate clause if it appears as a complement to a commentative
emotion predicate. An independent subordinate clause is always taken as a fact
to be commented on by the experiential predicate while an incompletive-
marked verbal clause generally represents an actual or potential occurrence of
the designated situation, which is commented on by the predicate. This difference can be seen by comparing (362a/b) with (364a/b). The incompletive-
marked verbal clause in (364a) is most likely to be understood as an actual occurrence of the proposition, while the incompletive-marked verbal clause in
(364b) can (also) be understood as a potential occurrence of the proposition.
Thus, if emotional predicates such as *ki'mak POSS óol* 'happy', *yah POSS óol*
'regret', etc. combine with an incompletive-marked verbal core, they convey
an emotional or evaluative attitude towards an actual or potential occurrence of
the proposition, while combination with an independent clause constitutes a
comment on a presupposed/factive situation.

Other propositional predicates from the group of emotional lexemes are
generally judged as bad when combined with an incompletive-marked verbal
core. This applies to the adjectives *ts'iik* 'furious, angry', *p'úuha'n* 'cross,
peeved', *ts'iikil-óol* 'furious, angry', and *lúub-óol* 'disappointed, depressed'.
These are constructed with independent clauses as in (368) and (369), i.e. they
can only constitute comments on presupposed/factive situations.

(368)   *Ts'iik-en /   p'úuh-a'n-en*
         furious-ABS.1.SG/   cross-RSLTV-ABS.1.SG
         **(táan)   in   w-il-ik   in   x-ka'na'.*
         [PROG   SBJ.1.SG   0-see-INCMPL   POSS.1.SG   F-two:mother]$_{VCI}$
         'I am furious/peeved that I am seeing my second mother.' (ACC)

(369)   *Lúub-óol-en*   *(*úuchik*)   *in*   *kíins-ik*
         fall-mind-ABS.1.SG   [by.means.of SBJ.1.SG   kill-INCMPL
         in   *chan   àalak'*   *pèek'.*
         POSS.1.SG little   CL.domestic1dog]vcɪ
         'I was very sad that I killed my little dog.' (ACC)

An incompletive-marked verbal core contrasts with a *káa*-subordinative
clause after some predicates of emotional or evaluative attitude. The pairs of
examples in (370) and (371) show that while the incompletive-marked verbal
cores in (370a)/(371a) again attain either an actual or a potential reading;
(370b)/(371b) are comments on hypothetical situations. Moreover, they make
clear that there is no difference in SRef vs. DRef in construction options.

(370) a. *Uts   t-in*   *t'àan   u*   *k'áax-al   ha'.*
          good LOC-POSS.1.SG   speech [SBJ.3   rain-INCMPL water]vCₒ
          'I like that it is raining / I like it to rain.' (ACC)

       b. *Uts t-in*   *t'àan   káa   k'áax-ak   ha'.*
          goodLOC-POSS.1.SG   speech [that   rain-SUBJ   water]vCɪ
          'I would like if/that it will rain / rained.' (ACC)

(371) a. *Uts   t-in*   *t'àan   u/*   *in*   *bin   Cancun.*
          good LOC-POSS.1.SG   speech [SBJ.3/ SBJ.1.SG   go   Cancún]vCₒ
          'I like him to go to Cancun/ I like to go/ going to Cancún.' (ACC)

       b. *Uts   t-in*   *t'àan*
          good LOC-POSS.1.SG   speech
          (*wáah*) *káa   xi'k/*   *xi'k-en*   *Cancun.*
          [(if)   that   go:SUBJ/ go:SUBJ-ABS.1.SG   Cancún]vCɪ
          'I would like if/that he/I went to Cancún.' (ACC)

Evaluative expressions containing perception verbs as matrix verbs (cf. (367)
above) cannot be combined with a *káa*-clause, so these only allow an actual or
potential interpretation of their 'embedded' proposition (372).[7]

---

[7] There is one exception to this. If the perception verb itself is modified so that the matrix clause has an irreal meaning, then a *káa*-clause is possible. See the following example:

Ba'li'   *k-in*   *w-il   káa   xi'k   te'x*   *uts-il-e'*!
how.many   IMPF-SBJ.1.SG   0-see   that   go:SUBJ you.all   good-ADVR-D3
'I wished I could see that you are fine!' (RMC_0168)

(372) a. *Hach   uts   in   w-il-ik*
      really good   SBJ.1.SG   0-see-INCMPL
      u   tàal   Pedro.
      [SBJ.3 come(INCMPL) Pedro]$_{VCo}$
      'I like (seeing) that Pedro comes/will come.' (ACC)

   b.*Hach   uts   in   w-il-ik*
      really good   SBJ.1.SG   0-see-INCMPL
      káa   tàak   Pedro.
      [that   come(SUBJ)   Pedro]$_{VCl}$
      intended: 'I would like (to see) if/that Pedro would come.' (ACC)

Now, lets take a look at two other groups of putative propositional predicates in the domain of emotion, which take the stimulus, (i.e. the proposition)
in subject function: causative emotion verbs and collocations (sect. 5.3.2.2 and
sect. 5.3.2.2.2.) and stimulus-oriented evaluative adjectives (sect. 5.2.1.4). In
principal members of both groups show the same range of subordination patterns that have been discussed before. (373) is an example of a causative emotion verb taking an independent subordinate clause in stimulus function.

(373)   *K-u   p'u'hs-ik-en*
      IMPF-SBJ.3   get.mad:CAUS-INCMPL-ABS.1.SG
      yan   a   tàal   way-e'.
      [DEB   SBJ.2 come here-D3]$_{VCl}$
      'It bothers me that you will come here.' (ACC)

(374) exemplifies a causative verb and a causative collocation taking a an incompletive-marked verbal core in stimulus function.

(374) a. *K-u   náays-ik   in   w-óol*
      IMPF-SBJ.3   calm.down:CAUS POSS.1.SG 0-mind
      u   k'áaxal   ha'.
      [SBJ.3 rain-INCMPL water]$_{VCo}$
      'It entertains/distracts me that it is raining.' (ACC)

   b. *K-u   sahak-kuns-ik-en*
      IMPF-SBJ.3   afraid-FACT-INCMPL-ABS.1.SG
      a   tàal   way-e'.
      [SBJ.2   come   here-D3]$_{VCo}$
      'It makes me afraid that you come here.' (ACC)

Further such verbs and collocations are *ki'makuns/t* POSS *óol* 'delight', *ha's*
POSS *óol* 'scare, frighten; cause admiration/impression', *hets'* POSS *óol* 'calm,

appease', *náaks* POSS *óol* 'bore, annoy', *péeks* POSS *óol* 'disturb, worry', *sahbes* 'frighten', *p'u'hs* 'bother, scare, make angry', *ts'íikkun* 'bother', *chi'chnakkun* 'disturb, bother', *su'lakkun* 'abash, embarrass', *sahakkun* 'frighten'.

Note that in (374)[8] the object or possessor-experiencer in the matrix predication is not referentially identical to the subject argument of the subordinate clause. Such a constellation of referential identity is judged as bad by most of my consultants (375a/b) and they propose alternative constructions with the respective base or intransitive predicates as matrix predicates (375a'/b').

(375) a.[?/]*K-u*   ki'mak-kuns-ik*   *in*   *w-óol*
     IMPF-SBJ.3   happy-FACT-INCMPL POSS.1.SG   0-mind
     (*in*)   *bin   Cancun*.
     [(SBJ.1.SG) go   Cancun]$_{(SF)VCo}$
     intended: 'It makes me happy to go to Cancun.' (NMP, RMC)

    a'.*Ki'mak in*   *w-óol   in*   *bin   Cancun*.
     happy   POSS.1.SG 0-mind [SBJ.1.SG go   Cancun]$_{VCo}$
     'I am happy going to Cancun.' (RMC)

    b.[?/]*K-u*   sahak-kuns-ik-en*
     IMPF-SBJ.3   afraid-FACT-INCMPL-ABS.1.SG
     (*in*)   *bin   Cancun*.
     [SBJ.1.SG go   Cancun]$_{(SF)VCo}$
     intended: 'It makes me afraid to go to Cancun'
     (ACC, NMP, SME, RMC)

    b'.*K-in*   sahak-tal   bin   Cancun*.
     IMPF-SBJ.1.SG afraid-PROC [go   Cancun]$_{SFVCo}$
     'I am afraid going to Cancun.' (ACC, RMC, SME)

The bases of the mentioned causative verbs belong to the commentative (375a') as well as the volitive type of matrix predicates (375b'). The latter type displays a 'split' pattern subordinate core under SRef, as will be shown in more detail in sect. 7.4.2. The causative derivation changes the semantics of the bases to the effect that the derived verbs join the class of the commentative predicates. They display the same range of subordination patterns as the commentative predicates do. (376) shows that a *káa*-clause, if it is accompanied by *wáah*, can follow a causative commentative matrix predicate.

---

[8] Some of the examples discussed in the reminder of this section have been checked by Jürgen Bohnemeyer which is greatfully acknowledged.

(376) *K-u*   *chi'chnak-kuns-ik-en*
       IMPF-SBJ.3   stir-INCMPL-ABS.1.SG
       wáah   káa   tàak   way-e'.
       [if   that   come:SUBJ   here-D3]$_{VCl}$
       'It makes me uncomfortable if he comes here.' (ACC)

(377) gives examples of a stimulus-oriented evaluative adjective as matrix
predicate occurring with all three complementation patterns discussed before.
Remember that such adjectives generally do not adjoin the experiencer as has
been described in sect. 5.2.1.4. Rather, the experiencer is understood to be identical to the speaker.

(377) a. *Ma'lòob   ts'o'k   a   tàal   way-e'.*
         good   [TERM   SBJ.2   come   here-D3]$_{VCl}$
         'It is good that you (already) have come here.' (ACC)

      b. *Ma'lòob   a   tàal   way-e'.*
         good   [SBJ.2   come   here-D3]$_{VCo}$
         'It is good that you come here.' (ACC)

      c. *Ma'lòob $^?$(wáah)   káa   tàak-ech   way-e'.*
         good   [(if)   that   come:SUBJ-ABS.2.SG   here-D3]$_{VCl}$
         'It would be good if/that you came/would come here.' (ACC)

Finally, there are emotional predicative expressions that for different reasons do not function as propositional predicates at all. First, there are a number
of predicates that do not take propositional stimuli for semantic reasons. Some
of these demand non-propositional stimuli, namely, *yàabilt* 'love', *yàakunt*
'love, care for'. Others may adjoin propositional clauses in a causal or temporal relation: *k'ùux(il(t))* 'get angry about', *ch'a' k'ùuxil* 'get annoyed',
ch'a'k'ùux(t) 'be angry at, hate', *hets'óol, hets'* (*POSS óol/POSS báah*) 'calm,
tranquil', *kaxt POSS báah* 'desperate', *háak'(a'n) POSS óol/háak'óol* 'be frightened, astonished', *péek POSS óol/péek-óol* 'get frightened; to be ill at ease'.
Thus, these do not function as complements to the respective predicates. Furthermore, intransitive verbs generally do not take subordinate clauses if there is
a derived transitive form (e.g., *ch'a'p'èek*) and neither intransitive nor transitive verbs take subordinate clauses if there is an adjectival base form (e.g.,
ki'maktal POSS óol, ki'makóoltik POSS báah, ts'íikil(t)).[9]
To summarize complementation patterns with commentative emotion predicates it can be noted that there are two major cases. First, these predicates may

---

[9] Note that this applies to experiencer- and part-oriented predicates. Stimulus-oriented predicates that are derived causatives are used as matrix predicates, as has been shown before.

combine with an independent clause to give an emotional comment on a pre-supposed or factive proposition. Second, they may take an incompletive-marked verbal core constituting a comment on an actual or a potential situation. Finally, it has been shown that some emotional predicates may also take a *káa*-clause, which codes a hypothetical situation that is commented on.

7.4.2 *Volition and volitive emotion*

As introduced in sect. 7.4, predicates containing an aspect of volition will be discussed here together because of their common behavior in subordination. Following Noonan (1985) desiderative predicates must be distinguished from predicates of fearing. Predicates conveying the attitude of interest/will or re-pugnance with respect to the realization of the subordinate proposition also be-long here. This group of complement taking predicates can be characterized as prototypically occurring with the most 'grammatical' complementation con-struction in a SRef constellation, namely, with the 'split' pattern core/complex. DRef leads to diverse types of more complex constructions. Nevertheless, there are also differences among this group of voliton and volitive emotion predi-cates. These concern the mentioned subgroups of desiderative vs. fear vs. in-terest predicates and each will be discussed in turn.

7.4.2.1 *Desire*

Desiderative predicates express a desire with respect to the subordinate propo-sition to be realized. Noonan (1985:121ff.) classifies desiderative predicates into three subgroups, each showing a characteristic behavior which is based on their individual semantics. The three types differ as to whether or not they can be applied to past situations or exclusively to future situations. The *hope*-class is characterized by the possibility of combining with complement clauses showing ITR. The *wish*-group can also be combined with ITR complement clauses, but a past reference of the complement clause normally results in a contrafactive reading under the matrix predicates meaning 'wish'. Finally predicates of the *want*-class take complement clauses with DTR, and the possi-bility of the realization of the situation expressed in the complement clause is bound to the future. *Want*-constructions are possible with both SRef and DRef. This latter criterion distinguishes the *want*-class from the interest predicates to be discussed in sect. 7.4.2.3, which are only possible with SRef.

Desiderative meanings are expressed in YM by *tàak* 'be anxious, want', *k'áat*[10]'want, wish', *óot* 'agree, accept, be willing', *ts'íibóol(t)* 'wish, desire', *k'áat-óolt* 'solicit, wish' and *pa't* 'wait, hope'. *Tàak* and *óot* belong to the *want*-group. They can only refer to a situation with future reference (378).

---

[10] Following an observation in Dixon (1995:215) *k'áat* 'want, wish' is cross-linguistically typi-cal in that it displays different subordination patterns according to SRef vs. DRef (cf. (126), (128)), contrary to English which uses an infinitive complement in both constellations.

(378) *Tíin   w-óot-ik-e'   h   tàal-ih.
       PROG-SBJ.1.SG   0-agree-INCMPL-CNTR   [PFV   come-ABS.3.SG]$_{VCI}$
       lit. 'I agree that he has come.' (NMP)

Among the mentioned desiderative predicates, *pa't* 'wait, hope' is the only one to combine with an independent clause referring to a past situation. Note that, in contrast to independent clauses subordinated to commentative emotion predicates, the truth status of the subordinate proposition in (379) is not presupposed/factive.

(379) Tíin   pa't-ik-e'   h   tàal-ih.
       PROG-SBJ.1.SG   wait-INCMPL-CNTR   [PFV   come-ABS.3.SG]$_{VCI}$
       'I hope he has come.' (ACC)

Ts'iibóolt 'wish, desire' and *k'áat* 'want, wish' fit with the *wish*-group by taking an independent complement clause, resulting in a contrafactive interpretation (380).

(380) a. *K-in*   ts'ibóol-t-ik
         IMPF-SBJ.1.SG   write:soul-TRR-INCMPL
         $^?$(wáah) ts'o'k   u   tàal   way-e'.
         [if   TERM   SBJ.3   come   here-D3]$_{VCI}$
         'I wished he had already come here.' (ACC)
      b. *In*   k'áat   ts'o'k   u   tàal   in   tàatah.
         SBJ.1.SG   wish   [TERM   SBJ.3   come   POSS.1.SG   father]$_{VCI}$
         'I wished my father had come.' (ACC)

Concerning DTR patterns, the YM desiderative predicates can be partitioned into three groups. First, there is the modal *tàak*, the most grammaticalized desiderative predicate. It is restricted to SRef constellations and exclusively takes an incompletive-marked verbal core (cf., e.g., (196.a) and Construction 15, sect. 5.2.2.1.1). Second, some desiderative predicates take a 'split' pattern complement under SRef, while DRef entails a *káa*-clause. *K'áat* 'want, wish' (cf. (133) vs. (126), *óot* 'agree, accept, be willing' (381), *ts'iibóolt*[11] 'wish, desire' (382), and *ts'iibóol* 'eager, be longing' belong to this group.

---

[11] Some of my consultants alternatively or preferably allow for an incompletive-marked verbal core with *ts'iib-óolt* 'wish, desire' under SRef and DRef. Andrade (1955:182, 237) and Vapnarsky (1995:89) however show the above 'split' pattern.

(381) a. *T-in   w-óot-ah   in   mèet-eh,*
PFV-SBJ.1.SG 0-agree-CMPL [SBJ.1.SG   do-SUBJ]$_{VCo}$
pero ma' bey-chah-i'.
but   NEG possible-PROC.CMPL-NEGF
'I was ready/wanted to do it, but it was not possible.' (RMC_0960)

b. *Ma' táan a   w-óot-ik*
NEG PROG SBJ.2   0-be.willing-INCMPL
káa ts'o'k-ok in   beh-il   t-a   w-éetel?
[that finish-SUBJ POSS.1.SG road-REL   LOC-POSS.2   0-with]$_{VCl}$
'Aren't you willing to be married to me?' (MUUCH_038)

(382) a. *Bíin   u   ts'íib-óol-t   x-ch'úup-tal   xib-o'b*
PRDV SBJ.3 write-soul-TRR [F-female-PROC.INCMPL male-PL]$_{SFVCo}$
bíin   u   ts'íib-óol-t   xib-tal   x-ch'úup-o'b.
PRDV SBJ.3 write-soul-TRR [male-PROC.INCMPL F-female-PL]$_{SFVCo}$
'The men shall wish to become women, the women shall wish to become men.' (Vapnarsky 1995:89)

b. *le   ken   òok-ok   k'ìin-e'*
when SR.FUT enter-SUBJ   sun-TOP
k-u   ts'íib-óol-t-ik   káa háahan sáas-ak
IMPF-SBJ.3 write-soul-TRR-INCMPL [that   hurriedly   light-SUBJ]$_{VCl}$
'when night was falling, she wished that it would dawn soon again'
(HK'AN_261.3)

Third, some predicates take an incompletive-marked verbal core under SRef. These are predicates conveying the meaning of 'plan' or 'intend' (383). With these predicates the proposition embodied in the incompletive-marked verbal core has a greater chance of realization than a proposition conveyed by the 'split' pattern combined with those desiderative predicates mentioned above. The propositional attitude verb *tukul* 'think' that shifts to the meaning 'plan' when combined with an incompletive-marked verbal core under SRef is shown in (383a). In this meaning *tukul* is exclusively future oriented and impossible with independent clauses as complements (cf. 7.3.2).[12] The verb *péek-óolt* 'plan' also takes an incompletive-marked subordination pattern (383b).

---

[12] Such a meaning shift connected to the respective pattern shift seems to be quite usual cross-linguistically.

(383) a. *H   háak'   túun bin   y-óol   ti'   u*
      PFV become.scared then QUOT POSS.3-mind LOC POSS.3
      yo'lal ba'x k-u   tukul-ik   u   mèent-ik-o'.
      reason what IMPF-SBJ.3 think-INCMPL [SBJ.3 do-INCMPL]$_{VCo}$-D2
      'He was very scared of what he planned to do.' (HK'AN_049)

     b. *Péek-óol-t   a   bis-ik   tàak'in!*
      move-mind-TRR   SBJ.2.SG carry-INCMPL money
      'Plan to take money with you!' (Bricker et al. 1998, s.v. *péek*)

Similarly, experiential collocations with *tàal* 'come' as *tàal ti'* POSS *tùu-kul/pòol* 'come into one's mind' take an incompletive-marked verbal core under SRef (384). They are assumed to be similar to plans and realistic future events.

(384)   *K-u   tàal   t-in   tùukul/pòol*
       IMPF-SBJ.3 come   LOC-POSS.1.SG thought/head
       in   bin meyah/ xíimbal.
       [SBJ.1.SG   go   work/   stroll]$_{VCo}$
       'It comes into my mind to go to work / for a walk.'
       (RMC_2280/ACC_0413)

The desiderative predicates *k'áat-óolt* 'solicit, wish' and *pa't* 'wait, hope' typically combine with DRef situations, and *k'áat-óolt* either takes a *káa*-clause (385a) or an independent clause (385b).

(385) a. *K-in   k'áat-óol-t-ik   káa k'áax-ak ha'.*
      IMPF-SBJ.1.SG wish-mind-TRR-INCMPL [that rain-SUBJ water]$_{VCl}$
      'I pray that it may rain.' (EMB_0808)

     b. *K-in   k'áat-óol-t-ik   ti'   dios*
      IMPF-SBJ.1.SG wish-mind-TRR-INCMPL LOC god
      ma'   in   k'oha'n-tal.
      [NEG SBJ.1.SG ill-PROC]$_{VCl}$
      'I pray to god not to fall ill' (MPK_051)

Pa't 'wait, hope' may take an incompletive-marked verbal core (386a) or a *káa*-clause (386b). Combination with an independent clause has been shown above in (379).

(386) a. *Káa t-u$_i$ pa't-ah   u$_j$ y-u'l.*
      CNJ PFV-SBJ.3 await-CMPL [SBJ.3   0-come.home]$_{VCo}$
      'And he waited that she would return.' (XWAAY_004)

b. *Ma' a   pa't-ik   káa séeb   k'áax-ak ha'*!
   NEG SBJ.2 await-INCMPL [that quickly rain-SUBJ water]$_{VCl}$
   'Don't expect that it will rain soon!' (NVV_007)

7.4.2.2 *Fear*

Predicates of fear express "an attitude of fear or concern that the complement proposition will be or has been realized" (Noonan 1985:119). Semantically they are the true converse of the *hope*-class of positive predicates of volition, since they may refer to past situations as well. The fear group includes *sahak(tal)* '(get) afraid' and *ch'a' sahkil* 'get afraid'. Furthermore, *su'lak(tal)* '(get) ashamed' and *ch'a' subtal* 'get ashamed', which have already been treated in sect. 7.4.1, behave like fear predicates when combined with subordinate clauses referring to future situations.

Fear predicates may combine with an independent clause conveying ITR as shown in (387). The option of inserting the conjunction *wáah* indicates that the truth status of the subordinate proposition is non-factive.

(387)   *Sahak-en*   (*wáah*) *ts'o'k   u   tàal-o'b*.
         afraid-ABS.1.SG [if   TERM   SBJ.3 come-3.PL]$_{VCl}$
         'I am afraid that they have come' (ACC)

In their reference to future situations *fear*-predicates combine with a 'split' pattern core under SRef as shown in (388) and (389).[13]

(388) a. *Sahak-en*   *in*   *k'áat*   *tèech wáah ba'x*.
         afraid-ABS.1.SG [SBJ.1.SG ask(SUBJ) you   any   thing]$_{VCo}$
         'I am afraid to ask you something' (ACC)

      b. *Sahak-en*   *tsikbal*.
         ashamed-ABS.1.SG [chat(INCMPL)]$_{SFVCo}$
         'I am afraid to talk' (ACC)

---

[13] Note that a combination of *fear*-predicates with an incompletive-marked verbal core under SRef results in a gerundial construction conveying a simultaneous interpretation of main clause and dependent core (cf. (124) in sect. 4.2.2). While in the following example (a) the incompletive-marked verbal core is understood as occurring simultaneously with respect to the main clause, (b) shows a 'split' pattern core conveying a potential reading in the future.

a. *K-in*   *ch'a'-ik*   *sahkil in*   *bin*   *xòok*.
    IMPF-SBJ.1.SG   take-INCMPL   fear   [SBJ.1.SG   go   read\INTRV]$_{VCo}$
    'I am getting afraid (when) going to school' (EMB)

b. *K-in*   *ch'a'-ik*   *sahkil*   *bin*   *xòok*.
    IMPF-SBJ.1.SG   take-INCMPL   fear   [go   read\INTRV]$_{SFVCo}$
    'I am afraid/ashamed to go to school' (ACC)

(389) a. *Su'lak-en*   *in*   *k'áat in*   *w-o'ch*
       ashamed-ABS.1.SG   [SBJ.1.SG   ask   POSS.1.SG   0-food
       ti'   *le*   *máak-o'b-o'.*
       LOC   DEF   person-PL-D2]$_{VCo}$
       'I am ashamed to ask food from other people' (RMC_2073)

   b. *Su'lak-en*   *tsikbal   yéetel   máak-o'b-o'.*
      ashamed-ABS.1.SG   [chat   with   person-PL-D2]$_{SFVCo}$
      'I am ashamed to talk to poeple.' (RMC_2074)

Fear predicates such as *sahak* 'afraid' and its derivational and periphrastical
forms may take propositional stimuli under DRef using a *káa*-clause. Again the
káa-clause has a hypothetical or unreal meaning.

(390)   *Sahak-en*   *káa p'a't-ak*   *pèek' way-e'.*
        afraid-ABS.1.SG   [that   leave:PASS-SUBJ   dog   here-D3]$_{VCl}$
        'I am afraid that they leave/abandon dogs here.' (ACC)

In summary it can be concluded that the subordination pattern most characteristic for fear predicates is the 'split' pattern with SRef and the *káa*-clause
with DRef.

7.4.2.3 *Interest*
Interest predicates can be divided into positive and negative groups, conveying
(lacking) interest/will and/or (lacking) energy that the subordinate proposition
will be realized. Predicates of interest are *sa'kóol* 'sedulous, active, industrious', *chuka'n/chukpah* POSS *óol* 'be patient, with stamina, with staying power',
tàal POSS *óol* 'feel like', *yàan* POSS *óol* 'feel good, to feel like', *pòoch* 'desirous; greedy'. For an example cf. (391).

(391)   *K-u*   *tàal*   *in*   *w-óol*   *xíimbal/*   *meyah.*
        IMPF-SBJ.3   come   POSS.3   0-mind   [stroll]$_{SFVCo}$/ [work]$_{SFVCo}$
        'I would like to go for a walk / to work.' (NMP_0420/RMC/EMB)

Predicates of lacking interest, referred to here also as repugnance predicates,
include *ma'k'óol* 'idle, lazy', *ma'óol* 'weary, listless, lethargic', *náak-óol* 'feel
bored', *lúub(a'n)* POSS *óol* 'feel/get weak, depressed, disheartened', *mina'n*
POSS *óol* 'not feel like', *máan* POSS *óol* 'lose heart; lose interest', *náak* POSS *óol*
'get bored, tired, weary'. Compare (392).

(392) a. *Ma'k'óol-en   in   p'o'*
    idle-ABS.1.SG [SBJ.1.SG wash(SUBJ)(ABS.1.SG)
    in   nòok'.
    POSS.1.SG   dress]$_{VCo}$
    'I am (too) lazy to wash my dresses.' (NMP)

   b. *Ma'k'óol-en   p'òo'.*
    idle-ABS.1.SG   [wash\INTRV]$_{SFVCo}$
    'I am (too) lazy to wash.' (NMP)

Both groups take a 'split' pattern core under SRef, as (391) and (392) show. Based on their semantics, interest predicates exclusively show DTR and SRef. This can be shown in cases like (393), that require the insertion of a perception verb in order to be related indirectly to a DRef situation. This underlines the fact that interest predicates can only immediately refer to one's own affairs. Using perception verbs in this function is again based on evidentiality, parallel to the case of *su'lak* 'ashamed' in (366).

(393) a. *Chuk-a'n   in   w-óol *(in   w-il)*
    suffice-RSLTV POSS.3 0-mind SBJ.1.SG 0-see(SUBJ)
    u   k'áax-al   ha'.
    [SBJ.3 rain-INCMPL water]
    'I am patient (enough) to see it raining' (EMB)

   b. *H   náak   in   w-óol *(in*
    PFV   leave.this.way\DEAG POSS.1.SG 0-mind   SBJ.1.SG
    w-u'y)   u   pa'x-al   le   guitara-o'.
    0-feel(SUBJ) [SBJ.3   play.music:PASS-INCMPL DEF   guitar-D2]$_{VCo}$
    'I am bored hearing the guitar being played' (ACC)

Furthermore, interest predicates cannot be related to independent clauses; a fact that is also related to their semantics. Interest predicates can only refer to future situations; never to past situations.

Most YM interest predicates exclusively take propositional stimuli, either as 'split' pattern cores/clauses or as nominal(ized) lexical NPs, governed by the preposition *ti'*, or more seldomly by *yéetel* (cf. sect. 5.2.1.2, sect. 5.2.1.3, sect. 5.3.1.1, sect. 5.3.1.2, etc.). Furthermore, there is no transitive verb in the group of interest predicates. Most items relevant here are verbal or adjectival expressions taking *óol* as their subject argument. Others are simple or compound adjectives taking the experiencer in subject function. Based on the fact that the stimuli participants concerned are generally propositional and given that the predicates are all adjectival or intransitive, the analysis that propositional stimuli of interest predicates are in fact purpose clauses is proposed. These constructions correspond to the motion-cum-purpose construction introduced in sect. 4.2.2, which also takes a 'split' pattern with purpose semantics (cf. (125)). YM purpose clauses may be complements as well as adjuncts. Thus, *ma'k'óol* 'idle, lazy', *ma'óol* 'weary, listless, lethargic', and *sa'kóol* 'sedulous, active, industrious', which are clearly monovalent adjectives, can take a 'split' pattern stimulus in the function of a purpose clause (cf. (392) above).

Finally, it has to be noted that some of the items grouped here are also possible with an incompletive-marked verbal core: *lúub(a'n)* POSS *óol* 'feel/get weak, depressed, disheartened', *mina'n* POSS *óol* 'not feel like', *yàan* POSS *óol* 'feel like'. In these cases consultants emphasize a simultaneous interpretation in contrast to a 'split' pattern subordination. Compare (394a) with (394b). These cases are assumed to be marginal, all the more so as consultants' judgments differ as to the acceptability of an incompletive-marked verbal core with interest predicates.

(394) a. *Mina'n   in   w-óol in   w-il-ik*
         NEG.EXIST POSS.1.SG 0-mind [SBJ.1.SG 0-see-INCMPL
         in   x-ka'na'.
         POSS.1.SG   F-two:mother]$_{VCo}$
         'I don't feel good in seeing my stepmother.' (RMC)

      b. *Mina'n   in   w-óol   in   w-il*
         NEG.EXIST POSS.1.SG 0-mind [SBJ.1.SG 0-see(SUBJ)
         in   x-ka'na'.
         POSS.1.SG   F-two:mother]$_{VCo}$
         'I do not feel like seeing my stepmother.' (RMC)

Some interest predicates can only be combined with action verbs in subordinate propositions (395). Note that the decisive criterion here is not control, since both *he'l* 'rest' and *chital* 'lie (down)' integrate with Test 5.

(395) a. *Yàan/ mina'n   in   w-óol meyah/ áalkab/*
         EXIST/ NEG.EXIST POSS.1.SG 0-mind work/   run/
         háanal/ báaxal/ tsikbal.
         eat/   play/   chat
         'I do (not) feel like working/ running/ eating/ playing/ talking'
         (RMC_1734/EMB/ACC)

      b. **Yàan/ mina'n   in   w-óol he'l-el/   chi-tal.*
         EXIST/ NEG.EXIST POSS.1.SG 0-mind rest-INCMPL / lie-PROC
         intended: 'I do (not) feel like resting/ lying down' (EMB)

To summarize the behavior of interest predicates with subordination it can be observed that they prototypically combine with a 'split' pattern. In contrast to desire and fear predicates they require SRef of the main participant in the subordinate core.

7.5 *Summary*
7.5.1 *Types of complementation*
Table 50 summarizes the predicate types and their complementation patterns described in the preceding paragraphs. The prototypical combination, showing the semantics of the matrix predicate according to its 'basic' meaning is highlighted by italics, while derivational meanings evolving from the combination with other patterns are also given. Furthermore, when several possible patterns preserve the 'basic' meaning of respective items of the group, the most widespread pattern(s) is/are highlighted.[14] Table 50 indicates the construction type of the complement clause, associated referential restrictions between the participants in the main and the subordinate clause, and the truth status of the subordinate clause. Additionally, the resulting semantics of the whole construction is mentioned and examples are given in the rightmost column.

Table 50 reflects two types of hierarchies, namely the *binding* hierarchy proposed in Givón (1980) and the *desententialization* hierarchy proposed in Lehmann (1988, sect. 3.1). The latter corresponds to the *deranking* hierarchy given in Croft 2001:357 (based on Cristofaro 1998/2003). While the *binding* hierarchy orders matrix predicates of different semantic classes according to the tightness of binding they exhibit with respect to their propositional argument, the *desententialization* or *deranking* hierarchy orders constructions of propositional arguments according to their degree of nominalization, i.e. it ranges from clause-like to NP-like (i.e., most desententialized or deranked).

With respect to the YM complementation patterns, the following order in the *desententialization* hierarchy can be identified. The independent clause is not *desententialized*, since it carries full A/M marking and person marking. The *káa*-clause then follows: it lacks the A/M marker (cf. Table 14) but is obligatorily marked for subjunctive status and preserves person marking. The ordering of the incompletive-marked verbal core and the 'split' pattern is somewhat intricate, mainly because the 'split' pattern has a different marking depending on the transitivity of the verb. With intransitive verbs in subordination, the incompletive-marked verbal core is clearly less *desententialized* than the semi-finite verbal core belonging to the 'split' pattern (cf. Table 15). The

---

[14] This applies to, e.g., the group of volitive emotion and volition predicates whose items combine with independent subordinate clauses depending on their specific semantics, e.g., items meaning 'want' do not show such a subordination pattern. Therefore, this group has not been highlighted in Table 50 despite there being a usual pattern for other items of the group, e.g., those meaning 'hope'.

former shows full person and status marking, while the latter has no subject (S, A) marking. Regarding the transitive constructions in both patterns, there is no 'quantitative' difference concerning person and status marking. Status marking only differs in whether its value is incompletive or subjunctive. Thus, the 'split' pattern is taken as more *desententialized* than the incompletive pattern.

As regards the *binding* hierarchy, Croft (2001:358) presents the following order which is based on the deranking status of the complement of the respective matrix predicates: utterance < knowledge/propositional attitude < perception < desiderative/manipulative < phasal/modal. This hierarchy largely confirms Givón's *binding* hierarchy. While Givón did not include perception verbs and modals, the Croft's hierarchy does not consider commentative emotion predicates. However, the latter are not differentiated from volitive emotion predicates in Givón's *binding* hierarchy, i.e., commentative emotionals are located at the same level as volitive emotionals.

The order of the diverse YM complement taking predicates (from top to bottom) given in Table 50 is created on the basis of the *desententialization* of the complement construction(s) with which the matrix predicates primarily combine, as was discussed before. The order in Table 50 largely confirms the orders proposed in Givón (1980) and Croft (2001). However, taking the 'split' pattern as more 'deranked' than the incompletive pattern leads to the observation that YM shows a reverse order concerning the last two groups of matrix predicates in the *binding* hierarchy, i.e., in YM, phase verbs and most modals take an incompletive-marked verbal clause while desideratives take the 'split' pattern. This point will be further discussed in sect. 7.5.3.

Futhermore, it can be seen at various points in Table 50 that the combination of a given predicate type with an unusual complementation type results in a meaning shift of the main predicate. This applies to, e.g., the predicate of propositional attitude *tùukul(t)* 'think' that changes its meaning to convey a plan when combined with an incompletive pattern under SRef. A meaning shift also occurs with the knowledge predicate *ohel* 'know' that conveys the modal meaning of ability when combined with the 'split' pattern. It also applies to the perception predicates that change to knowledge predicates when combining with an independent subordinate clause. Such regular changes of meaning corresponding to subordination patterns have been reported for other languages, too (cf., e.g., Givón 1990, ch. 13).

Matrix predicates	Construction type of subordinate clause	Reference of actants	Semantics of subordinate proposition	Semantics of whole construction
(acquisition of)	*independent clause*	*DRef*	*factive (presupp. or ass.)*	*knowledge of P as a fact*
knowledge	incompl. pattern	DRef	actual	imagination of P
			potential	volition that P (comes true)
		SRef	implicative	manner of achievement of P
	'split' pattern	SRef		ability with respect to P
propositional	*independent clause*	*both*	*potential*	*degree of commitment to the truth of P*
attitude	/ incompl. pattern	both		
	incompl. pattern	SRef	potential	plan of realizing P
commentative	*independent clause*	*both*	*factive*	*comment on P as a fact*
emotion	*incompl. pattern*	*both*	*actual; potential*	*comment on an actual or potential occ. of P*
	káa-clause	both	hypothetical	comment on a hypothetical occurrence of P
perception	*incompl. pattern*	*DRef (SRef)*	*simultaneous*	*immediate perception of occurrence of P*
	independent clause (prog)	both	simultaneous (inferred)	primary mental perception of P as a fact
	independent clause	both	factive (presupp. or ass.)	sec. mental perc. = knowledge of P as a fact
volitive emotion /	*'split' pattern*	*SRef*	*potential*	*volition that P be (not) realized*
volition	*/ káa-clause*	*DRef (SRef)*		
	incompl. pattern	both	potential; more realistic	plan/intention that P be realized
	independent clause	both	potential	volition that P be (not) realized

Table 50. Types of complementation with experiential matrix predicates

Figure 16 is the semantic map of experiential propositional meanings that reflects the semantic properties of the experiential predicates in combination with the prototypical subordination patterns. It visualizes the diverse shifts that have been mentioned as occurring with a shift in the subordinate pattern. One systematic meaning shift is that if commentative emotion predicates such as *ki'mak POSS óol* 'happy', *yah POSS óol* 'regret', etc. combine with an incompletive-marked verbal core, they convey an emotional or evaluative attitude towards an actual or potential occurrence of the proposition, while the combination with an independent clause constitutes a comment on a factive situation.

In addition, there is a shift from propositional attitude to plan that has been described for *tùukul(t)* 'think' changing from the combination with an independent clause to the combination with an incompletive-marked verbal core. A converse shift can be observed for perception verbs that combine with an incompletive-marked verbal core in their immediate perception sense while in combination with an independent clause they produce a cognitive meaning.

Finally, volitive emotion predicates, which canonically take a 'split' pattern, can combine with an incompletive-marked verbal core, which either shifts the meaning of the subordinate proposition to a more realistic statement, or the latter is interpreted as occurring simultaneously to the main predicate. Conversely, emotional attitude predicates can be combined with a *káa*-clause to comment on a hypothetical situation.

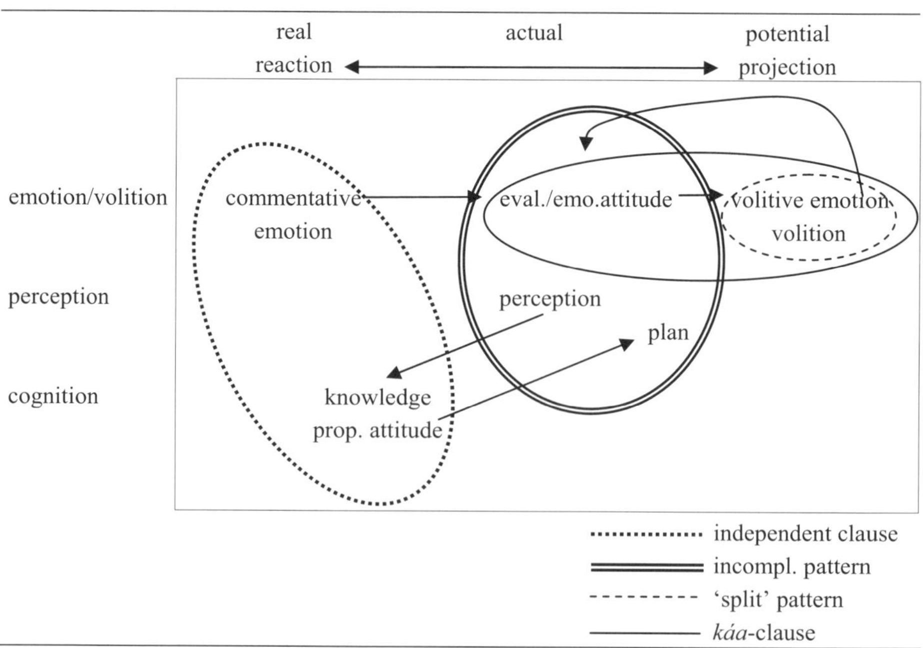

Figure 16. Experiential propositional meanings

7.5.2 *The evidential role of perception verbs in subordination*

It has been shown that several groups of experiential complement taking predicates may insert a perception verb to adjoin an incompletive-marked verbal core under DRef. This has been exemplified for some commentative emotion predicates in (365) and (366), for some interest predicates in (393) and for *sùuk* 'accustomed' in (331a).

The function of such a strategy is twofold as it has semantic as well as syntactic goals. First, the syntactic strategy works as follows: perception verbs are transitive verbs taking the experiencer in subject function and an incompletive-marked verbal core in direct object function. This valence frame makes them an ideal 'bridge' between a matrix predicate that is constrained to SRef constellations with reduced patterns of subordination and an incompletive-marked verbal core with DRef. Thus, inserting a perception verb which has a referentially identical experiencer to the matrix predicates does not violate the constraint on SRef. At the same time the complement clause in object function is the required incompletive-marked verbal core.

Second, 'bridging' SRef constraints also has a semantic function which is evidential in nature since it pertains to contexts where the superordinate experiential predicate cannot be directly related to the subordinate situation involving other participants. This is most obvious with predicates of interest which are semantically closely related to own-experience, but YM also turns out to be precise concerning evidential relations in relating other emotional meanings as matrix predicates to DRef situations such as with *ki'mak óol* 'happy' in (365) or *sùuk* 'accustomed' in (331a).

The perception verb *il* 'see' is most often used in such a function since it has a kind of 'neutral' or generalized role in attaining evidence for a DRef situation, which is surely related to the fact that vision is thought of as the primary perceptual mode. With respect to the subordination patterns of perception verbs, it has been shown that *il* is polysemous. In addition to its strict perception sense, it has the meaning of intellectual (acquisition of) knowledge. Such a general intellectual meaning is reflected in cases like those given in (331a), (366), and (393a). The other perception verb *u'y* 'hear' is only used in cases of auditory evidence. Compare (393b) and (396).

(396) *K-u   péek   in   w-óol   in   w-u'y-ik*
   IMPF-SBJ.3 move POSS.1.SG 0-mind [SBJ.1.SG 0-feel-INCMPL
   u   wáak'al   ts'òon.
   [SBJ.3.SG   explode\DEAG   gun]$_{\text{VCo}}$]$_{\text{VCo}}$
   'I get a fright hearing the explosion of guns.' (EMB)

The evidential nature of perception verbs in YM is also visible in their use in evaluation, which has been described in sect. 5.3.2.1.4 with respect to

Construction 34. Furthermore, note that the language is also precise in rendering auditory perception in contexts of communication, often using *u'y* 'feel, hear' in a purpose clause to code the listener (397).

(397) a. *Uts   ti'   k   t'àan*
       good   LOC   POSS.1.PL   speech
      káa   t'àan-ak-ech   k   u'y-e'.
      that   speak-SUBJ-ABS.2.SG   SBJ.1.PL   feel(SUBJ)-D3
      'We appreciate that you talk for us to listen.' (FCP_025)

     b. *ma'ch   in   k'áat-ik   in   w-u'y   ti'*
      not.ever SBJ.1.SG ask-INCMPL   SBJ.1.SG 0-feel(SUBJ) LOC
      'never did I ask to hear from him' (UUCHUL_08)

7.5.3 *Verbal categories in matrix and subordinate clause*

It is a common strategy in language for the dependent clause to lose more and more of its verbal categories such as tense, aspect, mood and person marking, and to become more and more a part of the superordinate clause through increasing grammaticalization. This process is reflected in the abovementioned *desententialization/deranking* hierarchy. However, not only the subordinate clause is deranked in grammaticalization, but also the matrix verb may undergo grammaticalization, losing (some of) its verbal categories. Thus, a full verbal matrix predicate may grammaticalize to a modal verb or to an auxiliary. The grammaticalization of the matrix verb generally implies a syntagmatic interweaving of the two propositions and leads, through stronger grammaticalization, to just one clause representing one proposition, as, for example, represented by the auxiliary periphrases of the SAE type. Here the auxiliary carries person marking and itself conveys modal, aspectual, or temporal meanings. The lexical predicate (full verb) is grammatically reduced to an infinitive or a participle.

YM displays another strategy of (complex) sentence formation under grammaticalization, e.g., with modals and phasals. This may account for the reversed order of the last two groups of matrix predicates in the *desententialization/deranking* hierarchy introduced above. In YM, phase verbs and modals take an incompletive-marked verbal clause while desideratives take the 'split' pattern. The reason for this seems to lie in the distribution of the person category over matrix and subordinate clauses. The desiderative predicates (with the exception of *tàak* which indeed belongs to the modals) are personal and their subject can, thus, control the subject (S/A) of the subordinate core. The modals, including *tàak*, as well as the impersonal phase predicates are not marked for person, and thus person needs to be marked in the subordinate clause. This is the reason why YM does not show its most deranked pattern with phasals and modals.

Impersonal 'superordinate' predicates are very common in YM, and it has been shown in sect. 6.4 that stimulus-oriented experiential verbs such as *tu'b* forget and *k'a'h* 'remember' and respective adjectives such as *sùuk* 'accustomed' that 'normally' add their experiencer as an indirect object, may occur in constructions motivated by the modal operator construction which leads to the 'backward control' of the indirect object experiencer by the subject of the subordinate clause.

As long as the matrix predicate is non-verbal, i.e., when it is a stative predicate or an auxiliary, it does not carry any grammatical markers of aspect or mood itself. Thus in examples like (132), (370b), (371b), mood information is only coded in the subordinate clause. This also applies to verbal matrix predicates as shows (376). This is due to the fact that the subjunctive only occurs in subordinate clauses/cores. The YM speaker may however modalize a verbal matrix predicate with the assurative marker *he' ...-e'*.

It becomes obvious that YM contrasts with the SAE type (which seems to be cross-linguistically the more dominant type in this respect) by coding verbal categories such as person and mood predominantly in the subordinate part of a more grammaticalized complex construction. The latter languages instead favor 'raising' constructions, thus, highlighting the personal participant in a syntactically prominent function (cf. 2.2.3).

CHAPTER 8

Person and body parts in experiential collocations

In ch. 5, it was shown that YM uses a number of person and body part nouns in experiential collocations and compounds. This chapter intends to shed light on the semantics of these and their function in rendering experience. It begins with the treatment of the person parts *óol* 'mind' and *ìik'* 'air' followed by those body parts that frequently occur in experiential body part constructions such as *pòol/ho'l* 'head' and *puksi'k'al* 'heart' and the body parts used in perception, namely, *ich* 'eye', *xikin* 'ear', *chi'* 'mouth', and *ni'* 'nose'.

8.1 *Person parts*
8.1.1 *óol*

The most frequently used part in person part collocations is clearly *óol* 'mind'. As a first assessment to a 'Gesamtbedeutung' *óol* might be equated with 'sensitive part of a person'. In the following discussion it will become clear that *óol* is related to all experiential subdomains discussed with the exception of perception. This latter subdomain features the body parts of perception which will be discussed below. Beyond pure experience, *óol* also occurs with property concepts, i.e., habitual emotional and cognitive characteristics/personal traits related to cognition, emotion and sensation, and as part of compounds as well as in collocations. It is used in the expression of attitudes/opinions, moods, internal contemplation, mental power and beliefs. In terms of Wierzbicka, it is related to the basic semantic concepts of feeling, wanting and thinking.

In Colonial Yucatec Maya *óol* is even more frequent than today. Barrera Vásquez et al. (eds., 1980) abounds with expressions containing *óol*. Nowadays, most of these have become largely obsolete or even unknown, as a systematic inquiry of *óol*-collocations from Barrera Vásquez shows. I tested about 200 instances of such *óol*-collocations with different consultants (from different age groups) and most of them were found to be unknown today. A concrete body part meaning for *óol* in Colonial times is 'lungs' (Vocabulario de Vienna apud Barrera Vásquez et al. eds. 1980, s.v. *ol*). Nowadays the expression for 'lungs' is *sak-óol* lit. 'white-lung/mind'. Further Colonial meanings include 'corazón formal, y no el material' and 'condición o propiedad, voluntad y gana, intento, intención' (Diccionario de Motul I apud Barrera Vásquez et al. eds. 1980, s.v. *ol*). Thus, the range of meanings of *óol* seems to be similar to Old

High German *muot* 'Kraft des Denkens, Seele, Herz, Gemütszustand, Gesin-
nung, Gefühl, Absicht, Neigung' (Pfeifer et al. 1993, s.v. *Mut*).

Many consultants are no longer able to separate *óol* from its collocations,
hence an isolated meaning is given only with difficulty: some consultants vol-
unteered Spanish equivalents as 'estado de amimo' or 'sentido (de expres-
sión)'. Interestingly some consultants spontaneously translated *óol* with Span.
estar 'be, exist', which is surely due to the lack of a copula in YM. On second
glance however, this seems to be not so far from its core meaning, given that
óol is the essential 'living, sensitive' part of a (human) being.

Nowadays *óol* is present in collocations of bodily sensation with the meaning 'pleasure, strength, energy'. Indeed, this may be one of the more basic
meanings of *óol*: consider (398) (cf. also (395) above) which features relatively
abstract predicates. In this meaning *óol* is on the verge of transition to the subdomain of emotion.

(398) a. *Chan   yàan   a   w-óol   behe'la'*?
         a.bit   EXIST   POSS.2   0-mind   today
         'Are you (feeling) better today?' (NMP_0056)

      b. *h   bin   in   w-óol káa   t-in   w-il-ah*
         PFV   go   POSS.1.SG   0-mind CNJ   PFV-SBJ.1.SG   0-see-CMPL
         ba'x   t-u   mèet-ah
         what   PFV-SBJ.3   do-CMPL
         'I lost interest when I saw what he did' (NMP_0054)

In (399) *óol* refers to mental consciousness.

(399) a. *hach bèey túun   kíimil-e'*
         very thus PROG.SBJ.3   die:ABSTR-D3
         h   sáat   u   y-óol
         PFV   lose\DEAG   POSS.3   0-mind
         h   p'áat   sak-kimen
         PFV   stay   white-dead
         'he seemed to die, he lost his mind, he got pale like a dead'
         (HK'AN_106.3)

    b. *H   xáan-lah-ih*
      PFV   take.long-PROC.CMPL-ABS.3.SG
      káa   sùut-nah   ti'   u   y-óol
      CNJ   turn\INTRV-CMPL LOC POSS.3   0-mind
      le   káa   t-u   y-u'b-ah
      DEF   CNJ   PFV-SBJ.3 0-feel-CMPL
      ts'o'k   u   ch'a'-ik   y-óol-e', ...
      TERM SBJ.3 fetch-INCMPL POSS.3-mind-CNTR
      'And it took long that he regained consciousness and when he felt
      better, (…)' (HK'AN_0107.1)

In sect. 5.2.1.3 it was discussed how *óol* is used to convert a bodily condition (e.g., hot, cold, ill, etc.) into a bodily sensation (e.g., feel hot, cold, ill, etc.). At this point it may be appropriate to draw the reader's attention to a Mayan cultural belief related to the 'feeling' of *chokol óol*. The Maya strongly believe that one should not drink something cold if one is feeling hot/has been heated up (by the sun/work in the sun). Doing so may cause an illness called *pasmar* 'congealing/congelation'.

(400)   *Wáah chokol a   w-óol-e'   k-u   tsa'y-al*
          if   hot   POSS.2 0-mind-TOP IMPF-SBJ.3 strike-INCMPL
          tèech hun-p'éel   k'oha'n-il u   k'àaba'-e'   pasmar.
          you   one-CL.INAN ill-ABSTR POSS.3 name-CNTR   congealing
          'If you are feeling hot this (may) cause an illness called 'pasmar'.'
          (NMP_0053)

Furthermore note, that in the Diccionario de San Francisco (Juan Pío Pérez, ca. 1855 apud Barrera Vásquez et al. eds. 1980, s.v. *chokó ol*) the meaning of *chokó ol* is an emotional one, i.e., 'irritarse, enojarse, airarse, encenderse en ira, abochornarse'. Contemporary sources (apud Barrera Vásquez et al. eds. 1980, s.v. *chokó oolal*) give both the bodily sensation as well as the emotion meaning while in my consultants dialect the latter meaning is not present. Here, as well as in other cases, it can be observed that formerly non-concrete, possibly metaphorical meanings, have been pushed aside or have even been lost in favor of a more concrete meaning of bodily sensation.

In collocations from the subdomain of emotion, the meaning of *óol* comes close to Germ. 'Mut', Engl. 'heart' as in e.g., (401). The German adverb *zumute* 'feel, be in a mood' also seems to be similar.

(401) a. *táan u   máan u   y-óol le   t'ùup-o'*
          PROG SBJ.3 pass   POSS.3 0-mind DEF youngest.sibling
          'the youngest brother lost heart' (T'UUP 259)

b. *Huan-e'   hach   lúub-a'n   y-óol*
Huan-TOP   really   fall-RSLTV   POSS.3-mind
'Juan is really down/depressed' (EMB_0528)

As concerns the expression of volition, *óol* seems to be etymologically connected to such a meaning (cf. above). Also Hanks (1990:87) and Bricker et al. (1998) mention the meaning 'will, desire' for *óol(al)* (402).

(402)   *tuméen ts'o'k   a   sen   bèet-ik   a   w-óolal*
because TERM   SBJ.2 very   do-INCMPL POSS.2 0-desire
'because here you have only done what you desired to do.'
(HLU'M_KÀAB_123.2)

In the dialect under investigation this meaning is not immediately present. Furthermore, there is no contemporary *óol*-collocation expressing volition (but note that (395) may contain a volitive aspect). Instead *óol* is part of compounds and derivatives that express volitive meanings, e.g., *ts'íibóolt* 'wish, desire' (403b), *óot* 'agree, accept, be willing' (403a).

(403) a. *Ma' táan   a   w-óot-ik*
NEG PROG SBJ.2   0-be.willing-INCMPL
káa   ts'o'k-ok   in   beh-il   t-a   w-éetel?
that   finish-SUBJ POSS.1.SG road-REL   LOC-POSS.2 0-with
'Aren't you willing to be married to me?' (MUUCH_038)
   b. *le   ken   òok-ok   k'ìin-e'*
when SR.FUT enter-SUBJ sun-TOP
k-u   ts'íib-óol-t-ik
IMPF-SBJ.3 write-soul-TRR-INCMPL
káa háahan   sáas-ak
that   hurriedly   light-SUBJ
'when night was falling, she wished that it would be dawn soon again' (HK'AN_261.3)

In the subdomain of cognition, there are compounds as well as collocations containing *óol*, e.g., *k'ah-óol* 'be acquainted with, know a person', *k'a'h POSS óol* 'remember', etc. The following collocations point to cognitive meanings such as imagination, opinion, mental effort, concentration, belief, and intelligence.

(404) a. *Ma' k'oha'n-ech-i'*
NEG sick-ABS.2.SG-NEGF
chéen u   ts'ib   a   w-óol!
just   POSS.3 mental.image POSS.2   0-mind
'You're not sick; its only your imagination!'
(Bricker et al. 1998, s.v. *óol*)

b. *Ts'a'   a   wool t-a   p'o' ba'x-o'.*
put(IMP) SBJ.2   0-mind LOC-SBJ.2 wash what-D2
'Concentrate on washing up.' (NMP_0023)

c. *Bèey in   w-óol*
thus   POSS.1.SG 0-mind
màas ma'lòob káa xi'k-ech   doktòor.
more   good   that   go.SUBJ-ABS.2.SG   doctor
'It seems to me it's better for you to go to the doctor.'
(BVS_13.01.22)

d. *k-u   y-òoks-ik   u   y-óol*
IMPF-SBJ.3   0-enter:CAUS-INCMPL   POSS.3 0-mind
ti'   ba'x   k-u   y-a'l-a'l
LOC   what   IMPF-SBJ.3   0-say-PASS.INCMPL
'he believes in what people say' (RMC_2219)

e. *ma' t-u   y-óol   yàan   ka'ch-i'*?
NEG LOC-POSS.3   0-mind EXIST   past-NEGF
'wasn't he in his right mind?' (HIJO_105)

In the sense investigated here, *óol* is primarily attributed to persons, i.e., it is
a person part. However, it has been shown above that it may also be construed
as part of another person part in some collocations, as, for example, with
puksi'k'al 'heart, stomach' (cf. (175)).

Óol is only partly conceived as 'active': it is not construed as the subject of
speech act verbs, and generally does not occur as the subject of a transitive
verb. It is however construed as the subject of some intransitive verbs, mostly
from the domain of motion such as *bin* 'go', etc.

8.1.2 *ìik'*

In its most 'neutral' sense *ìik'* 'air' refers to the air which is inhaled and is then
turned into the breath, which is also referred to by *ìik'* in YM (405).

(405) a. *k'a'm u   ch'a'-ik   y-ìik'*
loud   SBJ.3 take-INCMPL   POSS.3-air
'he is breathing with difficulty' (RMC_0560)

b. *h   bin   u   y-ìik'*
PFV   go   POSS.3   0-air
'he died (lit. his breath went away)' (RMC_2081)

Along with *óol, ìik'* is connected to a person's inner state or condition, especially in its cognitive or mental sense, though it occurs much less frequently than *óol* in experiential collocations (or as a lexical part of complex experiential expressions). Hanks (1990:87) characterizes *ìik'* as 'awareness' in its non-concrete sense. This awareness may also be oriented, as shown in the collocation *tu k'a'hsah yìik* 'he snapped him out of it, got his attention (lit. reminded his wind)'. In this sense *ìik'* is connected with the cognitive events of remembering and forgetting, as can be derived from (406a/b). Bricker et al. (1998) provides the meaning 'responsibility' for the compound *k'ah-ìik'* and thus identify a moral shading. The latter meaning has been confirmed by my consultants for the dialect under investigation.

(406) a. *Maria, k'a'hs   a   w-ìik'-e'*
Maria   remember:CAUS(IMP) POSS.2   0-air-CNTR
tu'x   t-in   líik's-ah   le   wàah-o'.
where   PFV-SBJ.3   guard-CMPL   DEF   tortilla-D2
'Maria, try to remember where I put the tortillas' (NMP_0169)

b. *Pedro-e'   hach   tu'b(ul)-ìik'*
Pedro-TOP   really   forget-air
'Peter is really forgetful' (RMC_2078)

c. *yàan   u   k'ahìik'*
EXIST   POSS.3   responsibility
'he thinks responsibly' (Bricker et al. 1998, s.v. *k'ah)*

Ìik' can also refer to inspiration as in (407). The context here is a battle where a person is asked to participate because of his ability to give the battle its *ìik'il*. Note that *ìik'* is marked here with the relational suffix *-il*, indicating 'unusual' possessorship since *ba'te'l* 'battle' takes possessor function here. In this sense, the meaning of *ìik'* comes close to the Colonial meaning which is described as 'el espíritu, vida y aliento, ánimo, fuerza y vida' (cf. Barrera Vásquez et al. eds. 1980, s.v. *ik'*).

(407)   *Yùum, tak   tèech k'abéet a   tàal t-u   táan ba'te'l*
        lord   as.far.as you   necessary SBJ.2 come LOC-POSS.3 front fight
        tuméen a   winklil ichil-o'n-e'   nohoch áantah k-u
        because POSS.2 body   in-1.PL-CNTR   big   help   IMPF-SBJ.3
        ts'a-ik   to'n. Leti'   u   mùuk'-il   le   ba'te'l-o';
        put-INCMPL us   that.one POSS.3 strength-REL DEF fight-D2
        u   mùuk'-óolal-il   yéetel u   ch'a'ìik'-il.
        POSS.3 strength-desire-REL and   POSS.3   breath-REL
        'Chief, even you have to come to the battle front, because your
        body among us will give us a big support. It's the force of the bat-
        tle, it's mental strength and inspiration.' (HK'AN_513-515)

Furthermore, *ìik'* is also connected to the cognitive and the bodily condition.
The (*k'ak'àas*) *ìik'* '(evil) wind' can affect a person's inner cognitive and bodily condition by giving him a kind of illness referred to in Spanish as 'enfer-
medad de ataque' by native speakers (408). The (*k'ak'àas*) *ìik'* can be transmitted by prostitutes or generally morally doubtful persons, especially women.
A person affected by such an illness is called *ìik'-il máak* 'air-REL person'.

(408)   *t-u   chuk-ah-ech   k'a-k'àas   ìik'*
        PFV-SBJ.3 catch-CMPL-ABS.2.SG   RED-evil   air
        'lit.: (an) evil wind caught you'

8.2   *Body parts*
8.2.1 *puksi'k'al*
Nowadays *puksi'k'(al)* seems to be used in YM psycho-collocations in a way
similar to the use of *corazón* 'heart' in Spanish. There are even collocations
which seem to be nearly calques of Spanish expressions, as in (409).

(409)   *le   x-ch'úuppal-o'   k-u   k'uch-ul*
        DEF   F-woman:child-D2 IMPF-SBJ.3 arrive-INCMPL
        t-in   puksi'k'-al
        LOC-POSS.1.SG   heart-REL
        'that girl touches my heart' (EMB_0697)

As a body part or organ, *puksi'k'(al)* is sometimes identified with the heart
(cf., e.g., Bricker et al. 1998, s.v. *puksíʔk'al*). In the dialect investigated,
puksi'k'al is identified with the whole inner torso area, from heart to stomach,
and people generally propose both meanings 'heart' and 'stomach'. It is identical to the heart in that it beats, but after having eaten some hot chilies it is also
the *puksi'k'(al)* that is burning, as in (410) where it means 'stomach':

(410)   *hach   k-u   y-èel-el   in   puksi'k'al*
        really IMPF-SBJ.3 0-burn-INCMPL POSS.1.SG   heart
        'my stomach is burning' (NMP_0353)

The Diccionario de Motul (cf. Barrera Vásquez et al. eds. 1980, s.v. *puksík'al*) gives both meanings, 'heart' and 'stomach', for Colonial Yucatec Maya ('el corazón material de cualquier animal racional o irracional' and 'el brío que uno tiene; órgano vital, estómago').

There seem to be a lot of recent/ad hoc combinations and expressions with psycho-collocations containing *óol*, which seems to indicate that the latter is no longer 'felt' to be metaphorical. Many of the psycho-collocations with *óol* can be ascribed to *puksi'k'(al)*. They may result in emotional or sensational expressions, taking *puksi'k'(al)* as the 'seat' of emotions on the one hand (411a) or in its body part sense 'stomach' (411b) on the other.

(411) a. *ki'mak y-óol   in   puksi'k'-al*
         happy   POSS.3-mind POSS.1.SG   heart-REL
         'my heart is happy' (NMP_0402)

      b. *k'àas-lah-a'n   u   y-óol   u   puksi'k'-al,*
         bad-PROC.CMPL-RSLTV POSS.3 0-mind POSS.3 heart-REL
         la'téen ma'ch   u   hàan-al
         therefore not.ever SBJ.3 eat-INCMPL
         'his stomach has got bad, therefore he does not eat' (NMP_0405)

Furthermore, there is a common expression combining *óol* and *puksi'k'*. This expression hints at the emotional significance of *puksi'k'(al)* and its strong associations to the meaning of 'love'. In this collocation, *óol* may mean 'most important part' and probably 'innermost part' (412).

(412)   *y-éetel bin   tuláakal u   yahil u   y-óol u*
        0-with   QUOT all   POSS.3 pain   POSS.3 0-mind POSS.3
        puksi'k'al-e' t-u   y-a'l-ah   ma'lòob-il
        heart-CNTR   PFV-SBJ.3 0-say-CMPL good-ADVR
        'with all his mental and psychic pain he agreed' (HK'AN_0290.2)

In some cases *puksi'k'al* and *óol* are interchangeable (compare (413) with (244)).

(413)   *k-u*   *yah-tal*   *t-in*   *puksi'k'al*
        IMPF-SBJ.3 ache-PROC LOC-SBJ.1.SG heart
        in   *w-il-ik*
        SBJ.1.SG   0-see-INCMPL
        ba'x k-u   *mèet-ik*   *le*   *xibpal-o'*
        what IMPF-SBJ.3 do-INCMPL DEF man:child-D2
        'it hurts me to see what that boy is doing (to me)' (RMC_1790)

8.2.2 *pòol / ho'l*

There are a number of cognitive collocations with the body part terms *pòol* or *ho'l*, both meaning 'head' (414). These seem to be less conventionalized than the expressions with *óol* and may be constructed ad hoc on certain metaphorical grounds. In general, *pòol* is more usual in psycho-collocations than *ho'l*, as shown in examples throughout ch. 8.

(414) a. *hach*   *h*   *p'áat*   *t-in*   *pòol*
         really PFV stay(CMPL) LOC-POSS.1.SG head
         'I kept it in my mind' (CPP_0021)

      b. *yàan*   *bakáan* *ba'x* *t-a*   *ho'l/pòol*
         EXIST   gee   what LOC-SBJ.2 head/head
         'you are rather intelligent' (NMP_0002)

The connection between *pòol* and the ability to learn quickly (or genius) is already present in Colonial Yucatec Maya, as shown in (415), which originates from the Diccionario de Motul.

(415)   *uts*   *u*   *pòol* *ti'*   *kambal*   *k'àay*
        good POSS.3 head   LOC learn\INTRV sing
        'he has the faculty of learning to sing' (Barrera Vásquez et al. eds. 1980, s.v. *pol*)

8.2.3 *Body parts of perception*

All body parts of perception are used for evaluation in Construction 14, the most common being *ich* 'eye', *xikin* 'ear', and *chi'* 'mouth'. Some consultants identify the respective body parts as the source of the evaluation, while examples from written sources such as (193) do not (always) vauch for such an assessment.

8.2.3.1 *ich*

The body part *ich* 'eye, face' is used with emotional adjectives in an evidential function, i.e., to underline that a given feeling can be noticed in the eyes or the face of a person. Some emotional expressions have been conventionalized in such a form, e.g., *óotsil* POSS *ich* 'sad', *ok'om-óol* POSS *ich* 'sad (looking)' (cf. (177)). Other emotional adjectives can be freely combined with *ich* to convey the mentioned evidential meaning (416).

> (416) a. *ts'íik   u   y- ich   tuméen   ts'-u   ha'ts'-al*
>   furious POSS.3 0- eye   because   TERM-SBJ.3 beat:PASS-INCMPL
>   'he is looking furious since he has been beaten' (RMC_1175)
>
>   b. *ma'   ki'mak   y-óol   y-ich-i'*
>   NEG   happy   POSS.3-mind   POSS.3-eye-NEGF
>   'he is not looking very happy' (RMC_1776)

Furthermore, Table 37 listed a number of incorporative verbs containing the body part noun *ich*. They are used to express certain (generally negative) feelings towards another person (cf. (266a)).

8.2.3.2 *xikin*

Along with its use related to evaluation based on auditory evidence (417) *xikin* also has a connection to intellectual understanding, as (418a) from Colonial YM (cf. also (194b)) and (418b) from Modern YM show. A metonymic relation between the auditory sense and intellectual faculties is especially frequent in Australian languages (cf. sect. 3.2.2.6 with special reference to Evans and Wilkins 1998)

> (417)   *Tuméen   uts   t-in   xikin le   máasewal   t'àan-a'.*
>   because   good   LOC-POSS.1.SG ear   DEF   Indian   speech-D1
>   'Because I like this Indian tongue.' (BVS_08.01.20)

> (418) a. *yàan   ti'   xikin*
>   EXIST LOC   ear
>   'know something' (Barrera Vásquez et al. eds. 1980, s.v. *yan*)
>
>   b. *Le   pàal-o'   ma'   hach   lòob   behla'ke'*
>   DEF   child-D2 NEG   really   evil   today
>   *tumen   núuk-pah-il   u   xikin.*
>   because answer-SPONT-ADJR   POSS.3 ear
>   'That child is not really evil today since it already understood.'
>   (NMP_0412)

8.2.3.3 *chi'*

The body part noun *chi'* 'mouth' is employed within collocations in its relation to communication. In this sense it may be metonymically extended to neighboring senses belonging to the domain of experience. In the contemporary collocation given in (419), *tsìik* 'respect' is attributed to *chi'*. Colonial Yucatec Maya displays metonymic expressions with *chi'* concerning cognition as in (420), and emotion (194a). Note that the former is experiencer-related while the latter is stimulus-related.

(419)   *x- pìil-e'*   *hach   mina'n   u   tsìik   u   chi'*
        F- Phyllis-TOP   really   NEG.EXIST   POSS.3   respect   POSS.3   mouth
        'Phyllis is very rude (lit.: her mouth has no respect at all).'
        (Bricker et al. 1998, s.v. *chi'*)

(420)   *kom   u   chi'   Pedro*
        short   POSS.3   mouth   Pedro
        'Pedro is short in intelligence'
        (Barrera Vásquez et al. eds. 1980, s.v. *kom*)

8.2.3.4 *ni'*

The body part noun *ni'* 'nose' is not usually used in forming experiential collocations. Instead, there are some incorporatives designating olfactory perception or the expression of a negative attitude towards someone/something, e.g., *ts'úuyni't* (bend:nose:TRR) 'wrinkle nose (at bad odor)', *úuts'ni't* (smell:nose: TRR) 'sniff', etc.

8.2.4 *Other*

Colonial Yucatec Maya was much richer in psycho-collocations, with a number of additional body part nouns playing a role (cf. (174) and (421) for illustration).

(421)   *he'pah-ih*   *in   kàal   y-iknal   Pedro*
        open:SPONT-ABS.3.SG   POSS.1.SG   neck   POSS.3-at   Pedro
        'I calmed down with/in presence of Pedro'
        (Barrera Vásquez et al. eds. 1980, s.v. *hepahal kal*)

In Colonial (422b) as well as in contemporary YM (422a) experience-related expressions containing the body liquid noun *k'i'k'* 'blood' can also be found. Note that YM uses here a recurrent internal bodily image in the sense of Wierzbicka (1999). Compare the parallel examples from English, Amharic and Wolof in sect. 3.5.2.2.

(422) a. *chokol k'i'k'   le   máak-o'*
         hot   blood   DEF   person-D2
         'that person easily upsets' (RMC_0737)

   b. *omni   in   k'i'k'-el*
      burn   POSS.1.SG   blood-REL
      'I got very angry' (Barrera Vásquez et al. eds. 1980, s.v. *oomankil*)

T'àan 'speech, language, word' as a person part occurs frequently in collocations and complex lexemes which refer to the expression of an evaluation or opinion (cf. Table 21, Table 37). It is also used in collocations related to cognition (305.d), cognitive ability and social/moral behavior, as (423) from Colonial YM shows.

   (423) a. *òoksabe'n   u   t'àan*
            trustworthy POSS.3   speech
            'he is trustworthy.' (Barrera Vásquez et al. eds. 1980, s.v. *oksabe'n u t'an*)

         b. *ahahbil   a   t'àan*
            clear   POSS.2   speech
            'your thought/reasoning is clear' (Barrera Vásquez et al. eds. 1980, s.v. *ahahbil*)

8.3   *Summary*

As has been concluded for many other languages (cf. sect. 3.5), YM uses person and body parts in figurative expressions in rendering experience, especially emotional experience. Body parts and liquids used in this respect are, for instance, *puksi'k'al* 'heart', *pòol/ho'l* 'head', *k'i'k'* 'blood', and *kàal* 'neck, throat' (in Colonial YM). They occur in metaphoric expressions (e.g., (409), (414)) and in collocations rendering bodily images (e.g., (421), (422)) to refer to emotional situations. Apart from this, YM frequently ascribes experience to person and body part terms instead of ascribing it to the person as a whole. This applies not only to the person part noun *óol* 'mind' but also for other person and body part nouns (cf., e.g., *chi'* 'mouth' in (419), *t'àan* 'speech' in (423), *xikin* 'ear' in (418), *ich* 'eye' in (416), and *puksi'k'(al)* 'heart' in (411).

   Furthermore, it has been shown that the person parts *óol* and *ìik'* occur in collocations and compounds from several experiential domains, i.e., *óol* covers the subdomains bodily sensation, emotion, volition, and cognition, and *ìik'* is primarily related to cognitive situations but also to bodily condition and health. Thus, *óol* can be identified as a language-specific category marker for experiences from the mentioned subdomains. This points to a more unified conceptualization of these subdomains in YM in contrast to a Western conceptualization which sets these subdomains apart.

   From the analyses given in sect. 8.1, a development from an originally concrete person part/liquid meaning to an expertum meaning can be noted for both *óol* and *ìik'*. This is a common development cross-linguistically and it exemplifies the conceptual closeness of person parts and experta, which is also testified by their common behavior in some experiential constructions (cf. Bickel 1997[P] for the Belhare possessive of experience construction featuring both body part and expertum nouns at the same position and, e.g., sect. 5.2.2.1.2.3 or sect. 5.3.3.2 for YM).

CHAPTER 9

Conclusions

The grammatical structure of the domain of experience in YM is largely influenced by the typological profile of the language. This has become obvious at many points in the above description and will be explained in the following concluding sections. Experiential constructions draw largely on more general construction types such as possessive constructions, adjectival and intransitive constructions, transitive constructions, and ditransitive constructions and most properties are inherited from these (sect. 9.1). Sect. 9.2 presents some general conclusions for a typological characterization of YM which can be drawn from the current work. These concern the system of predicate classes (sect. 9.2.1), the grammatical strategies of coding the experiencer (sect. 9.2.2) and finally, the question of the grammaticalization of the experiencer role (sect. 9.2.3).

9.1 *Experiential construction types*

In this chapter, the most frequently used YM constructions which express experiential situations will be discussed in light of the cross-linguistic background established in sect. 3.4.3. The hierarchical relations of the constructions considered in ch. 5 will be of special focus here. Since the aim is to show the major traits of the organization of the YM experiential constructions, the discussion will be restricted to the dominant patterns of the language and some very specific constructions will not be repeated here. The discussion in ch. 5 has shown that most experiential constructions are instantiations of rather general predicate constructions. As instantiations of general structures however, they are well defined through semantic and lexical constraints.

9.1.1 *Possessive constructions*

YM possessive constructions expressing experience involve several more specific possessive relations. The most predominant construction type codes the experiencer as possessor of a person part noun. Furthermore, the experiencer may be coded as the possessor of an expertum noun. A third more rare construction type codes the stimulus as the possessor of an expertum noun. These three cases will be discussed in the mentioned order.

The treatment of YM experiential person part constructions in ch. 5 has shown that such constructions are, to a large extent, parallel to experiencer-oriented constructions. This means that many predicate types[1] take a person part noun in the same function as an experiencer. In a constructional view, the language displays two general parallel patterns as depicted in Construction 42 and Construction 43.

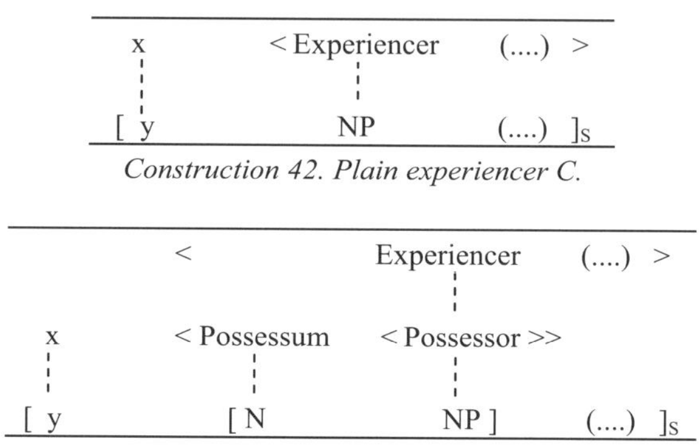

Construction 42. Plain experiencer C.

Construction 43. Possessed experiencer C.

This is true for the subject function of predicative adjectives (cf. sect. 5.2.1.2 and sect. 5.2.1.3) and intransitive verbs (cf. sect. 5.3.1.1 and sect. 5.3.1.2), and the direct object function of transitive verbs (cf. sect. 5.3.2.2.1 and sect. 5.3.2.2.2). Furthermore, constructions that take a person part noun in local function may be regarded as parallel to those that take an experiencer in indirect object function (cf. sect. 5.2.1.4 for stimulus-oriented adjectives, sect. 5.3.1.3 for stimulus-oriented intransitive verbs and sect. 5.2.2.1.2 for *yàan-*collocations).

In contrast to YM, in many African languages person part constructions frequently take a body part noun in actor function with a transitive verb (cf. sect. 3.4.3.3.3, (67) from Ewe and (77) from Bété). At this point there is a lack of parallel behavior between experiencer and person part constructions in YM.

YM body part nouns do not occur as subjects of a transitive verb (cf. sect. 5.3.2). This fits with the common selectional restrictions of YM transitive verbs, according to which there are no transitive verbs in YM that would restrict their subject participant to inanimate or abstract participants. In person part collocations, *óol* 'mind', *iik'* 'air; life, breath' and other person part nouns always take the undergoer function of a predicate, i.e., they are either in direct object function with transitive verbs or in subject function with inactives/inchoatives intransitive verbs and stative predicates.

---

[1] Note that this does not refer to a specific predicate which for the most part selects either the experiencer or the person part noun in a given function. However, there are also cases where a given predicate is open to take either the experiencer or the person part noun *óol* in a given function, e.g., *sahak* 'afraid', *chi'chnak* 'angry' etc.

The immaterial body part noun *óol* 'mind' is the main person part noun used in experiential person part constructions in the subdomains of bodily sensation and emotion, and is more seldomly used in the subdomain of cognition. Person part collocations with *óol* and some other person part nouns (e.g., *iik'* 'air; life, breath', *pòol/ho'l* 'head') are idiomaticized and the person part nouns are restricted concerning some regular operations such as topicalization. This points to the fact that they are semantically rather empty and together with the predicate form a complex unit. Since *óol* is very frequent in these collocations, combining with many predicates from the aforementioned subdomains, it has been analyzed as an experience marker.

This construction type may be compared to experiential possessive constructions in other languages where the possessor-experiencer either shows subject properties or has even developed into a subject experiencer (cf. sect. 3.6). The YM possessor-experiencer in the construction type just described is far from being a syntactic subject. Nevertheless, these constructions show some specific behavioral properties that have to be related to the natural pragmatic prominence of the experiencer. This has become obvious at two points. First, it was shown that instead of topicalizing the person part noun, the experiencer has to be topicalized (230) and, second, in sect. 6.2.2 it was discussed that the third person subject clitic (cross-referencing the person part noun) in idiomaticized collocations can be controlled in a subordinate clause if the controller in the matrix clause is referentially identical with the possessor-experiencer.

Furthermore, it has been shown that there are also non-idiomaticized body part collocations in the domain of experience, especially in the subdomain of bodily sensation. These do not, however, instantiate specifically experiential constructions. Rather, they instantiate a more general body part construction together with body part collocations from other semantic domains such as, e.g., physical ability, character traits, body shape, etc.

A comparable constructional difference related to person part constructions is reported in Clark (1996) for Mainland South-East Asian languages. These languages display two different person part constructions: a canonical possessive construction where the experiencer is coded as the possessor of the person part noun (cf. (424a/b) from Thai) and another construction where the experiencer is analyzed as the subject of a stative verb followed by a person part noun (424a'/b'). This is analyzed as forming a kind of complex. The canonical possessive construction is not possible with idiomaticized collocations which usually encode emotional and other 'abstract' states (424b). It can thus be noted that the distribution of the two Thai constructions is similar to that of the YM idiomaticized vs. non-idiomaticized person part constructions: While emotional expressions occur in idiomaticized constructions, items from the subdomain of bodily sensation occur in both construction types.

(424) a. *Taa   khăw   cèp.*
      eye   3   sore
      'Her/his eyes are sore.'

  a'.*Khăw cèp   taa.*
      3   sore   eye
      'She/he is sore in the eyes' or 'she/he has sore eyes.'

  b.**Cay   phŏm   sâw   mâak.*
      heart 1.SG   sad   very
      intended: 'My heart is very sad.'

  b'.*Phŏm sâw   cay   mâak.*
      1.SG   sad   heart very
      'I am very sad.' (Clark 1996:538f.)

Barrera Vásquez et al. (eds., 1980) suggests that body part constructions in the domain of experience were much more frequent in earlier stages of the language. It was noted at several points in ch. 5 that a given person part construction scheme had many more instantiations in Colonial YM, many of them with *óol* 'mind' as well. Nowadays however, most of these have become largely obsolete or even unknown, as a systematic inquiry of *óol*-collocations from Barrera Vásquez shows.

In sect. 3.4.3.6, it was mentioned that it is also cross-linguistically usual for expertum nouns to occur as possessed nominals which take either the experiencer or the stimulus in possessor function. Both construction types also occur in YM. The first one is largely parallel to the aforementioned person part constructions. Abstract predicators such as the existential predicate *yàan* (cf. sect. 5.2.2.1.2) or the transitive verb *ch'a'* 'take' (sect. 5.3.2.1.3) take both possessed person part as well as expertum nouns as their subject or object, respectively.

The second one, namely, that the stimulus is coded as the possessive attribute of an expertum noun, is cross-linguistically more unusual. This construction type was discussed for YM in sect. 5.2.2.1.2 in connection with the existential construction. If the experiencer is coded as an indirect object of the existence predicate, the possessor slot may be taken by the stimulus. This 'unusual' possessive relation is generally marked on the possessed nominal by means of the relational suffix *-il*.

In sum, it has become obvious that possessive constructions are one important means to expressing experiential situations in YM. This fits well with the grammatical relevance of the grammar of possession in the language. As regards the significance of person part collocations in YM in comparison to other languages, YM can be judged as taking an intermediate position between many African and Asian (including Papuan) languages which predominantly use such person part collocations and many European languages which mostly use experiential lexemes that are directly ascribed to the person as a whole.

9.1.2 *Adjectival and intransitive constructions*
In YM adjectival and intransitive constructions are largely parallel in terms of their participant structure. Therefore they can be discussed here under one heading. As is common cross-linguistically, YM displays simple and extended adjectival and intransitive construction types instantiated by experiential lexemes.

9.1.2.1 *Simple*
The simple adjectival and intransitive constructions take either the experiencer or a body part noun, or the stimulus in subject function (cf. sect. 5.2.1 and sect. 5.3.1). The most abstract pattern with an experiential adjective or intransitive verb and one argument is represented in Construction 44. In the following illustrations the parts of each construction which are inherited from a more generic construction are given in italics.

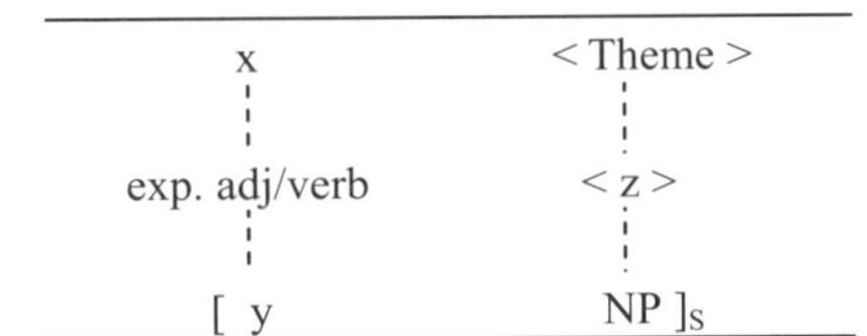

Construction 44. Simple adjectival/intransitive C. I

According to the semantic role which instantiates the Theme, this construction type is subclassified in the subgroup (Construction 5, Construction 21) which matches the constructional Theme with the EXPERIENCER (Construction 45) and another subgroup (Construction 11, Construction 26) which matches the constructional Theme with the STIMULUS (Construction 46). Thus, Construction 45 motivates Construction 5 and Construction 21. Construction 46 motivates Construction 11 and Construction 26.

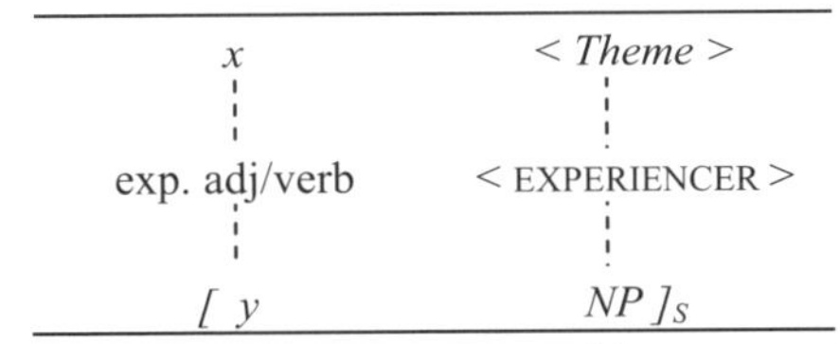

Construction 45. Simple adjectival/intransitive C. II

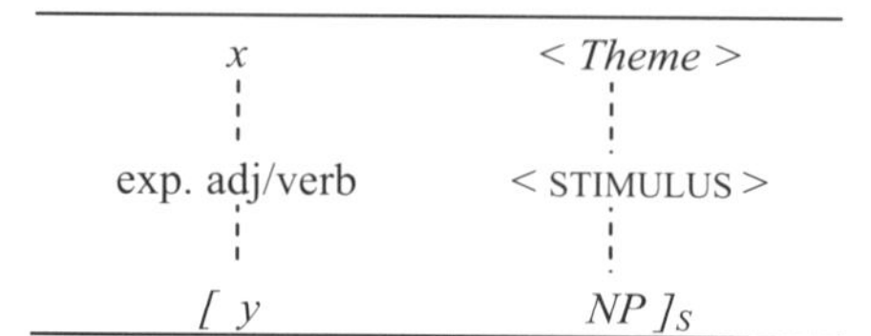

Construction 46. Simple adjectival/intransitive C. III

Following from the parallelism between experiencer and person-part orientation discussed in sect. 9.1.1, the person part noun is coded as a constructional Theme as well. Thus Construction 47 motivates Construction 8, Construction 9, Construction 10, Construction 23 , Construction 24, and Construction 25.

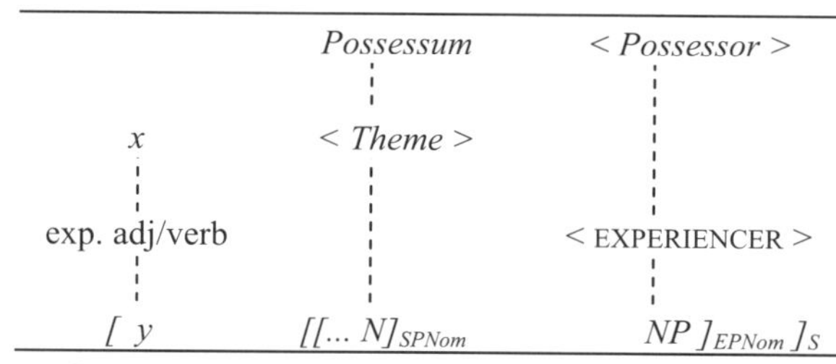

Construction 47. Simple adjectival/intransitive C. IV

Finally, there is a subtype of Construction 44 which matches the Theme argument with a possessed expertum nominal. Here the existence predicate *yàan* is the predicate. The experiencer is coded as the possessor of the expertum (Construction 18). Cases of coding an expertum nominal as an argument of an abstract predicator can also be found among the transitive constructions.

There are no non-oriented or subjectless constructions in YM. However, some modal auxiliaries displaying experiential meaning (e.g., *tàak* 'be anxious, want', *k'abéet/k'a'náan* 'need, necessary') are impersonal and take the modalized proposition in subject function. These do not take the experiencer as a direct dependant, but instead the experiencer is identified as the subject (S, A) of the subordinate core/clause (cf. sect. 5.2.2.1.1).

9.1.2.2 *Extended*

All adjectival and intransitive constructions, with the exception of the items from the subdomain of bodily sensation, are extendable by a Location or Goal argument, as is shown in Construction 48, which is an extension of Construction 44.

x	< Theme	Goal/Location >
exp. adj/verb	< z	w >
[y	NP$_1$	ti' NP$_2$]$_{PP}$]$_S$

Construction 48. Extended adjectival/intransitive C. I

Again, there are several possible subconstructions according to the alignment of EXPERIENCER and STIMULUS with the constructional arguments Theme and Goal/Location. Thus, Construction 6 and Construction 22 match the EXPERIENCER with the Theme and the STIMULUS with the Goal/Location, being motivated by Construction 49. Construction 12 is converse to these and aligns the STIMULUS with the Theme and the EXPERIENCER with the Goal/Location, being motivated by Construction 50.

x	< *Theme*	*Goal/Location* >
exp. adj/verb	< EXPERIENCER	STIMULUS >
[*y*	*NP$_1$*	*ti' NP$_2$]$_{PP}$]$_S$*

Construction 49. Extended adjectival/intransitive C. II

The construction type with an oblique encoding of the experiencer has a further extension indicated in Construction 50. YM displays adjectives and intransitive verbs which take the experiencer as an indirect object. Thus, these predicates map the lexical EXPERIENCER onto a constructional Indirectus argument (Construction 13 and Construction 27). The existential Construction 16 belongs to this type, too.

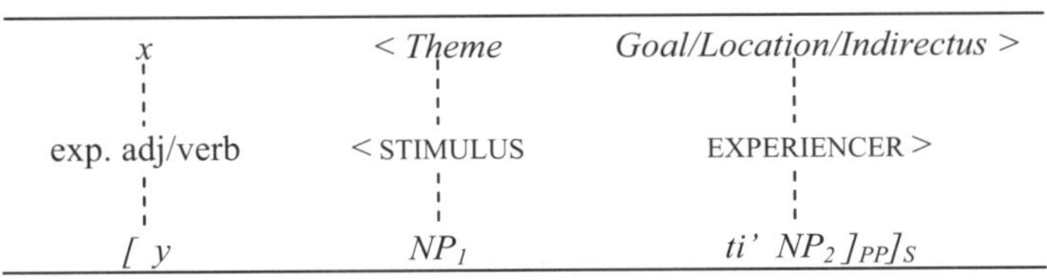

x	< *Theme*	*Goal/Location/Indirectus* >
exp. adj/verb	< STIMULUS	EXPERIENCER >
[*y*	*NP$_1$*	*ti' NP$_2$]$_{PP}$]$_S$*

Construction 50. Extended adjectival/intransitive C. III

Again, person part-oriented constructions are parallel to experiencer-oriented constructions. Construction 14, Construction 19, and Construction 29 are motivated by the general Construction 51. The adjectival Construction 14 is a common means for expressing evaluation (e.g. *uts ti' POSS óol* 'please, like', *uts ti' POSS chi'* 'taste good, like') in the language. Construction 19 is an existential person part construction.

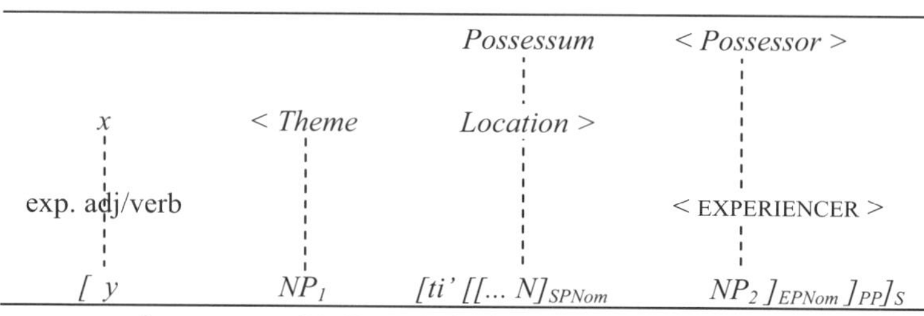

Construction 51. Extended adjectival/intransitive C. IV

9.1.3 *Transitive constructions*

The most abstract pattern with experiential transitive verboids and verbs is represented in Construction 52.

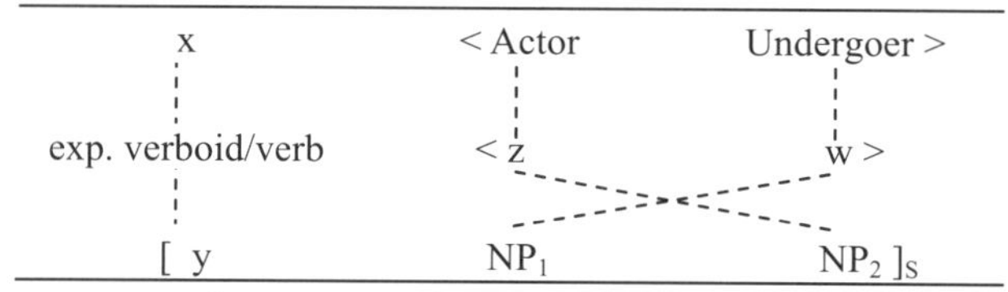

Construction 52. General transitive C. I

The general structure of Construction 52 is used in diverse ways within the experiential domain. Firstly, the constructions differ as to whether they use the argument slots for the encoding of the participants of the experiential situation or whether they use one argument slot for the (partial) encoding of the experience itself. The first type is the dominant one in the documented constructions and will be discussed first.

As is cross-linguistically common, the first construction type displays both alignments: the experiencer-as-Actor/stimulus-as-Undergoer scheme (cf. Construction 53 which motivates Construction 20 and Construction 30) and the converse stimulus-as-Actor/experiencer-as-Undergoer scheme (cf. Construction 54 which motivates Construction 36).

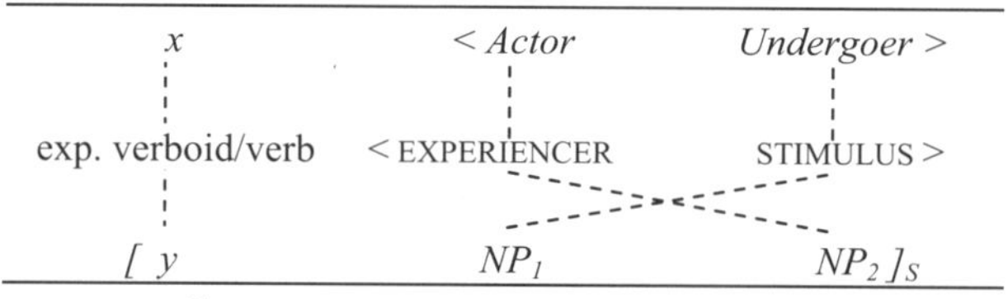

Construction 53. General transitive C. II

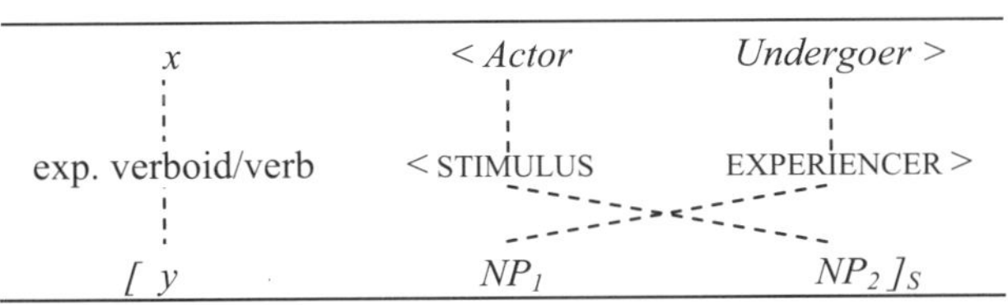

Construction 54. General transitive C. III

Only Construction 54 (and not Construction 53) has parallel possessor-experiencer constructions, which code the experiencer as the possessor of a person part noun (Construction 37, Construction 38, and Construction 39). The possessive construction type which codes a body part or expertum as Actor is ruled out in YM due to the reasons discussed in sect. 9.1.1.

In the second type of instantiation of Construction 52 within the domain of experience, the expertum nominal is coded in an argument slot. In this case, the predicate function is taken by a generalized experiential predicate (Construction 31) or by an abstract predicate (Construction 32). Both are experiencer-oriented constructions which take the expertum nominal in Undergoer/direct object function. Construction 31 is used to express bodily sensation with the verbs *u'y* 'feel' and *muk'yaht* 'suffer, feel' (cf. sect. 5.3.2.1.1.1). Construction 32 has *ch'a'* 'take' as abstract predicate and conveys inchoative meaning (cf. sect. 5.3.2.1.3).

Finally, YM has a transitive experiencer-oriented construction specifically conveying evaluation (cf. Construction 34 in sect. 5.3.2.1.4). This is a focus construction of the manner focus type which has an evaluative adjectival predicate as 'secondary predicate' in focus position while the experiencer is coded as the subject of a transitive perception verb, this being the main predicate of the construction. In contrast to other focus constructions of the manner type, focusing of the 'secondary predicate' is (nearly) obligatory with the evaluative construction. The described construction type is cross-linguistically typical for expressing evaluation of a stimulus, but in languages such as German it competes with a construction featuring a stimulus-oriented 'deagentive' perception/evaluation verb which takes the experiencer in indirect object or oblique object function (cf. Germ. *er mag Bohnen (gern)* vs. *ihm schmecken Bohnen (gut)* 'he likes beans', *er findet diese Hose schön* vs. *ihm gefällt diese Hose* 'he likes these trousers'). In contrast, in YM the aforementioned adjectival construction with a stimulus subject and the experiencer as possessor of a person part noun within a local phrase (cf. Construction 14) alternatively codes evaluation.

9.1.4 *Ditransitive constructions*

As is cross-linguistically common (cf. sect. 3.4.3.4), the ditransitive construction scheme is seldomly found among experiential constructions in YM. The most abstract ditransitive pattern is represented in Construction 55:

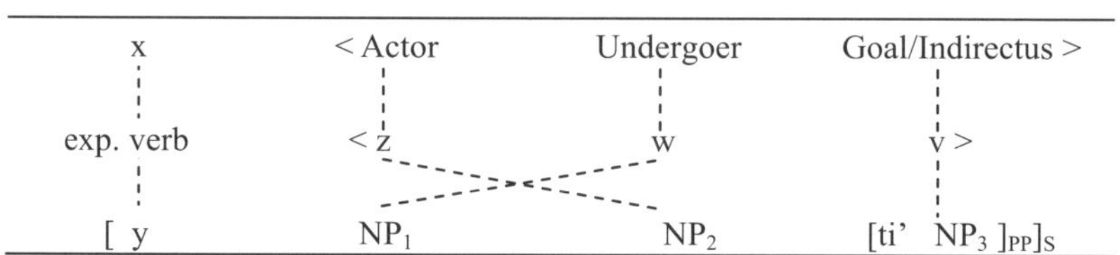

Construction 55. General ditransitive C.

YM has a few ditransitive experiential verbs from the subdomains of perception and cognition that map the EXPERIENCER onto the constructional Indirectus argument. The Actor argument is either a lexical STIMULUS or an AGENT, the Undergoer argument is either a lexical THEME or a STIMULUS depending on the verb semantics. This construction type was depicted in Construction 40, which is directly motivated by Construction 55.

Furthermore, YM uses some ditransitive experiencer-oriented collocations which display a general causative change-of-location verb (cf. sect. 5.3.3.2). There are two converse patterns as regards the fillers of the Undergoer and Goal argument slots. Either a body part/expertum noun is mapped onto the constructional Undergoer and the stimulus is mapped onto the goal argument, or the stimulus is matched with the Undergoer argument and the expertum noun is matched with the goal argument.

9.2 *Typological characterization of YM experiential constructions*

9.2.1 *Predicate classes in the domain of experience*

As has been outlined in sect. 4.1.8, YM provides for a set of grammatically instantiated predicate classes that host experiential predicates according to situation type features such as dynamicity, types of change, and causation as well as according to their relationality. A general distribution of basic experiential concepts with respect to word classes has already been given in sect. 5.4.1 and it has been shown that this distribution results in the hierarchy in Figure 17 which arranges the subdomains of experience according to the semantic properties of increasing dynamicity and increasing relationality in the following way:

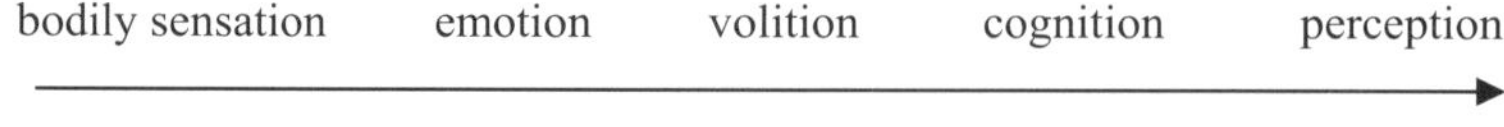

Figure 17. Hierarchy of experiential subdomains in YM

This arrangement concurs with the transitivity scale established in Tsunoda (1985) with respect to experiential verbs from the subdomains of emotion, cognition, and perception. In the following paragraphs, the preferences of the predicate classes of the language for encoding items of these subdomains are outlined.

The great majority of YM experiential adjectives are from the subdomains of emotion and bodily sensation, more seldomly from the subdomain of volition. They encode experiential states. With the exception of the adjectives designating bodily sensation, they may add an oblique stimulus complement.

The class of transitive verboids hosts basic stative members of the experiential subdomains emotion (*yàa(ku)mah* 'love', *p'èek* 'dislike, hate'), volition (*k'áat* 'wish, want'), and cognition (*ohel* 'know (proposition)', *k'ah-óol* 'acquaint, know (entity)'. It can be seen as the YM 'solution' for the expression of stative birelational concepts. Members of the subdomains of bodily sensation and perception are excluded from basic lexicalization as transitive verboids since they lack either birelationality or stativity. Thus, the fact that concepts of bodily sensation are monovalent can explain why these are not lexicalized as transitive verboids, but merely as adjectives or intransitive verbs. Concepts of perception are categorized as dynamic and birelational in YM as they are lexicalized as canonical transitive verbs and undergo regular passive formation. Passivization is not possible for transitive verboids without their first being verbalized. Stolz and Stolz (1993) has identified the lack of verbs which code emotional states as a typological characteristic of YM and its neighboring languages. The present work has shown that experiential states are instead coded by adjectives and transitive verboids.

As concerns the (sub)classes of intransitive verbs, it has been shown that there is a certain clustering of semantic subdomains according to formal subclasses. While those subclasses coding state changes, namely the inactive and inchoative intransitive verbs, are predominantly from the subdomains of bodily sensation and emotion, active intransitive experiential verbs are mostly from the subdomains of cognition and emotion. In both subclasses, the subdomain of volition is only marginally represented. The subdomain of perception is marginally represented by intransitive verbs of active perception. However, the verbs do not take oblique stimulus arguments, rather they have to be transitivized in order to take the stimulus in direct object function.

Since YM provides for a rich inventory of derivational operations, all basic predicates can regularly change to one or more other classes, providing for a possible change of the associated parameters of dynamicity, cause, change or relationality. Thus, emotional activities are expressed by active intransitive verbs that are often derived from adjectives. State changes in the subdomains of bodily sensation and emotion are conveyed by inchoative verbs derived from adjectives. Transitive experiential causatives (i.e. experiencer-object verbs) are factitives derived from adjectives or causatives derived from inactive intransitive verbs.

The class of transitive verbs hosts basic concepts of the subdomains of cognition and perception. All emotional concepts occurring in this class are morphologically derived. This is not only true for the aforementioned experiencer-object verbs, but also for the experiencer-subject verbs.

As has been outlined in sect. 5.3.2.2.1, YM experiencer-object verbs differ from their SAE-counterparts in their semanto-syntactic behavior. They exclusively designate caused state changes (and not states, as some of the SAE-couterparts do) and they form a regular passive with dynamic semantics, while the stative SAE experiencer-object verbs form stative or adjectival passives. The YM derivational structure of this part of the lexicon is converse to that of SAE languages: while in the latter languages the experiencer-object verbs are basic and the adjectival forms are derived, in YM the adjectival forms are basic and the experiencer-object verbs are derived. Thus, the YM adjectival base forms can be considered the true counterparts of the SAE stative or adjectival passive forms. According to what has been said in sect. 3.4.2.3, YM typologically clusters with languages such as Korean and Tamil regarding this part of the experiential lexicon.

Furthermore, since most basic forms in the subdomain of emotion are adjectives and, to a minor degree, intransitive verbs, YM does not exploit deagentive or anticausative derivation, e.g., by reflexivization, a process which has been identified in sect. 3.4.2.3 as being frequently used in other languages for conveying emotions. In YM, there is no class of 'reflexiva tantum'. Instead, reflexive constructions, which are syntactically complex transitive constructions in YM (employing the relational nouns *báah* 'self', *óol* 'mind' as direct objects), are exploited to form transitive imperatives of otherwise non-controllable basic experiential forms (cf. sect. 6.2.5).

Experiential nouns are to a large extent derived from adjectival or (to a lesser degree) from verbal bases. As in many other languages, they occur as expertum nouns in constructions with abstract predicators such as the existential predicate *yàan* (cf. sect. 5.2.2.1.2) or the transitive verb *ch'a'* 'take' (sect. 5.3.2.1.3).

Finally, ditransitive experiential verbs are rather marginal in YM and designate mainly cognitive concepts. The language has no three-place emotional verbs (as, e.g., Germ. *jdn. um etw. beneiden, jdm. etw. neiden* 'envy sb. [for] sth.').

9.2.2 *Experiencer coding and syntactic prominence*

The investigation in ch. 5 and ch. 6 has revealed a rather large variety of experiencer coding options in YM. Depending on the larger construction type, the YM experiencer takes the grammatical functions of subject, direct object, indirect object, or possessive attribute of a person part or expertum noun.

These construction types, including the associated grammatical coding of the experiencer however, are not chosen at random with respect to the experiential subdomains established in sect. 3.2.2. Given basic lexicalization patterns, experiencers of emotional concepts and concepts of bodily sensation are predominantly constructional Undergoers or Themes. Experiencers of cognition and perception are predominantly constructional Actors. Experiencers of volition occur in both patterns.

These general tendencies are cross-linguistically very common (cf. sect. 3.4.3). What is striking in YM is the highly regular system of derivation. The impact of this property is that the mentioned associations of experiential subdomains with constructional arguments may be changed to the effect that experiencers from virtually all subdomains may be coded as constructional Actors, or – conversely – as constructional Undergoers.

Concerning the positioning of the YM experiencer on the hierarchy of grammatical relations (Figure 3), it seems to be cross-linguistically remarkable that experiencers located in the middle part of Figure 3, such as indirect object experiencers, may be even more backgrounded, attaining positions at the low end of Figure 3 such as the adnominal relation of the possessor or a grammatical function in the subordinate clause. This has been shown in sect. 6.4 for indirect object experiencers of some adjectival and intransitive constructions. This is especially remarkable since the diachronic development of experiencers tends to locate them in higher positions in Figure 3 (cf. sect. 3.6). This unusual behavior of YM experiencers has been explained in sect. 6.4 as being due to the basic relation-prominent character of YM. It was shown that the possessor of a verbal argument as well as the subject in a subordinate core/clause can 'control' a possible indirect object which may be in the valency of the main verb. This common behavior of possessors and subjects was traced back to the fact that the subjects of transitive and intransitive verbs are former possessors of nominalized constructions representing a *genitivus subjectivus*.

Finally, experiencers from all subdomains may be coded as possessive attributes of body part or expertum nouns with stative as well as with dynamic predicates. In these possessive constructions, the experiencer is a canonical possessor. However, possessors in idiomaticized collocations have been shown to be pragmatically more prominent than canonical possessors. This can be deduced from the observation that the third person subject clitic (cross-referencing the person part noun) can be controlled ('equi-deleted') in idiomaticized collocations in a subordinate clause if the controller in the matrix clause is referentially identical with the possessor-experiencer (sect. 6.2.2).

9.2.3 *Grammaticalization of experiencer role*

As in many other languages, the experiencer in YM is mapped onto other grammatically relevant categories. These were described as constructional arguments in ch. 5, such as Possessor, Actor of a transitive verb, Undergoer of a transitive verb and Theme, Goal or Indirect object of an intransitive verb.

In a number of languages, the indirect object function is predominantly occupied by the experiencer (usually in addition to other roles such as recipient or beneficiary). In such languages, the indirect object may be judged as a grammaticalization of the experiencer role. YM also codes some experiencers as indirect objects. However, the number of experiencers coded in this way is rather small compared to experiencers in other grammatical functions. This is accompanied by a rather low degree of implementation of the indirect object in the language in general. In sect. 6.4, it was shown that the coding of an experiencer, a recipient or a beneficiary as indirect object can be overridden by its coding as the possessive attribute of a further argument of the main verb. Thus, that fact that the number of indirect object experiencers is comparatively low, together with the overall low degree of implementation of the indirect object function, provides evidence that the experiencer role is not grammaticalized as an indirect object in YM.

A specific experiential coding exists in the form of experiential body part constructions. A number of idiomaticized person part collocations form these special experiential constructions, mostly featuring the person part noun *óol* as experience marker. This type of construction shows a special behavior distinguishing it from other person part constructions (e.g., those for non-idiomaticized collocations). In these constructions, the experiencer is coded as a possessor and has been termed 'possessor-experiencer'. These constructions can be judged as a genuine means to convey experience.

This however is not a case of grammaticalization of the experiencer. Rather, *óol* as an experience marker is a lexical means of signaling experience. Its occurrence in person part collocations and compounds can be compared to the classifying function of experiential person parts nouns in psycho-collocations in some South-East Asian languages, as mentioned in Matisoff (1986). Such a strategy provides for a greater semantic transparency of the lexical inventory of the domain of experience.

References

Academia de la lengua maya de Yucatán, A.C. [s.d.]. *Diccionario Maya Popular. Maya – Español, Español – Maya*. Mérida, Yucatán, México.

Aikhenvald, Alexandra Y., R.M.W. Dixon and Masayuki Onishi (eds). 2001. *Noncanonical Marking of Subjects and Objects* [Typological Studies in Language 46]. Amsterdam, Philadelphia: John Benjamins.

Allen, Cynthia L. 1995. *Case Marking and Reanalysis: Grammatical Relations from Old to Early Modern English*. Oxford: Clarendon Press.

Amberber, Mengistu. 2001. Testing emotional universals in Amharic. In *Emotions in crosslinguistic perspective*, J. Harkins and A. Wierzbicka (eds), 35-67. Berlin, New York: de Gruyter.

Ameka, Felix. 1990. The grammatical packaging of experiencers in Ewe: a study in the semantics of syntax. *Australian Journal of Linguistics* 10:139-181.

Anagnostopoulou, Elena. 1999. On experiencers. In *Studies in Greek syntax*, A. Alexiadou, G. Horrocks and M. Stavrou (eds), 67-93. Dordrecht: Kluwer Academic Publishers.

Andrade, Manuel J. 1955. *A Grammar of Modern Yucatec*. [Microfilm Collection of Manuscripts on Middle American Cultural Anthropology, Series 7, 41]. Chicago: University of Chicago Library.

Andrade, Manuel J. and H. Máas Collí (eds). 1991. *Cuentos Mayas Yucatecos, Tomo II*. Mérida: Universidad Autónoma de Yucatán.

Andrade, Manuel J. and Refugio Vermont-Salas. 1971. *Yucatec Maya Texts: Preliminary Transcription and Translation* [recorded by M.J.A.; transcribed and translated by R.V.-S.]. [Microfilm Collection Manuscripts on Cultural Anthropology 41]. Chicago: University of Chicago Library.

Arzápalo, Marín Ramón. 1995. *Calepino de Motul: diccionario Maya-Español; 3 tomos*. México: Universidad Nacional Autónoma de México.

Asher, R.E. 1982, *Tamil* [Lingua Descriptive Studies 7]. Amsterdam: North-Holland.

Athanasiadou, Angeliki and Elżbieta Tabakowska (eds). 1998. *Speaking of Emotion: Conceptualisation and Expression*. Berlin, New York: Mouton de Gruyter.

Barcelona, Antonio (ed.). 2000. *Metaphor and Metonymy at the Crossroads: A Cognitive Perspective* [Topics in English Linguistics 30]. Berlin, New York: Mouton de Gruyter.

Barðdal, Jóhanna. 2002. 'Oblique subjects' in Icelandic and German. *Working Papers in Scandinavian Syntax* 70:61-99.

Barrera Vásquez, Alfredo et al. (eds). 1980. *Diccionario Maya Cordemex*. Mérida: Ediciones Cordemex.

Bauer, Winifred. 1983. Experience verbs in Maori. *Te Reo* 26:3-28.

Becher, Jutta. 2003. *Experiencer constructions in Wolof* [HAAP 2]. Hamburg: Universität Hamburg, Institut für Afrikanistik und Äthopistik.

Belletti, Adriana and Luigi Rizzi. 1988. Psych-verbs and θ–theory. *Natural Language and Linguistic Theory* 6:291-352.

Belz, Julie A. 1992. Sight, space and symbolism: motivating German case alternation in metaphorical extensions of physical domains. *The American Journal of Semiotics* 9(4):77-87.

Berg, Helma van den. 1995. *A grammar of Hunzib (with texts and lexicon)*. München: Lincom.

Bertinetto, Pier Marco. 1997. *Il dominio tempo-aspettuale: Demarcazioni, intersezioni, contrasti*. Torino: Rosenberg & Sellier.

Bhaskararao, Peri and Karumuri Venkata Subbarao (eds). 2004. *Non-nominative subjects, 2. vols*. Amsterdam: Benjamins.

Bickel, Balthasar. 1997[A]. Aspectual scope and the difference between logical and semantic representation. *Lingua* 102:115-131.

Bickel, Balthasar. 1997[P]. The possessive of experience in Belhare. In *Tibeto-Burman languages of the Himalayas*, D. Bradley (ed.), 135-155. Canberra: Pacific Linguistics (A-86).

Bickel, Balthasar. 2000. Unlogischer Aspekt: zur Bedeutungsstruktur von Aspekt und Aktionsart, besonders im Belharischen. In *Probleme der Interaktion von Lexik und Aspekt (ILA)* [Linguistische Arbeiten 412], W. Breu (ed.), 1-20. Tübingen: Niemeyer.

Bickel, Balthasar. 2004. The syntax of experiencers in the Himalayas. In *Non-nominative subjects, vol. 1*, P. Bhaskararao and K. V. Subbarao (eds), 77-111. Amsterdam: Benjamins.

Blair, Robert. 1964. *Yucatec Maya Noun and Verb Morphosyntax*. PhD Disseration, Indiana University (Bloomington).

Blair, Robert and Refugio Vermont Salas. 1965/1967. *Spoken (Yucatec) Maya*. Chicago: University of Chicago, Department of Anthropology [Reprint: 1979, Columbia, Miss.: Lucas Brothers].

Blake, Barry J. 1994. *Case*. Cambridge: Cambridge University Press.

Blansitt, Edward L. Jr. 1978. Stimulus as a semantic role. In *Valence, semantic case and grammatical relations* [Studies in Language Companion Series 1], W. Abraham (ed.), 311-325. Amsterdam: Benjamins.

Blevins, Juliette. 1995. The syllable in phonological theory. In *Handbook of phonological theory*, J. Goldsmith (ed.), 206-244. London: Basil Blackwell.

Bloomfield, Leonard. 1970 [1933]. *Language*. London:Allen and Unwin.

Bohnemeyer, Jürgen. 1998[S]. Sententiale Topics im Yukatekischen. In *Deskriptive Grammatik und allgemeiner Sprachvergleich*, D. Zaefferer (ed.), 55-85. Tübingen: Niemeyer.

Bohnemeyer, Jürgen. 1998[T]. *Time Relations in Discourse: Evidence from a Comparative Approach to Yucatec Maya*. PhD Dissertation, Tilburg University.

Bohnemeyer, Jürgen. 2001. Argument and event structure in Yucatec verb classes. In *The Proceedings of SULA* [University of Massachusetts Occasional Papers in Linguistics, 25], J.Y. Kim and A. Werle (eds), 8-19. Amherst, MA: GLSA.

Bohnemeyer, Jürgen. 2002. *The Grammar of Time Reference in Yukatek Maya.* [LINCOM Studies in Native American Linguistics 44]. München: Lincom Europa.

Bohnemeyer, Jürgen. 2004. Split intransitivity, linking, and lexical representation: the case of Yukatek Maya. *Linguistics* 42:67–107.

Bolinger, Dwight. 1977. *Meaning and Form.* London, New York: Longman.

Bolinger, Dwight. 1984. Surprise. In *Language and Cognition: Essays in Honor of Arthur J. Bronstein.* L. J. Raphael, B. Carolyn and M. R. Valdovinos (eds), 45-58. New York, London: Plenum Press.

Bossong, Georg. 1998. Le marquage de l'experient dans les langues de l'Europe. In *Actance et valence dans les langues de l'Europe* [Empirical Approaches to Language Typology; EUROTYP 20-2], J. Feuillet (ed.), 259-294. Berlin, New York: Mouton de Gruyter.

Bresnan, Joan. 2001. *Lexical-functional syntax.* Oxford & Malden (Mass.): Blackwell Publishers.

Bricker, Victoria R. 1979. Wh-questions, relativization, and clefting in Yucatec Maya. In *Papers in Mayan linguistics*, L. Martin (ed.), 107-136. Columbia, Miss.: Lucas Brothers.

Bricker, Victoria R. 1981[I]. Grammatical introduction. In *Yucatec Maya Verbs (Hocaba Dialect)* [with a grammatical introduction by Victoria R. Bricker; translated by James Ward], E. Po'ot Yah (ed.), vi-xvii. Tulane: Center for Latin American Studies, Tulane University.

Bricker, Victoria R. 1981[S]. The source of the ergative split in Yucatec Maya. *Journal of Mayan Linguistics* 2(2):83-127.

Bricker, Victoria, Eleuterio Po'ot Yah and Ofelia Dzul de Po'ot 1998. *A Dictionary of the Maya Language as Spoken in Hocabá, Yucatán.* Utah: University of Utah Press.

Bugenhagen, Robert D. 1990. Experiential constructions in Mangap-Mbula. *Australian Journal of Linguistics* 10(2):183-215.

Bugenhagen, Robert D. 1995. *A Grammar of Mangap Mbula: an Austronesian Language of Papua New Guinea.* [Pacific Linguistics C-101]. Canberra: Australian National University Press.

Bugenhagen, Robert D. 2001. Emotions and the nature of persons in Mbula. In *Emotions in crosslinguistic perspective*, J. Harkins and A. Wierzbicka (eds), 69-114. Berlin, New York: de Gruyter.

Bühler, Karl. 1934. *Sprachtheorie: die Darstellungsfunktion der Sprache.* Stuttgart, New York: Fischer.

Chomsky, Noam. 1981. *Lectures on government and binding.* Dordrecht: Foris.

Chomsky, Noam. 1995. *The Minimalist Program.* Cambridge: The MIT Press.

Chun, Soon A. and David A. Zubin. 1990. Experiential vs. agentive constructions in Korean narrative. *Berkeley Linguistics Society: Proceedings of the annual meeting* 16 [General session and parasession on the legacy of Grice]: 81-93.

Clark, Marybeth. 1996. Where do you feel? Stative verbs and body-part terms in Mainland Southeast Asia. In *The grammar of inalienability: a typological perspective on body part terms and the part-whole relation*, H. Chappell and W. McGregor (eds), 529-563. Berlin, New York: Mouton de Gruyter.

Classen, Constance. 1993. *Worlds of Sense: Exploring the Senses in History and Across Cultures*. London: Routledge.

Comrie, Bernard. 1976. *Aspect: An Introduction to the Study of Verbal Aspect and Related Problems*. Cambridge: Cambridge University Press.

Comrie, Bernard. 1981. *Language Universals and Linguistic Typology: Syntax and Morphology* [2. ed. 1989]. Oxford: Blackwell.

Comrie, Bernard. 2001. 'Love your enemies': affective constructions in two Daghestanian languages. In *Perspectives on semantics, pragmatics, and discourse: a festschrift for Ferenc Kiefer*, I. Kenesei and R.M. Harnish (eds), 59-72. Amsterdam: Benjamins.

Comrie, Bernard and Helma van den Berg. 2003. Experiencer constructions in Daghestanian languages. Handout from the Conference on Case, Valency and Transitivity, Nijmegen, June, 17-19, 2003.

Craig, Colette G. 1977. *The structure of Jacaltec*. Austin, London: University of Texas Press.

Cristofaro, Sonia. 2003. *Subordination*. Oxford: Oxford University Press.

Croft, William. 1983. Grammatical relations vs. thematic roles as universals. *Chicago Linguistics Society* 19:76-94.

Croft, William. 1990. *Typology and Universals*. Cambridge: Cambridge University Press.

Croft, William. 1991. *Syntactic Categories and Grammatical Relations: the Cognitive Organization of Information*. Chicago, London: The University of Chicago Press.

Croft, William. 1993. Case marking and the semantics of mental verbs. In *Semantics and the Lexicon,* J. Pustejovsky (ed.), 55-72. Dordrecht etc.: Kluwer Academic Publishers.

Croft, William. 1998. Event structure in argument linking. In *The Projection of Arguments: Lexical and Compositional Factors*, M. Butt and W. Geuder (eds), 21-63. Stanford: CSLI.

Croft, William. 2001. *Radical Construction Grammar: Syntactic Theory in Typological Perspective*. Oxford: Oxford University Press.

Cruse, D.A. 1986. *Lexical semantics*. Cambridge etc.: Cambridge University Press.

Dabrowska, Ewa. 1994. Dative and nominative experiencers: two folk theories of the mind. *Linguistics* 32(6):1029-1054.

DeLancey, Scott. 1997. Mirativity: The grammatical marking of unexpected information. *Linguistic Typology* 1:33-52.

Diewald, Gabriele. 1999. *Die Modalverben im Deutschen. Grammatikalisierung und Polyfunktionalität* [Reihe Germanistische Linguistik, 208]. Tübingen: Niemeyer.

Dik, Simon. 1978. *Functional grammar* [North-Holland Linguistic Series, 37]. Amsterdam: North-Holland.

Dik, Simon. 1997. *The theory of Functional Grammar, 2. vols.* [edited by Kees Hengeveld]. Berlin: Mouton.

Dik, Simon C. and Kees Hengeveld. 1991. The hierarchical structure of the clause and the typology of perception-verb complements. *Linguistics* 29:231-259.

Dineen, Anne. 1990. *Shame/embarrassment* in English and Danish. *Australian Journal of Linguistics* 10(2):217-229.

Dixon, R.M.W. 1989. Subject and object in universal grammar. In *Essays on grammatical theory and universal grammar*, Arnold (et al. eds), 91-118. Oxford: Clarendon Press.

Dixon, R.M.W. 1995. Complement clauses and complementation strategies. In *Grammar and Meaning: Essays in Honour of Sir John Lyons,* F. R. Palmer (ed.), 175-220. Cambridge: Cambridge University Press.

Dixon, R.M.W. and Alexandra Y. Aikhenvald. 2000. Introduction. In *Changing Valency: Case Studies in Transitivity*, R.M.W. Dixon and A.Y. Aikhenvald (eds), 1-29. Cambridge: Cambridge University Press.

Doi, Takeo. 1981. *The Anatomy of Dependence*. Tokyo: Kodansha.

Dowty, David. 1979. *Word Meaning and Montague Grammar*. Dordrecht: Reidel.

Dowty, David. 1991. Thematic proto-roles and argument selection. *Language* 67:547-619.

Drossard, Werner. 1991. Verbklassen. In *Partizipation: das sprachliche Erfassen von Sachverhalten*, H. Seiler and W. Premper (eds), 150-182. Tübingen: Gunter Narr Verlag.

Dryer, Matthew S. 1986. Primary objects, secondary objects, and antidative. *Language* 62:808-845.

Durbin, Marshall and Fernando Ojeda.1978. Basic word-order in Yucatec Maya. In *Papers in Mayan Linguistics*, vol. 2 [University of Missouri Miscellenous Publications in anthropology 6], N. C. England (ed.), 69-77. Columbia: University of Missouri, Department of Anthropology.

Ekman, Paul. 1992. An argument for basic emotions. *Cognition and Emotion* 6(3/4):169-200.

Ekman, Paul and Richard J. Davidson (eds). 1994. *The Nature of Emotion: Fundamental Questions*. Oxford: Oxford University Press.

Enfield, Nick J. 2001. Linguistic evidence for a Lao perspective on facial expression of emotion. In *Emotions in crosslinguistic perspective*, J. Harkins and A. Wierzbicka (eds), 149-166. Berlin, New York: de Gruyter.

Evans, Nicholas and David Wilkins.1998. *The knowing Ear: An Australian Test of Universal Claims about the Semantic Structure of Sensory Verbs and their Extension into the Domain of Cognition* [AKUP 32, Neue Folge].Universität zu Köln: Institut für Sprachwissenschaft.

Fabricius-Hansen, Catherine. 1991. Verbklassifikation. In *Semantics: an International Handbook of Contemporary Research*, A. von Stechow and D. Wunderlich (eds), 692-709. Berlin: de Gruyter.

Fesmire, Steven, A. 1994. Aerating the mind: the metaphor of mental functioning as bodily functioning. *Metaphor and symbolic activity* 9(1):31-44.

Feuillet, Jack (ed.). 1998. *Actance et valence dans les langues de l'Europe*. [Empirical Approaches to Language Typology; EUROTYP 20-2]. Berlin, New York: Mouton de Gruyter.

Filip, Hana. 1996. Psychological predicates and the syntax-semantics interface. In *Conceptual Structure, Discourse, and Language*, A. Goldberg (ed.), 131-147. San Diego: CSLI Publications.

Fillmore, Charles J. 1968. The case for case. In *Universals in Linguistic Theory*, E. Bach and R. Harms (eds), 1-88. New York: Holt, Rinehart and Winston.

Fillmore, Charles J. 1971. Some problems for case grammar. In *Georgetown University Round Table on Linguistics and Language Study 1971*, R. J. O'Brien (ed.), Georgetown: Georgetown University Press.

Fillmore, Charles J. 1977. The case for case reopened. In *Syntax and Semantics VIII: Grammatical Relations*, P. Cole and J. M. Sadock (eds), 59-81. New York: Academic Press.

Fillmore, Charles J. 1988. The mechanisms of 'Construction Grammar'. *Berkeley Linguistics Society: Proceedings of the annual meeting* 14:35-55.

Fillmore, Charles J., Paul Kay and Mary C. O'Connor. 1988. Regularity and idiomaticity in grammatical constructions: the case of *let alone*. *Language* 64:501-538.

Foley, William A. and Robert D. Van Valin. 1984. *Functional Syntax and Universal Grammar* [Cambridge Studies in Linguistics 38]. Cambridge: Cambridge University Press.

Frajzyngier, Zygmunt. 2001. *A Grammar of Lele*. Stanford: CSLI.

Frei, Henri. 1962. L'unité linguistique complexe. *Lingua* 11:128-140.

Geertz, Clifford. 1973. *The Interpretation of Cultures: Selected Essays*. New York: Basic Books.

Gerdts, Donna B. and Cheong Youn. 1988. Korean psych constructions: advancement or retreat?. *Papers from the 25th Regional Meeting of the Chicago Linguistics Society* 24:155-175.

Givón, Talmy. 1975. Cause and contol: on the semantics of interpersonal manipulation. In *Syntax and semantics, vol. 4*, J. P. Kimball (ed.), 59-89. New York: Academic Press.

Givón, Talmy. 1979. *On Understanding Grammar* [Perspectives in Neurolinguistics and Psycholinguistics]. New York: Academic Press.

Givón, Talmy. 1980. The binding hierarchy and the typology of complements. *Studies in Language* 4:333-378.

Givón, Talmy. 1984. *Syntax: a Functional-typological Introduction, vol 1*. Amsterdam: Benjamins.

Givón, Talmy. 1990. *Syntax: a Functional-typological Introduction, vol. 2*. Amsterdam: Benjamins.

Goldberg, Adele E. 1992. The inherent semantics of argument structure. *Cognitive Linguistics* 3:37-74.

Goldberg, Adele E. 1995. *Constructions: a Construction Grammar Approach to Argument Structure*. Chicago, London: University of Chicago Press.

Goldberg, Adele E. 1999. The emergence of the semantics of argument structure constructions. In *The Emergence of Language*, B. MacWhinney (ed.), 197-212. Mahwah, NJ: Lawrence Erlbaum.

Goossens, Louis. 1989. *Metonymy in Metaphorization: from Body Parts (and other Donor Domains) to Linguistic Action*. [Series A, Paper No. 256]. Duisburg: L.A.U.D.

Grimshaw, Jane. 1990. *Argument Structure*. Cambridge etc: The MIT Press.

Gupta, Sagar Mal and Jyoti Tuladhar. 1979. Dative subject constructions in Hindi, Nepali and Marathi and Relational Grammar. *Contributions to Nepalese Studies* 7(1/2):119-153.

Halliday, Michael A.K. 1985. *An Introduction to Functional Grammar*. London etc.: Edward Arnold.

Hanks, William F. 1990. *Referential Practice: Language and Lived Space among the Maya*. Chicago, London: The University of Chicago Press.

Harkins, Jean. 1995. Desire in language and thought: a study in crosscultural semantics. PhD Dissertation, Australian National University (Canberra).

Harkins, Jean. 2001. Talking about anger in Central Australia. In Harkins and Wierzbicka (eds), 197-216.

Harkins, Jean and Anna Wierzbicka. (eds) 2001. *Emotions in crosslinguistic perspective* [Cognitive Linguistics Research, 17]. Berlin & New York: de Gruyter.

Harris, Alice and Lyle Campbell. 1995. *Historical syntax in cross-linguistic perspective*. Cambridge: Cambridge University Press.

Härtl, Holden 2001. *Cause and change: thematische Relationen und Ereignisstrukturen in Konzeptualisierung and Grammatikalisierung* [studia grammatica, 50]. Berlin: Akademie Verlag.

Haspelmath, Martin. 1993. *A grammar of Lezgian* [Mouton Grammar Library, 9]. Berlin: Mouton De Gruyter.

Haspelmath, Martin. 2001. Non-canonical marking of core arguments in European languages. In Aikhenvald et al. (eds), 53-83.

Havers, Wilhelm. 1911. *Untersuchungen zur Kasussyntax der indogermanischen Sprachen* [Untersuchungen zur indogermanischen Sprach- und Kulturwissenschaft, 3]. Straßburg: K. J. Trübner.

Haviland, John B. 1988. It's my own invention: a comparative grammatical sketch of Colonial Tzotzil. In *The great Tzotzil dictionary of Santo Domingo Zinacantán with grammatical analysis and historical commentary; vol. I: Tzotzil-English*, R. M. Laughlin (ed.), 79-121. Washington: Smithsonian Institution Press.

Heine, Bernd; Claudi, Ulrike and Friederike Hünnemeyer. 1991. *Grammaticalization: a conceptual framework*. Chicago, London: The University of Chicago Press.

Hockett, Charles F. 1958. *A course in modern linguistics*. New York: The MacMillan Company.

Hofling, Charles A. 1990. Possession and ergativity in Itzá Maya. *International Journal of American Linguistics* 56:542-560.

Holland, Dorothy and Naomi Quinn (eds). 1987. *Cultural models in language and thought*. Cambridge: Cambridge University Press.

Hopper, Paul and Sandra Thompson. 1980. Transitivity in grammar and discourse. *Language* 56:251-299.

Horie, Kaoru. 1985. Lexico-syntactic analysis of verbs of cognition, conception and perception. *Sophia Linguistica* 18:39-48.

Hübler, Axel. 1998. *The expressivity of grammar: grammatical devices expressing emotion across time*. Berlin etc.: Mouton de Gruyter.

Inoue, Kazuko. 1974. Experiencer. *Descriptive and Applied Linguistics* (Tokyo) 7:139-162.

Izard, Carroll. 1977. *Human emotions*. New York: Plenum Press.

Jackendoff, Ray. 1987. The status of thematic relations in linguistic theory. *Linguistic Inquiry* 18:369-411.

Jackendoff, Ray. 1990. *Semantic structures*. Cambridge, Mass.: MIT Press.

Jaisser, Annie. 1990. DeLIVERing an introduction to psycho-collocations with *siab* in White Hmong. *Linguistics of the Tibeto-Burman Area* 13(1):159-178.

Jakobson, Roman. 1960. Closing statement: linguistics and poetics. In *Style in language*, Th. A. Sebeok (ed.), 350-377. Cambridge, Mass.: MIT Press; New York, London: J. Wiley & Sons.

Jo, In-hee. 1988. Double subject constructions and marked case assignment in Korean. *Working Papers in Linguistics* 37:11-27.

Johnson, Mark. 1987. *The body in the mind*. Chicago: University of Chicago Press.

Johnson-Laird, Philip N. and Keith Oatley. 1989. The language of emotions: an analysis of a semantic field. *Cognition and Emotion* 3(2):81-123.

Johnson-Laird, Philip N. and Keith Oatley. 1992. Basic emotions, rationality, and folk theory. *Cognition and Emotion* 6(3/4):201-223.

Karttunen, Lauri. 1971. Implicative verbs. *Language* 47:340-358.

Kaufman, Terrence. 1990. Algunos rasgos estructurales de los idiomas Mayances. In *Lecturas sobre la lingüística Maya*, N. C. England and St. R. Elliot (eds), 59-114. La Antigua, Guatemala: Centro de Investigaciones Regionales de Mesoamérica.

Kay, Paul. 2002. An informal sketch of the formal architecture for construction grammar. *Grammars* 5:1-19.

Kay, Paul and Charles J. Fillmore. 1999. Grammatical constructions and linguistic generalizations: the *What's X doing Y?* construction. *Language* 75:1-33.

Keenan, Edward L. 1976. Towards a universal definition of 'subject'. In *Subject and topic*, Ch. N. Li (ed.), 303-333. New York etc.: Academic Press.

Keenan, Edward L. and Bernard Comrie. 1977. Noun phrase accessibility and universal grammar. *Linguistic Inquiry* 8(1):63-99.

Kemmer, Suzanne. 1993. *The Middle voice* [Typological Studies in Language, 23]. Amsterdam, Philadelphia: John Benjamins.

Kiparsky, Paul and Carol Kiparsky. 1970. Fact. In *Progress in Linguistics: a collection of papers* [Janua Linguarum series maior, 43], M. Bierwisch and K. E. Heidolph (eds), 143-173. The Hague, Paris: Mouton.

Klaiman, Miriam H. 1980. Bengali dative subjects. *Lingua* 51:275-295.

Klein, Katarina and Silvia Kutscher 2002. *Psych-verbs and lexical economy* [Theorie des Lexikons, 122]. Düsseldorf: Universität Düsseldorf.

König, Ekkehard and Martin Haspelmath. 1998. Les constructions à possesseur externe dans les langues de l'Europe. In Feuillet (ed.), 525-606.

Kornacki, Paweł. 2001. "Concepts of anger in Chinese". In Harkins and Wierzbicka (eds), 255-290.

Kövecses, Zoltán. 1986. *Metaphors of anger, pride and love*. Amsterdam, Philadelphia: Benjamins.

Kövecses, Zoltán. 2000. *Metaphor and emotion: language, culture, and body in human feeling*. Cambridge: Cambridge University Press.

Kuno, Susumu. 1987. *Functional syntax: anaphora, discourse and empathy*. Chicago: Chicago University Press.

Kuno, Susumu and Etsuko Kaburaki. 1977. Empathy and syntax. *Linguistic Inquiry* 8:627-672.

Lakoff, George. 1987. *Women, fire, and dangerous things: what categories reveal about the mind*. Chicago: Chicago University Press.

Lakoff, George. 1993. The contemporary theory of metaphor. In *Metaphor and thought*, A. Ortony (ed.), 202-251. Cambridge: Cambridge University Press.

Lakoff, George and Mark Johnson.1980. *Metaphors we live by*. Chicago: University of Chicago Press.

Lakoff, George and Zoltán Kövecses. 1987. The cognitive model of anger inherent in American English. In Holland and Quinn (eds), 195-221.

Lambrecht, Knud. 1994. *Information structure and sentence form: a theory of topic, focus, and the mental representation of discourse referents*. Cambridge: Cambridge University Press.

Langacker, Ronald W. 1987. *Foundations of cognitive grammar, vol. I: theoretical prerequisites*. Stanford, Cal.: Stanford University Press.

Langacker, Ronald W. 1990. *Concept, image, and symbol: the cognitive basis of grammar* [Cognitive Linguistics Research, 1]. Berlin & New York: Mouton de Gruyter.

Langacker, Ronald W. 1991. *Foundations of cognitive grammar, vol. II: descriptive application*. Stanford, Cal.: Stanford University Press.

Larsen, Thomas W. and William M. Norman. 1979. Correlates of ergativity in Mayan Grammar. In *Ergativity: towards a theory of grammatical relations*, F. Plank (ed.), 347-370. London etc: Academic Press.

Lazard, Gilbert. 1999. Mirativity, evidentiality, mediativity, or other?. *Linguistic Typology* 3:91-109.

Leavitt, John. 1996. Meaning and feeling in the anthropology of emotion. *American Ethnologist* 23(3):514-539.

Lehmann, Christian. 1983. Rektion und syntaktische Relation. *Folia Linguistica* 17:339-378.

Lehmann, Christian. 1984. *Der Relativsatz: Typologie seiner Strukturen, Theorie seiner Funktionen, Kompendium seiner Grammatik* [LUS, 2]. Tübingen: G. Narr.

Lehmann, Christian. 1988. Towards a typology of clause linkage. In *Clause combining in grammar and discourse*, J. Haiman and S. A. Thompson (eds), 181-225. Amsterdam: Benjamins.

Lehmann, Christian. 1989. Language description and general comparative grammar. In *Reference grammars and modern linguistic theory*, G. Graustein and G. Leitner (eds), 133-162. Tübingen: Niemeyer.

Lehmann, Christian. 1990[L]. Towards lexical typology. In *Studies in typology and diachrony: papers presented to Joseph H. Greenberg on his 75th birthday*, W. Croft, K. Denning and S. Kemmer (eds), 161-185. Amsterdam, Philadelphia: Benjamins.

Lehmann, Christian. 1990[Y]. Yukatekisch. *Zeitschrift für Sprachwissenschaft* 9(1/2):28-51.

Lehmann, Christian. 1991. Predicate classes and PARTICIPATION. In Seiler and Premper (eds), 183-239.

Lehmann, Christian. 1993[P]. Predicate classes in Yucatec Maya. *Función* (Guadalajara) 13/14:195-272.

Lehmann, Christian. 1993[G]. The genesis of auxiliaries in Yucatec Maya. In *Proceedings of the International Congress of Linguistics* (1992), B. Crochetiere (et al. eds), 15(2):313-316.

Lehmann, Christian. 1994. Predicates: aspectual types. In *The encyclopedia of language and linguistics*, R.E. Asher and J.M.Y. Simpson (eds), 3297-3302. Oxford etc.: Pergamon.

Lehmann, Christian. 1996[C]. Control in Yucatec Maya. In *La sémantique des relations actancielles à travers les langues*, J. François (ed.), 105-127. Strasbourg: Université de Strasbourg 2.

Lehmann, Christian. 1996[O]. Ein Schriftsystem für das Yukatekische. Paper presented at the conference "Konvergenz und Individualität – die Mayasprachen zwischen Hispanisierung und Indigenismus", Bremen, July 5-7, 1996.

Lehmann, Christian. 1998. *Possession in Yucatec Maya* [LINCOM Studies in Native American Linguistics, 4]. Unterschleissheim: LINCOM Europa.

Lehmann, Christian; Shin, Yong-Min and Verhoeven, Elisabeth. 2000[D]. *Direkte und indirekte Partizipation: zur Typologie der sprachlichen Repräsentation konzeptueller Relationen* [LINCOM Studies in Language Typology, 4]. München: LINCOM Europa.

Lehmann, Christian; Shin, Yong-Min and Verhoeven, Elisabeth. 2000[P]. *Person prominence and relation prominence: on the typology of syntactic relations with particular reference to Yucatec Maya* [LINCOM Studies in Theoretical Linguistics, 17]. München: LINCOM Europa.

Lehmann, Christian; Shin, Yong-Min and Verhoeven, Elisabeth. 2000[U]. Unfolding of situation perspectives as a typological characteristic of languages. *STUF* 53(1):71-79.

Lehmann, Christian; Shin, Yong-Min and Verhoeven, Elisabeth. 2000[Z]. Zur interlingualen Ebene in der typologischen Analyse. *Göttinger Beiträge zur Sprachwissenschaft* 3:57-71.

Lehmann, Christian and Verhoeven, Elisabeth. 2005. Noun incorporation and participation: a typological study on participant association with particular reference to Yucatec Maya. In *Aspects of participation: typological studies on concomitance and incorporation* [Studia Typologica 7], C. Lehmann (ed.), 105-188. Berlin: Akademie.

Lehmann, Christian and Elisabeth Verhoeven. 2006. Extraversive transitivization in Yucatec Maya and the nature of the applicative. In *Case, valency, and transitivity*, L. Kulikov, A. Malchukov and P. de Swart (eds), 465-493. Amsterdam: Benjamins.

Levin, Beth and Malka Rappaport-Hovav 1995. *Unaccusativity*. Cambridge, MA: MIT Press.

Levinson, Stephen C. 1994. Vision, shape and linguistic description: Tzeltal body-part terminology and object description. In *Space in Mayan languages* [Special issue of Linguistics, 32.4], J. Haviland and S. C. Levinson (eds), 791-855. Berlin: Mouton der Gruyter.

Lightfoot, David. 1979. *Principles of diachronic syntax*. Cambridge: Cambridge University Press.

Longacre, Robert E. 1976. *An anatomy of speech notions*. Lisse: Peter de Ridder.

López Otero, Daniel. 1914. *Gramática maya: Método teórico práctico*. Mérida de Yucatán: La Moderna.

Lucy, John. 1992. *Grammatical categories and cognition: a case study of the linguistic relativity hypothesis* [Studies in the Social and Cultural Foundations of Language, 13]. Cambridge: Cambridge University Press.

Lucy, John. 1994. The role of semantic value in lexical comparison: motion and position in Yucatec Maya. *Linguistics* 32(4/5):623-656.

Lutz, Catherine A. 1982. The domain of emotion words on Ifaluk. *American Ethnologist* 9(1):113-128.

Lutz, Catherine A. 1987. Goals, events, and understanding in Ifaluk emotion theory. In Holland and Quinn (eds), 290-312.

Lutz, Catherine A. 1988. *Unnatural emotions: everyday sentiments on a Micronesian Atoll and their challenge to Western theory*. Chicago etc.: The University of Chicago Press.

Lyons, John. 1977. *Semantics, 2 vols*. Cambridge: Cambridge University Press.

Manney, Linda. 1990. Mental experience verbs in Modern Greek: a cognitive explanation for active vs. middle voice. *Berkeley Linguistics Society: Proceedings of the annual meeting* 16 [General session and parasession on the legacy of Grice], 229-240.

Maratsos, Michael P.; Katis, Demetra and Annalisa Magheri. 2000. Can grammar make you feel different. In *Evidence for linguistic relativity*, S. Niemeier and R. Dirven (eds), 53-70. Amsterdam: Benjamins.

Matisoff, James A. 1986. Hearts and minds in South-East Asian languages and English: an essay in the comparative lexical semantics of psycho-collocations. *Cahiers de linguistique asie-orientale* 15:5-57.

McElhanon, Kenneth A. 1975. Idiomaticity in Papuan (non-Austronesian) languages. *Kivung* 8(2):103.144.

McElhanon, Kenneth A. 1977. Body image expressions in Irianese and Papua New Guinea languages. *Irian* 6:3-27.

McElhanon, Kenneth A. 1978. On the origin of body part image idioms in Tok Pisin. *Kivung* 11(1):3-25.

McQuown, Norman A. 1967. Classical Yucatec (Maya). In *Handbook of Middle American Indians. Vol. 5: Linguistics* R. Wauchope (ed.), 201-247. Austin: University of Texas Press.

McVeight, Brian. 1996. Standing stomachs, clamoring chests and cooling livers: Metaphors in the psychological lexicon of Japanese. *Journal of Pragmatics* 26:25-50.

Merlan, Francesca C. 1982. *Mangarayi* [Lingua Descriptive Studies 4]. Amsterdam: North Holland.

Merlan, Francesca C. 1994. *A grammar of Wardaman: a language of the Northern Territory of Australia*. Berlin etc.: Mouton de Gruyter.

Michaelis, Laura and Knut Lambrecht 1996. Toward a construction-based theory of language function: the case of nominal extraposition. *Language* 72(2):215-247.

Mohanan, K.P. and Tara Mohanan. 1990. Dative subjects in Malayalam: semantic information in syntax. In Verma and Mohanan (eds), 43-57.

Mourelatos, Alexander. 1981. Events, processes and states. In *Tense and aspect* [Syntax and Semantics, 14], Ph. Tedeschi and A. Zaenen (eds), 191-212. New York: Academic Press.

Mosel, Ulrike and Even Hovdhaugen. 1992. *Samoan reference grammar*. Oslo: The Institute for Comparative Research in Human Culture.

Niemeier, Susanne. 2000. Straight from the heart – metonymic and metaphorical explorations. In Barcelona (ed.), 195-213.

Niemeier, Susanne and René Dirven (eds). 1997. *The language of emotions: conceptualization, expression and theoretical foundation*. Amsterdam & Philadelphia: Benjamins.

Noonan, Michael. 1985. Complementation. In *Language typology and syntactic description, vol. II: Complex constructions*, T. Shopen (ed.), 42-140. Cambridge etc.: Cambridge University Press.

Osmond, Meredith. 1997. The prepositions we use in the construal of emotion: Why do we say *fed up with* but *sick and tired of?*. In Niemeyer and Dirven (eds), 111-133.

Owen, Micheal G. 1968. The semantic structure of Yucatec verbs. PhD Dissertation, Yale University.

Palmer, Frank Robert. 1994. *Grammatical roles and relations*. Cambridge: Cambridge University Press.

Payne, Doris L. and Immanuel Barshi. (eds). 1999. *External possession*. Amsterdam, Philadelphia: Benjamins.

Pesetzsky, David. 1987. Binding problems with experiencer verbs. *Linguistic Inquiry* 18:126-140.

Pesetzsky, David. 1995. *Zero syntax: experiencer and cascades*. Cambridge etc: The MIT Press.

Pfeifer, Wolfgang et. al. 1993. *Etymologisches Wörterbuch des Deutschen*. München: DTV.

Pfeiler, Barbara. 1995. Variación fonológica en el maya yucateco. In *Vitalidad e influencia de las lenguas indígenas en Latinoamérica*, R. Arzápalo and Y. Lastra (eds), 488-497. México, D.F.: Universidad Autónoma de México, Instituto de Investigaciónes Antropológicas.

Polinsky, Maria and Eric Potsdam. 2002. Backward Control. *Linguistic Inquiry* 33(2):245-282.

Postal, Paul M. 1971. *Cross over phenomena*. New York: Hole, Rinehart and Winston.

Primus, Beatrice. 1999. *Cases and thematic roles: ergative, accusative and active* [Linguistische Arbeiten 393]. Tübingen: Niemeyer.

Reh, Mechtild. 1998[E]. Experiens-Konstruktionen in afrikanischen Sprachen: Erkenntnisinteressen, Ansätze, Ergebnisse. Reh (ed.), 1-22.

Reh, Mechtild. 1998[L]. The language of emotion: an analysis of Dholuo on the basis of Grace Ogot's novel 'Miaha'. In Athanasiadou and Tabakowska (eds), 375-408.

Reh, Mechtild. 1998[M]. The role of metaphor in grammar: experiencer constructions. In Reh (ed.), 25-40.

Reh, Mechthild (ed.). 1998. Experiens-Kodierung in afrikanischen Sprachen typologisch gesehen: Formen und ihre Motivierungen. Hamburg: Universität Hamburg, Institut für Afrikanistik und Äthopistik.

Reh, Mechthild and Ulrike Frühwald. 1996. Zur Versprachlichung experientieller Sachverhalte in afrikanischen Sprachen. Bericht an die DFG. Universität Hamburg, Institut für Afrikanistik und Äthopistik.

Reh, Mechthild and Christiane Simon. 1998. Experiens-Konstruktionen in Mande-Sprachen. In Reh (ed.), 41-88.

Rice, Ann Sally. 1987. Towards a cognitive model of transitivity. PhD Dissertation, University of California, San Diego.

Russell, James A. 1991. Culture and the categorization of emotions. *Psychological Bulletin* 110(3):426-450.

Russell, James A. 1995. Facial expression of emotion: what lies beyond minimal universality?. *Psychological Bulletin* 118(3):379-391.

Russell, James A.; Fernández-Dols, José-Miguel; Manstead, Antony S.R. and J.C. Wellenkamp (eds). 1995. *Everyday conceptions of emotion: an introduction to the psychology, anthropology and linguistics of emotion.* Dordrecht etc.: Kluwer Academic Press.

Sasse, Hans-Jürgen. 2002. Recent activity in the theory of aspect: accomplishments, achievements, or just non-progresssive state?. *Linguistic typology* 6:199-271.

Schultze-Berndt, Eva. 2000. *Simple and complex verbs in Jaminjung: a study of event categorization in an Australian language* [MPI Series in Psycholinguistics, 14]. PhD Dissertation, Katholieke Universiteit Nijmegen.

Schultze-Berndt, Eva. 2002. Constructions in language description. *Functions of language* 9(2):269-310.

Seefranz-Montag, Ariane von. 1983. *Syntaktische Funktionen und Wortstellungsveränderung: die Entwicklung "subjektloser" Konstruktionen in einigen Sprachen* [Studien zur Theoretischen Linguistik, 3]. München: Wilhelm Fink Verlag.

Seiler, Hansjakob. 1984. Die Dimension der Partizipation (Valenz, Transitivität, Kasusmarkierung, usw.) [Vorlesungsmitschrift]. Köln: Institut für Sprachwissenschaft.

Seiler, Hansjakob. 1988. *Die universalen Dimensionen der Sprache: Eine vorläufige Bilanz* [AKUP 75]. Köln: Institut für Sprachwissenschaft.

Seiler, Hansjakob. 2000. *Language Universals Research: a Synthesis* [Language Universals Series 8]. Tübingen: Gunter Narr.

Seiler, Hansjakob and Premper, Waldfried (eds). 1991. *Partizipation: das sprachliche Erfassen von Sachverhalten* [Language Universals Series, 6]. Tübingen: Gunter Narr Verlag.

Shibatani, Masayoshi. 2001. Non-canonical constructions in Japanese. In Aikhenvald (et al. eds), 307-354.

Shin, Yong-Min. 2004. *Possession und Partizipantenrelation: eine funktional-typologische Studien zur Possession und ihren semantischen Rollen am Beispiel des Deutschen und Koreanischen* [Diversitas Linguarum, 5]. Bochum: Brockmeyer.

Silverstein, Michael. 1976. Hierarchy of features and ergativity. In *Grammatical categories in Australian languages*, R.M.W. Dixon (ed.), 112-171. Canberra: Australian Institute of Aboriginal Studies.

Skopeteas, Stavros 2002. Lokale Konstruktionen im Griechischen: Sprachwandel in funktionaler Sicht. PhD Dissertation, University of Erfurt (Germany).

Skopeteas, Stavros and Elisabeth Verhoeven. 2005. Postverbal argument order in Yucatec Maya. *Sprachtypologie und Universalienforschung (STUF)* 58, 4:347-373.

Smailus, Ortwin. 1989. *Grammática del Maya Yucateco Colonial*. Hamburg: Wayasbah.

Smith, Carlota. [2]1997. *The parameter of aspect*. Dordrecht: Kluwer.

Sneddon, James Neil. 1996. *Indonesian: a comprehensive grammar*. London & New York: Allen & Unwin.

Stadler, Michael; Seeger, Falk and Arne Raethel. 1975. *Psychologie der Wahrnehmung*. München: Juventa.

Stolz, Christel and Thomas Stolz. 1993. Ein Herz und eine Seele: Psycho-Kollokationen in Mesoamerika. Talk held at the Workshop "From Body to Emotion and Cognition", Cologne, 2.-3. July 1993.

Sweetser, Eve. 1990. *From etymology to pragmatics: metaphorical and cultural aspects of semantic structure*. Cambridge: Cambridge University Press.

Talmy, Leonard. 1985. Lexicalization patterns: semantic structure in lexical forms. In *Language typology and syntactic description, vol. III: grammatical categories and the lexicon*, T. Shopen (ed.), 57-149. Cambridge: Cambridge University Press.

Taylor, John R. 1989. *Linguistic categorization: prototypes in linguistic theory*. Oxford: Clarendon Press.

Tenny, Carol L. 1987. Grammaticalizing aspect and affectedness. PhD Dissertation, MIT (Cambridge: Mass).

Tomasello, Michael. 2000. Do young children have adult syntactic competence? *Cognition* 74:209-253.

Tozzer, Alfred M. 1921. *A Maya grammar, with bibliography and appraisement of the works noted* [Papers of the Peabody Museum of American Archaeology and Ethnology, Harvard University, 9], [reprint 1927, New York: Kraus Reprint Corporation; New York: Dover Publications]. Cambridge, Mass.: Peabody Museum.

Tsunoda, Tasaku. 1981. Split case-marking patterns in verb-types and tense/aspect/mood. *Linguistics* 19:384-438.

Tsunoda, Tasaku. 1985. Remarks on transitivity. *Journal of Linguistics* 21:385-396.

Van Valin, Robert D. 1993. A synopsis of role and reference grammar. In *Advances in role and reference grammar* [CILT, 82], R. D. Van Valin (ed.), 1-164. Amsterdam & Philadelphia: J. Benjamins.

Van Valin, Robert D., Jr. and Randy LaPolla. 1997. *Syntax: structure, meaning, and function*. Cambridge: Cambridge University Press.

Van Valin, Robert D., Jr. and David P. Wilkins. 1993. Predicting syntactic structure from semantic representations: *remember* in English and its equivalents in Mparntwe Arrernte. In R. D. Van Valin (ed.), 499-534.

Van Valin, Robert D., Jr. and David P. Wilkins. 1996. The case for 'effector': case roles, agents, and agency revisited. In *Grammatical constructions: their form and meaning*, M. Shibatani and S. A. Thompson (eds), 289-322. Oxford: Clarendon.

Vapnarsky, Valentina. 1995. Las voces de las profecías: Expresiones y visiones del futuro en may yucateco. *Trace* (CEMCA, México), 28: 88-105.

Velázquez Castillo, Maura. 1996. *The grammar of possession: inalienability, incorporation and possessor ascension in Guaraní* [SLCS, 33]. Amsterdam, Philadelphia: J. Benjamins.

Vendler, Zeno. 1967. *Linguistics in Philosophy*. Ithaca: Cornell Univ. Press.

Verma, Manindra K. and K.P. Mohanan (eds). 1990. *Experiencer subjects in South Asian languages.* Stanford: The Center for the Study of Language and Information, Stanford University.

Viberg, Åke. 1984. The verbs of perception: a typological study. In *Explanations for language universals*, B. Butterworth, B. Comrie and Ö. Dahl (eds), 123-162. The Hague etc.: Mouton.

Voorst, Jan van. 1992. The aspectual semantics of psychological verbs. *Linguistics and Philosophy* 15:65-92.

Wierzbicka, Anna. 1988. *The semantics of grammar.* Amsterdam etc.: Benjamins.

Wierzbicka, Anna. 1990. The semantics of emotions: fear and its relatives in English. *Australian Journal of Linguistics* 10:359-375.

Wierzbicka, Anna. 1992. Defining emotion concepts. *Cognitive Science* 16:539-581.

Wierzbicka, Anna. 1994. Cognitive domains and the structure of the lexicon: the case of emotions. In *Mapping the mind: domain specificity in cognition and culture*, L. Hirschfeld and S. A. Gelman (eds), 431-452. Cambridge: Cambridge University Press.

Wierzbicka, Anna. 1995. Everyday conceptions of emotion: a semantic perspective. Russell (et al. eds), 17-47.

Wierzbicka, Anna. 1996. *Semantics: primes and universals.* Oxford: Oxford University Press.

Wierzbicka, Anna. 1999. *Emotions across languages and cultures: diversity and universals.* Cambridge: Cambridge University Press.

Wierzbicka, Anna. 2001. A culturally salient Polish emotion: *Przykro* (pron. *pshickro*). In Harkins and Wierzbicka (eds), 337-357.

Zwicky, Arnold. 1987. Constructions in monostratal syntax. *Chicago Linguistic Society* 23:389-401.

Zwicky, Arnold. 1994. Dealing out meaning: fundamentals of syntactic constructions. *Berkeley Linguistics Society: Proceedings of the annual meeting* 20:611-625.

Index

Studies in Language Companion Series

A complete list of titles in this series can be found on the publishers' website, *www.benjamins.com*

60 **GODDARD, Cliff and Anna WIERZBICKA (eds.):** Meaning and Universal Grammar. Theory and empirical findings. Volume 1. 2002. xvi, 337 pp.

59 **SHI, Yuzhi:** The Establishment of Modern Chinese Grammar. The formation of the resultative construction and its effects. 2002. xiv, 262 pp.

58 **MAYLOR, B. Roger:** Lexical Template Morphology. Change of state and the verbal prefixes in German. 2002. x, 273 pp.

57 **MEL'ČUK, Igor A.:** Communicative Organization in Natural Language. The semantic-communicative structure of sentences. 2001. xii, 393 pp.

56 **FAARLUND, Jan Terje (ed.):** Grammatical Relations in Change. 2001. viii, 326 pp.

55 **DAHL, Östen and Maria KOPTJEVSKAJA-TAMM (eds.):** Circum-Baltic Languages. Volume 2: Grammar and Typology. 2001. xx, 423 pp.

54 **DAHL, Östen and Maria KOPTJEVSKAJA-TAMM (eds.):** Circum-Baltic Languages. Volume 1: Past and Present. 2001. xx, 382 pp.

53 **FISCHER, Olga, Anette ROSENBACH and Dieter STEIN (eds.):** Pathways of Change. Grammaticalization in English. 2000. x, 391 pp.

52 **TORRES CACOULLOS, Rena:** Grammaticization, Synchronic Variation, and Language Contact. A study of Spanish progressive -ndo constructions. 2000. xvi, 255 pp.

51 **ZIEGELER, Debra:** Hypothetical Modality. Grammaticalisation in an L2 dialect. 2000. xx, 290 pp.

50 **ABRAHAM, Werner and Leonid KULIKOV (eds.):** Tense-Aspect, Transitivity and Causativity. Essays in honour of Vladimir Nedjalkov. 1999. xxxiv, 359 pp.

49 **BHAT, D.N.S.:** The Prominence of Tense, Aspect and Mood. 1999. xii, 198 pp.

48 **MANNEY, Linda Joyce:** Middle Voice in Modern Greek. Meaning and function of an inflectional category. 2000. xiii, 262 pp.

47 **BRINTON, Laurel J. and Minoji AKIMOTO (eds.):** Collocational and Idiomatic Aspects of Composite Predicates in the History of English. 1999. xiv, 283 pp.

46 **YAMAMOTO, Mutsumi:** Animacy and Reference. A cognitive approach to corpus linguistics. 1999. xviii, 278 pp.

45 **COLLINS, Peter C. and David LEE (eds.):** The Clause in English. In honour of Rodney Huddleston. 1999. xv, 342 pp.

44 **HANNAY, Mike and A. Machtelt BOLKESTEIN (eds.):** Functional Grammar and Verbal Interaction. 1998. xii, 304 pp.

43 **OLBERTZ, Hella, Kees HENGEVELD and Jesús SÁNCHEZ GARCÍA (eds.):** The Structure of the Lexicon in Functional Grammar. 1998. xii, 312 pp.

42 **DARNELL, Michael, Edith MORAVCSIK, Michael NOONAN, Frederick J. NEWMEYER and Kathleen M. WHEATLEY (eds.):** Functionalism and Formalism in Linguistics. Volume II: Case studies. 1999. vi, 407 pp.

41 **DARNELL, Michael, Edith MORAVCSIK, Michael NOONAN, Frederick J. NEWMEYER and Kathleen M. WHEATLEY (eds.):** Functionalism and Formalism in Linguistics. Volume I: General papers. 1999. vi, 486 pp.

40 **BIRNER, Betty J. and Gregory WARD:** Information Status and Noncanonical Word Order in English. 1998. xiv, 314 pp.

39 **WANNER, Leo (ed.):** Recent Trends in Meaning–Text Theory. 1997. xx, 202 pp.

38 **HACKING, Jane F.:** Coding the Hypothetical. A comparative typology of Russian and Macedonian conditionals. 1998. vi, 156 pp.

37 **HARVEY, Mark and Nicholas REID (eds.):** Nominal Classification in Aboriginal Australia. 1997. x, 296 pp.

36 **KAMIO, Akio (ed.):** Directions in Functional Linguistics. 1997. xiii, 259 pp.

35 **MATSUMOTO, Yoshiko:** Noun-Modifying Constructions in Japanese. A frame semantic approach. 1997. viii, 204 pp.

34 **HATAV, Galia:** The Semantics of Aspect and Modality. Evidence from English and Biblical Hebrew. 1997. x, 224 pp.

33 **VELÁZQUEZ-CASTILLO, Maura:** The Grammar of Possession. Inalienability, incorporation and possessor ascension in Guaraní. 1996. xvi, 274 pp.

32 **FRAJZYNGIER, Zygmunt:** Grammaticalization of the Complex Sentence. A case study in Chadic. 1996. xviii, 501 pp.